Federico Buccellati, Sebastian Hageneuer,
Sylva van der Heyden, Felix Levenson (eds.)
Size Matters – Understanding Monumentality Across Ancient Civilizations

Histoire | Volume 146

Federico Buccellati, Near Eastern Archaeologist, is a researcher at the Freie Universität Berlin as well as at the Alexandria Archive Institute. He has served as Field Director of the Mozan/Urkesh Archaeological Project since 2008, and is deputy-director of the International Institute for Mesopotamian Area Studies (IIMAS). His research interests lie in 3rd and 2nd millennium Syro-Mesopotamia, particularly architecture and the archaeological record, as well as theoretical and digital aspects of archaeology.

Sebastian Hageneuer, Near Eastern Archaeologist, works as a research assistant at the Archaeological Institute at the Universität zu Köln. In 2010, he received his degree in Near Eastern Archaeology. Since 2013, he is part of a research group that focuses on the significance of size in the architecture of the Ancient Near East. His research focuses on the history and current methods of architectural reconstruction.

Sylva van der Heyden is an art historian with special interests in the 18th and 19th century, reception history, graphic prints and objects made of unusual material. She was part of a research group in the Excellence Cluster TOPOI (Berlin), which dealt with the topos of the greatness of ancient Rome and worked in this context on her doctoral thesis with the support of a scholarship from TOPOI.

Felix Levenson, Near Eastern Archaeologist, studied Religious Studies and Near Eastern Archaeology at the Freie Universität Berlin. During his PhD research he held the Elsa-Neumann scholarship of the Land of Berlin. He has done fieldwork in Syria, Jordan, Azerbaijan, Saudi Arabia and Iraq. His research interests reach from architectural energetics over pottery technology to social and cognitive archaeology, as well as heritage management. He is currently focused on »networks of knowledge« between Mesopotamia and Ancient Iran in the 4th millenium BCE and on memory work and the creation of historical narratives in the Ancient Near East.

Federico Buccellati, Sebastian Hageneuer,
Sylva van der Heyden, Felix Levenson (eds.)

**Size Matters –
Understanding Monumentality
Across Ancient Civilizations**

[transcript]

We would like to thank the Cluster of Excellence 264 TOPOI for funding this project and this book. Furthermore, we would like to warmly thank the speaker of TOPOI's reserach group B-2, Prof. Eva Cancik-Kirschbaum, for her support.

Bibliographic information published by the Deutsche Nationalbibliothek
The Deutsche Nationalbibliothek lists this publication in the Deutsche Nationalbibliografie; detailed bibliographic data are available in the Internet at http://dnb.d-nb.de

Cover layout: Birgit Nennstiel
Cover illustration: Birgit Nennstiel
Proofread by Katherine Thomas
Contributions by Hageneuer/van der Heyden and Delitz/Levenson translated from German by Katherine Thomas
Printed by Majuskel Medienproduktion GmbH, Wetzlar
Print-ISBN 978-3-8376-4538-5
PDF-ISBN 978-3-8394-4538-9
https://doi.org/10.14361/9783839445389

Content

Part I
Theoretical Framework and Methodology

Responses to the Theoretical Framework and Methodology

Part II
Case Studies

Preface

Felix Levenson on behalf of the editors

How often have any of us sat in a conference or workshop session with back-to-back lectures and without the proper time to discuss the matters that are central to the theme of the session? How often did you wish to have less time for presentations and more time for discussion?

The *Cluster of Excellence 264 TOPOI* gave us the chance to broaden our horizons and look beyond the traditional borders of our own research field by inviting fellows from a wide range of disciplines and different parts of the world, but mainly by encouraging junior scholars – like myself – to experiment with different formats of workshop and knowledge transfer.

With the concept of the symposium and also the published volume we took a gamble. The planning phase was long and changed drastically throughout the entire process. The first draft was a three-day-long conference with lectures in several, even parallel sessions and keynote-lectures each evening. We considered inviting many established scholars of the ancient world and spending more time listening to presented papers than discussing the matters that had driven our own research for the past five years.

As interesting this would surely have been, we feared getting stuck with the same questions or hearing answers we could read about by looking at published work. Instead, we were eager to provide a forum where concrete discussions could take place, as well as give new and young voices a chance to share their opinions and their own research questions.

We chose specifically to forge a symposium-style meeting to serve the needs of our research group, but also to provide a chance for junior researchers to connect with scholars working on the same types of questions. It quickly became apparent that a 'traditional' concept of 20-minute presentations and 10-minute discussions – which more often than not turns into "only one quick question because we are running out of time" – was not the format we were looking for.

The idea was to have a conference at which no one reads a single paper – which may, however, seem a contradiction in terms. Nevertheless, the concept of the established *Dahlem Konferenzen* is exactly what we searched for and that is why it served as a blueprint for the symposium. We needed to make a few changes because we did not want to have a five-day schedule or parallel sessions, but we still did not envisage any read papers. The plan was to have different sessions for different topics and themes which were led by research questions we shared with the *TOPOI* researchers of our group in advance. These questions were then released in a *Call for Discussants*, which was specifically directed towards junior researchers, PhD students, and post-docs. In addition to these researchers, we were able to invite, thanks to the generosity of *TOPOI*, some more senior scholars from the world of monumentality research to kick-off each discussion session, which was moderated in turn by a senior scholar.

There were many applications and good feedback in advance, but until the symposium itself, my fellow organisers and I were still afraid that our experiment would backfire – there would be no real discussion and we would sit around in silence for a long time. But our gamble paid off and we had a very successful symposium with four individual discussion sessions on the first two days and a general discussion on the third. This symposium contrasts starkly with the type of congress at which fragments of worth are lost among a 'phalanx of predictable material'.

This volume of conference proceedings, or rather the results of the symposium *SIZE matters* held in Berlin on October 9–11 2017, marks the end of the DFG-funded research of the *Cluster of Excellence 264 TOPOI*'s research group B-2 'Monumentalized Knowledge', which dealt with the concept of monumentality in antiquity as well as monumental architecture throughout the world, with projects based in the Near East, Rome, Eurasia, and Germany. This broad scope of projects helped our research immensely and also contributed to the success of the symposium.

Due to the symposium's concept, this volume is not only a collation of different papers on monumentality but a volume presenting the results of the discussions of the symposium and the desire of the contributors to engage in interdisciplinary debate on phenomena that do not separate disciplines, but rather allow the finding of elements common to them.

I am grateful to all the contributors, discussants, and guests for three days of thrilling scientific exchange, to *TOPOI* for providing the funding, to my co-organizers Anton Gass, Federico Buccellati, Sylva van der Heyden, and Sebastian Hageneuer, who joined us in editing the book. Particular thanks and all our gratitude goes to Prof. Eva Cancik-Kirschbaum for supporting the idea and concept and helping in every possible way, from the conceptualization of the symposium to the finished book.

Uruk, 15.03.2019

Sebastian Hageneuer

Bernhard Herb Felix Levenson   Hauke Ziemssen   Kyra Gospodar Marcello Mogetta Martin Gussone René Ohlrau

Eva Cancik-Kirschbaum   Ricardo Eichmann Jordan Pickett Anton Gass Alexander Syrovatko

Mirko Novák   Ioulia Kaouraio

Silke Haps   Sandra Feix   Hanna Erftenbeck   Marina Daragan

Anna Wolf Christian Freigang   Kirrily White   Laura Cousin   Sylva van der Heyden

Reinhard Bernbeck   Güzin Eren   Sabrina Autenrieth

Federico Buccellati   Stella Nair   Rachel Lane   Mónica Pacheco   Alice Mandell

Introduction

Federico Buccellati, Sebastian Hageneuer, Sylva van der Heyden, and Felix Levenson

The symposium 'SIZE matters – Extra Large Projects in the Ancient World', held in Berlin on October 9–11, 2017 marked the end of the five-year research period of the Research Group B-2 'Monumentalized Knowledge' of the Cluster of Excellence 264 TOPOI – The Formation and Transformation of Space and Knowledge in Ancient Civilizations. The Research Group was one of the most diverse groups in TOPOI with research projects ranging from the 'Size of Rome', Scythian tombs in the Eurasian steppes, 'Big Buildings – Big Architecture?' in the ancient Near East and to the 'Ritual Landscape of the Royal Tomb of Seddin' in Brandenburg (Germany). Each project had its own focus and scope, nevertheless there were recurring questions that linked the different projects and were the starting point of many discussions held during our five-year research period. Firstly, there were questions of the terminological framework – What is monumentality? Does size really matter? These questions were followed by others, such as – Who profits from big architecture? What does it actually cost? Who built monuments and how were they built?

Having explored these questions within our own research foci, we decided to think outside the box and broaden our scope even further, inviting a wide range of scholars to participate in a symposium related to size and monumentality. Might other disciplines and other scholars working on similar problems have found alternative solutions?

The result of the symposium is an inter- and multidisciplinary volume dealing with the topic of Size and Monumentality in Ancient Architecture, which focuses not only on a single geographic or cultural region but covers much of the ancient world, including Mesoamerica (Pacheco), Syria (Butterlin; Hof), Babylonia (Cousin), Sumer (Hageneuer & Schmidt), Italy (Mogetta), and Ancient Judeah (Smoak & Mandell), also giving a broad overview (White & Lane), and even touching on sociology (Delitz & Levenson) and economics (Bernbeck).

The volume is divided in two main parts: a first section examining concepts relating to size and monumentality, followed by a series of case studies which were presented by speakers at the symposium. The symposium itself was organised inversely. First, case studies were presented in sessions with a short discussion following each session, then a longer discussion was held on the final day touching on many of the theoretical and methodological aspects which linked all of the papers presented. After the symposium the editors (for more on the symposium itself see the preface to this volume) used the material from that final discussion to elaborate a theoretical framework and a discussion of relevant methodological approaches to monumentality, not only with the goal of introducing the volume and the case studies presented therein, but also to discuss approaches and problems associated with the study of monumentality in the ancient world.

The article by Felix Levenson considers theoretical aspects of monumentality as relating to size, as well as elements of labor and the type of construction under consideration. Federico Buccellati gives an overview of methods used in the study of monumentality, discussing their applicability in research environments as well as the strengths and weaknesses of the methods as they relate to the study of monumentality. Sebastian Hageneuer and Sylva van der Heyden discuss object biography as it relates to diverse moments of a structure, beginning with the pre-construction moment and ending with reproductions of constructions considered monumental. These articles do not aim to present a 'final definition' of monumentality – they instead present the complexity of the topic, discussing the many facets (as seen from a wide range of scholarly viewpoints) and commonalities which link these approaches. Additionally, we asked several scholars for their responses to this discussion of theories and methods in order to keep the spirit of the symposium from which the volume stems.

The second section of the volume presents twelve case studies which reflect the spatial, temporal, and inter-disciplinary breadth of the symposium and the study of monumentality in general. These case studies show how individual scholars or teams approached the question of monumentality in very interesting and challenging contexts; when considered against the backdrop of the first section, they show how specific examples fit into an overarching framework while also presenting unique aspects which call into question certain elements of that framework.

Articles in this volume

Heike Delitz and Felix Levenson describe four heterogeneous structures in an attempt to investigate sociological aspects of monumentality through a comparison between societies with and without 'big' monumental structures. The sociological approach is twofold: from the perspective of a collective existence and from one where artefacts are socially active. The authors make the case that the absence of monumentality does not reflect a lack of ability to create such structures, but is rather the result of a decision to abstain from their construction.

Reinhard Bernbeck takes a look at the economics of the building process, focusing on labor where he follows Chayanovian ideas on the logic of drudgery and shows how diverse practices and especially institutional arrangements in ancient Mesopotamian societies tried in different ways to reduce tensions in projects with large amounts of laborers. Here he defines the 'utility-drudgery-threshold' as an aid to explanation.

Sabrina N. Autenrieth and Dieuwertje van Boekel investigate why the destruction of architectural monuments and pictorial works by humans always takes place at times of change. Starting with their definition of monuments – containers of memories – they shed light on the possible reasons for the destruction of monuments by choosing examples from the whole range of possible sites and periods: Neolithic UK, pre-classic Mesoamerica, 16th century Low Countries, Germany in 1989, contemporary Afghanistan, and Syria.

In their worldwide case study about the operation of monumentality in low-occupation-density settlements in prehistory, Kirrily White and Rachael Lane discuss the way in which these monuments can be formed by being part of a larger area or a system. In their opinion, monumental objects were not only single points of interest, but were able to expand to regional space and thus stabilize regional populations by connecting these stable points into a larger network of memory, ordering the settlement and cultural territories across a wider landscape. This study is insofar interesting, as rather than discussing individual structures it focuses on how such structures interrelate in a broader system in the wider landscape.

Pascal Butterlin, on the other hand, focuses his study on the Massif Rouge, a multi-phased high terrace in Mari/Syria and the comparison to other Early Dynastic high terraces. In his study, Butterlin suggests that the Massif Rouge is a very particular case, as although it seems to follow the general scheme of sizes at least in the beginning, it does not follow the invention of second storeys like comparable terraces in southern Mesopotamia. He concludes that the development of local building traditions is rooted in local religious topographies, so to say in a form of local monumentality.

Laura Cousin takes a look at the magnificent city of Babylon of the 1st millennium BCE, where she not only considers monumental architecture but also textual evidence describing its monumentality. She argues that Babylon's architecture shows colossal buildings, but its monumentality also stems from the symbolic meaning connected to them. This symbolic meaning is part of the monumentality of ancient Babylon and is clearly expressed by the inscriptions about the city even before its bloom in the 1st millennium BCE.

Catharine Hof takes the cistern of Resefa in Syria – without question a large-scale technological system – as the focus of monumental research. Her research sheds light on the intention of the construction, the building process, and its impact on society. The assignment of monumentality to this structure, although it is almost invisible, is based on its purpose: to win clean water under the most unfavorable circumstances.

Marcello Mogetta's analysis of Cosa focuses primarily on two structures: the Forum and the so-called Capitolium. Three aspects are brought to the fore – construction materials and labor, chronological sequence, and questions relating to identity. Mogetta uses Cosa as an example showing how innovation in construction practices was not centered on Rome, but could also originate in provincial towns. A discussion relating to identity highlights the arrival of a group of colonists who noticeably alter the needs and construction abilities of the community.

Mónica Pacheco Silva examines Oaxaca in the heartland of Mesoamerica and draws a picture of an area without big architecture but with a completely reworked landscape, which she argues is a truly monumental endeavor. She points out, "[...] urbanized society does not necessarily express itself in monumental architectonics [...]" and underscores the important role of the natural environment and its own monumentality.

Sebastian Hageneuer and Sophie Schmidt investigate the energetic cost of buildings in ancient Uruk and Habuba Kabira, examining the volume of the structures as well as the effort required for their construction. Such an analysis needs to include not only the volumes themselves, but also to consider the diverse materials employed. In order to include the diverse costs of the different materials used, the authors use weighted factors for different material classes. Through this juxtaposition of diverse structures and their material components, their aim is to discover a definition of monumentality.

Jeremy Smoak and Alice Mandell tackle a different kind of monumentality in their chapter as they explore the monumentality of inscriptions in Jerusalem's urban spaces and thereby also texts themselves. They argue that considering inscriptions and texts as monumentality exceeds mere typology and style and is more about the function and "communicative power of the text". Texts and inscriptions respectively convey, they argue, memories of "more distant generations within a larger political or social narrative" than architecture, and thereby become part of the cultural memory.

Part I
Theoretical Framework and Methodology

Monuments and Monumentality – different perspectives

Felix Levenson

"Monumentality (or the XXL phenomena) is not confined to physical scale: the creation of monumental architecture involves a combination of great technical ingenuity, extraordinarily high levels of skill, the devotion of vast amounts of time to build them, the type and range of the resources invested and the sheer size of the task."
Brunke et al. 2016: 250

"Monuments [...] are in the eye of the beholder."
Hole 2012: 457

"Monumentality is something more than the shape, or size, or visibility, or permanence of the monument – though these variables absolutely carry their own significance. Monumentality lies in the meaning created by the relationship that is negotiated between object and person, and between object and the surrounding constellation of values and symbols in a culture."
Osborne 2014a: 14

"Monumental architecture embraces large houses, public buildings, and special purpose structures. Its principal defining feature is that its scale and elaboration exceed the requirements of any practical functions that a building is intended to perform."
Trigger 1990: 119

"Monumental ist, was den Maßstab sprengt, Proportionen außer Kraft setzt und die Regel der Angemessenheit um der Wirkung willen bewusst verletzt."
Kirk 2008: 14

"Monuments are ideological statements about social and political relations."
Pollock 1999: 175

"True monumentality is indeed not expressed in the size, but in the relationship to the figure of the observer and, put in highly emotive terms, the inner imbuement [Durchdrungenheit] of a work."
Küster 2009

The task of finding a general and unifying definition for such a complex idea as the 'monumental' is an impossible one. Reading about the cultural phenomenon of monumentality makes one wonder if it actually exists or if it is just something made up anew every time somebody wants to talk about it. This is not only true in modern discussions about this architectural phenomenon but particularly for its study in the archaeological scientific literature. Studying monumentality in a way means studying the unknown, for there is no satisfactory definition of the term. I personally would not agree with all the above statements about monumentality or monuments, nevertheless I do not want to deny the legitimacy of each and every one of them, as Osborne already pointed out in his work (see above). It is the goal of this paper to make the variability and diversity of the terminology and the discussion about it visible.

The discussion of monuments, monumentality, and extra-large projects is in resurgence at the moment, and not only in Berlin – where it seems impossible to construct an airport[1], or in the ever-faster growing megacities of South-West Asia, or with reference to the new skyscrapers in the United Arab Emirates (cf. Osborne 2014b and Brysbaert et al. 2019). In 2012 James Osborne held a conference in Buffalo with the title *Approaching Monumentality in Archaeology* which was published in 2014 under the same title by SUNY Press, and asked – as our forum did – what can archaeology learn from so-called monumental structures and 'extra-large projects' about their societies (cf. Osborne 2014a). While both volumes are on the topic of monumentality, they are of a different nature. In his introduction Osborne starts his explanations with the discussion of an Elamite figurine of a lioness, known as the Guennol Lioness (formerly Guennol Lion),[2] which undoubtedly gained its importance and/or monumentality from its horrendous selling price. Though monumentality is not – as Osborne showed in his introduction (Osborne 2014a) – confined to built structures such as buildings, dams etc., in the present book it will only be discussed in relation to architecture. Even the contribution by Smoak/Mandell, which also deals with the monumentality of texts (Smoak/Mandell this volume), is based in the realm of built structures as it deals with inscriptions as objects rather than focusing on their contents.

Before I go into a discussion of the terminology of the monumental, monuments, and *lieux des mémoires*, I want to point out the main difference between Osborne's volume and the debates held in our discussion forum. The organization of our forum allowed us to have long and uninterrupted discussions[3] about most

---

1 The new Berlin airport's (BER) construction was started in 2006 after a 15-year planning period. It was initially intended to be opened in 2011, but as of today it still remains a construction site.

2 The name Guennol relates to the previous owner's family name which is Martin and Guennol in Welsh, where the family came from. The lioness gained its fame when it was auctioned in 2007 for $57.200.000.

3 For more on the organization of the forum, see Levenson (this volume).

themes of this volume. For our forum one of the most important conversations was about energetics and the possibility of quantifying monumentality – something that Osborne denies. He speaks more about monumentality as the meaning a structure gains through negotiations between objects and people (Osborne 2014a: 13). What Bourdieu (1992: 163–70) calls symbolic power is what defines a monument for Osborne. However, he ends with the notion that "Monuments, it turns out, are in the eye of the beholder." (Hole 2012: 457) Although I agree with this assessment, I will try to elaborate on how this differs between monuments, monumentality, and communal monuments (see below).

So, what do we mean when we speak about monumentality in relation to the built environment? How can we define monumental architecture and how can we identify monumental structures from the past? Firstly, it is of utmost importance to realize that *nothing is monumental, and everything is monumental* and that there is a distinction between a monument (Denkmal) and something monumental (see below, for a more detailed account of the sociology of the monumental and also cf. Delitz/Levenson this volume).[4]

In the 18th century CE the word monument (from Latin, *monere* – to admonish, to warn, to remind but *not* to remember) referred to sites of memory and places of remembrance. These *lieux de mémoire* (Nora 1989) initially had no connotation of size. The relation to an architectural structure was also not necessary. Megastructures were not included in the term until the 19th century CE when these aspects became relevant to national representation and historical legitimization. At the beginning of the 20th century CE there was a movement that tried to connect the notion of monumentality to the sacred in opposition to the profane (cf. Meyer 1938). This concept is linked to the works of Pseudo-Longinus (1966) and Kant (1990; 1995) on the sublime.[5]

From the beginning of the 20th century CE onward monuments were understood as communicators between past and future, they "[...] are human landmarks, which men have created as symbols for their ideals, for their aims, and for their actions. They are intended to outlive the period which originated them and constitute a heritage for future generations." (Brunke et al. 2016: 252) In the 19th and 20th centuries CE monuments that were erected in Europe were mainly linked to structures and symbols from classical Roman and Greek antiquity. The next shift in the history of monumentality in architecture took place during and after World War II – after the time Mussolini enacted his plans to redesign Rome's urban

---

4 Even though linguistically 'monumental' is the adjective to 'monument', 'monumental' not only describes the attributes of a monument but also has its own separate meaning (cf. Delitz/Levenson in this volume). The German term 'Denkmal' is the closest match to the English 'monument'; however, it mainly relates to statues and memorials and not necessarily buildings.

5 Kant described the sublime as that "which is beyond all comparison great" and as "awe-inspiring greatness" (Kant 1995: § 65).

space, after Adolf Hitler's architect Albert Speer transformed central Berlin to create a massive parade route to showcase Germany's military strength, and after Stalin transformed Moscow's skyline with 'socialist' skyscrapers. This motivation is also clearly visible in the cinematography of Leni Riefenstahl's films – especially her Olympia films which glorified the 1936 Olympic Games in Berlin. She uses the monumental structures as a frame, showing them in a specific fashion and thereby making them accessible and visible to everybody, not just to an elite that is able to be in the front rows of the Nazi-parades in Nürnberg or the Olympic Games in Berlin. It is clear that in this case there was an intentional creation of monumentality for the masses and the commoners as well as the political elites. After this instrumentalization of big architecture for political purposes, this kind of architectural expression of quoting ancient monuments and rebuilding them on an extra-large scale fell out of favor, especially in Germany. The era of 'democratic architecture' began (Howell-Ardila 1998). This involved the usage of certain building materials such as concrete, glass and steel. The architecture was very clear and straightforward without extra-large structures, which were even avoided whenever possible. The new German Bundestag in Bonn built in 1992, for example, was a smallish inconspicuous building (see Figure 1).

Figure 1: Plenary building of the German Bundestag in Bonn (Photo Courtesy of WorldCCBonn)

It was only after the reunification of the Federal German Republic and the German Democratic Republic that it became desirable to invest in big architecture again, whether this was a conscious decision or only a 'mood of the country' remains unclear. The rebuilding of the center of Berlin, however, is a striking example of this phenomenon. Just to give some examples:

The Reichstag in Berlin became the seat of the German parliament again and was renovated in such a way that in 1999 it was given back its dome, this time by the 'star-architect' Norman Foster (see Figure 2), after being wrapped in an aluminium-coated fabric by artists Christo and Jeanne-Claude – like a *rite de passage*.

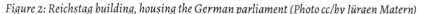

Figure 2: Reichstag building, housing the German parliament (Photo cc/by Jürgen Matern)

The move of the German parliament was enacted in 1999, nine years after German reunification. It was by far not the only change to the urban sphere in Berlin. Potsdamer Platz, right on the border between West and East Berlin, has been completely restructured and was Europe's largest intraurban building site in the 1990s. The shift is therefore apparent: there was a step back towards a reconnaissance of antique architecture and social conservatism which in Berlin culminated in the Humboldtforum, an extra-large building on the site where the Berliner Stadtschloss used to be, which 'quotes' the façade of the old palace. As in the 19th century CE, political power is shown through the means of architecture and the monumental. This shift in the meaning and connotation of monumentality and the monumental is also apparent in the *Denkstil* (Fleck 1980) of the time. The Frankfurt School,[6] for example, influenced thought about architecture a lot in Germany, as did Foucault's work on prisons and mental institutions in France.[7]

---

6 A group of German philosophers and theorists based in Frankfurt a. M.; well-known members include e. g. Theodor W. Adorno and Max Horkheimer.

7 See Foucault (1998). For further discussions on the sociology of the monumental see Delitz/Levenson in this volume.

What makes the monumental?

There is something distinct and yet very indistinct about monuments and monumentality. As I have stated above, there is no single and unifying definition of this phenomenon, yet all things we consider seem to have something in common – somehow, we always seem to be able to decide whether something is monumental or not (see below). In the following I will try to elaborate on this phenomenon.

Affection makes a monument, for there must be either a perceptual impact on a personal or cultural level or a personal or cultural investment in the monument. Either way, social involvement in making or perceiving the monument is more important than, for example, size in the making of monumentality, which as I will explain below is something completely different.

Society makes monumentality. This might not be so difficult to comprehend for 'living' societies where we can talk to witnesses, but for ancient people this seems almost impossible. How can we ever tell what was impressive for the 5th millennium BCE Urukean? Or how do we know what the Roman triumph arches or Trajan's Column (cf. Hageneuer/van der Heyden this volume) meant to a Roman citizen of the early 2nd century CE? For the archaeologist, the question of how to deal with this situation arises – how can a feeling or a sense be proven archaeologically? We have to ask what factors are actually detectable in the archaeological record that can hint us towards an understanding of a concept of ancient monumentality and of ancient monuments.

Events create monumental spaces. Something that can be best captured by the German term *Ortsmonumentalität* describes a structure or built environment that gains its monumentality and thereby its importance from the place it was constructed upon (Brunke et al. 2016: 255). The structure can possibly be very little or very big, this has no influence on its monumentality. This monumentality is purely related to space and position. We have to ask ourselves then, how do certain spaces become so important and so impregnated with meaning and memory? I argue that this is due to events that took place there. This may seem simple and straightforward, but the question "What is an event?" is no less complex that the questions "What is a monument?" and "What is monumentality?" (cf. e. g. Žižek 2014). In a nutshell, I suggest that it would not have mattered what was built on ground zero after the attacks of 9/11, it would have been monumental due the place and position which were embedded in cultural memory (see below) by an event.

One can already see in its history that monumentality is a very dynamic term with a fluid meaning, even when dealing with structures or monuments from our time or from a time with very good written and photographic documentation. It becomes even more problematic when we as Western scholars try to study foreigners as exemplified in ethnographic studies or deal with antiquity as in archaeology. As this volume deals mainly with antiquity I will focus on the latter.

In archaeological literature dealing with architecture the term monumental is most commonly used in relation to large built structures or structures in a particularly meaningful place, an acropolis for example or religious or prestigious buildings for an elite class (see Sievertsen 2010 for one example from the 'Ubaid period [5th millennium BCE] in Mesopotamia). Connotations of the sublime, remembrance and effort do not play a major role even though they do in the texts by Vitruvius (1999) in the 1st century BCE.

There are several factors that need to be considered to allow something to be talked about as monumental, as Brunke et al. (2016) state. These include:

1. *Size*: the spatial dimensions of the object cause it to stand out significantly vis-à-vis the surrounding norm.
2. *Position*: the object's exposed position relative to the surrounding buildings causes it to stand out, e. g. it was sited on a mound or hill or in the center of a settlement, or at a location, possibly even a peripheral location, that developed into a center as a result of the object's presence.
3. *Permanence*: the object dominated the surrounding area over a long period of time.
4. *Investment*: construction of the object involved abnormally large investment relative to the technical or economic potential (skills, knowledge, tools, cultural techniques) of the population and/or its size; construction may even have involved investments and hence risks on a level disproportionate to the population's capacities.
5. *Complexity* […]: the technical knowledge, the artisanal skills and the organizational and logistical effort required to construct the object exceed both qualitatively and quantitatively the levels entailed in construction of a structure reflecting the norm for the surrounding area. Thus, for example, an object that is 'large' in terms of its dimensions but that was formed through the agglomeration of many smaller objects, which themselves reflect the norm for the surrounding area, may not necessarily be 'large' in terms of the complexity of the project object, its impressive size notwithstanding.[8] (Brunke et al. 2016: 255)

Different monumentalities

I would argue that none of the above alone makes a monument monumental, but that a combination of these factors could probably be used as a marker of a more objective approximation of the term. It is clear, however, that the common factor in all these five points is that monumentality is in any case a relational term that

---

8 Highlights by the author.

defines something through its otherness and opposition to the 'norm'.[9] Therefore, one could argue that everything is monumental for someone due to their personal memory and/or its personal meaning for someone. There are always several monumentalities that exist separately and independently but describe the same monument or structure. There are, for example:

1) *Intended* and built monumentality.
   Every structure has been built with an intent. In many cases, especially in public buildings with a political or religious meaning, this intent is linked to an intended monumentality. The intended function was sometimes to impress viewers, or to intimidate. Cathedrals, for example, were meant to showcase the sublime divinity of God.

2) *Perceived* monumentality, which differs from people to people and peoples to peoples or societies to societies.
   The perceived monumentality or social meaning of a structure not only differs between people or peoples, but also from the intended monumentality. The new Berlin airport for example (see above and below), which has been in the process of being built since 2006, has become a monument to the inability of the State of Berlin to finish a project and has thus gained its monumentality. The intended positive association with the airport has changed into a perceived negative one.

3) *Received* monumentality.
   Received monumentality is the most complex of the three concepts. It is a middle ground between 1) and 2). But it is more than that; it is also the reception of the monument or the monumental through time and its changes within. Received monumentality is the outside perception of the way monumentality is perceived. It is in a way the outsider looking into an already established system and analyzing it, like an ethnographer studies unknown people.

There is a chain of dependencies and dependences. Thus the intent forms the perception, or at least is intended to do so; however, it is important to note that the intent is only there for one generation or less, and is exclusively limited to those who intend (beginning from the 'idea' until the practical implementation of the building process). Even those within the same generation who are not the decision makers are excluded from the 'intent-group'. The following generations can therefore only perceive this intent. In this scheme, intent is a priori temporary. Speaking as an archaeologist: intent is always a hypothetical which we are trying

---

9 Again, this leaves us with the problem of defining the norm as an objective category, which it is not, and which is very difficult indeed. This unfortunately is neither the time nor the place to go into further detail.

to prove as well as possible with studies like this. What we can, however, assume is that the real recipient of the 'elite's' intentions is not the monument or intended monumental structure itself; the aim is to control the perception of the 'general population' – the observers. Intent does not leave the inherent social system.

Perception depends on the social position of the percipients, their social involvement, and social setting. Perception, as described above, changes over time and differs between different social groups. The perception of the monument and its monumentality is thereby highly influenced by the perception of the intending party; however, it never means the same to everyone.

Reception depends on the perception and is therefore also fluid and dynamic. It is, so to say, the perceived perception of someone else or of an alien social system.

Figure 3: Graphic model of the interrelationships between intended, perceived and received monumentality

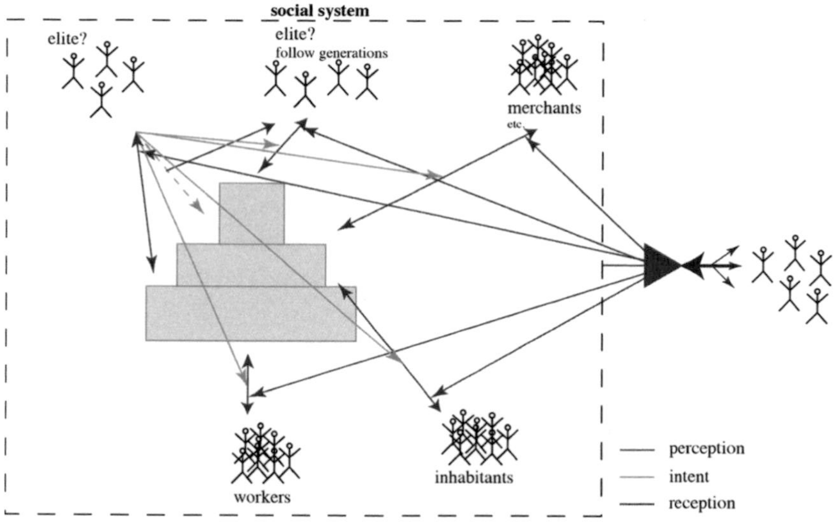

The Austrian author Robert Musil wrote:

"Denkmale haben außer der Eigenschaft, daß man nicht weiß, ob man Denkmale oder Denkmäler sagen soll, noch allerhand Eigenheiten. Die wichtigste davon ist ein wenig widerspruchsvoll; das Auffallendste an Denkmälern ist nämlich, daß man sie nicht bemerkt. Es gibt nichts auf der Welt, was so unsichtbar wäre wie Denkmäler. Sie werden doch zweifellos aufgestellt, um gesehen zu werden, ja geradezu, um die Aufmerksamkeit zu erregen; aber gleichzeitig sind sie durch irgend etwas gegen Aufmerksamkeit imprägniert, und diese rinnt Wassertropfen-auf-Ölbezug-artig an ihnen ab, ohne auch nur einen Augenblick stehenzubleiben. Man kann monatelang eine Straße gehen, man wird jede Hausnummer, jede Auslagenscheibe, jeden Schutzmann am Weg kennen, und es wird einem nicht entgehen, wenn ein Zehnpfennigstück auf dem Gehsteig liegt; aber man ist bestimmt jedesmal sehr überrascht, wenn man eines Tages nach einem hübschen Stubenmädchen ins erste Stockwerk schielt und dabei eine metallene, gar nicht kleine, Tafel entdeckt, auf der in unauslöschlichen Lettern eingegraben steht, daß an dieser Stelle von achtzehnhundertsoundsoviel bis achtzehnhundertundeinige-mehr der unvergeßliche Soodernichtso gelebt und geschaffen habe." (Musil 2017)[10]

This illustrates monumentality as a personal and subjective phenomenon most adequately. A monument is only important and thereby monumental due to a personal connection to it or at least due to the knowledge of the same.

Lieux de mémoire, monuments, and monumentality

It is important to state at this point that we are in fact talking about modern scholarly concepts that we are trying to reflect onto ancient societies. Therefore, it is of primary importance to have crystal clear definitions, which I now will discuss *in medias* res.

I want to draw a clear distinction between monuments and structures with monumentality in the sense of the above, and I want to do this by describing a process from personal monument, or *lieu de mémoire* for that matter, via monumentality to communal monuments (cf. Osborne 2014a: 3).

Everything is a monument for somebody (at least potentially), but the monumental is made by the society and by the acceptance of a monument as a communal monument. A monument does not, by this definition, need to be monumental in accordance to the definition provided by Brunke et al. (2016), nor can it be objectively described – it is in its nature to be subjective.

However, the monumental – or communal monument if you will – can be quantified and has an effect on at least a group of people. What Musil wrote connects much more with the notion of a monument than with the monumental. But if a monument does not have to be monumental, one needs to ask if something monumental has to be a monument.

I would argue that this link does exist, as I already mentioned 'communal monuments'. I would even go one step further in calling them 'cultural monuments' in that they represent *lieux des mémoires* of cultural memory, whereas the

---

grave of a beloved pet, for example, is surely a *lieu de mémoire* for an individual but not part of cultural memory and not monumental.

Monumental structures are canonized and culturally memorized.[11] To stick to the pet example, one could say that the grave of any beloved pet is not remembered by a society or a people, the grave of the beloved fictional pet-dog Lassie, however, would probably enter the realm of cultural memory for a few generations. Therefore, communal monuments cannot be built, they can only become such over time and by the resonance they create in their perceivers. Although some things – like e. g. Lassie's grave – will be instantly perceived as communal monuments, they only reveal their true importance after at least two generations.

Graveyards also represent this phenomenon. Each of the individual graves represents a monument, an individual's *lieu de mémoire*, whereas the graveyard as a whole is a cultural *lieu de mémoire*. This can be best described as an interrelationship between the part and the whole. The study of graves is an ideal example of how to study the social identity of the deceased and their social group. It is also one of the only ways one can identify canonized social and thereby cultural memory (Roßberger 2014: 202; see also Laneri 2014). Grave goods also reflect how this social identity and memory were materialized (cf. Halbwachs 1985) and may provide analogies towards the study of monumentality, cultural memory, and identity.[12]

Cultural memory – as Aleida (2002) and Jan Assmann (1988a; 1992) describe it – is a fluid and dynamic – ever-changing – concept which nevertheless belongs in the sphere of Braudel's (1979) *longue durée*.

Monuments are being created through circumstance and events (see below) and belong to Braudel's *eventements*. Monumentality, however, is intended and intentionally planned, whereas communal monuments are the reaction of perceived monumentality, hence they have something I call received monumentality – as cultural memory they belong to the *longue durée*. There is a progression in the step from where monumentality is intentionally planned from top-down, to communal monuments that are made by society and are therefore bottom-up. Monumentality not only has a quantifiable axis, but also a temporal one.

Monumentality is, by this definition, also a means of creating extra and special meaning for institutions like palaces or temples and their structures. This might also be considered a way of inventing a tradition that puts institutions deeper into cultural memory (see below).

---

11 This might be best compared to what Aby Warburg described as Mnemosyne (Warburg 2012).

12 This will hopefully be further explored in the research group "Making the dead visible" at the University of Durham and in other projects focusing on the re- and assessment of ancient tombs and graveyards. For further details see e. g. Bradbury et al. (2016).

Tackling monumentality with labor

So how can we even speak about monumentality in a way that is scientifically adequate and acceptable in the archaeological record? I do *not* believe it is possible to give a formula for this and I think every case and every structure needs to be discussed separately and individually. However, there are certain questions one might ask that would lead the discussion in the right direction.[13] I will try to exemplify this by looking at labor (for further insights on labor see Bernbeck in this volume).

Figure 4: Relationship between 'regular' labor and drudgery

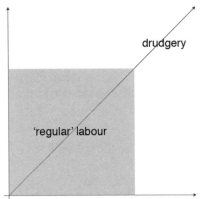

The energetics and labor needed for a building project can be studied objectively. First one needs to calculate the materials needed, then one tries to reconstruct the person power available by using maxima and minima. This plus an estimated timeframe lets us calculate the labor each and every worker had to do in order to finish the building process. Following Marx' distinction between abstract and concrete labor (Marx 1971), there is a certain amount of labor a worker is able to do in one day, this is considered 'regular'. Everything beyond 'regular' work becomes *drudgery (Schinderei)*. As Bernbeck describes in this volume, there are certain strategies that can be used to avoid drudgery to a degree, so the workload remains bearable for the workforce. One could, however, argue that the 'creation of monumentality' and 'meaning' starts with drudgery and that a structure built within

---

13 For a more detailed view on the methodology of studying monuments and monumentality in the archaeological record, see Buccellati (this volume), for energetics see Buccellati (2016) and Hageneuer/Schmidt (this volume).

the realm of 'normal' or 'regular' work cannot be monumental. This is, of course, only one of the possibilities of convergence with the term of monumentality.

The argument is that the ill-treatment of the workmen or dealing with the 'utility-drudgery threshold' (Bernbeck in this volume) adds to the *materiality* of the building and also shows the political power of the ruling class to use energy at their free will (cf. Trigger 1990). There is a discussion in the literature about whether political power is essential to the concept of monumentality (see Osborne 2014a: 9; Trigger 1990 and above) or if the creation of monumental architecture, which in any case needs to be seen as a communal effort, is in fact one of the creating forces of political power (Joyce 2004; Pauketat 2000).

Trevor Watkins even argues that the creation of monumental structures was a key factor in constituting societies (Watkins 2010). In his argument labor is again the main point. The creation of a structure is more important than the structure in its finished state (see e. g. Russell 1998). In short, banding together to create/ make something that is not essential for survival constitutes the Neolithic Revolution (Benz/Gebel/Watkins 2017; Gebel 2017; Helwing/Aliyev 2014; Watkins 2008; 2010; 2017). Labor is only one of the ways to tackle the issue of monumentality among others (cf. Buccellati in this volume), but nevertheless a promising one (cf. Bernbeck this volume).

Motivation behind the monumental

In the realm of the power of politics in relation to temporality, monumentality takes on two roles – an interior and an exterior.

(1) The interior motivation for extra-large projects (or monumental projects) may lie in the building process itself. Contrary to the modern-day view of building sites and building time, the long duration of a project was an indicator for the power of a ruling elite or a king. A prominent example would be gothic cathedrals whose building processes endured for several generations, sometimes even for centuries (e. g. Cologne Cathedral, which was left as a building site for centuries to become a symbol of the 'unfinished' and humankind's hybrid, before it was finally finished by the Prussian emperor [see Hageneuer/van der Heyden in this volume] or Milan Cathedral).

Figure 5: *Cologne Cathedral under construction in 1856 (Grefe 1988) (left) and Milan Cathedral (Photo cc/by Jiuguang Wang) (right)*

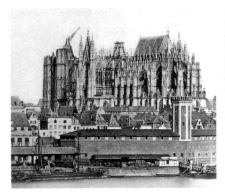

Figure 6: *The Sagrada Família in Barcelona under construction in ca. 1915 (Photo Courtesy of Templo Expiatorio de la Sagrada Familia)*

I argue that it was a show of power to be able to employ a lot of people for a long time – the king makes the palace. This is recorded countless times for the construction process of the gothic cathedrals. A project that is perceived benevolently in its never-ending building process is Sagrada Família in Barcelona, which has always been financed by the people and not by the Roman-Catholic church.

(2) Exterior motivation is different and works better with shorter construction times. I would argue that these kinds of extra-large projects (or monumental projects) were used to impress outsiders and were comparatively cheap. This might be best exemplified by the ziggurats of Ancient Mesopotamia. These were big buildings and in the eyes of the 'modern scholar' without a doubt monumental. They were also part of every city of a certain scale – so they were not unique or special – they were probably even an expected feature that every merchant, traveler or visitor would expect to see and, as Brunke (2016; 2018) shows, they were relatively cheap. In this case one could probably presume that these structures were intended as monumental structures to show power – the palace makes the king.

In both cases the structures are prestigious, either to the people building them or to the people perceiving them.

Figure 7: Ur-Namma Ziqqurat in Uruk-Warka (Photo by Felix Levenson)

However, monumentality does not necessarily have to be intended by the planner or architect. Function and action can make something monumental after the fact. Structures can be instrumentalized and become symbols of their institutions – independent of size. The architecture thereby becomes a symbol with the institution it is housing and its symbolic power (monumentality) is much more closely linked to the importance and the perception of said institution than of the structure itself.

Permanence and memory

Meaning, memory, and also fame play a major role when we are trying to look beyond mere size and volume of materials, as do time and temporality. Brunke et al. (2016) list *permanence* as one of the key aspects of monumentality and this permanence may reach into different aspects of life. Permanence in this context means an eternally enduring process, action, or status. There is for example:

1) *Permanence* of one structure or intended permanence of one structure (Hageneuer/Levenson 2018)
2) *Permanence* of a building space and/or place (Lohmann 2018)
3) *Permanence* of a memory (permanent reception)

This permanence of place and/or memory shows itself primarily in the fact that these memories or places can hand down monumentality to whatever structure is built on that space or built with a certain memory. Churches are a good example for this again. For instance, St. Peter's in Rome inherited its monumentality by being built on exactly the spot where St. Peter is said to have died. The structure would be monumental beside these facts, no matter how big, expensive, or sublime it would have been. An even better example might be the Church of the Holy Sepulchre in Jerusalem, because it is not big and is not as elaborate as St. Peter's; however its monumentality would not fade even if the structure were long gone, as long as the memory remains.

Figure 8: St. Peter's in Rome (Photo cc/by Jean-Pol Grandmont) (left) and the Church of the Holy Sepulchre in Jerusalem (Photo cc/by Jorge Láscar) (right)

So, does a non-permanent structure, or better a structure with no intention of being permanent, have the ability to become monumental? Temporary offices built from shipping containers, refugee camps built from corrugated iron, or visiting platforms for big building sites or other structures – like the Info-Box for the Potsdamer Platz building site or the Humboldt-Box in front of the Humboldforum to give just two examples from Berlin – have a special relevance but no air of permanence, though they do live in the memories of many people (although maybe not the temporary offices). I would argue that even structures that were not intended to be permanent can have, gain, or change their monumentality during their lives. However, this is much more difficult to study or to reconstruct in the archaeological record, as temporary structures are often not recognizable in the archaeological record; however, they can still act as a cultural memory.

Thus far we have only considered physical permanence. The situation changes drastically when one starts to consider mental permanence or permanence of memory as well. I would argue that even if the structure has long gone, it can still be monumental or even a communal monument (in spirit), if the same people still hold its memory and remembrance, which again is just a mind game because memory and oral traditions cannot be proven archaeologically. As I mentioned above, these traditions might be made up to evoke a false memory of an 'alternate' history which legitimizes institutions. This comes back to what the British historian Eric Hobsbawm describes as the invention of tradition (Hobsbawm 1983). One could also think of the Seven Wonders of the World, of which only one still physically exists; however, the other six have no less sense of monumentality.

Figure 9: Info-Box at the building site of the Potsdamer Platz in Berlin, with a fragment of the Berlin Wall (Photo cc/by Helen Schiffer)

Besides temporary structures that were in fact removed after a certain time (see above), it might also be worth considering structures that were intended as temporary, but gained so much monumentality, fame, and importance that they were never removed and sometimes even became emblems, like e. g. the Eiffel tower in Paris or the Crystal Palace in London (cf. Wiggington 1997: 44–45). The architecture from world expositions in general is a good example for the monumentality and meaning of temporary architecture.

In ancient Egypt the creation myth involves the emergence of the world from a permanent, infinite, and lifeless sea, which is often associated with the Nile River but also with groundwater (Assmann/Kucharek 2008; Quirke 2015). Besides being made from stone, tombs and temples were also built on deep foundations. Jan Assmann describes the choice of material as a choice of permanence over events, or speaking in Braudel's terms of *longue durée* over *eventements* (Assmann 1988b; 1991; Braudel 1979). He also believes that the depth of the foundations is related to the groundwater and to the notion of connecting the temples to the infinite, eternal, and permanent sea from which the world emerged (Assmann 2018).[14]

This permanence is clearly a factor to be considered when looking at monumentality. This kind of 'invisible permanence' draws on the same principles as the monumentality of temporary structures, for it only exists in the mind or memory of the beholder.

Large technical structures and infrastructure

One other kind of structure that needs discussion are large technical infrastructures like dams, aqueducts, cisterns, streets etc., but also reshaped landscapes and big grave buildings (for cisterns see Hof in this volume; for reshaped landscapes see Pacheco in this volume). These large technical infrastructures are irrefutably a big part of the realm of monumentality, but – at least in the popular discussion of monumentality – are often skipped due to their supposed lack of prestige or symbolic power (Bourdieu 1992). Nevertheless, the energetic investment in such structures is quantifiably higher than that made for almost any palace, temple, or domestic structure.

I am not sure how large technical infrastructure fit into the discussion of monuments and monumentality. Certainly, they fit many aspects of monumentality that I have considered, but they nonetheless have a different quality. Their importance might be best measured in their social impact and entanglement (cf. Levenson forthcoming). Thus large technical infrastructure starts as an innovation, something that makes life easier and is therefore admired by many. There it gains its importance and its monumentality. However, it also creates dependen-

---

14   This is a notion which is very common in Egyptology; however to my knowledge there is no textual evidence of this idea, nor is there archaeological evidence that the foundations were dug deliberately deeper than necessary for the structural integrity of the temple or tomb above.

cies and entraps us (cf. Hodder 2016). I argue that, similar to the way we use a scaling approach (cf. Buccellati this volume) to investigate monumentality in 'regular' projects, we can also determine the monumentality of infrastructural projects, whose entrapment and interdependencies are even more obvious and graver than, for example, those of palaces, temples, or other public buildings, because their function is inherently more important for the survival of a people.

Conclusion

So, how can we tell when and how a structure becomes monumental? What properties change in a structure to make it stand out from all the others? And to come back to the primary question, what is monumentality and how can we maybe find a convergence to the term?

This question will remain forever without a satisfactory answer, because it is subjective and individual. There are, however, certain elements that I have tried to show that might encase the term and build a framework around it, thus facilitating a more fruitful discussion of this highly interesting phenomenon in the future.

I have tried to show that monumentality is a fluid and dynamic concept, which correlates strongly with the concept of cultural memory. As I have already stated above there is no way of defining it satisfactorily. But somehow, we seem to always recognize, perceive, and receive the monumental and build monumentality (monumental architecture). There are certain factors that may allow us to empirically quantify the degree of monumentality by studying the energetics (energy costs) of a certain structure in comparison to others in the same region during the same period, or by looking at the social implications of different perceptions and receptions; however the intent remains speculative and can only ever be proven circumstantially. The result would thereby be not a mere calculation of labor costs but also a measurement of the social involvement in the construction. How many men and women were employed? Where did the material come from? How was it transported? How long did it take? Was it paid labor? Forced labor? Voluntary labor? The answers may allow us to speak more objectively of a monumentality that we can 'quantify' through the archaeological record.

There is, however, one more question worth asking. After having discussed how to deal with intended monuments or monumental structures, it is necessary to consider how to deal with unintended monumentality or, to be more precise, with structures that were consciously intended not to be monumental, like the German Plenary Building (Figure 1), which was built in the era where everyone (especially in Germany) made an effort to avoid anything even vaguely resembling what was at this time considered monumental. This had a strong connection to the Frankfurt School and the teachings of Theodor W. Adorno and Max Horkheimer (cf. e. g. Adorno 1995; 1967). Again, this shows us the fluidity of the phenomenon of monumentality and the subjectivity of the matter. It is therefore necessary to have a broad perspective when looking at architecture and its potential monumentality. The *Denkstil* of the era is one of the major things to be considered (cf. Fleck 1980 and above). There used to be an artwork by Maurizio Nannucci (*1939) posted above the entrance of the Altes Museum in Berlin that said, "All art has been contemporary" in neon letters. Keeping that in mind when looking at our theme, I argue that it is important to understand every structure as potentially monumental, therefore it is of the utmost importance to create tools and techniques to objectify and thereby make monumentality quantifiable.

Bibliography

Adorno, T. W. (1967): Ohne Leitbild, Frankfurt a. M.: Suhrkamp.

Assmann, A. (2002): Erinnerungsräume – Formen und Wandlungen des kulturellen Gedächtnisses, München: Beck.

Assmann, J. (1988a): "Kollektives Gedächtnis und kulturelle Identität." In: J. Assmann/T. Hölscher (eds.), Kultur und Gedächtnis, Frankfurt a. M.: Suhrkamp, pp. 9–19.

Assmann, J. (1988b): "Stein und Zeit. Das 'monumentale' Gedächtnis der altägyptischen Kultur." In: J. Assmann/T. Hölscher (eds.), Kultur und Gedächtnis, Frankfurt a. M.: Suhrkamp, pp. 87–114.

Assmann, J. (1991): Stein und Zeit – Mensch und Gesellschaft im alten Ägypten, München: Fink.

Assmann, J. (1992): Das kulturelle Gedächtnis, Frankfurt a. M.: Suhrkamp.

Assmann, J./Kucharek, A. (eds.) (2008) Ägyptische Religion. Totenliteratur, Frankfurt a. M.: Verlag der Weltreligionen.

Assmann, J. (2018): Heliopolitanische Kosmogonie, Public Lecture in Berlin held on July 27 2018.

Benz, M./Gebel, H. G./Watkins, T. (2017): "The construction of Neolithic corporate identities." In: M. Benz/H. G. Gebel/T. Watkins (eds.), Neolithic Corporate Identities, Studies in Early Near Eastern Production, Subsistence, and Environment 20, Berlin: ex oriente.

Bourdieu, P. (1992): Language and Symbolic Power, Cambridge: polity.

Bradbury, J./Davies, D./Jay, M./Philip, G./Roberts, C./Scarre, C. (2016): "Making the Dead Visible: Problems and Solutions for 'Big' Picture Approaches to the Past, and Dealing with Large 'Mortuary' Datasets." In: Journal Archaeological Method and Theory 23, pp. 561–591.

Braudel, F. (1979): La Méditerranée et le Monde méditerranéen à l'époque de Philippe II, Paris: Libraire Armand Colin.

Brunke, H./Bukowiecki, E./Cancik-Kirschbaum, E./Eichmann, R./van Ess, M./ Gass, A./Gussone, M./Hageneuer, S./Hansen, S./Kogge, W./May, J./Parzinger, H./Pedersén, O./Sack, D./Schopper, F./Wulf-Rheidt, U./Ziemssen, H. (2016): "Thinking Big. Research in Monumental Constructions in Antiquity." In: eTopoi Journal of Ancient Studies Special Volume 6, pp. 250–305.

Brysbaert, A./Klinkenberg, V./Gutiérrez-Garcia, M./Vikatou, I. (eds.) (2019): Constructing monuments, perceiving monumentality and the economics of building – Theoretical and methodological approaches to the built environment, Leiden: Sidestone Press.

Buccellati, F. (2016): Three-dimensional Volumetric Analysis in the Archaeological Context – The Palace of Tupkish at Urkesh and its Representation, Bibliotheca Mesopotamica, Malibu: Undena Publications.

Fleck, L. (1980): Entstehung und Entwicklung einer wissenschaftlichen Tatsache. Einführung in die Lehre vom Denkstil und Denkkollektiv, Frankfurt a. M.: Suhrkamp.

Foucault, M. (1998[1975]): Surveiller et punir. Naissance de la prison, Paris: Editions Flammarion.

Gebel, H. G. (2017): "Neolithic corporate identities in the Near East", In: M. Benz/H. G. Gebel/T. Watkins (eds.), Neolithic Corporate Identities, Studies in Early Near Eastern Production, Subsistence, and Environment 20, Berlin: ex oriente.

Grefe, U. (1988): Köln in frühen Photographien 1847–1914, München: Schirmer.

Hageneuer, S./Levenson, F. (2018) "Das Steinstiftgebäude in Uruk – ein gescheitertes Experiment?" In: K. Rheidt/W. Lorenz (eds.), Groß Bauen – Großbaustellen als kulturgeschichtliches Phänomen, Basel: Birkhäuser, pp. 109–121.

Halbwachs, M. (1985): Das kollektive Gedächtnis, Frankfurt a. M.: Suhrkamp.

Helwing, B./Aliyev, T. (2014): "A Monumental Neolithic? New Results of the Ongoing Azerbaijanian-German Investigations in the Mil Steppe, Azerbaijan." In: P. Bieliński/M. Gawlikowski/R. Koliński/D. Ławecka/A. Sołtysiak/Z. Wygnańska (eds.), Proceedings of the 8th ICAANE (Vol. 2). Wiesbaden: Harrassowitz, pp. 247–258.

Hobsbawm, E. (1983): "Introduction: Inventing Traditions" In: E. Hobsbawm/T. Ranger (eds.), The Invention of Tradition, Cambridge: Cambridge University Press, pp. 1–14.

Hodder, I. (2016): Studies in Human-Thing Entanglement, self publishing online.

Hole, F. (2012): "West Asian Perspective on Early Monuments." In: R. L. Burger/R. M. Rosenswig (eds.), Early New World Monumentality, Gainsville: University Press of Florida.

Howell-Ardila, D. (1998): "Berlin's Search for a 'Democratic' Architecture: Post-World War II and Post-unification." In: German Politics & Society 16, pp. 62–85.

Joyce, R. A. (2004): "Unintended Consequences? Monumentality as a Novel Experience in Formative Mesoamerica." In: Journal of Archaeological Method and Theory 11, pp. 5–29.

Kant, I. (1990): Kritik der Urteilskraft, Hamburg: Meiner.

Kant, I. (1995): Schriften zur Anthropologie, Geschichtsphilosophie, Politik und Pädagogik. 2. Register zur Werkausgabe, Frankfurt a. M.: Suhrkamp.

Kirk, T. (2008): "Monströse Monumentalität – Monumentale Monstrositäten." In: Bauwelt 48, pp. 1–25.

Küster, U. (2009): "Monumentalität contra Gigantismus. Alberto Giacometti hat auf das, was um ihn herum geschah, stärker reagiert als bisher angenommen." In: du! – Zeitschrift für Kultur 69, pp. 89–93.

Laneri, N. (2014): "Locating the Social Memory of the Ancestors: Residential Funerary Chambers as Locales of Social Remembrance in Mesopotamia During the Late Third and Early Second Millenia BC." In: P. Pfälzner/H. Niehr/E. Pernicka/S. Lange/T. Köster (eds.), Contextualising Grave Inventories in the Ancient Near East – Proceedings of a Workshop at the 7th ICAANE in April 2010 and an International Symposium in Tübingen in November 2010, both organized by the Tübingen Post-Graduate School "Symbols of the Dead," Qatna Studien Supplementa. Wiesbaden: Harrassowitz, pp. 201–216.

Levenson, F. (forthcoming): "Studying architectural energetics – body and mind in its social setting." In: N. N. (ed.), Proceedings of the 11th ICAANE in Munich, Wiesbaden: Harrassowitz.

Lohmann, D. (2018): "Superlative baulicher Art. Zum 'Trilithon' und der Inszenierung von Größe im antiken Jupiterheiligtum in Baalbek." In: K. Rheidt/W. Lorenz (eds.), Groß Bauen – Großbaustellen als kulturgeschichtliches Phänomen, Basel: Birkhäuser, pp. 149–163.

Marx, K. (1971): Das Kapital, Marx-Engels-Werke, Berlin: Dietz Verlag.

Meyer, P. (1938): "Ueberlegungen zum Problem der Monumentalität als Antwort an Hans Schmidt." In: Werk 25/4, pp. 123–128.

Musil, R. (2006): Posthumous Papers of a Living Author, New York: Archipelago.

Musil, R. (2017[1957]): "Denkmale." In: Nachlass zu Lebzeiten, Hamburg: Rowohlt, pp. 62–66.

Nora, P. (1989): "Between Memory and History. Les Lieux de Mémoire." In: Representations 26, pp. 7–24.

Osborne, J. F. (2014a): "Monuments and Monumentality." In: J. F. Osborne (ed.), Approaching Monumentality in Archaeology, IEMA Proceedings. Albany: State University of New York Press, pp. 1–19.

Osborne, J. F. (ed.) (2014b): Approaching Monumentality in Archaeology, IEMA Proceedings. Albany: State University of New York Press.

Pauketat, T. R. (2000): "The tragedy of the commoners." In: M.-A. Dobres/J. Robb (eds.), Agency in Archaeology, London: Routledge, pp. 113–129.

Pollock, S. (1999): Ancient Mesopotamia – The Eden that never was, Case Studies in Early Societies, Cambridge: Cambridge University Press.

Pseudo-Longinos (1966): Vom Erhabenen, Darmstadt: Wissenschaftliche Buchgesellschaft.

Quirke, S. (2015): Exploring Religion in Ancient Egypt, London: Wiley-Blackwell.

Roßberger, E. (2014): "Things to remember – Jewelery, Collective Identity and Memory at the Royal Tomb of Qatna." In: P. Pfälzner/H. Niehr/E. Pernicka/S. Lange/T. Köster (eds.), Contextualising Grave Inventories in the Ancient Near East – Proceedings of a Workshop at the 7th ICAANE in April 2010 and an International Symposium in Tübingen in November 2010, both organized by the Tübingen Post-Graduate School "Symbols of the Dead," Qatna Studien Supplementa, Wiesbaden: Harrassowitz, pp. 201–216.

Russell, J. M. (1998): "The Program of the Palace of Assurnasirpal II at Nimrud. Issues in the Research and Presentation of Assyrian Art." In: American Journal of Archaeology 102, pp. 655–715.

Sievertsen, U. (2010): "Buttress-recess architecture and status symbolism in the Ubaid period." In: R. Carter/G. Philipp (eds.), Beyond the Ubaid. Transformation and Integration in the Late Prehistoric Societies of the Middle East, Studies in Ancient Oriental Civilizations. Chicago: Chicago University Press, pp. 201–226.

Trigger, B. (1990): "Monumental architecture. A thermodynamic explanation of symbolic behaviour." In: World Archaeology 22, pp. 119–132.

Vitruvius (1999): Ten Books on Architecture. Cambridge: Cambridge University Press.

Warburg, A. (2012): Der Bilderatlas MNEMOSYNE, Gesammelte Schriften – Studienausgabe, Berlin: De Gruyter.

Watkins, T. (2008): "Supra-regional networks in the Neolithic of southwest Asia." Journal of World Prehistory 21, pp. 139–171.

Watkins, T. (2010): "New Light on Neolithic Revolution in south-west Asia." In: Antiquity 84, pp. 621–634.

Watkins, T. (2017): "Neolithic corporate identities in evolutionary context." In: M. Benz/H. G. Gebel/T. Watkins (eds.), Neolithic Corporate Identities, Studies in Early Near Eastern Production, Subsistence, and Environment 20, Berlin: ex oriente.

Wiggington, M. (1997): Glas in der Architektur, Stuttgart: Deutsche Verlagsanstalt.

Žižek, S. (2014): Event, London: Penguin Books.

Monumentality: Research Approaches and Methodology

Federico Buccellati

Having discussed a terminological framework for monumentality in the previous chapter, the next step is to focus on the means by which monumentality can be explored in diverse archaeological and historical contexts. One of the most important and debated problems related to the term 'monumentality' in such contexts is the question of perspective.[1] When the modern public sees a monument as 'monumental' they do so from their own perspective – while this certainly has validity, also within our discipline, as scholars we strive to understand ancient architecture within the context of the ancient society that constructed the edifice. This challenge, which lies at the core of archaeology in general, is particularly relevant when considering the longevity of architecture: as our modern built environment is heavily conditioned by architecture built by previous generations, adapted and repurposed to suit current needs and institutions, so too were ancient buildings reused over generations and modified to suit the changing needs of ancient societies. Thus, studies on ancient monumentality are, on the one hand, hampered by these changing constellations of meaning, but on the other hand benefit from them as they show the link between diverse functions (e. g. institutions) and monumental structures over a wider chronological span.

This chapter aims to investigate the methodological approaches and tools that scholars have at their disposal to explore monumentality in ancient societies. These are fruitful only in some contexts, and provide only incomplete answers to questions relating to monumentality; nevertheless it is only by means of such approaches and tools that questions relating to monumentality can be addressed through documentation in the archaeological and/or historical record. Many of these approaches are used to explore diverse research questions in a wide gamut of archaeological contexts – the aim here is only to elucidate how they can be used to explore monumentality, what problems are inherent in their use, what other complementary approaches might be used, and to give a limited range of examples. Thus a detailed explanation of the diverse methods will not be provided, rather only each method's applicability to the question at hand.

---

1 See also the chapter by Levenson this volume.

The tools can be grouped under six general categories as follows: (1) construction process, (2) context, (3) building as source, (4) perspective, (5) interpretation (in a narrow sense), and (6) building as object.[2] Several tools could be considered as pertaining to more than one category, and in such cases the most pertinent has been chosen.

1.   Understanding the construction process

One of the most useful tools in understanding monumentality in ancient contexts is to analyze the construction of an edifice. Such an approach lends itself to understanding the investment, in terms of labor-time and resources, required for a construction. To understand the steps required in a construction, a *chaîne opératoire* can be produced to discern the individual steps in the whole process. By combining the understanding of these steps together with calculations based on the time required for the individual steps, the cost (in terms of energy) required for a construction can be calculated based on a precisely measured edifice. Parallel to an examination of the materials, for some contexts a study of the workforce is possible, both in terms of skills and composition of the labor force.

1.1 Chaîne opératoire

Chaîne opératoire is a well-known method for investigating the process of production, behavior and use of technology; it is primarily applied to objects, particularly lithics (Lemonnier 1986; Bar-Yosef et al. 1992; Gamble 1998; Bleed 2001; Martinón-Torres 2002; Schlanger 2005; Bar-Yosef and Van Peer 2009). One of the strengths of this method is the combination of technological process and the production organization which reflects social processes. A term employed in English is 'operational sequence', and this is often used as a synonym for *chaîne opératoire* despite a few differences. One aspect of the *chaîne opératoire* method which differentiates it from 'operational sequence' or 'operational chains' of the English-language literature is the focus on the cognitive processes involved (Julien/Karlin 1994; Bleed 2001: 105–108). Bleed (2001: 118) suggests that the *chaîne opératoire*, arising as it does from the French Humanist tradition, places more emphasis on the cognitive aspect of such modeling, as opposed to the sequence models more prevalent in the American tradition: such sequence models tend to focus more on material aspects (Bleed 2001: 114).

---

2 A list of methodological approaches and tools was made by the participants in the Size Matters workshop during the final discussion and formed the point of departure for this article. These approaches and tools were then subsequently divided into these categories by the author.

A further term which is sometimes used in conjunction with *chaîne opératoire* is 'behavioral chain' but this term brings time and space into the analysis of the activity (Schiffer 1975a), which produces a specific study of a specific event in a specific space, as opposed to the *chaîne opératoire* which produces a more general sequence which can be applied to various events in various places. Behavioral chains reach this level of abstraction in a second stage, in their contribution to the formation of cultural transformations ('c-transforms') and the interaction of humans or objects through natural agents ('n-transforms' – the cases in behavioral chains where the energy source is non-human, for example) (Schiffer 1975b: 1999).

Four studies which approach architecture using such a methodology are: F. Buccellati for Syro-Mesopotamian Architecture (2016), V. Izzet for Etruscan Architecture (2007), K. Ryan for Dorset Architecture (2009) and C. B. Smith for the Egyptian Pyramids (2006).[3] There are some methodological differences between the application of the *chaîne opératoire* to lithics as opposed to architecture which should be noted. The first is the diverse end-products: in a sense, lithic production can be compared to the production of each of the individual elements making up a building – mudbricks, roofing beams, stone blocks, plaster etc. These elements are, however, not entirely 'understood' unless considered in the wider perspective of the construction as a whole. The second difference between lithics and architecture is the diversity in the skills of the actors and the materials that they use, even when considering the complexity of the construction project as a whole. While in lithic production actors, tools used, operation locations and materials are rather limited, the study of architecture entails much greater diversity. Finally, the last link in an operational chain dealing with lithics is the moment of discard; the last link when applying this method to architecture is more difficult to distinguish.

Despite such differences, which can greatly complicate the analysis of a structure, the *chaîne opératoire* method can be of considerable use when looking at monumentality since it helps scholars discern individual choices made during a construction project. Some choices will be conditioned by material availability, the topographic context, or other compelling factors. Some of the choices, however, may turn out to be a choice between two viable options, and it is in analyzing these alternatives and the final decision taken that the monumentality (as perceived by the ancient society) of a structure may come to light.

1.2 Energetics

By using energetics as a tool to explore the concept of monumentality, one is led to examine specific elements of the constructed space, looking in detail at the reasoning behind specific choices made at the moment of planning and construction.

---

3 See also Knappett (2011) on the chaîne opératoire method.

Sometimes the reasoning behind the decision is based on an improvement to be had on the technological level, but in some cases a social or ideological level can be posited.[4]

The following quote regarding Mayan architecture can help in understanding the relevance of energetics in this context:

> "Architecture, as a collection of raw and manufacture components, is translated into the composite cost of procuring and transporting those materials, manufacturing necessary parts, and assembling the final product." (Abrams 1994: 2)

Further:

> "The analyses focus on the comparison and interpretation of collective measures of architectural cost rather than on the more symbolic or psychologic dimensions of the architecture, although these factors are in reality not disarticulated" (Abrams 1994: 7)

An example of the usefulness of energetics in determining value is related to how one can ascribe meaning to specific choices made in constructing a monumental building. In a discussion of construction and considerations of the materials, one sees how the use of stone in the building meant a greater expenditure of work or energy than would have been the case had the building been built entirely of mud-bricks. One is led to ask why this material was used; there are clearly technological benefits to stone, primarily its ability to block humidity rising from the ground into the walls and damaging them. However it is a further interpretative step to say that stonework is linked to the definition of the structure, be it either to say that the use of stone (in parts of the structure or its entirety) is a symbolic necessity or to say that only the economic/energetic resources available to a specific person or institution could have constructed buildings out of stone – both considerations which tie directly into our definition of a building as 'monumental'. It is energetic analysis as a tool which allows one to show that a certain choice (use of stone, fresco, or secco painting of plastered walls, wide rooms necessitating unusually large roofing beams) implies a cost which can be put in relation to other similar calculations. These other calculations can be derived from the same structure, or from a typologically similar structure, or can even allow for a hypothetical comparison to a case where a different choice had been made for the same building. Thus a stone-paved courtyard can be compared, in terms of energetic cost, to other beaten-earth courtyards in the same building, or to other stone-paved courtyards in another typologically similar structure, or one can compare the stone-paved

---

4 As to some of the problems inherent in this line of questioning, see Meijer (2008).

courtyard to the hypothetical case of the same courtyard paved in baked brick.[5] There is, in other words, a correlation between costs and the final result: one may say that monumentality comes at a price – and to the extent that we can gauge this price (always keeping in mind the limitations of the data available as well as all of the factors that a 'cost' based approach leaves out), we get a better handle on what the monumentality meant to those who produced it.

1.3 Costly signaling

Linked to studies of energetics are analyses based on costly signaling; this approach attempts to see expensive (in a broad sense, including imported materials, advanced technical know-how, or labor-intensive work) elements of architecture as being vehicles of communication. This approach is derived from biology, where animals lay claim to desirability through physical attributes or works. It has been applied to literary texts by R. Corbey and A. Mol in an article where they analyze the weapons within the saga of Beowolf as elements of costly signaling (Corbey/Mol 2011). Its usefulness in the study of monumental structures lies in the focus on 'costliness' as communication, whereby the cost of aspects of a building (materials used, decoration, or size to name a few) are examined as a 'signifier' (in the sense of Saussure's *signifiant*). Combined, for example, with energetics, this type of analysis can aid scholars looking at how investments in certain rooms or areas of a structure, as well as the specific choices made during construction regarding materials used and techniques employed, may have been aimed at impacting specific audiences. Whereas energetics looks at the costs of building the structure as a whole in terms of materials and labor costs, a costly signaling approach considers the impact of the most costly elements in terms of audience, allowing scholars to add a consideration of the human aspect or human impact to the more abstract and material-oriented energetic analysis.

1.4 Organization

A further aspect of monumentality is the way in which the necessary workforce was organized. While not all monumental structures were built by workers organized under a higher authority, and not all work done by such a higher authority is necessarily monumental, still the workforce should be taken into account when ascribing 'monumentality' to a construction.[6]

---

5 For more on energetics see also the articles by Hageneuer and van der Hyden, as well as by Hageneuer and Schmidt, in this volume, as well as the online resource www.EnCAB.net by the author.

6 For more on labor refer to the chapters by Levenson and by Bernbeck in this volume.

There are several ethnographic studies detailing how workers can be organized within pre-industrial societies, and some textual information from the Old Babylonian period (c. 1800–1600 BCE) in particular (Burke 2008: 146). Without detailed records it is difficult to propose specific models for individual construction projects. However, these studies do give general parameters for various systems, and can be useful when considering the general parameters of worker organization within monumental construction projects.[7]

Two workforce systems play a primary role in many pre-industrial construction projects: the *corvée*-system and slavery. These two systems can be identified in the Garshana archives (Heimpel 2009: 45–90) in great detail; this archive dates to the Ur III period of Mesopotamia (c. 2100–2000 BCE), and the extensive archive provides a fascinating look into the day-to-day workings of a large building project. It is important to keep in mind, however, that the *corvée*-system is a modern term which is used to define a work relationship which predates the term by millennia, and is thus to be seen as an analogy which should be used only in so far as it helps understand this ancient work relationship.

The *corvée*-system is considered a form of 'custodial recruitment', and is sub-divided into two types: 'American' and 'African' *corvées* (Udy 1959: 79–81). 'American' *corvées* are more common in North and South America, and are primarily a political organization with only minimal or no economic support. Thus a political figure can command the participation of members of the society in public projects; each person normally is obliged to contribute only a certain amount to public projects over a set period of time. 'African' *corvées*, on the other hand, are more tied to the economic control of the official over the resources of the community. Thus the people working in an 'African' *corvée*-system contribute to the economic resources which belong to the community, for example by tilling communal land or as a shepherd of communal flocks.

The Garshana archives indicate that at least part of the workforce there came from a *corvée*-system, most likely of the 'American' type, since the control over the workers seems to be primarily political as opposed to economic. In this type of *corvée*-system the workers possessed their own means of production for periods when they were not working for the state (Schloen 2001: 263).[8] One difference in the *corvée*-system which seems to be at work in Garshana is that it draws on family structures as opposed to drawing directly on individuals. Further evidence of the *corvée*-system in the Ancient Near East can be seen in the Old Babylonian period (Yokoyama 1994) as well as in the Amarna texts.[9]

---

7   See, for example, the author's work on the Palace of Tupkish (Palace AP) at Tell Mozan, ancient Urkesh (Buccellati 2016).

8   *Pace* Diakonoff (1972, 1976).

9   Moran 2000 EA 365, Biridiya Letter 7 of 7.

The second group of workers participating in the work were slaves (Udy 1959: 86–87; Heimpel 2009: 45–90), who belonged directly to the political organization of the state or to the families who supplied workers under the *corvée*-system described above. Thus the use of slaves is not in parallel to the *corvée*-system, but is rather integrated as a part of the workforce, be it under the *corvée*-system or directly as state-controlled labor.

2. Considering context

A further category of conceptual tools used in understanding ancient monumentality is the wider context in which a building can be examined. Here the structure being analyzed is considered as one element within a typological category, and as such it demonstrates conformity or diversity to a general model extrapolated from the group as a whole. Such an approach lends to the individual building the strength of a wide range of examples from the same cultural and geographic context, allowing conclusions drawn in other cases to be applied (judiciously) to the example under investigation. Another means of analyzing context is to look beyond the cultural borders of the edifice in question, and to draw conclusions by analogy from other contexts with similarities which justify such an intercultural comparison.

2.1 Typology

Typological analysis is one of the mainstays of archaeological research, and plays an important role in the study of monumentality as well. Two aspects are particularly pertinent to understanding monumentality: recognizability and standardization vs innovation. Recognizability and standardization refer to aspects of a structure which are taken from other buildings, 'citing', as it were, the other structure and thus assuming (or attempting to assume) traits of the other structure; thus elements taken from another monumental structure confer monumentality to a new building by inference. Innovation, on the other hand, is the inclusion of a 'new' element (including both elements which had never been used or those imported from foreign contexts), making the structure unique and thus, in the case of monumental architecture conferring monumentality through the prestige of novelty.

When using typology as a method to study monumentality, there is the danger of creating a circular argument – collecting buildings which are monumental, and then showing that the collection demonstrates traits of monumentality. To counteract this risk, typological studies are best paired with other types of analysis which allow one to define a limited number of structures as monumental and then to see the position of these structures within the wider architectural field.[10]

A typological study of a class of buildings can be used to demonstrate their similarities – similarities which are apparent in the archaeological record, and which would have been evident to the ancient peoples as well. Using a typological study can aid in identifying elements of recognizability among classes of buildings, and, when used together with other methods, can attempt to define certain elements as being tied to monumentality. One of the best examples of this type of analysis is the study on Mesopotamian Palaces by J.-C. Margueron (1982); one particularly relevant graphic composition can be found in Figure 366, where Margueron places the floorplans of a series of palaces in the same scale and with their original orientation on a single page, graphically demonstrating similarities in overall building size as well as commonalities of orientation.

Typologies group buildings which are in the same class by identifying the presence of common elements, as discussed under recognizability. What is not common, but is rare or unique or a foreign import in one or more of these buildings can also be a marker of monumentality, as these elements can be signs of innovation. An example of this is the unique building material used in the Stone-Cone Building *(Steinstiftgebaeude)* in Uruk, as described by Hageneuer and Levenson (2018).

2.2 Analogy

The use of analogy is similar to typology, but draws on examples from different contexts that parallel the building under question but do not offer a direct link. Such examples can be of particular use when examining what is missing from a certain context, and may be drawn from ethnographic as well as archaeological contexts from other cultural regions.[11] An example of the benefit of ethnographic studies as a source for archaeological interpretation is the 'Fortress of the Elephant Hunter' in Burkina Faso, a structure where room function, rooftop usage, gardens and cultic practices can all be seen as analogies to better interpret elements found in the archaeological record (Buccellati 2014b; Schneider 1991). Analogies can be employed to argue that a building is monumental based on parallels from other contexts; this would be particularly useful for situations where monumentality is not immediately apparent and a case needs to be made. The 'Fortress

---

10 On some examples of monumentality and the 'copying' of architecture in a 'poorer' form (and thus perhaps not monumental) see Micale (2016).

11 A very interesting discussion of the value of ethnographic analogies can be found in a dialogue between Gould, Watson and Wylie (Watson/Gould 1982; Wylie 1982). For a recent treatment of the subject and bibliography see Bernbeck (2017: 251–322).

of the Elephant Hunter' could be used to describe a monumentality in which a single edifice contains all of the community and all structured functions of that community. An analogous example is the modern town of Whittier, Alaska, USA, where a town of over 200 people currently inhabit a single building (Begich Towers; in 1960 the towers housed 800 residents). This building serves not only as the residence for the community, but also includes schools, markets, a police station, and the town administrative offices.

3. Buildings as a source

Another approach to understanding the monumentality of buildings is in an analysis of the building as a source which can speak to the institution which it houses, attempting to understand the monumentality of a certain structure through the social role of the institution housed within. The building also acts as a frame for what is occurring within the building on a practical level, considering also audiences – thus the built environment enables the function of certain spaces as well as enhancing certain spaces through perceptual impact. These functions can also be seen in a diachronic manner, laying claim to monumentality through the duration of the activity (over generations). Finally, the impact of the structure on the surrounding urban environment is also an indicator of the monumentality of a certain structure.

3.1 Building as home to an institution

One approach to monumentality rests on the understanding of the social institution which the structure embodies, as the architecture develops into a symbol for that institution. The structure itself, then, becomes a way of examining the 'value' of the institution which it houses, and vice-versa (this is particularly apparent when considering temple complexes and royal palaces). This relationship between the social and the physical worlds is by far the most difficult to explore, meaningfully as archaeologists, and the most difficult to tie back to data from the archaeological record. Yet it is worthwhile despite these risks, since it is through these types of questions that the social aspect of ancient society can be discussed, and if such questions are not confronted by archaeologists, who have a unique grasp of the data from the archaeological record, then who should attempt such questions?[12]

---

12 Of course, one might argue that such questions should not be asked at all; such an argument is made for religion by Oppenheim in his famous chapter "Why a 'Mesopotamian Religion' should not be written" (1977: 172–182).

Perhaps the most fruitful approach here is not to find examples which show that important institutions or individuals from the elite are housed within monumental buildings, but to focus on those cases where this relationship does not hold: monumental buildings which do not house significant institutions or members of the elite, or, conversely, where important institutions or individuals from the elite are housed in seemingly un-monumental structures.[13]

3.2 Building as frame

The next approach is to consider the building as a frame for certain activities.[14] The installations or the presence of elements of material culture (e. g. seal impressions) are some of the primary elements which one can use to define the diverse functions present in specific areas of a building. By studying the built spaces where these functions were carried out, both in terms of construction materials as well as position within the building, conclusions as to monumentality can be drawn. One of the most stark examples of this is the presence of the king within a royal palace, leading to an emphasis on the throne room and private quarters; *babanu* and *bitanu* are two terms used in the literature discussing Mesopotamian architecture to refer to the reception area and living area of the king (Heinrich 1984; Margueron 2005; Kertai 2015).

A further approach contributing to considering the building as a frame lies in how the building uses the senses to produce a reaction in a viewer.[15] One example of this is the formal courtyard in the Royal Palace of Tupkish (Palace AP, dating to c. 2150 BCE) at Tell Mozan, ancient Urkesh (Buccellati 2016: 69); this courtyard was paved in massive white limestone blocks, and would most likely have been approached from a roofed area. The transition from the relative dark of the roofed area to the paved courtyard area, which is nearly blinding on a sunny day, would have made a great impact on the visitor, and, as it was the route to reach the king, would have been a monumental approach enhancing the perceived power of the king.

---

13 Examining such a relationship also raises the question of what the opposite of 'monumentality' is; perhaps 'vernacular', although any public building would be the opposite of vernacular, be it monumental or not. 'Common' does not fit either, as monumental buildings are not necessarily unique – if anything, their monumental character is enhanced by emulating other monumental structures.

14 This section is clearly closely tied to the preceding section on building as institutional home; the difference lies in the type of data available, as references to an institution would rely heavily on textual sources while a focus on activities draws primarily on the archaeological record.

15 For more on sensory perception see section 4.2 Touch, hearing and smell below.

3.3 Use analysis

The functions of the institution, as embodied in the installations and finds uncovered, can also speak to a building's monumentality when considered diachronically. The continued presence of certain functions over a long period is primarily to be found in temple architecture, where long architectural traditions of sacred architecture in the same location can often be discerned.

One of the most prominent examples of this type of continued presence is the E-Abzu temple of Eridu, modern Tell Abu Shahrain, dedicated to the god Enki. Here archaeologists uncovered a sequence of more than 14 different temple phases in the same location beginning around 5400 BCE and ending 2000 years later (Delougaz 1938; Frankfort/Roaf/Matthews 1996: 18; Oates 1960). Such a sequence shows an astounding continuity of tradition – even if the first structures were very limited in terms of the architecture, they are monumental because they form the beginning of a long architectural tradition.

3.4 Contextualization within the urban landscape

Buildings can also be seen as sources when viewed as individual elements within a wider urban context. A building's monumentality may be defined by what is removed in order to make space for the new building as well as its ability to affect what lies around it. What buildings or structures were removed to make room for the new construction? How does the new building affect the road/path network within the settlement? Is access to the primary entrance to the new structure privileged? Is the position of the building designed to highlight its visibility within the settlement and/or the surrounding rural areas? These questions aim to focus on the importance of the building as seen in relation to what is affected by its construction and presence within the urban landscape.

One particularly interesting example of monumentality as defined by urban context is the site of Tell Chuera. A very intensive geophysical survey allowed archaeologists to determine the road network within the city, thereby placing the monumentality of buildings within a wider urban context (Meyer 2013b; 2013a; 2007a). These monumental buildings had been uncovered in the course of archaeological excavations (the well-known *Steinbauten* of Tell Chuera), but these structures were examined individually. The geophysical survey allowed scholars to understand the buildings as a single complex, linked by a network of radial streets which underlined the structures' visibility and importance. It is also worth noting that the geophysical survey allowed archaeologists to explore these interconnections through excavation, making this urban monumentality at the site a research question in its own right (Meyer 2007b). The exploration of this particular organization of the urban space led to further research on a known type of urban planning, called *Kranzhuegel* sites (Akkermans/Schwartz 2002: 256–259; Meyer 2006), thus contributing not only to our understanding of the organization of urban space at Tell Chuera but also giving insight into a wider cultural phenomenon – and its implications for monumentality.

4. Perspective

The monumentality of a structure can also be proposed on the basis of the perceptual impact that a visitor would have; this would be primarily visual, but could also include other senses such as touch, hearing or smell. These senses can communicate on a wide variety of different levels (Ankerl 1981: 45–46).[16] Ankerl's work (1981) combining architecture and sociology provides great insight into the combination of space and communication. For him, architecture is a "system of multilinearly interlinked spaces" (Ankerl 1981: 171), and a proper analysis of these links and spaces can help define the style and function of a building, even in the absence of the users' self-expression in this regard.[17] This makes his work of particular use to archaeologists, since his interpretation of architecture is based on many of the same elements of material culture that are available to (and limit) archaeological research.

4.1 Visibility and the viewer

The work of Richard Bradley (Bradley 1997; 2000; 2009) shows how the correlation between viewpoint and landscape can be examined within a semantic framework – a similar approach might prove fruitful when applied to questions regarding the monumentality of buildings. Such an analysis would examine visibility in two directions, from the building to the surrounding area (be it the urban context of the building and/or the surrounding rural area) as well as from the surrounding area to the building. How much of the building could be seen from the outside (and vice-versa) can lead to questions regarding presentation, communication, and the iconography of power. Furthermore, such an approach can also examine who is doing the viewing – who could access portions of the building with views outside the walls, such as rooftop areas? How much could be seen from the outside through the external doorway? Was the access leading to the external doorway accessible to all, or was it limited? Some of these questions have been posed

---

16 *Pace* Preziosi, who limits perception to optical perception: "In connection with the nature of its perceptual address, architecture employs visually palpable means to broadcast its messages" (Preziosi 1983: 211).

17 Ankerl's book was not well received (Michelson 1984; Sydie 1984; Ankerl/Michelson 1985), but the criticism focuses primarily on other aspects of his book. Relevant for this study is his discussion of these "multilinearly interlinked spaces" which was not criticized by reviewers.

regarding the Palace of Tupkish at Mozan, ancient Urkesh (Buccellati 2014a) and the Temple Terrace at Urkesh (Buccellati 2010) by the author, and show how perception in general and visibility in particular can be examined with regard to the question of monumentality. Here 3D reconstructions can be of use in order to test and visualize the hypotheses developed.[18]

A second tool relating to visibility studies is the use of isovists to determine what is visible from a wide range of points (Benedikt 1979; Batty 2001). This tool can be employed to investigate enclosed spaces (but not necessarily roofed spaces) to examine how visible certain elements are within a space. Using this tool one can map a space in relation to a single point, determining how central, in terms of visibility, that point is. For example, an altar is visible from virtually every point within a sacred space, while a side chapel has more limited visibility. In this way the 'centrality' of certain points can be determined and codified in a way that allows for comparison to other points in the same space or when compared to other spaces. Additionally, such an approach can help codify the relationship between two points, for example between the position of a visitor entering a throne room and the king (or visitor and deity in the case of religious contexts), as is the case with so-called bent-axis approaches. A particularly successful use of this tool is the study of the courtyard of the Neo-Assyrian Palace of Sargon at Khorsabad (706 BCE) by A. McMahon (2013). Here McMahon shows how the approach from the entry gate (Gate B) is not centered on the entrance to the palace itself, but reveals, to the entering visitor, the perimeter wall of the palace. McMahon interprets this use of visibility as "a nuanced, innovative use and manipulation of space at the interface between the ideology of monumentality and the praxis of visual experience" (McMahon 2013: 172).

4.2 Touch, hearing and smell

The sense of touch can be examined in the layout of the rooms, for example a high number of small rooms increases the haptic space and decreases the optical space by increasing the number of walls. Put another way, the visitor cannot see very far, but has a lot of surface area within reach. The high level of surface area means that there is more space along the walls for storage, be it for shelving or larger objects on the floor along the wall.

The sense of sound[19] is much more difficult to project based on the architectural footprint as we have it, since sound would be most affected by the elements of the building which are no longer present: doors, the roof, windows, and the

---

18 There is a great deal of literature on 3D reconstructions of architecture; here I will only cite Wendrich's study on the Temple of Karnak (2014) as it relates directly to monumentality.

19 For a seminal study of sound in Neo-Assyrian palaces, see McMahon (2016).

presence of textiles in the rooms which would have affected how sound traveled as well. Such considerations should also be made for people outside the structure, who would have been able to walk up to the outer walls and presumably hear some of the sounds emanating from inside, primarily from the courtyards.

The final sense to be discussed here is that of smell. The placement of kitchen or workshop areas would have had a direct impact on portions of the structure which would have been affected when the wind carried in smells of cooking, smelting, or kiln fires. As wind direction is often determined by the topography of the city and by local geography, it is possible to estimate the space in which wind conditions might have carried such odors.

These elements,[20] considered for various portions of the building, can help understand how architecture shapes and is shaped by social space. Such an approach, in addition to studies on interaction and space syntax (Hillier 1988; Deblauwe 1992; 1994; 1997; Seamon 2013), can lead to a deeper understanding not only of the architecture itself but also of the uses for which it was designed, as well as how changes over time show shifting functions of the rooms. Such an approach can aid in the study of monumentality by examining how a structure focuses the senses on specific functional areas or social spaces within the building itself. A building is most often monumental because of what it contains, and such an approach allows scholars to define how individual elements of the structure bring those functions or areas to the fore.

5. Interpreting architecture

While all of the methods presented here are interpretive, two approaches are interpretive in a more narrow sense: reception and reconstruction. Reception studies examine the impact the building had on an (ancient) societal level, looking at how the building impacted future constructions in other contexts, how the urban landscape was affected post-construction, and depictions or descriptions of the structure in artistic or written sources. In the modern context, the reconstruction of the building (as a model, virtual or real, or in drawn reconstructions) also explores ancient monumentality by attempting to communicate that attribute of the building to modern audiences. The problems in 'translation' highlight differences in modern and ancient understandings of monumentality, bringing new research perspectives. Clearly, the two approaches are inexorably linked, as reconstructions impact directly on how ancient monumentality is perceived and vice-versa, but each is a separate approach to the interpretation of ancient monumentality.

---

20 There is a wide range of literature on the subject; for further reading and a more extensive bibliography, see Hamilakis (2013); Neumann (2014); Pink (2015); Turner (2012).

5.1 Reception

One criterion for monumentality is the impact of the structure on the cultural sphere it occupies; do similar buildings which postdate it echo some part of its monumental nature?[21] Does the structure impact the urban environment for a long period of time? Do textual or artistic sources refer to the structure as iconic or emblematic in some way? Many of these points have been raised above, in particular under typology and contextualization within the urban landscape – the particular emphasis here is the conscious choice to copy or emulate in some way a particular structure, giving monumentality to that original structure through this act of appropriation.

5.2 Reconstruction

There are a variety of techniques for reconstruction, all with the aim of reproducing to a certain degree of accuracy the ancient building as it would have been seen in ancient times. Many of these techniques produce three-dimensional models, either real or virtual, but the question of reconstruction predates such modern methods. In fact, reconstructions of ancient buildings produced by archaeologists have influenced modern architects, thus showing how ancient material culture can (through the less-than-perfect medium of archaeological interpretation)[22] be a source of inspiration for modern material culture (Micale 2007; 2010) and demonstrating how reconstruction and reception are inexorably linked. This impact on the modern world is often tied to monumentality, as it is ancient monumental structures which inspire modern monumental structures, such as the Tate Modern in London (Micale 2013; Pedde 2010).

6. Building as object

The last group of tools relate to architecture as an object. The material used in the construction of the building is also an aspect of the energetics and the perception approaches, yet the material as such and how it relates to questions of prestige or costly signaling are best considered separately. In keeping with the title of the conference which was at the origin of this volume (Size Matters), the dimensions of a building play an important role in many cultural contexts with regard to monumentality; thus scalarity – both larger and smaller than a 'norm' – can be an indi-

---

21 As reception is discussed in more detail in the following chapter by Hageneuer and van der Heyden I have limited the discussion here to a few questions relating to the other methods discussed.
22 See also Hageneuer (2016).

cator of monumentality. Finally, an examination of the life of a building through its object biography explores not only the initial form and function of a building but considers also how the building changes (in a myriad of ways) over time.

6.1 Materiality

The symbolic valence of materials is particularly difficult for archaeologists to determine since what is missing is not only the ability to interview the inhabitants of these buildings but also a series of other potentially symbolic elements which might have altered or enhanced the symbols available to us. An example of this is color in the form of fresco or secco wall painting (e. g. Til Barsip), which is only rarely preserved in the architectural remains in the ancient Near East[23] but which possibly played a major role in defining the significations, connotations, and usages of architectural space (Preziosi 1983: 210). Further considerations of material are made by Preziosi in his study of Minoan architecture:

> "If the Minoan corpus resembles other architectonic systems, then it will likely be the case that certain materials may come to take on more direct signification than is evident here. It may turn out that for the Minoan, the use of certain materials may have had connotations of its own. One may imagine, for example, that such is the case with respect to contrasts in texture and finishing of stone; it is generally the case that the major (western) facades of great public structures such as the palatial compounds were composed of finely hewn and squared hard limestone (vs. many private structures). The presence of such material may thereby have perceptually cued (or enhanced the geometric perception of) certain social and functional contrasts." (Preziosi 1983: 210)

6.2 Multi-scalarity

While the title of this book is Size Matters, size is not the primary criterion for monumentality, as the examples above and the other chapters in this volume show.[24] Small buildings can certainly be monumental, even perhaps more monumental than others which are larger in size. The examples above from Uruk and Eridu show that the use of a costly material or a humble structure which begins a 2000-year tradition of religious structures can be just as monumental, if not more, than their counterparts.

The concept of size is also relative. When determining that a building is 'large' or 'small' one must keep in mind that such determinations are relative, and the

---

23 On wall decorations see Nunn (1988); Albenda (2005).

24 For a discussion on size and monumentality see also Osborne (2014: 4–8).

context from which such a definition is drawn must be made explicit. The Citadel of Khorsabad (706 BCE) dwarfs the Palace of Tupkish at Tell Mozan (c. 2150 BCE), but each are large structures for their chronological period and cultural context.

6.3 Object biography

Object biography is one of the broadest methods for the study of material culture, and can incorporate many if not most of the methods discussed here. Due to its broad scope it will be discussed in detail in the following chapter by Hageneuer and van der Heyden; it is included as a heading in this chapter for the sake of completeness, as it is a method with which monumentality in architecture can be explored.

Concluding remarks

Monumentality, as an over-arching concept, is difficult to concisely define, and asking whether a structure is or is not monumental can, at times, lead to unending (and unfruitful) debate. The panorama of methodological approaches and tools given here is meant not only as an overview but also as an attempt to draw a boundary within which discussions of monumentality can take place. These limits are not inherent to the buildings we study, nor are they distilled from a totality of cultural contexts – they are instead boundaries inherent in our field, as they describe the mechanisms by which a discussion of monumentality can take place while remaining firmly anchored in archaeological, philological, and historical data. As with any boundary, however, the mere definition of a limit is also a challenge to go beyond – new methodological approaches and tools with which to explore monumentality are certainly awaiting discovery, and by expanding the reach of these discussions they will enrich our understanding of monumentality and the distant past.

Bibliography

Abrams, E. (1994): How the Maya Built Their World: Energetics and Ancient Architecture, Austin: University of Texas Press.

Akkermans, P./Schwartz, G. (2002): The Archaeology of Syria: From Complex Hunter-Gatherers to Early Urban Societies (c. 16,000–300 BC), Cambridge; New York: Cambridge University Press.

Albenda, P. (2005): Ornamental Wall Painting in the Art of the Assyrian Empire, Leiden; Boston: Brill; Styx.

Ankerl, G. (1981): Experimental Sociology of Architecture: A Guide to Theory, Research and Literature, New Babylon: Studies in the Social Sciences 36, The Hague; Paris; New York: Mouton.

Ankerl, G./Michelson, W. (1985): "Comment on Review of Experimental Sociology of Architecture – How Do Critics Skim a Book? [& Reply]" In: Contemporary Sociology 14/2, pp. 150–152.

Bar-Yosef, O./Van Peer, P. (2009): "The Chaîne Opératoire Approach in Middle Paleolithic Archaeology." In: Current Anthropology 50/1, pp. 103–131.

Bar-Yosef, O./Vandermeersch, B./Arensburg, B./Belfer-Cohen, A./Goldberg, P./ Laville, H./Meignen, L. et al. (1992): "The Excavations in Kebara Cave, Mt. Carmel [and Comments and Replies]." In: Current Anthropology 33/5, pp. 497–550.

Batty, M. (2001): "Exploring Isovist Fields: Space and Shape in Architectural and Urban Morphology." In: Environment and Planning B: Planning and Design 28/1, pp. 123–150.

Benedikt, M. L. (1979): "To Take Hold of Space: Isovists and Iaovist Fields." In: Environment and Planning B: Planning and Design 6/1, pp. 47–65.

Bernbeck, R. (2017): Materielle Spuren des nationalsozialistischen Terrors. Zu einer Archäologie der Zeitgeschichte, Histoire 115, Bielefeld: transcript.

Bleed, P. (2001): "Trees or Chains, Links or Branches: Conceptual Alternatives for Consideration of Stone Tool Production and Other Sequential Activities." In: Journal of Archaeological Method and Theory 8/1, pp. 101–127.

Bradley, R. (1997): Rock Art and the Prehistory of Atlantic Europe: Signing the Land, New York: Routledge.

Bradley, R. (2000): The Good Stones: A New Investigation of the Clava Cairns, Edinburgh: Society of Antiquaries of Scotland.

Bradley, R. (2009): Image and Audience: Rethinking Prehistoric Art, Oxford, England: Oxford University Press.

Buccellati, F. (2010): "The Monumental Temple Terrace at Urkesh and its Setting." In: J. Becker/R. Hempelmann/E. Rehm (eds.), Kulturlandschaft Syrien: Zentrum und Peripherie Festschrift für Jan-Waalke Meyer, AOAT 371, Münster: Ugarit-Verlag, pp. 71–86.

Buccellati, F. (2014a): "Diachronic Developments at the Central Monumental Complex of Ancient Urkesh (Tell Mozan)." In: Proceedings of the 8th International Congress on the Archaeology of the Ancient Near East: 10 April-4 May, 2012 University of Warsaw, 1, Wiesbaden: Harassowitz, pp. 313–322.

Buccellati, F. (2014b): "Understanding Households – a Few Thoughts." In: F. Buccellati/T. Helms/A. Tamm (eds.), House and Household Economies in 3rd Millennium B. C. E. Syro-Mesopotamia, BAR International Series 2682, Oxford, England: BAR International Series, pp. 35–42.

Buccellati, F. (2016): Three-Dimensional Volumetric Analysis in an Archaeological Context: The Palace of Tupkish at Urkesh and Its Representation, Bibliotheca Mesopotamica 30, Malibu: Undena Publications.

Burke, A. (2008): 'Walled up to Heaven' – the Evolution of Middle Bronze Age Fortification Strategies in the Levant, Studies in the Archaeology and History of the Levant 4, Winona Lake: Eisenbrauns.

Corbey, R./Mol, A. (2011): "'By Weapons Made Worthy': A Darwinian Perspective on Beowulf." In: E. Slingerland/M. Collard (eds.), Creating Consilience: Integrating the Science and the Humanities, New York: Oxford University Press, pp. 372–384.

Deblauwe, F. (1992): "A Study of Accessibility and Circulation Patterns in the Sin Temple of Hafagi from the Third Millennium B.C." In: Mesopotamia 27, pp. 89–118.

Deblauwe, F. (1994): "Spacings and Statistics, or a Different Method to Analyze Buildings. A Test with Mesopotamian Houses from the Late Bronze and Iron Ages." In: Akkadica 89–90, pp. 1–8.

Deblauwe, F. (1997): "Discriminant Analysis of Selected Spatial Variables Derived from Mesopotamian Buildings of the Late Bronze Age till the Parthian Period." In: Mesopotamia 32, pp. 271–288.

Delougaz, P. (1938): "A Short Investigation of the Temple at Al-'Ubaid." In: Iraq 5, pp. 1–11.

Diakonoff, I. (1972): "Socio-Economic Classes in Babylonia and the Babylonian Concept of Social Stratification." In: D. O. Edzard (ed.), Gesellschaftsklassen im alten Zweistromland und in den angrenzenden Gebieten, München: Beck, pp. 41–52.

Diakonoff, I. (1976): "Slaves, Helots and Serfs in Early Antiquity." In: J. Harmatta/G. Komoroczy (eds.), Wirtschaft und Gesellschaft im alten Vorderasien, Budapest: Akademiai Kiado, pp. 45–78.

Frankfort, H./Roaf, M./Matthews, D. (1996): The Art and Architecture of the Ancient Orient, New Haven: Yale University Press.

Gamble, C. (1998): "Palaeolithic Society and the Release from Proximity: A Network Approach to Intimate Relations." In: World Archaeology 29/3, pp. 426–449.

Hageneuer, S. (2016): "The Influence of Early Architectural Reconstruction Drawings in Near Eastern Archaeology." In: O. Kaelin (ed.), Proceedings of the 9th ICAANE, 1, Wiesbaden: Harassowitz, pp. 359–370.

Hageneuer, S./Levenson, F. (2018): "Das Steinstiftgebäude in Uruk – ein gescheitertes Experiment?" In: K. Rheidt/W. Lorenz (eds.), Groß Bauen – Großbaustellen als kulturgeschichtliches Phänomen, Basel: Birkhäuser, pp. 109–121.

Hamilakis, Y. (2013): Archaeology and the Senses: Human Experience, Memory, and Affect, New York: Cambridge University Press.

Heimpel, W. (2009): Workers and Construction Work at Garshana, CUSAS 5, Bethesda: CDL Press.

Heinrich, E. (1984): Die Paläste im alten Mesopotamien, Berlin: Walter de Gruyter.

Hillier, B. (1988): The Social Logic of Space, Cambridge: Cambridge University Press.

Izzet, V. (2007): The Archaeology of Etruscan Society, Cambridge; New York: Cambridge University Press.

Julien, M./Karlin, C. (1994): "Prehistoric Technology: A Cognitive Science?" In: C. Renfrew/E. Zubrow (eds.), The Ancient Mind: Elements of Cognitive Archaeology, Cambridge; New York: Cambridge University Press, pp. 152–164.

Kertai, D. (2015): The Architecture of Late Assyrian Royal Palaces, Oxford: Oxford University Press.

Knappet, C. (2011): "Networks of Objects, Meshworks of Things" In: T. Ingold (ed.), Redrawing Anthropology: Materials, Movements, Lines, Burlington; Farnham: Ashgate, pp. 45–63.

Lemonnier, P. (1986): "The Study of Material Culture Today: Toward an Anthropology of Technical Systems." In: Journal of Anthropological Archaeology 5, pp. 147–186.

Margueron, J.-C. (1982): Recherches sur les palais mésopotamiens de l'Âge du bronze, Paris: Geuthner.

Margueron, J.-C. (2005): "Du bitanu, de l'étage et des salles hypostyles dans les palais néo-assyriens." In: Syria 82, pp. 93–138.

Martinón-Torres, M. (2002): "Chaîne Opératoire: The Concept and Its Applications within the Study of Technology." In: Gallaecia 21, pp. 29–43.

McMahon, A. (2013): "Space, Sound, and Light: Toward a Sensory Experience of Ancient Monumental Architecture." In: American Journal of Archaeology 117/2, pp. 163–179.

McMahon, A. (2016): "A Feast for the Ears: Neo-Assyrian Royal Architecture and Acoustics." In: J. MacGinnis/D. Wicke/T. Greenfield (eds.), Assyrian Provinces Conference Proceedings, Cambridge: McDonald Institute, pp. 129–139.

Meijer, D. (2008): "Cracking the Code? Aspect and Impact in Mesopotamian Architecture." In: H. Kuehne/R. Czichon/F. J. Kreppner (eds.), Proceedings of the 4th ICAANE, 1, Wiesbaden: Harrassowitz, pp. 431–436.

Meyer, J.-W. (2006): "Zur Frage der Urbanisierung von Tell Chuera." In: P. Butterlin/J.-C. Margueron/M. Lebeau/J.-Y. Monchambert/J. L. Montero-Fenollos/B. Muller (eds.), Les espaces syro-mésopotamiens: dimensions de l'expérience humaine au Proche-Orient ancien. Volume d'hommage offert à Jean-Claude Margueron, Subartu 17, Turnhout: Brepols, pp. 79–90.

Meyer, J.-W. (2007a): "Town Planning in 3rd Millennium Tell Chuera." In: J. Bretschneider/J. Driessen/K. van Lerberghe (eds.), Power and Architecture: Monumental Public Architecture in the Bronze Age Near East and Aegean, Leuven; Dudley: Peeters, pp. 129–142.

Meyer, J.-W. (2007b): "Veränderungen der Grabungsstrategie in Tell Chuera (Syrien) aufgrund der Ergebnisse der geomagnetischen Prospektion." In: M. Posselt/B. Zickgraf/C. Dobiat (eds.), Geophysik und Ausgrabung: Einsatz und Auswertung zerstörungsfreier Prospektion in der Archäologie, Rahden/ Westf.: Leidorf, pp. 223–236.

Meyer, J.-W. (2013a): "Stadtgründung, Stadtstruktur und Zentralität – Zur Stellung von Tell Chuera bei der Urbanisierung Nordostsyriens." In: D. Bonatz/L. Martin (eds.), 100 Jahre archäologische Feldforschungen in Nordost-Syrien – eine Bilanz, Wiesbaden: Harassowitz, pp. 117–132.

Meyer, J.-W. (2013b): "Urbanisierung, Stadtplanung und Wirtschaftsweise in 'marginalen Gebieten' Nordostsyriens." In: E. Cancik-Kirschbaum/J. Klinger/G. G. W. Müller (eds.), Diversity and Standardization. Perspectives on Social and Political Norms in the Ancient Near East, Berlin: de Gruyter, pp. 81–98.

Micale, M. G. (2007): "Riflessi d'architettura Mesopotamica Nei Disegni e Nelle Ricostruzioni Architettoniche Di Assur e Babilonia: Tra Realtà Archeologica e Mito Dell'architettura Monumentale." In: J. Córdoba/M. Mañé/F. Escribano (eds.), Further Approaches to Travellers and Scholars in the Rediscovering of the Ancient Near East, II, ISIMU 10, Madrid: Universidad Autónoma de Madrid, pp. 117–140.

Micale, M. G. (2010): "Designing Architecture, Building Identities. The Discovery and Use of Mesopotamian Features in Modern Architecture between Orientalism and the Definition of Contemporary Identities." In: P. Matthiae/F. Pinnock/L. Nigro/N. Marchetti (eds.), Proceedings of the 6th ICAANE, Rome, 5th-10th May 2008, Wiesbaden: Harassowitz, pp. 93–112.

Micale, M. G. (2013): "Architecture and Ancient Near East in Drawings, Buildings and Virtual Reality: Issues in Imagining and Designing Ancient and Modern Space." In: L. Feliu/J. Llop/A. Millet Albà/J. Sanmartín (eds.), Time and History in the Ancient Near East. Proceedings of the 56th Rencontre Assiriologique Internationale, Barcelona, 21–25 July 2010, Winona Lake: Eisenbrauns, pp. 379–390.

Micale, M. G. (2016): "Lo spazio sacro e la sua rappresentazione: considerazioni storico-metodologiche sull'interpretazione e sulla ricostruzione dell'architettura templare di Siria." In P. Matthiae (ed.), L'archeologia del Sacro e l'archeologia del culto. Ebla e la Siria dall'Eta' del Bronzo all'Eta' del Ferro, Roma: Bardi Edizioni, pp. 415–443.

Michelson, W. (1984): "Architecture and Communication: A Framework." In: Contemporary Sociology 13/3, pp. 264–66.

Moran, W. (2000): The Amarna Letters, Baltimore: Johns Hopkins University Press.

Neumann, K. (2014): "Resurrected and Reevaluated: The Neo-Assyrian Temple as a Ritualized and Ritualizing Built Environment." Ph. D. Thesis, Berkeley, CA: UC Berkeley.

Nunn, A. (1988): Die Wandmalerei und der glasierte Wandschmuck im alten Orient, Leiden: Brill.

Oates, J. (1960): "Ur and Eridu, the Prehistory." In: Iraq 22/1-2, pp. 32–50.

Oppenheim, A. L. (1977): Ancient Mesopotamia: Portrait of a Dead Civilization, Chicago: University of Chicago Press.

Osborne, J. F. (2014): "Monuments and Monumentality." In: J. F. Osborne (ed.), Approaching Monumentality in Archaeology, IEMA Proceedings, Albany: State University of New York Press, pp. 1–22.

Pedde, B. (2010): "Reception of Mesopotamian Architecture in Germany and Austria in the 20th Century." In: P Matthiae/F. Pinnock/L. Nigro/N. Marchetti (eds.), Proceedings of the 6th ICAANE, 1, Wiesbaden: Harrassowitz, pp. 121–129.

Pink, S. (2015): Doing Sensory Ethnography, Los Angeles; London: Sage.

Preziosi, D. (1983): Minoan Architectural Design: Formation and Signification, Berlin; New York: Mouton.

Ryan, K. (2009): "The Significance of Choice in the Late Dorset Technology of Domestic Architecture." Ph. D. Thesis, Toronto: University of Toronto.

Schiffer, M. B. (1975a): "Behavioral Chain Analysis: Activities, Organization, and the Use of Space." In: Fieldiana. Anthropology 65, pp. 103–119.

Schiffer, M. B. (1975b): "Archaeology as Behavioral Science." In: American Anthropologist, New Series, 77/4, pp. 836–848.

Schiffer, M. B. (1999): "Behavioral Archaeology: Some Clarifications." In: American Antiquity 64/1, pp. 166–168.

Schlanger, N. (2005): "The Chaîne Opératoire." In: C. Renfrew/P. Bahn (eds.), Archaeology: The Key Concepts, London; New York: Routledge, pp. 25–31.

Schloen, J. D. (2001): The House of the Father as Fact and Symbol. Studies in the Archaeology and History of the Levant 2, Winona Lake: Eisenbrauns.

Schneider, K. (1991): Die Burg des Elefantenjägers: Geschichte des 'Grossen Hauses' von Bindouté Da (Lobi, Burkina Faso), Stuttgart: F. Steiner.

Seamon, D. (2013): "Environmental Embodiment, Merleau-Ponty, and Bill Hillier's Theory of Space Syntax: Toward a Phenomenology of People-in-Place." In: R. Bhatt (ed.), Rethinking Aesthetics: The Role of Body in Design, New York: Routledge, pp. 204–213.

Smith, C. B. (2006): How the Great Pyramid Was Built, New York: Harper Paperbacks.

Sydie, R. A. (1984): "Review of Ankerl – Experimental Sociology of Architecture." In: The Canadian Journal of Sociology 9/4, pp. 473–476.

Turner, B. (2012): Routledge Handbook of Body Studies, Abingdon, Oxon; New York: Routledge.

Udy, S. (1959): Organization of Work: A Comparative Analysis of Production among Nonindustrial Peoples, New Haven: Human Relations Area Files Press.

Watson, P. J./Gould, R. (1982): "A Dialogue on the Meaning and Use of Analogy in Ethnoarchaeological Reasoning." In: Journal of Anthropological Archaeology 1/4, pp. 355–381.

Wendrich, W. (2014): "Visualizing the Dynamics of Monumentality." In: J. F. Osborne (ed.), Approaching Monumentality in Archaeology, IEMA Proceedings, Albany: State University of New York Press, pp. 409–430.

Wylie, A. (1982): "An Analogy by Any Other Name Is Just as Analogical." In: Journal of Anthropological Archaeology 1/4, pp. 382–401.

Yokoyama, M. (1994): "The Administrative Structure and Economic Function of Public Service (Ilkum) of the Old Babylonian State in the Old Babylonian Period." Ph. D. Thesis, Los Angeles, CA: UCLA.

Perceiving monumentality

Sebastian Hageneuer & Sylva van der Heyden

Finding consensus

In addition to the question of what monumentality is and whether it can be deduced from a particular size of built structure, participants in the 'Size-Matters' forum were concerned with the comparability of monumental structures across the various disciplines. At first glance it is not obvious why Early Iron Age burial mounds in the Eurasian steppe and French gothic cathedrals should be included in a category of monumentality. However, on closer consideration participants repeatedly encountered terminology and methodological tools related to the question of monumentality that recurred in the most dissimilar disciplines. In a closing session, these terms were named, discussed, and ordered by the participants, and finally presented as a kind of guideline or *Biography of Monumentality*. This list and the naming of the same as a biography allowed the academics from archaeological, philological, and art-historical disciplines to reach a consensus before parting.[1]

The *Biography of Monumentality* is divided into three periods/ages[2] beginning with the *process* of discovery and implementation, followed by the *outcome*, and ending with *perception* in the afterlife of the structure concerned. Numerous terms that can refer to monumentality, either individually or in groups, are categorized in each period. Under the term *process*, the researchers included:

---

1 Both during and after the workshop, there was intensive discussion about the terminology used in this article. We agreed on the vocabulary used so as to render the processes and considerations transparent and universally accessible, as those involved in the workshop and this publication represent a wide range of archaeological disciplines and diverse academic traditions from around the world.

2 For the term periods or ages we adopt Kopytoff's vocabulary: "What, sociologically, are the biographical possibilities inherent in its 'status' and in the period and culture, and how are these possibilities realized? Where does the thing come from and who made it? What has been its career so far, and what do people consider to be an ideal career for such things? What are the recognized 'ages' or periods in the thing's 'life'?" (Kopytoff 1986: 66).

Motivation and Approach, Agency (negation), Energetics (resources, manpower, know-how, organization), Labor, Impact, Perception of Process, Representation of Process and Timespan (dynamics and tempo; linear and cyclical time or trajectory).

The next period begins after a 'turnkey moment', after the building phase has been completed. The following terms were grouped under *outcome*:

Perception of Outcome, Structure and Form, Divergence from Intention of Process e.g. Failure, Impact, Decline, Abandonment, Redefinition, Destruction, Maintenance (linked to process, post-turnkey).

And finally, the following terms were listed under the last point *perception*:

Form, Materiality, Judgment (audience, value attribution), Reception and Appropriation, and finally Reproduction and Authenticity.

In the following we as authors have struggled greatly with the term and concept 'biography'. Should it be possible to ascribe a biography to the monumentality of a building? How can the start- and endpoints of a biography of a building be defined, if architecture is seen as an object? Our attempt to apply the *Biography of Monumentality* with its allocated parameters to a monument by way of example was a complete failure. Closer consideration quickly led us to recognize that no monument could fulfill the extensive conditions of the biography construct. Even the most rewarding objects that initially promised to provide an exemplary and diverse biography, such as the Cathedral of Syracuse or the Temple of Athena (Bayliss 2001: 228–232; Gruben 2001: 285–294; Sgariglia 2009), had to be excluded from the investigation. The heterogeneous nature of the sources and the insufficient data – a situation that applies even to contemporary and well-documented monuments – do not permit a description of all the stages between the idea and the afterlife of a monument as a *Biography of Monumentality*.

This discussion makes clear why the attempt was bound to fail: the idea of the biography is attractive but it ignores the fact that there cannot be one valid, final biography for each built monument. In this vein, Igor Kopytoff explains in his groundbreaking essay *Cultural Biography of Things* that each person and each thing has many different biographies. These biographies are *per se* incomplete, as they are always viewed with a different focus, which then only takes a few details of the life story into consideration while blocking out others (cf. 1986: 67–68). Accordingly, what we here term a *Biography of Monumentality* can be designated as one more biography in the innumerable plethora of biographies of an object, albeit with a focus on built monumentality. In its diversity and subjectivity, the term biography thus has similarities with the term monumentality, the wide spectrum of which has been demonstrated by Levenson (see Levenson in this volume).

We further argue that, in contrast to objects that can be removed from their cycle of thing-human relations by being museumized or by disappearing, architectures remain present, even when they are no longer visible. This is because architectures consist in part of material and in part of 'ideas, thoughts, emotions, desires' and, to put it another way, monumental buildings are 'larger-scale phenomena' (cf. Olsen 2003; Hodder 2016: 9).

In this volume we are concerned with monumentality that derives from architectures. In the following we therefore use the terms architecture, monument, and built structure/areas, but also mention the term objects, which is then used synonymously.

So as not to blindly fixate on the term biography, which is frequently the subject of critical discussion (see, for instance, the comments on this text), the term *Thesaurus of Monumentality* was also discussed against the background of the aforementioned list of terms. The treasury (Lat. *thesaurus*) of the entirety of terms relevant to a topic is, in line with its original meaning, rather to be found in the comprehensive chapter on *Research Approaches and Methodology* in this volume by Federico Buccellati.

At this point we want to discuss the perception of monumentality from two perspectives in order to do justice to the interdisciplinarity of the discussion forum. Firstly, Sebastian Hageneuer tackles the question of the perception of the monumentality of a building. He thereby sheds light on the building process using the methodological tools of an archaeologist. Sylva van der Heyden focuses on the reception of architecture and asks – as an art historian – whether monumentality can also be displayed and perceived through reproductions. We are fortunate to be able to refer here to the two introductory chapters by Levenson and Buccellati and, equipped with the aforementioned terms, will clarify and carve out two views of the term monumentality by way of example.

Perceiving monumentality through the process of building

From an archaeological stance, we document the remains of buildings with a constant interest in the process by which they emerged. We want to understand not only what we have in front of us, but also what value the architecture had at the time of its planning, existence, and afterlife. As archaeologists it is not uncommon for us to stand in front of the results of our excavations and to ask ourselves whether the ancient builders felt something similar (in whatever sense). In the case of monumental architecture technical questions concerning the planning, execution, resources, or maintenance are supplemented by conceptual questions

inquiring into contemporary intention, perception, reception, and meaning, especially in comparison or contrast to our own. This section of a so-called object biography (cf. Kopytoff 1986: 66–68) thus largely describes what happened before and
during the creation of a monument, but it also to some extent relates to an immediate perception in the afterlife of the building. The final consensus of the forum
was to distinguish between *process* and *outcome*, although several cases were cited
in which monuments never reached a 'finished' status but were nonetheless used.
Examples here include the Temple of Jupiter in Baalbek/Lebanon (Lohmann 2018)
and Cologne Cathedral, which was 632 years in the building (Hardering 2014: 125).

In the following I attempt to describe the concepts and examples of monumentality in three steps. First, before building we find a planning and conceptual phase
when the motivation of the actors plays a particularly significant role. Second,
this is followed by the phase during building, that is, the concrete implementation
and organization of such a project. Finally, I discuss the phase after building and
describe the use and also the afterlife of the architecture.

Before the building

Before a monument exists it has to come into existence in the mind, be planned for,
and its construction organized. Here questions arise concerning actors and their
motivation. Were the buildings discussed here deliberately created in a way that
we today term monumental and why was this actually necessary?

A very early example of a monumental building is the Göbekli Tepe complex
in Turkey, which was possibly the result of collective effort and dates from the
10th millennium BCE (pre-pottery Neolithic) (Schmidt 2000; 2001; 2009). More
than ten circular compounds have been discovered, structured with elaborately
designed, T-shaped pillars in stone up to 4 m in height. The engravings depict
diverse human forms and animals. The excavators interpret the form of the stone
pillars as suggesting that they are anthropomorphic statues rather than buttresses
(Notroff/Dietrich/Schmidt 2014: 87–88). This building work could only have been
erected as a collaborative project. No other comparative complex has yet been
found and dating reveals that it is certainly one of the oldest monumental buildings of human history. The population of the time lived as hunters and gatherers
and in which numbers they were present at the creation of this circular compound
is as yet unclear. However, it has been suggested that various groups met for this
'collective work event', motivated by the desire for regular social exchange and
joint celebrations (Notroff/Dietrich/Schmidt 2014: 93–99). These building projects
thus started in the community and it is assumed that they were common in the
Neolithic (e. g. Mischka 2012: 141), especially as it is not possible to exactly classify
and define a hierarchy or form of political leadership for this time. The motivation
behind the building thus seems to have been the consolidation of communities.

If Notroff, Dietrich, and Schmidt (2014) are right, then monumentality may have developed from a sense of community in the pre-pottery Neolithic in Turkey, and could therefore have been a by-product.

The creation in later times of complexes that are termed monumental is usually attributed only to more highly organized groups (elites, royalty, religious organizations) (Trigger 2007: 564), even though – as just discussed – contrasting examples have recently been identified. Nonetheless the emerging complexity of political entities seems to be associated with the creation of such monuments. Furholt, Hinz, and Mischka go so far as to state that the creation of monumental buildings was not the result of a complex society but was the process of establishing such a society (2012: 13–15); they thus find themselves in complete contradiction to Notroff, Dietrich, and Schmidt. For example, we link the emergence of the first monumental structures in the 4th millennium BCE in Sumerian Uruk (Late Uruk Period) with the apparently simultaneous hierarchisation of society and the associated leading elite, whatever form they took (Hageneuer/Levenson 2018: 110–111, Pollock 2013). According to Furholt, Hinz, and Mischka the creation of the monumental buildings discovered in Uruk could also have been constitutive for the establishment of state structures and increased hierarchization (2012: 15).

A thousand years later, in the 3rd millennium BCE, so-called ziggurats emerged throughout Mesopotamia (Trigger 2007: 572). These monumental high temples dedicated to the gods were a tradition preserved until the 1st millennium BCE and culminated in the famous Tower of Babel. The creation, maintenance, and restoration of these buildings, truly monumental in size, were always in the hands of the king. This responsibility could serve to legitimize his monarchy and was therefore his duty. In this way, traditionally operating leaders were rendered responsible for the creation of monumental objects, for instance the Pyramid of Khufu or Gilgamesh's town-walls (also see Levenson in this volume: External Motivation).

There is evidence to show that large-scale projects such as the construction of the Egyptian pyramids and the Mesopotamian ziggurats of the 3rd millennium BCE were built under strict direction and supervision (Trigger 2007: 570–571). The leading ruler was undoubtedly diversely motivated. On the one hand, the buildings served as a very visible sign of rulership and a clear demonstration of power. On the other hand, through the construction of the immense buildings a link between the worldly and godly spheres was created. The focus here was not so much on collaborative building, but rather on the creation of monuments linked to individuals, serving their own legitimation or commemoration with clearly defined goals and expectations. Trevor Watkins adds that "the role of collective memory is generally said to be vital for maintaining the community's sense of common identity". These monuments were thus necessary for the formation of a shared identity (2012: 37).

Whoever (agency) for whatever reason (motivation) in whatever way (approach) erected a monument must have been confronted with logistical and material problems. Monumental projects need not be physically large (cf. Hageneuer/Levenson 2018) but they do need to contrast with the norm, which must have required considerable effort and a vast amount of resources and organization (cf. Bukowiecki/ Wulf-Rheidt 2018). We thus have to think right through the process of constructing monumental buildings and ask how it was practically possible.

During the building

The method of architectural energetics can help us to grasp monumentality in numbers (Buccellati 2016: 173–175; 196–198). Here the specific elements of the construction process of a building or complex are determined and subdivided into groups. For instance, the construction of a typical central hall of the Uruk era is broken down into the elements: mud bricks, mud plaster, wood (window and roof material, doors) and reeds (roof and window covering). This makes it possible not only to determine the individual building processes, but also to calculate the energy expended (cf. Hageneuer/Schmidt in this volume; Buccellati 2016; Hageneuer/Levenson 2018). This can be undertaken using contemporary texts, ethnographic parallels, or other archaeological sources (Buccellati 2016: 83–85; 173). The focus is not only on the individual elements of the building but also on the process of obtaining raw materials, transport, and processing, right up to the payment of the individual workers on a building site (cf. Brunke 2018). This entire interlinked process is also termed a *chaîne opératoire* (Buccellati 2016: 79–83), describing a course of occurrences that captures the total building process. Once this *chaîne opératoire* is established, then the energy expenditure for the materials, transport, processing, and maintenance of an individual project can be added together and the corresponding projects can be given an 'energetic cost'. These results clarify the effort and scope of the projects, but also help with direct comparisons.

The construction of the Flavian Palace of Emperor Domitian on the Palatine Hill in Rome serves as an example illustrating the immense effort involved in a brick building. E. Bukowiecki and U. Wulf-Rheidt have shown that over 1.8 million bricks of various sizes were used just for the shell of the building (2018: 55). This vast number of bricks had to be carefully organized and brought to the building site in a relatively short construction period. Calculations suggest that the bricks had to be transported from a distance of up to 80 km; this was also true of the wood required at the building site. The authors believe that for economic reasons the wood required was used to make floats, which were then also used to deliver the mud bricks (Bukowiecki/Wulf-Rheidt 2018: 56).

Apart from the transport of materials from the vicinity to Rome, the organization of the building site itself was a challenge. The authors have calculated that within the ten-year construction period at least 34,250 ox carts must have been required to cover the 1km distance from the landing stage on the Tiber up to the building site of the palace (Bukowiecki/Wulf-Rheidt 2018: 57). As space on the building site was also limited, the transport of materials to Rome, their delivery to the building site and their further processing needed to be smoothly and efficiently organized by those in charge of the building. The organization of the building site was also determined by regulations governing specific cases, as shown by S. Prignitz who discusses a building contract regulation from Tegea in Arcadia on the Peloponnese (2018). This demonstrates that the organizational effort could become multi-layered and complex. It can be surmised that this influenced contemporary builders and observers considerably.

The creation of monumental buildings cannot have escaped the notice of the observers of such building sites and works, as it can be assumed that these projects were always organized and carried out in large groups. They must therefore have exercised an enormous influence on society and the economy (see also Mogetta in this volume). As D. Lohmann (2018) has been able to demonstrate, for example, the construction of the Temple of Jupiter in Baalbek/Lebanon was an immense economic factor that promoted the development of what had been a small peripheral fortress in the Hellenistic period to a Roman town. The building work lasted at least two centuries and provided constant and reliable jobs, which in turn clearly brought increased prosperity and community to the town (also see Levenson in this volume: Internal Motivation). The author even suggests that certain extensions to the building plans and the conspicuous and prolonged unfinished state of the building may have been deliberate (Lohmann 2018: 150).

Another interesting point about the Temple of Jupiter in Baalbek concerns the presentation of the temple itself. The architectural survey reveals that the walls and podium were made of solid monumental stone blocks (Lohmann 2018: 157–160). Amazingly, the size of the stone blocks increased towards the top in order to create a monumental effect by deliberately disrupting normal visual habits (Lohmann 2018: 160). Monuments can thus create impacts and generate feelings, and they not only do this to us but also did so during the lifetimes of those who built them and contemporary beholders (see Delitz/Levenson in this volume).

The impact on viewers of such creations was particularly intensive if the building remained 'unfinished' over decades or centuries. If the unfinished state of the architecture was not intended, then this was initially perceived as a flaw and the building project and those in charge of it were negatively connoted. However, if the work was then completed, they ascended to monumental fame. A well-documented example from the post-antiquity era is the building of Cologne Cathedral, where an unfinished building dominated the townscape for almost 300 years between the first and second phases of construction. Numerous pictorial records show the state in which the building remained for generations after construction work stopped in 1559. The half-built South Tower of the cathedral with an enormous, abandoned crane on its upper floor was testimony to the incompleteness of the building, and also became a landmark of the city. This was a sight that caused Johann Wolfgang von Goethe (1749–1832) to be conscious of 'apprehension'[3], the unfinished building reminded him "of the inadequacy of man, as soon as he ventures to want to achieve something outsized" (Goethe 1998b: 180). In 1842 the foundation stone of the second construction phase of Cologne Cathedral was laid and within 38 years, by 1880, the building was completed. The resumption of building occurred under the protection of the Prussian king and Cologne Cathedral was thus rededicated and became a national monument to commemorate the French occupation of the Rhineland in 1813 (cf. Nipperdey 1981). Today it appears in every architectural guide as a leading example of the Gothic in Germany.

Post-Construction

What happens with a monument that has been built and can now be used? As described above, it is not actually necessary for the building work to be completed, but from a certain point the functions of the monument – as determined by those in charge of the building – begin. These functions can be diverse and may change again over time.

Furholt, Hinz, and Mischka state that "there seems to be a broad consensus on the importance of monuments as a stage for the transmission of socially relevant meanings, of social memories" (2012: 13). Monumental architecture can thus serve as the cultural memory of a society, some examples of which we still marvel at (the Pyramid of Khufu) or talk about today (the Tower of Babylon). The permanence of monuments clearly plays an important role (e. g. Mischka 2012), even though the significance and function of the buildings can change over time (Furholt/Hinz/Mischka 2012: 16). The aforementioned example of Cologne Cathedral demonstrates the way in which permanence can play a role. Even though it was unfinished, the cathedral with the crane was a landmark of the city for almost 300 years. Today the cathedral is still constantly subject to building work, a situation that continues to conjure weary smiles from the people of Cologne.

If monuments or monumental places are deserted (abandonment), no longer maintained (decline) and are in this way, or indeed deliberately, destroyed (destruction), then this represents an abrupt break in the life history of the monument – both positively and negatively. If one chooses destruction and artificial

---

3 The term *apprehension* can have two different meanings: firstly, the perception of an object through the senses; secondly, as Goethe uses the term, a spontaneous, negative but not aggressive reaction to things, people, and experiences (cf. Herwig 1978: 778–779).

decomposition as something that brings an architecture's biography to an end, then it is right to talk of a physical end. However, this can only be putatively valid. Academic reappraisal, techniques, and methods are particularly suitable for bringing the forgotten back into the light of day and public awareness, as has been the case, for instance, with the Tower of Babel (Schmid 1995; Wullen/Schauerte 2008). After its destruction the monument was forgotten, so that at the beginning of the 20th century the Tower of Babel was only familiar thanks to the bible and the writings of Herodotus. It was not until 1912 that Robert Koldewey (1855–1925) excavated the actual remains of the monument; ever since there has been an unending series of proposals for reconstructions (Minkowski 1959; Schmid 1995). Thus even an absent monument can be present just through the reception of the disappeared architecture (cf. Lindemann 2008).

Clearly, destruction need not be the end of the lifespan of a monument providing that after a timeout (however this may be defined) a revival of the monument is possible; this may be based on visible built elements, excavated architectural findings, discolourations in the soil, or written and pictorial sources (see Autenrieth/van Boekel in this volume).

Even a redefinition of the purpose or specific character of a monument, which initially brings its original function to an end, can actually signify the rescue or revival of endangered architecture. Here the Cathedral of Syracuse or the Temple of Athena can be illustrative. The Temple of Athena, built in 480 BCE in Doric style, was not only used as a central argument in the evidence brought against Verres by Cicero (Cicero 1995: 393–394, In Verrem II.4.122), but also happened to be converted into a Christian place of worship. At the naming of the building as the Cathedral of Santa Maria delle Colonne in 640 CE its conversion from a temple to a three-nave basilica had been completed. Temple conversions were not uncommon at this time in the Mediterranean area, although not as widely spread as the building of new churches and chapels on the ruins of temples, as Bayliss shows (2001: 230).

It is significant that the modern built structures did not hide the ancient temple but the different structural elements rather existed in visible juxtaposition, almost like an archaeological window (Figure 1).

Thus visitors could and can easily reconstruct the antique building for themselves. The Prussian architect Heinrich Gentz (1766–1811), for instance, made a detailed recording in his diary of his visit on 9 May 1792 to the "Cathedral-church, the former Temple of Minerva", meticulously describing and reconstructing the existing and former architecture (cf. Gentz 2004: 104–105).

Of course the aspects described here can only illustrate a small part of what monumentality means or may have meant. Similar résumés can be found in Furholt, Hinz, and Mischka (2012: 13–20), Osborne (2014: 1–19), or Brunke et al. (2016: 250–254). All attempt to summarize and order the archaeological view of

Figure 1: Cathedral of Syracuse, Sicily, detail of the side aisle (Photo by Sylva van der Heyden)

monumentality.[4] Monumentality is initially perceived in an unconsciously emotional fashion. All the senses contribute to the manner of unconscious perception (see Buccellati in this volume). In the attempt to define monumentality we thus also unavoidably interpret an entire history of research. The question therefore arises as to how and in what way we receive monumentality. To again draw on Kopytoff and make use of the image of the biography of an object, we should not stop at the (putative) end of the life of a monument but should inquire into the form in which monumentality has survived into modern times and how it has been received and changed.

Perceiving monumentality through reproduction

Fundamentals

Monumentality is ascribed to objects, an ascription that is generated by the perception of a beholder. There are therefore an infinite number of monumentalities and no objective definition of them (see Levenson in this volume). The situation is clearer with objects that are produced and constructed as monuments. They have the task, e. g. as with a memorial – and now we return to built space – of transporting memoria, and thus act as an agent of something that can be perceived as monumentality. One possible way in which this monumentality is manifested is in the reception of a built monument through reproducing it, perceiving the reproduction, and discussing its authenticity.

With his essay *The Work of Art in the Age of Mechanical Reproduction*,[5] Walter Benjamin has for decades dominated the discourse on the concept of reproduction (1993). In this text Benjamin states that every artwork is reproducible but that the unique being of the original cannot be reproduced (cf. Benjamin 1993: 10–11) because the "here and now of the original underlies the concept of its authenticity" (Benjamin 1993: 12; translation: Jennings et al. 2002: 103). Benjamin postulates two kinds of reproduction, a manual and a technical.[6] It proves positive for the beholder that technical reproductions "can place the copy of the original in sit-

---

4   To look into monumentality in other fields besides archaeology and architecture see for example: Rehding, A. (2009): Music and monumentality. Commemoration and wonderment in the nineteenth-century Germany, Oxford: Oxford University Press; Garval, M. D. (2004): A dream of stone. Fame, vision and monumentality in nineteenth-century French literary culture, Newark: University of Delaware Press; Hung, W. (1995): Monumentality in Early Chinese Art and Architecture, Stanford: Stanford University Press.

5   *Das Kunstwerk im Zeitalter seiner technischen Reproduzierbarkeit.*

6   Benjamin uses the term manual reproduction to refer to the copying by hand of an artwork, whereby the original retains its authority in the face of the reproduction. With the term technical

uations which the original itself cannot attain. Above all it enables the original to meet the recipient halfway [...]" (Benjamin 1993: 12–13; translation: Jennings et al. 2002: 103). At the same time, however, the technical reproduction devalues the artwork in its here and now, in its authenticity, and jeopardizes its historical testimony. Benjamin links "the authenticity of an artwork not with an ascription of authenticity but with its materiality which has experienced the unfolding of time itself" (Mager 2017: 31). Materiality in this context means the tangible matter and its erosion, the light that is reflected differently on different materials, the echo that can be perceived in different ways by the viewer (see Buccellati in this volume).

Monumentality can thus be generated from historical testimony and from materiality (see Levenson in this volume). If a technical reproduction lacks these two important aspects, then further questions must be posed. Can reproductions of monuments give a perception of monumentality? Can a copy of Trajan's Column transport monumentality in the same way as Trajan's Column itself?

Hypothesis

One possible way to perceive monumentality is to create or possess an image, a copy, a reproduction of the original monument and to enter into an exchange, as Osborne puts it, "an ongoing, constantly renegotiated relationship between thing and person" (2014: 3). Is this possible and if so, how? This idea was the subject of critical discussion in the workshop, as it seems that the limits of the imagination are quickly exceeded if the reproduction of a monument is not true to scale. To what extent is it then possible to refer to monumentality if the physical size or architectural scale of a Trajan's Column is not mirrored? If the reproduction is much smaller than the original monument? Does size matter? What parameters should be applied to monumentality if physical size is not an argument? What happens in the perception of a monument if the original three-dimensionality of a built object becomes two-dimensional in the course of a reproduction?

On 5 September 1786, Johann Wolfgang Goethe made a note in his diary about a visit to the Hofgarten Gallery in Munich, where he stopped on his way to Italy and saw "the Colonna Trajani as a model" with "the figures gilded silver on lapis lazuli" (Goethe 1976: 17–18) (Figure 2).

In Munich Goethe encountered a reproduction of the column monument, which he described as "a beautiful piece of work" (Goethe 1976: 17–18) and which produced a visual imprint and impression. However, his contact with the monument in Rome was far more multifaceted. Here Goethe also had a bodily expe-

---

reproduction Benjamin refers to all techniques that allow mass replication: casting, embossing, woodcuts, copperplate, etching, lithography and photography.

Figure 2:
Luigi Valadier,
Bartholomäus Hecher,
Peter Ramoser, Trajan's
Column, 1774–1780,
203 cm high, marble,
bronze, guilded silver,
lapis lazuli (Inv.
Res.Mü.Sch. 1221,
Residenzmuseum
München, © Bayerische
Schlösserverwaltung)

rience of the monumentality of Trajan's Column. On 23 July 1787 he climbed the steps to the top and abandoned himself to the inestimable view of Rome to be had from the 30 m high platform (cf. Goethe 1998: 371). In retrospect he actually only reports on the view that he enjoyed from Trajan's Column, he records no reception of the monument itself. Why this was probably not possible is clarified by the following facts.

The location of the 35 m high monument has not changed since its construction in 113 CE in the Forum of Trajan, in a narrow courtyard bookended by two library buildings. As viewers of the monument have to look up at a very sharp angle from ground level, the view of the column is limited and only the lower portions of the frieze can be seen. After the complex was completed it was possible to examine the frieze in sections from the terraces of the libraries. If these elevated locations had not existed a reception of the historical frieze would have been completely impossible (cf. Hölscher 2017: 32–33). This limited but, according to Hölscher, functional method of reading is aided by the fact that the figures on the frieze increase in size from the bottom to the top (see Baalbek and the stone blocks that get bigger towards the top). Hölscher suggests that Trajan's Column is a complex message with limited perceptibility (Hölscher 2017: 33) and it is therefore possible to adopt new forms of perception. A "macro-perspective" allows the entire monument, including the aesthetic message, to be appreciated, without it being possible or necessary to recognize the details. A "micro-perspective" allows a view of details or individual scenes of the frieze. This partial perception is supplemented by integrative extrapolation and a conviction of completeness with which the observer can assume that the entire frieze is equally detailed, convincing, and complete as the few, easily visible scenes at the bottom end of Trajan's Column (cf. Hölscher 2017: 34–35).

A constant motif running through history is the longing to possess something more than just the memory of the object. Something that helps to preserve the image of the monument and the impression of the monumentality that, e. g., the beholder of Trajan's Column has assimilated. Beyond that, diverse motivations for possessing an image of the monument – in the period constituted by the examples, from about 1770 to 1830 – are: reminders (souvenirs), scientific objects for collections or study, didactic models, vehicles to influence the development of taste, and symbolic appropriation.[7]

---

7 Transferred to the present day these can be supplemented with gain or pecuniary interest through (illegal) art dealing.

Trajan's Column by Valadier

The monument Trajan's Column and the monumentality of Trajan's Column were honored with a range of technical reproductions.[8] In Rome between 1774 and 1780, Luigi Valadier (1726–1785), Bartholomäus Hecher (around 1729–1807), and Peter Ramoser (1722–1802) completed an almost 2 m high Trajan's Column made of bronze and gilded silver, and decorated with lapis lazuli (cf. Galinier 1999: 203). On a much reduced scale but with pinpoint accuracy, every detail of the frieze was transferred to the copy[9] and much appreciated by contemporaries such as Johann Wilhelm von Archenholz (1741–1812):

> All the figures and objects that this wonderful memorial contains, without exception, can be seen meticulously imitated on a small scale in this model, whereby not even the slightest detail has been forgotten. [...] This small model is, without reckoning the valuable materials, most estimable because one has an overview of the whole in one go and can easily follow the curvatures of the line. (von Archenholz 1785: 265–266)

Valadier's copy of Trajan's Column is only 2 m high as opposed to 35 m, but it does not appear less monumental than the original in view of the skill of the craftsmanship, the time it took to produce, and the precious materials used.[10] The entirety of the monument can be much more comprehensively perceived in this reduced form. Here no cognitive supplementation or 'extrapolation' is required. In 1783 the column was acquired by the Bavarian Elector Karl Theodor (1724–1799) in Rome and moved to Munich. There it was initially placed in the recently completed Hofgarten Gallery, where Goethe noticed it, before being moved to its present location in the treasury of the residence. The Hofgarten Gallery built by Karl Theodor is considered to be one of the first public art galleries; here the foremost idea was clearly to make this scaled-back Trajan's Column accessible to the public. In addition to this didactic and encyclopedic aspiration, the focus seems also to have been on the dynastic legitimization of the ruling line through the representative monument (cf. Granzow 2015: 524–548).

---

8 Further details about the intentions behind the creation of reproductions and their function are not discussed here. See on this subject the Ph. D. project by Sylva van der Heyden at the Technische Universität Berlin under the working title *Die Medialisierung von Monumentalität. Die Darstellung der Größe Roms im späten 18. und frühen 19. Jahrhundert in zwei- und dreidimensionalen Medien.*

9 According to copperplates by Pietro Santi Bartoli (publ. 1672).

10 See on down-scaled monumentality and materiality J. Osborne in the introduction to the conference paper (2014) and Geoffroy-Schneiter, B. (2015): Micromonumentality – A Tribute to Miniature Works of African Art, Milan: 5 Continents Editions.

Casts of the frieze of Trajan's Column

The reproduction of Trajan's Column was also motivated by other aspirations, as revealed by consideration of the casts made of the column. The casts of the entire frieze made at the same scale as the original do most justice to the notion that monumentality can only be perceived, received, and interpreted through an equally large copy.[11] The best known of these casts are exhibited in the Victoria & Albert Museum in London and in the National Museum of Romanian History in Bucharest.[12] (Figure 3 & 4)

The casts were prepared piece by piece, which involved erecting scaffolding around the entire column, an undertaking that was only possible for and by the elite. Monarchical, imperial, and national interests were always behind the reproductions. The first casts were commissioned in 1540 by Francis I of France (1494–1547); this was followed in 1665–1671 by a commission by Louis XIV of France (1638–1715). A turning point and new dimension in the reception of Trajan's Column was achieved in 1797 when Napoleon (1769–1821) attempted to move the entire column to Paris. As this proved impossible without destroying it, in 1810 a new, higher column was erected in Place Vendôme in the style of Trajan's Column, intended as a memorial to Napoleon's victorious activities (Battle of Austerlitz). "Linked inextricably to Napoleon's display of power and his preoccupation with France's past was an element of demonstrating the First Empire's preeminence over Imperial Rome." (Rowell 2012: 59) In 1833 a statue of Napoleon was placed on top of the Vendôme Column, thus copying the appearance of Trajan's Column in the early centuries after its construction.[13] The hegemonic interests expressed in the struggle over Trajan's Column and the possession of as complete an iconographic program as possible are also demonstrated in the following centuries. In 1861–62 a cast of the frieze was made for Napoleon III (1808–1873), in 1938 Mussolini (1883–1945) commissioned a cast, and in the 1960s a cast was taken to Bucharest[14] under orders from Nicolae Ceauşescu (1918–1989) (Galinier 1999: 201–202; Galinier 2017: 234–235; Hölscher 2017: 17).

---

11 I am not dealing with the preparation, use and dissemination of the partial casts of the frieze in museums and university collections.

12 The casts in the collection of the Victoria & Albert Museum are presented as dissected parts of the column and were made c. 1864 in Paris. The casts of the frieze in Bucharest are cut into 125 pieces and are arranged on the walls of a court surrounding a copy of the base of Trajan's Column. Other casts of the complete frieze are found in Rome (Museo della Civiltà Romana) and Saint-Germain-en-Laye (Musée des Antiquités Nationales).

13 At its construction, a statue of Trajan was placed on the top of Trajan's Column; this was lost at some point and in 1588 was replaced by a statue of St. Peter.

14 Other sources date the order for the replica in 1939, suggesting it was finished in 1943. Due to World War II the casts came to Romania only in 1967 (cf. Museteanu 2004: 35).

Figure 3: The West Court (The Ruddock Family Cast Court) at the Victoria and Albert Museum, London, with the Trajan's Column in two parts (Photo by Sylva van der Heyden)

Figure 4: Casts of Trajan's Column at the Muzeul Naţional de Istorie a României, Bucharest (Photo cc/by Jorge Láscar)

In all these cases, knowledge about the monument, the reason for its construction, and the idea of the memoria is necessary to achieve reception – in particular if viewers get closer to the frieze than was envisaged in the original context.

Trajan's Column by Piranesi

A change of medium: how can a 35 m high antique monument, covered with reliefs, be appropriately and accurately reproduced in a two-dimensional medium? Giovanni Battista Piranesi (1720–1778) found a simple but ingenious answer to this problem: *Trofeo o sia magnifica colonna coclide di marmo [...]*, an etching that presents a reproduction of Trajan's Column on a kind of over-dimensional, monumental folding panel, an impressive 3 m in length (Figure 5). Piranesi etched Trajan's Column from the base to the crowning figure on six separate plates; other panels show architectural and sculptural details of the column. This truly imposing reproduction of the column demands particular attentiveness from the beholder. To view and consume this 3 m version one requires an especially large table or the use of the floor. Moving around this image or crouching down next to it is a bodily experience, and the monumentality of the work has a perceptible impact. In this example the reproduction is also, despite the reduction in size, monumental. This observation raises new questions: Does Piranesi appropriate the monumentality of the column for himself by making his work monumental as well, even as a copy?

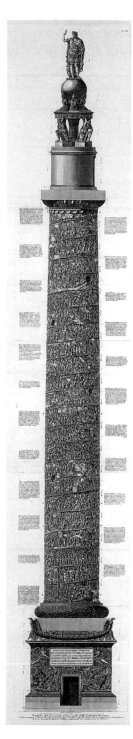

Figure 5: Giovanni Battista Piranesi, Veduta del prospetto principale della Colonna Trajana, assembled from six plates printed on six sheets [in: Trofeo o sia magnifica colonna coclide di marmo composta di grossi macigni ove si veggono scolpite le due guerre daciche fatte da Traiano], 1774–1779, 285.5 × 47.0 cm, etching (Inv. 1926,0511.35, Collection, British Museum, © Trustees of the British Museum)

Calling this print monumental relates to the technical term that is used for prints that were created in the Renaissance era and gives credit to the sheer size of the assembled panels.[15]

The medium furthermore permits particularly intensive and comparative study of the frieze and thus awakens fresh amazement at the skilled craftsmanship revealed in the sculptures of Trajan's Column. Monumentality can thus be perceived through observation of both the pictorial object and the pictorial medium.

Synthesis of the chapter

Reception, judgment, and appropriation are processes that cannot be thought of without each other. They occur during and after the first contact with a monument. By accepting monumentality it can be consciously perceived, accepted, or rejected. The reproduction of a monument cannot occur without prior appropriation, just as the appropriation can only occur after observation and judgment.

Considering these processes individually, judgment is a significant factor for the 'survival' of the monument. If viewers decide against the monument, perhaps for political or hegemonic reasons, these architectural structures will be rejected, rededicated, converted, built over, or destroyed (see Delitz/Levenson and Autenrieth/van Boekel in this volume). On the other hand, it has only been possible to investigate certain monumental architectures because over the centuries relevant actors judged them in a way that permitted appropriation. In addition to Trajan's Column, considered in such detail above, the Pantheon in Rome provides another striking example, regarded among scholars of antiquity as the epitome of Roman architecture (Hirt 1822: 283) and as a perfect representation of the "transformation of associations linked with it, both formally aesthetic and functional" (Martini 2006: 8). The Pantheon was built under Emperor Hadrian between 118 and 126 CE as a rotunda. In the 7th century it was granted to Pope Boniface and dedicated as a Christian church to Mary and the Martyrs. The Catholic Church took over the building in a visible fashion by removing statues and inscriptions and erecting altars in the interior. The rotunda is viewed as unique and influential in the history of architecture and there are many examples of its reception.[16] The diverse history on the one hand and the unusual cupola architecture on the other guarantee a pronounced and sustained reception.

---

15 Cf. Silver, L./Wyckoff, E. (eds.) (2008): Grand Scale: Monumental Prints in the Age of Dürer and Titian, New Haven: Yale University Press.

16 E. g. Villa Rotunda in Vicenza by Andrea Palladio, 1566–1569; St. Hedwig's Cathedral in Berlin by Georg Wenzeslaus von Knobelsdorff and J. L. Legeay, 1747–1773; Cenotaph for Newton by Étienne-Louis Boullée, 1784; Rotunda of the University of Virginia by Thomas Jefferson, 1822–1826; Rotunda of the Altes Museum in Berlin by Karl Friedrich Schinkel, 1825–1830.

The monumental character of the building is especially highlighted in its reception. In his novel *Titan*, the poet and writer Jean Paul (1763–1825) has his protagonist enter the Pantheon and wonder:

> there reared itself around them a holy, simple, free world structure with its heavenly arches soaring and striving upward, an odium of the tones of the sphere-music, a world in the world! And overhead the eye-socket of the light and of the sky gleamed down, and the distant rack of clouds seemed to touch the lofty arch over which it shot along! And round about them stood nothing but the temple-bearers, the columns! The temple of all gods endured and concealed the diminutive altars of the later ones. (Paul 1803: 40; translation: Paul 1877: 198)

Remarkably, despite his impressive depiction of an experience of the Pantheon's interior, Jean Paul never visited Rome. Jean Paul provides an "example of a poetic reception of antique architecture without actual beholding" (Heres 1977: 205) and must have drawn on pictorial templates based on engravings by Giovanni Battista Piranesi, Giuseppe Vasi (1710–1782), or Jean Barbault (1718–1762) for his descriptions (Heres 1977: 199). The reception of monumentality – and precisely that is what Jean Paul conveys in the scene in the Pantheon – must thus have occurred via technical reproductions.

We know that the situation was similar with Herodot's description of the Tower of Babel (Feix 1963: 181). The ancient historian describes the composition and structure of the tower right down to the smallest detail. Later archaeologists such as Victor Place (1818–1875) or Leonard Woolley (1880–1960) attempted to adhere to Herodot's descriptions in their reconstructions of the ziggurats that they found during their excavations; however they discovered that it was almost impossible to harmonize the descriptions with what was physically achievable (Hageneuer 2016: 363–366). In 1994 Stephanie Dalley published an article in which she demonstrated that Herodot most probably never visited Babylon and that his descriptions were probably based on local sources (Dalley 1994: 45). With these two examples, the Pantheon and the Tower of Babel, it again becomes clear that an incessant reception of existing and no longer existing monuments through very different mediums can displace direct perception. The idea of monumentality survives all forms of the biography of its (initial) carrier and can be perceived and received with the help of very differently characterized mediums.

Returning to the three-way division of the biography of monumentality as drawn up by the participants of the workshop (*process*, *outcome*, and *perception*), the analogy to Kopytoff's object biography was obvious but only applies to the extent that there is not *the* one biography of monumentality. However, as long as the monumental is also seen as an object this approach makes sense because it is a reminder of the different stages in which monumentality can be perceived and researched.

Our dual view on the topic has demonstrated that there are points of agreement on the part of both archaeology and art history in approaching and using the concept of monumentality. During the writing process the focus of the article repeatedly shifted. We discovered that our own sections often required the perspective of the other and thus represent, at least in part, an intersection of views. As Levenson describes in his terminology chapter, our article also demonstrates that there is more than one definition of monumentality and there is more than one subjective approach to the topic. Ultimately, that is exactly what this volume wishes to reflect. Starting with this introductory chapter and the corresponding critical comments, we would like to draw attention to the problematic nature of the term monumentality. The following case studies are then intended to demonstrate the broad range of examples investigated under monumentality.

Bibliography

Archenholz, J. W. von (1785): England und Italien, vol. 1, Leipzig: Dyk.

Bayliss, R. (2001): "Provincial Cilicia and the Archaeology of Temple Conversion." Ph. D. Thesis, Newcastle: University of Newcastle upon Tyne.

Benjamin, W. (1993): Das Kunstwerk im Zeitalter seiner technischen Reproduzierbarkeit: Drei Studien zur Kunstsoziologie, Frankfurt a. M.: Suhrkamp.

Brunke, H. (2018): "Großbaustellen in Sumer – Aufwand und Kosten." In: K. Rheidt/ W. Lorenz (eds.), Groß Bauen – Großbaustellen als kulturgeschichtliches Phänomen, Basel: Birkhäuser, pp. 27–36.

Buccellati, F. (2016): Three-dimensional Volumetric Analysis in an Archaeological Context: The Palace of Tupkish at Urkesh and its Representation, Urkesh/ Mozan Studies 6, Malibu: Undena Publications.

Bukowiecki, E./Wulf-Rheidt, U. (2018): "Ziegel für den Kaiser: Römische Palastbauten als logistische Meisterleistungen." In: K. Rheidt/W. Lorenz (eds.), Groß Bauen – Großbaustellen als kulturgeschichtliches Phänomen, Basel: Birkhäuser, pp. 47–61.

Cicero, M. T. (1995): Die Reden gegen Verres. In C. Verrem, ed. by M. Fuhrmann, vol. 1, Zürich: Artemis & Winkler.

Dalley, S. (1994): "Nineveh, Babylon and the hanging gardens: Cuneiform and classical sources reconciled." In: Iraq 56, pp. 45–58.

Dobres, M.-A./Robb, J. (2000): Agency in Archaeology, London: Routledge.

Feix, J. (1963): Herodot Historien, vol. 1, München: Heimeran.

Furholt, M./Hinz, M./Mischka, D. (2012): "'As time goes by' – Meanings, Memories and Monuments." In: M. Furholt/M. Hinz/D. Mischka (eds.): "As time goes by?" – Monumentality, Landscapes and the Temporal Perspective, Bonn: Habelt, pp. 13–20.

Galinier, M. (1999): "La Colonne Trajane et les pouvoirs européens: Reproductions et imitations." In: C. Llinas (ed.), Moulages. Actes des rencontres internationales sur les moulages, 14–17 février 1997, Montpellier: Éditions de l'Université Montpellier III, pp. 201–209.

Galinier, M. (2017): "La Colonne Trajane, 'Miroir' des Princes, ou la fortune idéologique du monument de Trajan." In: F. Mitthof/G. Schörner (eds.), Columna Traiani – Traianssäule: Siegesmonument und Kriegsbericht in Bildern. Beiträge der Tagung in Wien anlässlich des 1900. Jahrestag der Einweihung, 9.–12. Mai 2013, TYCHE Sonderband 9, Wien: Holzhausen, pp. 229–249.

Gentz, H. (2004): Reise nach Rom und Sizilien 1790–1795: Aufzeichnungen und Skizzen eines Berliner Architekten, ed. by M. Bollé/K.-R. Schütze, Berlin: Willmuth Arenhövel.

Goethe, Johann Wolfgang (1976): Tagebuch der Italienischen Reise 1786: Notizen und Briefe aus Italien mit Skizzen und Zeichnungen des Autors, ed. and commented on by C. Michel, Frankfurt a. M.: Insel.

Goethe, J. W. von (1998): "Italienische Reise." In: Johann Wolfgang von Goethe, Werke. Hamburger Ausgabe, textual criticism and commentary by E. Trunz, vol. 11, München: Deutscher Taschenbuch Verlag.

Goethe, J. W. von (1998b): "Von deutscher Baukunst (1923)." In: Johann Wolfgang von Goethe, Werke. Hamburger Ausgabe, textual criticism and commentary by E. Trunz, vol. 12, München: Deutscher Taschenbuch Verlag.

Granzow, J. (2015): "Die Hofgartengalerie zu München." In: B. Savoy (ed.), Tempel der Kunst: Die Geburt des öffentlichen Kunstmuseums in Deutschland 1701–1815, Köln; Weimar; Wien: Böhlau, pp. 524–548.

Gruben, G. (2001): Griechische Tempel und Heiligtümer, München: Hirmer.

Hageneuer, S. (2016): "The Influence of Early Architectural Reconstruction Drawings in Near Eastern Archaeology." In: R. A. Stucky/O. Kaelin/H.-P. Mathys (eds.), Proceedings of the 9th ICAANE, vol. 1, Wiesbaden: Harrossowitz, pp. 359–370.

Hageneuer, S./Levenson, F. (2018): "Das Steinstiftgebäude in Uruk – ein gescheitertes Experiment?" In: K. Rheidt/W. Lorenz (eds.), Groß Bauen – Großbaustellen als kulturgeschichtliches Phänomen, Basel: Birkhäuser, pp. 109–121.

Hardering, K. (2014): "Der Dom zu Köln, 'kein Gebäude... wie alle andern auf der Welt'." In: Wallraf-Richartz-Museum und Fondation Corboud (eds.), Die Kathedrale: Romantik – Impressionismus – Moderne, München: Hirmer, pp. 121–151.

Heres, G. (1977): "Römische Bauwerke in Jean Pauls 'Titan'." In: Staatliche Museen zu Berlin. Forschungen und Berichte, 18, Archäologische Beiträge, pp. 199–205.

Herwig, G. (1978): "Apprehension." In: Akademie der Wissenschaften der DDR/Akademie der Wissenschaften in Göttingen/Heidelberger Akademie der Wissenschaften (eds.), Goethe-Wörterbuch, vol. 1, Stuttgart; Berlin; Köln; Mainz: Kohlhammer, col. 778–779.

Hirt, A. (1822): Die Geschichte der Baukunst bei den Alten, vol. 2, Berlin: G. Reimer.

Hodder, I. (2016): Studies in Human-Thing Entanglement, self publishing online.

Hölscher, T. (2017): "Ideologie der Realität – Realität der Ideologie: Narrative Struktur, Sachkultur und (Un-)Sichtbarkeit eines bildlichen Kriegsberichts." In: F. Mitthof/G. Schörner (eds.), Columna Traiani – Traianssäule: Siegesmonument und Kriegsbericht in Bildern. Beiträge der Tagung in Wien anlässlich des 1900. Jahrestag der Einweihung, 9.–12. Mai 2013, TYCHE Sonderband 9, Wien: Holzhausen, pp. 15–35.

Jennings, M. W./Eiland, H./Smith, G. (eds.) (2002): Walter Benjamin: Selected Writings, vol. 3, 1935–1938, Cambridge: Belnap Press.

Kopytoff, I. (1986): "The cultural biography of things: Commoditization as process." In: A. Appadurai (ed.), The Social Life of Things: Commodities in Cultural Perspective, Cambridge: University Press, pp. 64–92.

Lindemann, B. W. (1998): "Der Turm in der Baukunst." In: M. Wullen/G. Schauerte (eds.), Babylon – Mythos, München: Hirmer, pp. 245–252.

Lohmann, D. (2018): "Superlative baulicher Art: Zum 'Trilithon' und der Inszenierung von Größe im antiken Jupiterheiligtum in Baalbek." In: K. Rheidt/W. Lorenz (eds.), Groß Bauen – Großbaustellen als kulturgeschichtliches Phänomen, Basel: Birkhäuser, pp. 149–163.

Mager, T. (2016): Schillernde Unschärfe: Der Begriff der Authentizität im architektonischen Erbe, Berlin; Boston: Walter de Gruyter.

Martini, W. (2006): Das Pantheon Hadrians in Rom: Das Bauwerk und seine Deutung, Stuttgart: Steiner.

Minkowski, H. (1959): Aus dem Nebel der Vergangenheit steigt der Turm zu Babel: Bilder aus 1000 Jahren, Simbach, Inn: Deutsche Heraklith AG.

Mischka, D. (2012): "Temporality in the Monumental Landscape of Flintbek." In: M. Furholt/M. Hinz/D. Mischka (eds.), "As time goes by?" – Monumentality, Landscapes and the Temporal Perspective, Bonn: Habelt, pp. 133–143.

Mitthof, F./Schörner, G. (eds.) (2017): Columna Traiani – Traianssäule: Siegesmonument und Kriegsbericht in Bildern. Beiträge der Tagung in Wien anlässlich des 1900. Jahrestag der Einweihung, 9.–12. Mai 2013, TYCHE Sonderband 9, Wien: Holzhausen.

Museteanu, C. (2004): "The National History Museum of Romania: Achievements and Perspectives." In: Medelhavsmuseet 2004/1, pp. 34–39.

Nipperdey, T. (1981): "Der Kölner Dom als Nationaldenkmal." In: Historische Zeitschrift 233/3, pp. 595–613.

Notroff, J./Dietrich, O./Schmidt, K. (2014): "Building Monuments, Creating Communities – Early Monumental Architecture at Pre-Pottery Neolithic Göbekli Tepe." In: J. F. Osborne (ed.), Approaching Monumentality in Archaeology, IEMA Proceedings, Albany: State University of New York Press, pp. 83–105.

Olsen, B. (2003): "Material Culture after Text: Re-Membering Things." In: Norwegian Archaeological Review 36/2, pp. 87–104.

Osborne, J. F. (2014): "Monuments and Monumentality." In: J. F. Osborne (ed.), Approaching Monumentality in Archaeology, IEMA Proceedings, Albany: State University of New York Press, pp. 1–19.

Paul, J. (1803): Titan, vol. 4, Berlin: Matzdorff.

Paul, J. (1877): Titan: A Romance, translated from the German by C. T. Brooks, New York: Henry Holt.

Pollock, S. (2013): "Differenzierung und Klassifizierung in Gesellschaften des 4. und 3. Jahrtausends v. Chr." In: N. Crüsemann/M. van Ess/M. Hilgert/B. Salje (eds.), Uruk: 5000 Jahre Megacity, Petersberg: Michael Imhof, pp. 149–155.

Prignitz, S. (2018): "Die altgriechische Bauvergabeordnung aus Tegea." In: K. Rheidt/W. Lorenz (eds.), Groß Bauen – Großbaustellen als kulturgeschichtliches Phänomen, pp. 37–46.

Rowell, D. (2012): Paris: The 'New Rome' of Napoleon I, London; New Delhi; New York; Sydney: Bloomsbury.

Schmid, H. (1995): Der Tempelturm Etemenanki in Babylon, Baghdader Forschungen 17, Mainz am Rhein: von Zabern.

Schmidt, K. (2000): "Zuerst kam der Tempel, dann die Stadt: Bericht zu den Grabungen am Gürcütepe und am Göbekli Tepe 1996–1999." In: Istanbuler Mitteilungen 50, pp. 5–40.

Schmidt, K. (2001): "Göbekli Tepe, Southeastern Turkey: A preliminary Report on the 1995–1999 Excavations." In: Paléorient 26, pp. 45–54.

Schmidt, K. (2009): "Göbekli Tepe. Eine Beschreibung der wichtigsten Befunde, erstellt nach den Arbeiten der Grabungsteams der Jahre 1995–2007." In: K. Schmidt (ed.), Erste Tempel – Frühe Siedlungen. 12000 Jahre Kunst und Kultur. Ausgrabungen und Forschungen zwischen Donau und Euphrat, Oldenburg: Isensee, pp. 187–223.

Sgariglia, S. (2009): L'Athenaion di Siracusa: Una lettura stratigrafica tra storia e segni. The Athenaion at Syracuse: A stratigraphic analysis based on history and archaeological evidence, Siracusa: Lettera Ventidue.

Trigger, B. G. (2007): Understanding early civilizations: A comparative study, Cambridge: University Press.

Watkins, T. (2012): "Household, Community and Social Landscape: Maintaining Social Memory in the Early Neolithic of Southwest Asia." In: M. Furholt/M. Hinz/D. Mischka (eds.), "As time goes by?" – Monumentality, Landscapes and the Temporal Perspective, Bonn: Habelt, pp. 23–44.

Wullen, M./Schauerte, G. (eds.) (2008): Babylon – Mythos & Wahrheit. Mythos: eine Ausstellung der Kunstbibliothek, Staatliche Museen zu Berlin mit Unterstützung der Staatsbibliothek zu Berlin, München: Hirmer.

Responses to the Theoretical Framework and Methodology

Monumentalbaukunst –
Architektur als erweiterter Denk- und Erfahrungsraum

Jörg H. Gleiter

In den einleitenden Zitaten zu Monuments and Monumentality – Different Perspectives führen die Autoren an, dass man aufgrund der Komplexität der Monumentalität nie gerecht werden und sie daher nicht näher definieren könne. Gleichfalls wird festgestellt, dass Monumentalität sich verbindet mit dem Großen als „XXL phenomena", mit dem, „was den Maßstab sprengt" und die „Regeln der Angemessenheit um der Wirkung willen bewusst verletzt." (Levenson in diesem Band)

Es ist die Architektur, mit der man Monumentalität unmittelbar in Verbindung bringt. Sie steht im Zentrum der Architektur als Baukunst, man spricht auch von Monumentalbaukunst, womit sie sofort auch im Zentrum der Wandlung der Konzeption von Baukunst in der Moderne steht. Mit der Moderne wurde die Monumentalität zu einer offenen Frage, ob die Architektur als Baukunst immer monumental, im klassischen Sinne also massiv und groß sein muss. Gerade in Hinblick auf die Architektur, auf einem Gebiet also, wo man es am wenigsten erwarten würde, soll hier die Frage gestellt und zugleich positiv beantwortet werden, ob nicht auch Kleines monumental sein kann.

Tatsächlich ist die Monumentalität des Kleinen einer der großen Beiträge der Moderne und ihrer Wandlung des Begriffs von Baukunst. Als Beispiele dafür können die Meisterhäuser (1926) von Walter Gropius in Dessau stehen. Sie sind von geringer Größe und doch von monumentaler Wirkung. Wobei in der Moderne, wie hier schon vorweggenommen werden soll, weniger die Konzeption als die Art und Weise der Manifestation von Monumentalität sich änderte. Mit der Verschiebung der Perspektive auf das Kleine verbindet sich die Hoffnung, die nötige Distanz zu finden, um dem Phänomen Monumentalität begrifflich näherzukommen.

Übergroß

Kann Kleines monumental sein? „Das Kunstwerk ist revolutionär, das Haus konservativ" (Loos 1962: 315). Das ist irritierend und umso mehr, als dies Adolf Loos
1910 auf dem ersten Höhepunkt der Debatten um die Moderne und die Neukon-
zeption der Architektur als Baukunst formuliert hatte, was gleichzeitig auch die
Zeit ist, in der er seine ersten schlichten, ornamentlosen Häuser baute. Dass das
Haus konservativ ist, heißt aber nicht, dass sich nichts ändern und alles gleich-
bleiben soll, im Gegenteil, wie Loos' Architektur zeigt, heißt konservativ, dass das
moderne Haus in einer spezifischen historischen Traditions- und Entwicklungs-
linie der Monumentalbaukunst steht – trotz allem, vielleicht auch gerade wegen
des Wandels in der Erscheinung, das heißt gerade weil es klein, ornamentlos und
weiß ist.

Auch Loos stand unter dem Einfluss von Gottfried Sempers Konzeption der
Monumentalbaukunst. Die Auflösung der Wand durch das Bauen mit Stahl und
Glas wurde Semper zum Auslöser für die Reflexion über die Theorie der Architektur im Allgemeinen und der Monumentalbaukunst im Besonderen. Vier Elemente
können nach Semper benannt werden, die die Monumentalbaukunst charakteri-
sieren: Einerseits übergroße Masse und Dauerhaftigkeit, andererseits Historizität und feierliche, mythische Stimmung. Wobei übergroße Masse und Dauerhaftigkeit der Kategorie des Raumes, Geschichtsbezug und mythische Stimmung der
Kategorie der Zeit zugeordnet werden können. Man muss aber auch feststellen,
dass so gültig Sempers Definition im klassischen Verständnis war, so sehr stand
sie der Entwicklung der Architektur der Moderne im Weg.

Monumentalität in der Architektur ist kein Selbstzweck. Sie verband sich mit
den Verfahren zur Überhöhung der Architektur zur „wahren Atmosphäre der
Kunst". Sie erlaubte die Transzendierung von Material und konkreter Form und
so die Öffnung der Architektur als erweiterter Denk- und Erfahrungsraums. Monumentalität war der Schlüssel zur Öffnung der Architektur für Bedeutung und
kulturelle Semantiken durch Bezugnahme auf räumlich wie zeitlich Abwesendes.
Daher der Begriff Monumentalbaukunst im Sinne des „Kunstschaffens" und des
„Kunstgenusses". „Vernichtung der Realität, des Stofflichen, ist nothwendig", so
Semper, „wo die Form als bedeutungsvolles Symbol als selbständige Schöpfung
des Menschen hervortreten soll." (Semper 1878: 216).

Es gehörte zur Überzeugung Sempers, dass übergroße Masse und Dauerhaftigkeit, Historizität und mythische Atmosphäre unumgängliche Voraussetzun-
gen sind, damit Architektur ebenbürtig mit den darstellenden Künste wird. Es ist
paradox und trifft doch den Kern von Sempers Konzeption von Architektur, dass
gerade übergroße Massen Auslöser für die Öffnung hin zu geistigen Inhalten sind.
Wobei es weniger die Art des Gemachtseins oder das Wunder der Konstruktion
der großen Bauwerke sind, als die Oberflächenbehandlung und die Weise ihrer

Wirkung, nämlich ihre erhabene, über die Präsenz der Dinge hinausreichende Wirkung, die im Vordergrund stehen. Das in räumlicher wie auch zeitlicher Hinsicht Übergroße und als solches Unheimliche löst erhabene Gefühle im Betrachter aus und macht die Architektur zu einem erweiterten Denk- und Erfahrungsraum. Transzendierung der Architektur mittels der Erfahrung des Erhabenen, das ist das Programm der Monumentalbaukunst.

Erhaben

Sempers Monumentalbaukunst als praktische Ästhetik erschließt sich aus Immanuel Kants Analytik der ästhetischen Urteilskraft. Erhabene Gefühle werden nach Kant von sinnlichen Ereignissen ausgelöst, die „über alle Vergleichung groß" sind und daher, weil eben zu groß, von der menschlichen Vernunft nicht erfasst werden können. Auslöser für das Erhabene können unheimliche Naturereignisse sein wie der unendliche Sternenhimmel, die stürmische See oder Blitz und Donner. Das Übergroße und Unheimliche löst emotionale Reaktionen aus, regt aber auch die menschliche Vorstellungskraft an.

Es geht vom Unerklärlichen und Erschütternden, was im ersten Moment Gefühle der Unlust auslösen, eine den Intellekt dynamisierende Kraft aus. Denn was ihn ängstigt, für das versucht der Mensch im freien Spiel der Einbildungskraft eine Erklärung zu finden. Er sucht die Kausalitäten hinter den Erscheinungen und versucht, für die ängstigenden Phänomene eine Erklärung zu finden und ihnen eine Rationalität nach seinen Maßstäben unterzuschieben. Dieses Verfahren bezeichnete Kant als Subreption (Kant 1996: 180). Indem er die Phänomene erklärbar macht, aber nicht der Realität, sondern der Idee nach, erhebt sich der Mensch so über das im ersten Moment Unverstandene und Unheimliche, der anfängliche Schrecken schlägt in der geistigen Erhebung in lustvolle Bestätigung der eigenen Existenz um.

Hier kommt die Monumentalbaukunst ins Spiel. Schaut man sich diese genauer an, so können Gebäude wohl übermäßig groß oder „beinahe zu groß" sein, wie Kant sagte, sie bewegen sich aber immer innerhalb der menschlichen Rationalität, sie sind ja von ihm konzipiert und erbaut. So kann, im Unterschied zu den Phänomenen der Natur, von der monumentalen Größe der Gebäude nur bedingt eine Erfahrung des Erhabenen ausgehen. Und wenn, kann es nicht allein an der räumlichen Kategorie von Masse und Dauerhaftigkeit liegen. Damit kommt die andere Dimension ins Spiel: Die Zeit in ihrer besonderen Erscheinung als historische Zeit. Sie trägt wesentlich zur Erfahrung des Erhabenen bei. Es sind hier besonders die Ornamente und Stile, mittels derer die Monumentalbaukunst an das Älteste und Vorvergangene appelliert. Sie führen uns geistig zurück an die dunklen Anfänge der Menschheitsgeschichte, den Mythos und damit in zeitliche

Dimensionen, die die menschliche Vorstellungskraft überschreiten. Es ist die Historizität und die mythische Atmosphäre der Monumentalbaukunst, die eine schwindelerregende, die materielle Präsenz des Bauwerks transzendierende, erhabene Wirkung erzeugen.

Dynamisch

Es macht die klassische Monumentalbaukunst aus, dass sie mittels Stile die heroische Geschichte herbeizitiert, die sich je länger je mehr im Dunkel der Vorgeschichte verliert. Dafür stehen die Gebäude des Historismus wie die Semperoper in Dresden (1878) oder Paul Wallots Berliner Reichstagsgebäude (1894), wie überhaupt die Monumentalbaukunst des ausgehenden 19. und beginnenden 20. Jahrhunderts. Deren erhabene Wirkung beruht so sehr auf einer Rhetorik historischer Zeitlichkeit wie der Räumlichkeit großer Baumassen.

Man versteht jetzt auch, warum sich die Architekten der Moderne mit der Abschaffung der klassischen Ornamente so schwergetan haben: So sinnvoll dies im Kontext der neuen technologischen, materiellen und gesellschaftlichen Veränderungen schien, mit ihnen fiel auch die Zeitdimension weg und damit im Sinne der Monumentalbaukunst die Möglichkeit zur Transzendierung der Präsenz der Architektur und ihrer Öffnung als erweiterter Denk- und Erfahrungsraum. Ohne eine alternative Strategie würde eine ornamentlose und damit referenzlose Architektur auf die Banalität der reinen materiellen Präsenz reduziert. Wo die Moderne auf andere, scheinbar weniger dauerhafte Materialien zurückgriff wie Stahl und Glas, würde die Monumentalbaukunst nur noch auf einen ihrer vier Parameter reduziert, auf die schiere Größe und damit allein auf die moderne Bauaufgabe, das Hochhaus.

Im Zentrum der Moderne stand die Rekonzeptualisierung der Monumentalbaukunst. Der Wandel erfolgte dann im Übergang vom historischen Zeitkonzept zu einer Konzeption immanenter Zeitlichkeit. Dafür stehen die Verfahren der Dynamisierung der Architektur. Das hieß: Aufgabe sowohl der Symmetrie wie auch einfacher platonischer Körper, dagegen kubistische Verschränkung und Durchdringungen der platonischen Körper, Verschiebungen und Transpositionen, Staffelung, Schichtung und Rotation der Elemente im Raum, Spiel mit der Spur als Erinnerung und Rückführung der ikonischen, ornamentalen Bildhaftigkeit auf die Indexikalität von Zeichen. Es trat die immanente Zeitlichkeit der Architektur als Thema hervor, die Prozessualität der architektonischen Verfahren, oftmals bei gleichzeitiger Verunklärung der sie bewegenden, damit magisch beeinflussenden Kräfte – alles Voraussetzung dafür, dass auch Kleines monumental werden und doch gleichzeitig in der Tradition der Monumentalbaukunst stehen konnte.

Bibliographie

Kant, I. (1996), Kritik der Urteilskraft, ed. by W. Weischedel, Frankfurt a. M.: Suhrkamp.

Loos, A. (1962): "Architektur", in: A. Loos, Sämtliche Schriften in zwei Bänden, ed. by F. Glück, Wien; München: Herold.

Semper, G. (1878): Der Stil in den technischen und tektonischen Künsten oder praktische Ästhetik, vol. 1, Die textile Kunst für sich betrachtet und in Beziehung zur Baukunst, München: Bruckmann. doi:10.3931/e-rara-11736.

Monumentality in context – a reply from Egyptology

Richard Bußmann

Monuments have shaped and are still shaping contemporary views on the past. Gothic cathedrals, the Chinese Wall, and Egyptian pyramids open a window into past civilizations and the lives of people who imagined the world differently from us today. Cross-cultural research into early complex societies tends to be focused on monuments of the elite, partially because these seem to embody the essence of a society, and partially because comparison requires flying from society to society at some distance above ground, where monuments stand out, while their context begins to disintegrate (Trigger 2003).

In their introduction, the editors of this volume show that monuments have complex stories to tell. Levenson distinguishes between intended (builder), perceived (people for whom a monument was built) and received (cultural memory) dimensions of monumentality, implying that these need not coincide. He also considers forms of monumentality other than built environment. Buccellati suggests an agenda for the study of built monuments, which embraces labor organization, typological variation, institutional history, use analysis, phenomenology, spatial context, echoes in later representations, and object biography. Many of these themes are well designed to bring people back into the discussion of monuments. Departing from this agenda, Hageneuer and van der Heyden offer examples of life cycles of monuments, from their planning, building and afterlife to modern three-dimensional reproductions.

The approaches adopted by the editors rightly make it clear that monuments were not static buildings, but embedded in dynamic processes and various types of social interaction. I would add that historical context, both of the making and the reception of monuments, is a key dimension for approaching monuments. Since pyramids and cultural memory are mentioned in the introductory chapters, I would like to respond to these themes from the point of view of my discipline, which is Egyptology.

The pyramids of Egypt are an example of what one could describe as a mismatch between intended, perceived, and received monumentality. In the cultural memory of Egypt in the West, pyramids have long played a recurrent, but rather modest role. Travelers speculated about the historical meaning of the pyramids, specifically the pyramid of Khufu who was portrayed by Herodotus as a despotic and hubristic ruler. However, religious knowledge of ancient Egypt mattered more to European scholars and enthusiasts than pyramids alone did (Ucko/Champion 2003; Assmann 2006). In contrast, today the pyramids are icons of ancient Egypt. They are actively promoted by the tourist industry, and traveling to Egypt has become sufficiently affordable for many to experience these monuments physically.

The pyramid of Khufu belongs to a small group of extraordinarily gigantic pyramids built in the early Fourth Dynasty, around 2600 BCE. These pyramids had gradually developed from smaller versions and ultimately from much simpler forms of the royal tomb (Lehner 1997). Although the pyramids of the Fourth Dynasty are undeniably technological masterpieces, knowledge of how to build them and how to organize labor rested on centuries of experience. A carpet of settlements, workshops, and barracks, located at the foot of the Giza plateau, is archaeological evidence of labor management and the accommodation of service personnel (Möller 2016: 117–157). Papyrus documents, recently discovered at a harbor site on the shore of the Red Sea and belonging to an official involved in the logistics of pyramid construction (Tallet 2017), also show that pyramid building was an enormous but essentially manageable effort.

Khufu's pyramid was just one element of a much grander social project. It was set centre stage in a planned cemetery, cascading from the royal pyramid and its associated boats to the pyramids of the queens, large tombs to the east of the royal pyramid for the princes, and finally a set of smaller tombs to the west for high-ranking courtiers (Jánosi 2005). The Khufu cemetery continued a tradition of large-scale cemetery planning apparent already under his predecessor Sneferu at Dahshur and Meidum (Alexanian 1995). A few centuries earlier, at the beginning of Pharaonic history, the royal tomb was surrounded by rows of subsidiary tombs of almost equal size, suggesting that the king was imagined as a primus inter pares (Vadou 2008). While the Khufu pyramid at Giza surely emphasizes the centrality of the deceased ruler, the king is presented here as entangled in a more complex set of relationships than the earliest Pharaohs were. The actual monument at Giza, one could argue, is the building into stone of a ranked court community focused on the royal family.

Gordon Childe (1945) argued that the monumentality of royal tombs reflected the transition of a society towards territorial statehood. According to Tobias Kienlin (2007), monumentality and ritual expenditure, in the case of the early European Bronze Age tomb of the 'Fürst' of Leubingen, were a means of establishing social coherence in a period of transition, when previous forms of social organization were being reshaped. Along similar lines, Mirsolav Bárta (2013) has seen the Giza pyramids as symbolizing the transition to a fully-fledged administration in Egypt. I have argued elsewhere that the gigantic pyramids might reflect the beginning of the territorial integration of the country and that the planned arrangement on the cemetery foregrounds the royal family as the core of court society, thus emphasizing dynastic inheritance patterns (Bussmann 2014; 2015). Whatever the most adequate interpretation, historical context matters for explaining why and how gigantism at Giza happened in this particular period.

With the shrinking size of pyramids in the following centuries, building efforts gradually shifted towards the temples attached to the east of pyramids, where offerings were made to the deceased kings (Posener-Kriéger 1976). Involvement in the royal funerary cult was a lucrative business. According to their official titles and inscriptions, courtiers were rather eager to get a share of the revenues. Consequently, it was not the size of a pyramid that mattered to the courtiers, but the social practices centered on the royal funerary cult.

As a final note on pyramids, and returning to Buccellati's comment on the relevance of institutional history, the matrix of Egyptian 'high culture' developed in the context of the royal tomb. It is only over a millennium later that temples of deities started playing a significant role for central administration and royal display (Kemp 2006: 111–135). In fact, speculative thought in the 3rd millennium BCE revolved around the question of what a king is rather than what a deity is. Theology was a much later offspring in Egypt (Assmann 1983). This development was paralleled by a steady increase in the size of temples, until these dominated the landscape along the Nile in the 1st millennium BCE, when early travelers from ancient Europe made their first encounters with the people of Egypt. Today religious and administrative buildings are often dwarfed by the buildings of private companies and banks, a reflection of the capitalist organization of societies. Comparing and contrasting monuments through time and across cultures can thus reveal the different institutional settings of societies and help with explaining the varying strategies for the display of core values.

The pyramids and temples of ancient Egypt are bound up in what Egyptologist Jan Assmann (1991; 1996) has referred to as the 'monumental discourse'. The monumental discourse encompasses stone-lined buildings, the hieroglyphic inscriptions and visual scenes displayed on their walls, and handwritten religious texts, in short: formalized knowledge, access to which was restricted to the elite. The term 'discourse' highlights a self-referential dimension of this history, meaning that a monument can respond to a previous monument rather than to a reality outside the discourse. Simplifying a little, building a pyramid can be a statement about continuing an existing order rather than about the actual power of an individual king. For this reason, monuments do not speak directly to a visitor or a reader, but require contextual analysis within the language – material, visual, or written – in which a society communicates.

The monumental discourse lies at the heart of the cultural memory of ancient Egypt. Following Assmann (1992), one can distinguish between individual memorizing, social memory based on face-to-face communication, and long-term cultural memory, which requires formalized institutions for the transmission of knowledge, predominantly in writing. The cultural memory of Egypt is thus an elite practice, both in terms of what is remembered and who is remembering today. Discussions of cultural memory have opened up important lines of research, including on the relevance of the past for the contemporary world. However, a cultural memory of Egypt based on the monumental discourse runs the risk of forgetting social contexts in the past and presenting knowledge as a history of ideas devoid of the people who produced and consumed them. Seen from this angle, cultural memory almost emerges as a counter paradigm to an object biography, if the latter is understood as the history of changing social networks, structured around an object, and the various meanings assigned to an object by different people (Gosden/Marshall 1996).

Finally, the cultural memory of ancient Egypt has political implications. In Egypt, antiquity tourism, centered on monuments, plays an important role in the national economy (Hassan 2003). The flourishing antiquity market, with all its disastrous consequences, shows that authentic objects from the past have huge monetary value also outside Egypt. Interpretation and the administration of Pharaonic monuments has long been dominated and funded by Western institutions (Jeffreys 2003; Carruthers 2015). The process of the 'decolonization' of Egyptology, as the historian Donald Reid (1985) has called it, is still on its way. Afrocentrists emphasize the African nature of ancient Egypt, stressing the superiority of a 'black' civilization to enforce political rights (Diop 1955). Although these positions represent a selected and narrow range of motivations for engaging with ancient Egypt, the afterlife of Pharaonic monuments clearly is a history of power relationships up to the present day.

Bibliography

Alexanian, N. (1995): "Die Mastaba II/1 in Dahschur-Mitte." In: Anonymous (ed.), Kunst des Alten Reiches: Symposium im Deutschen Archäologischen Institut Kairo am 29. und 30. Oktober 1991, Mainz: Philipp von Zabern, pp. 1–18.

Assmann, J. (1983): Re und Amun. Die Krise des polytheistischen Weltbilds im Ägypten der 18.–20. Dynastie, Göttingen: Vandenhoeck & Ruprecht.

Assmann, J. (1991): Stein und Zeit. Mensch und Gesellschaft im Alten Ägypten, München: Fink.

Assmann, J. (1992): Das kulturelle Gedächtnis. Schrift, Erinnerung und politische Identität in frühen Hochkulturen, München: C. H. Beck.

Assmann, J. (1996): "Der literarische Aspekt des ägyptischen Grabes und seine Funktion im Rahmen des 'monumentalen Diskurses'." In: A. Loprieno (ed.),

Ancient Egyptian Literature: History and Forms, Leiden; New York; Köln: E. J. Brill, pp. 97–104.

Assmann, J. (2006): Erinnertes Ägypten. Pharaonische Motive in der europäischen Religions- und Geistesgeschichte, Berlin: Kadmos.

Bárta, M. (2013): "Kings, Viziers, and Courtiers: Executive Power in the Third Millennium BC." In: J. C. Moreno García (ed.), Ancient Egyptian Administration, Leiden: Brill, pp. 153–175.

Bussmann, R. (2014): "Scaling the state: Egypt in the third millennium BC." In: Archaeology International 17, pp. 79–93. DOI: 10.5334/ai.1708

Bussmann, R. (2015): "Pyramid Age: Huni to Radjedef." In: W. Grajetzki/W. Wendrich (eds), UCLA Encyclopedia of Egyptology http://digital2.library.ucla.edu/viewItem.do?ark=21198/zz002k2rxm (last accessed April 12, 2019)

Carruthers, W. (ed.) (2015): Histories of Egyptology: Interdisciplinary Measures, New York; London: Routledge.

Childe, G. (1945): "Directional Changes in Funerary Practices during 50,000 years." In: Man 45, pp. 13–19.

Diop, C. A. (1955): Nations nègres et culture, Paris: Éditions africaines.

Gosden, C./Marshall, Y. (1999): "The Cultural Biography of Objects." In: World Archaeology 31/2, pp. 169–178.

Hassan, F. A. (2003): "Selling Egypt: Encounters at Khan el-Khalili." In: S. MacDonald/M. Rice (eds.), Consuming Ancient Egypt: Encounters with Ancient Egypt, London: UCL Press, pp. 111–122.

Jánosi, P. (2005): Giza in der 4. Dynastie: die Baugeschichte und Belegung einer Nekropole des Alten Reiches. Band. 1: die Mastabas der Kernfriedhöfe und die Felsgräber, Wien: Österreichischen Akademie der Wissenschaften.

Jeffreys, D. (ed.) (2003): Views of ancient Egypt since Napoleon Bonaparte: Imperialism, Colonialism and Modern Appropriations, London: UCL Press.

Kemp, B. J. (2006): Ancient Egypt: Anatomy of a Civilization, 2nd revised ed., London: Routledge.

Kienlin, T. (2007): "Der 'Fürst' von Leubingen: Herausragende Bestattungen der Frühbronzezeit als Bezugspunkt gesellschaftlicher Kohärenz und kultureller Identität." In: C. Kümmel/B. Schweizer/U. Veit (eds.), Körperinszenierungen – Objektsammlung – Monumentalisierung: Totenritual und Grabkult in frühen Gesellschaften, Münster: Waxmann, pp. 181–206.

Lehner, M. (1997): The Complete Pyramids, London: Thames and Hudson.

Moeller, N. (2016): The archaeology of Urbanism in Ancient Egypt: From the Predynastic Period to the End of the Middle Kingdom, New York: Cambridge University Press.

Posener-Kriéger, P. (1976): Les archives du temple funéraire de Néferirkarê-Kakaï (Les papyrus d'Abousir): traduction et commentaire, Cairo: Institut français d'Archéologie orientale.

Reid, D. M. (1985): "Indigenous Egyptology: The Decolonization of a Profession." In: Journal of the American Oriental Society 105, pp. 233–246.

Tallet, P. (2017): Les papyrus de la mer Rouge I: Le 'journal de Merer' (Papyrus Jarf A et B), Cairo: Institut français d'Archéologie Orientale.

Trigger, B. G. (2003): Understanding Early Civilizations: A Comparative Study. Cambridge: Cambridge University Press.

Ucko, P./Champion, T. (eds.) (2003): The Wisdom of Egypt: Changing Visions Through the Ages, London: UCL Press.

Vaudou, É. (2008): "Les sépultures subsidiaires des grandes tombes de la Ire dynastie égyptienne." In: Archéo-Nil 18, pp. 148–168.

Part II
Case Studies

The Social Meaning of Big Architecture, or the Sociology of the Monumental

Heike Delitz & Felix Levenson

> "Buildings are treated as art, technical or investment objects. Rarely as social objects."
> *Markus 1993: 26*

> "Never in my life have I experienced the subtleties of such monochromy. The body, the mind, the heart gasp, suddenly overpowered [...]. The feeling of a superhuman fatality seizes you. The Parthenon, a terrible machine, grinds and dominates [...]. As by the violence of a combat I was stupefied by this gigantic apparition [...]; dropping down onto one of those steps of time, head sunk in the hollow of your hand, you are stunned and shaken."
> *Corbusier 1987: 212, 217*

Introduction

Le Corbusier, as one of the principal authors of classical Modern Architecture, describes how architectural works can be "terrible machines", machines that induce affects such as fear, humility and pride, and provide institutions with substance and perpetuity. For this very reason, they attract the wrath of the people, the anger of the subjected. Within European history, the storming of the Bastille provides a case in point. It is in "the form of cathedrals and palaces that the Church and State speak to and impose silence upon the multitudes" argues the French social theorist Georges Bataille. And, he continues, architectural monuments themselves often arouse "real fear". They appear as the "true rulers". Thus the "enmity of the people", which ends in destruction, is not directed towards the buildings as a substitute, it really is targeting the architecture (Bataille et al. 1970: 15–18).

So-called monumental buildings are omnipresent in the archaeological context. On the one hand, they simply have the greatest chance of surviving the millennia.

On the other hand, archaeological cultures have a lasting fascination, precisely because of their big architecture. Admittedly, there are just as many counter-examples and signs of systematic destruction that bear witness, *ex negativo*, to the social power of big architectures. One example is provided by the successive destruction and rebuilding of the Mycenaean palaces (see e. g. Maran 2006, 2012). Precisely through the destruction and reconstruction of these artifacts, societies transformed themselves and new societies emerged – and this was concurrent, it did not occur in advance and it was not unrelated.

What is then the social and cultural meaning of (relatively) 'big' architectures, what are their social and societal effects – promoting inequalities and instituting society –, how do they impact on bodies, interactions, and institutional prestige? The paper traces the social meaning of architectures, using the term architecture to refer here equally to infrastructure, open spaces, and urban structures.[1] A specific sociological perspective is adopted whereby architecture is generally viewed more as a *medium of the social* or a *mode of collective existence* than just a mere expression of the same (Delitz 2010b; 2018). Thus instead of assuming that architectures symbolize, represent, or reflect social power or inequality, we understand architectural activities, artifacts, and perceptions as ones in which the social structures, institutes, and transforms itself.

The background of such a perspective is based on those traditions of sociological thinking that share an understanding of each society as being culturally instituted: social meanings, inequalities, and power relations are ultimately socially and culturally constructed meanings – they have no basis *in re*. We are therefore dealing here with imagined institutions, as Cornelius Castoriadis puts it – who is able to draw essentially on the structuralist theory of society developed by Claude Levi-Strauss (Castoriadis 1987; Lévi-Strauss 1969: XX; 1987: 21: "Mauss still thinks it possible to develop a sociological theory of symbolism, whereas it is obvious that what is needed is a symbolic origin of society"). This is also true of the meaning that we assign to economic inequalities. The categorization of individuals into classes or milieux, for instance, involves invented categories. They have to be repeatedly symbolically embodied, rendered perceptible, as it is only in this way that imagined meanings have *material* existence. They require vivid, perceptible bodies – also in the form of architectural and infrastructural artifacts. Thus rather than assuming a fundamental social structure in contrast to which all symbolic practices and artifacts are mere symbolic expressions – like Marxism

---

1   Here the term architecture is not aesthetically defined and is not dependent on a distinction being made to normal 'buildings' – it includes all architectural activity and its artifacts. See Cache (1995) for a formal definition of architecture of this sort that allows the inclusion of the architecture of other societies, architecture that does not fit with classical value judgments about 'advanced civilizations' – a definition that is thus not ethnocentrically conceived.

assumes economic inconsistencies to be the basis of social structure, or like the action theory that assumes society is based on individual actors –, the premise of this discussion of the effect of monumental architecture is as follows.

Every social meaning (including economic and political inequalities, which are often the focus when monumental architectures are discussed) is culturally or symbolically produced, and shifts are always possible – transformations of societies in the medium of symbolic, meaningful artifacts. Through imagined, societally specific meanings, individuals become specific subjects with specific desires, affects, and ideas; cultural, power relations are created and individuals are classified.

In other words, of course 'elites' or those holding hegemonic positions are the builders of concrete monumental architectures, and of course they 'represent' their power in large artifacts. This is similarly true for the craftspeople involved – they too are proud of the big architecture and use it as a demonstration of their social status, for instance towards the agricultural serfs of the High Middle Ages.[2] It is, however, equally possible to state that political, economic, religious, or producing 'elites', including the respected craftspeople and master builders, are only able to establish themselves in and maintain these positions, if they manage to present themselves as such through the artifacts – without which no 'power' exists. Furthermore, they too are subjects of their society, socially formed, and they too share the dominant self-concepts, world images, and desires of their collective existence.

Our concern here is twofold. Firstly, we pursue a sociological theory that is generally interested with the issue of collective existence, with the forming of subjects or the socially *constituted subject*.[3] Secondly, we are concerned with a sociological theory that understands artifacts as socially meaningful, as indispensible, as socially active. Architectures are, in general, modes to create or to institutionalize, and to transform 'power' and social disparities. The social institutes itself in the mode of architecture. Certain forms of socialization display monumental architectures – and others do not. And the answer to the question of what leads a society to invest enormous resources in architecture lies in their own existence. In order to classify, assign, and subordinate individuals, the hegemonic positions within a society always have to employ particular artifacts; and the unavoidable and ever-present architecture is one of the most impressive and most effective means – as can be seen, for instance, in the quotations initially mentioned.

The following section of the paper outlines the importance of architecture for the constitution of collectives, of social life, or of society in general. The second section then discusses the significance of 'big' architectures in particular – and

2 On the pride of the master builders in the construction of the cathedrals, see Warnke (1984: 128–145).

3 On this basic decision of post-structuralist thinking see Balibar (2003).

also the significance of an apparent lack of such artifacts and buildings. Four different societies are considered as examples: the Tuareg as a case-study of a nomadic society with mobile tent architecture (1); the Achuar as an example of architectural dispersal and non-concentration (2); medieval society with the cathedrals in the 11th and 12th centuries (3); and the archaeological case of Uruk as one of the first *urban empires* (4).

1. Architecture as a mode of collective existence

What is a society and, in particular, what is the basis of an unequal distribution of power – of social divisions? It must firstly be said that societies cannot of course be reduced to social classifications and inequalities – the genders, classes, milieus, and generations. Although this is a fundamental requirement of collective existence, societies also at the very least comprise imaginaries of collective identities, of solidarity-based relations and boundaries towards others; of specific relationships between nature and culture; and religious or politically and legally formulated imaginaries of the foundation on which the collective in question is based, which justifies its norms and values, structures the daily routine and much more besides. From the sociological perspective adopted here, all these social meanings are *inventions* – institutions that are based on nothing. They express nothing else, cultural meanings have rather an ordering function. Social divisions like the categorization of individuals in classes, races, castes, or estates are imaginary, invented, and culturally stabilizing meanings.

The starting point of such an assertion (by Castoriadis [1987] and other authors) is the belief that each social reality exists in constant change, in becoming. In reality subjects and interactions are incessantly changing; furthermore every society is unpredictable, changes can always transpire. The social is continual change:

The perpetual selfalteration of society is its very being, which is manifested by the positing of relatively fixed and stable forms-figures and through the shattering of these forms-figures which can never be anything other than the positing-creating of other forms-figures (Castoriadis 1987: 372).

Each society must deny its becoming, and equally the unpredictability of its alteration. It must also deny its own contingency – the fact that each institution, its deepest commitments and holiest meanings and values represent a historical invention that was unnecessary. In this sense every society is an imagined fixation. It is based on the imagination of a collective identity in time. As every society is also heterogeneous, is divided, and does not constitute a harmonious whole, each also exists only as an imagined unity of members. And each society, or collective existence, is – thirdly and finally – only rendered possible out of the belief that it is based on a foundation that commits and justifies. Societies share the (again hegemonic) imaginary that there is something unquestionable on which their own values, norms, and desires are founded. Castoriadis refers to the primary social meaning or the "central imaginary" (Castoriadis 1987: 129) – the ultimate meaning that can never be disputed and never be justified, but that justifies everything. Such imaginary "social significations [...] denote nothing at all, and they connote just about everything" (Castoriadis 1987: 143). Thus the belief of being created by God or of owing life to a totem ancestor is based on an empty meaning of this sort. In the same way the idea of human dignity, to which democratic societies are dedicated, can be understood as an ultimate, foundational meaning of this sort – as a social basis or a founding outside.[4] Ultimate meanings are always presented as something that precedes the society, that lies outside it – as though they had created the society, rather than the opposite being the case. These meanings justify all others. Thus the imaginary 'God' justifies the Christian (Jewish, Islam) division of time, the structuring of daily routines around prayer times, hopes and fears associated with the life hereafter and contempt for this life, the way in which non-believers are treated, and so on (Castoriadis 1987: 129, 140). It should be added that every specific imaginary about the out-of-society foundation, the unity of members, and their identity in time is hegemonic – none is simply shared by all, each is disputed, and the particular positions and actors are always interested in determining society – in becoming the hegemon.[5] In short, societies are – on the part of hegemonic or ruling positions and probably never without controversy or dispute – imaginarily fixed, assigned a particular history. They are equally imaginarily unified, claiming an identity for their members. And their foundations are also in the realm of the imaginary.

All these meanings only exist as such if perceptible – they are only socially effective if they are symbolically embodied. Collectives have to portray themselves in symbolic practices and artifacts in order to become visible to themselves. The "social-historical is, or comes into existence as, a figure, hence as spacing, and as the otherness-alteration of the figure, temporality" (Castoriadis 1987: 219). The built form of a society is therefore not neutral or passive and is not a secondary shell of the social. Architecture is not just an expression, "neither adding anything nor taking anything away" (Castoriadis 1987: 118). It is rather the case that collectives constitute themselves *in the medium* of their cultural artifacts, their architectures, as this *specific* society with *these* categorizations of individuals, *this* relationship to nature, *this* history, and so on.

In a nutshell: architecture is one of the cultural or symbolic modes *in which* collectives incessantly create themselves. It is in this mode that power relations

---

4 See for the central imaginary as the 'founding outside' of a society Delitz/Maneval (2017).

5 As Laclau and Mouffe (1985) augment; see on their 'postfoundational thought' e. g. Marchart (2010).

are established, individuals are rendered unequal and 'territorialized' (Deleuze/ Guattari 1987: Ch. XII), are organized and fixed on the ground. In comparison to other cultural mediums – here language and its lack of precursors should be particularly emphasized, architecture is characterized by its perpetual presence, its non-linguisticality, its affectivity. The social effectiveness of its impact on the body, its force, and its dimensions should not be underestimated. In this context one of Castoriadis' comments can be applied to architecture, gauging its social significance. "The 'dimensionality' of the social-historical is not a 'framework' in which the social-historical is spread out and in which it unfolds; it is itself the mode of self-unfolding of the social-historical." (Castoriadis 1987: 219)

In light of the cultural self-constitution of society, in light of the hegemonic assignation of the collective, of the power relations and subjections, it is difficult to exaggerate the social significance of 'monumental' architectures in particular, of large buildings and other large-scale building techniques,[6] that is, urban development and infrastructure. A distinct political, a specific 'power sharing', is established in the affectivity of the large buildings, the adulation that they command, the fear and awe, the affect of invincibility and permanence.[7] And it is just the same with artifacts that allow the infrastructural development of a territory. They 'furnish' the territory, structure it, enable the institution of interactions. "The wall is the basis of our coexistence. Architecture builds its space of compatibility on a mode of discontinuity", as Bernard Cache, for example, expresses it (Cache 1995: 25).

Even the choice of materials is socially significant and should be considered as such – as a *choice*. Each building material has its own logic. Each allows a different static construction, different forms and surfaces, determines the durability and aesthetics – the symbolic potential of the architecture (Simondon 2017). And it is just the same with the affectivity of buildings and the institutions brought into existence in them. From the perspective of affect theory, the artifacts themselves create aversion, fear, anger, or adulation, rather than just triggering an emotion that already lies in the subject.[8] Wood, concrete, natural stone, felt, and wool do not just lead to differing visual and acoustic perceptions, they provide the institutions with different qualities of power – and thus with differing inequalities

---

6   "Urban development is per se large-scale building techniques. For a dense mass of people, housing must be built closely together, connected by a mesh of street networks and protected by security architecture of walls and fortifications. From the very beginning there is a monumental strain thereby." This involves "the mass, the density, the multiplicity – and the concentration of power" (Popitz 1995: 117).

7   On this definition of the political – the division of power in state and anti-state societies – see Gauchet (1994, 1999).

8   On this relational affect concept – following Spinoza's Ethics – see, e. g., Seyfert (2011) on institutional theory (where the focus is, broadly speaking, on affects – institutionalized ways to affect and be affected), and the critical overview of the 'affective turn' in Leys (2011).

and subjections. And in this context it is not only big architecture that is of social relevance, but literally every architecture. After all, even societies that do not feature monumental architecture connect it with a particular categorization of individuals, a particular political. The apparent 'lack' of large, impressive architecture is also socially significant. Because this too is a way to classify individuals in the mode of architecture, a specific kind of institutionalization of power and inequality – one that takes issue with societies with monumental architecture and large-scale building techniques.

A note challenging (archaeological, ethnological, sociological) evolutionism

Before we begin to consider these contrasting forms of society (societies with and societies without big architecture), we want to put aside the evolutionary perspective which regards big architectures as always being characteristic of 'advanced cultures'. A lack of monumental architecture is often correspondingly understood as a sign of a more primitive, archaic form of society. The same evolutionary logic presents nomadic societies as ones that are pre-sedentary, not yet sedentary – as ones that precede fixed buildings and are 'simpler'. Structural anthropology in particular raises objections to such perspectives, ones that judge all forms of society according to their own image and assign to the others a 'lack', a 'not yet developed' status.

Countering this evolutionary and thus ethnocentric perspective, Claude Lévi-Strauss demonstrated the exceptional complexity of the institutions of apparently 'simple' totemic societies. They are just as contemporary as modern societies, they do not precede them, and they are anything but primitive. And instead of speaking of these societies as ones that lack something – instead of addressing them as 'societies without history' or 'without writing' – structural anthropology is concerned to use only positive terms when describing all societies. Societies that apparently have no history are of course also part of history. They too change. They 'have' a history – and are incessantly struggling against it. They are not without history; they are rather *opposed* to history. Lévi-Strauss writes in this context of "cold societies". Their aim is "to make it the case that the order of temporal succession should have as little influence as possible on their content. No doubt they do not succeed perfectly; but this is the norm they set themselves." (Lévi-Strauss 1966: 234) Totemic societies imagine their origin and identity in timeless myths; and they classify individuals through the ahistorical range of natural genera. In comparison, modern societies are those that are permanently oriented towards the new and tell themselves stories about historical events. They render the new the "moving power of their development" (Lévi-Strauss 1966: 234).

In the same way, now related to the political, Pierre Clastres spoke of societies that resist the state, that keep the state latent. They are, as Clastres expresses it, "societies against the State", instead of them 'lacking' the state. The apparently neutral assessment that a society has no history or lacks a state apparatus is actually a normative judgment that renders other forms of society social 'embryos' – solely on the ground that they 'are not the occident'.

Primitive societies are societies without a State. This factual judgment, accurate in itself, actually hides an opinion, a value judgment. What the statement says, in fact, is that primitive societies are missing something – the State – that is essential to them, as it is to any other society: our own, for instance. Consequently, those societies are incomplete; they are not quite true societies. (Clastres 1989: 188–189)

When other societies are classed 'negatively', an 'ethnocentric' perspective is at play (Clastres 1989: 189; see also Delitz 2010a). Societies that exhibit no state are making constant efforts to avoid one: in this sense they have a state, but keep it permanently latent and prevent power from accumulating through their institutions. These societies are constantly working to prevent "any one of the sub-groups [...] from becoming autonomous". They are "societies against the State" (Clastres 1989: 211).

It is appropriate to apply the same terminological strategy to the question of monumental architecture. Societies – like the nomadic – that exhibit no monumental architecture must rather be described as ones that defend themselves against monumental buildings and artifacts. Collective strategies are associated with this: the accumulations of power that accompany monumental and impressive architecture are to be avoided. The intention is to moderate social inequalities and hierarchies in the mode of architecture. For example, alongside the nomadic societies whose tent architecture is *per se* low and soft, offering little resistance (Delitz 2010a), we can consider the Kabyles who use building rituals and involve the entire village collective to always erect the same small buildings (Maunier 1926). The case is similar with collectives like the South-American Achuar, who institute a "residential atomism" in the scattering of their settlements and exhibit ritual rules governing the size and material of the houses (Descola 1994: 9). It follows that the archaeological classification of 'advanced cultures' should be revised: all cultures are advanced cultures, no society is primitive, and this is also true for those without monumental buildings. However, it is fair to say that the resistance against monumental buildings was probably more directed towards their physicality. Their symbolic and identifying function was deferred to other artifacts, ritual actions, or even natural landscape features, like e. g. mountains. In such societies these artifacts, rituals, and/or landscape features became monumental and their monuments, but they are invisible to the future and foreign scholar.[9] Active resistance against diversity and 'cultural riches' can be found in other ways. Reinhard Bernbeck (2010: 136–138), for example, argues in the case of Neolithic

---

9 For the concept of landscape as a monument see e. g. Tilley (1994) and Bradley (1998).

Tol-e Baši in Iran that the local people resisted the diverse possibilities of the pottery decoration of the surrounding area in order to remain a non-hierarchical, equal society.

2. Divergent architectural modes of collective existence: with and 'against' monumentality

The comparison between fixed, monumental architectures with foundations on the one hand, and apparently ephemeral, low architectures constructed from soft materials on the other hand, is revealing of both forms of collective existence. When considering the social significance or function of monumental artifacts it is worthwhile contrasting and comparing. As architecture is a non-linguistic mode of social structuring, as the buildings address the bodies and the eyes, as they are omnipresent and encompass socialization in its entirety, it seems methodologically promising to compare contrasting architectural modes of collective existence: how do societies that currently exhibit no monumental architecture function – how do they imagine their history, what social inequalities take hold here, how do institutions achieve legitimacy or affect?

In the following we pursue this end by discussing two examples that contrast to collectives with monumental architecture. The first is a nomadic society, namely the Tuareg with their low, small, and soft architectures. The other is the Achuar as an example of a society that has no monumental architecture and no large-scale building techniques, but that practices systematic architectural scattering and whose architecture consists of plant-based building materials that require periodic renewal. Only subsequently do we turn to two collectives that attract attention with their monumental architecture: firstly, the medieval European societies with large cathedrals; secondly the seleucid Uruk.

2.1 Nomadic architecture: dynamic, low, and ephemeral instead of fixed and cemented

The Tuareg are an example of a mobile, nomadic society. They exhibit *per se* no monumental architecture. Rather, they are familiar with low, mobile tents that fundamentally resemble one another in terms of size, ornamentation, construction, and function. Made of soft materials and always low with a single storey, this architecture does not suggest permanence nor does it establish social inequalities. On the contrary, it enables movement. And in fact the affect, the pride of the Tuareg is found in *speed*, in fast movement (Deleuze/Guattari 1987: 395–398), which is made possible by the tents and by the animals they ride. Tent architecture is a specific mode of collective existence. Such architecture gives the collective a flat, soft, and mobile structure. It engenders acoustic and visual sensations and bodily movements that differ from those generated by fixed buildings – the visual divisions between the generations, classes, and genders are less and there are no acoustic divisions at all. Nevertheless there are strict divisions between the sexes, marked in the interiors of the tents; and there are divisions between status groups, which have become established since colonization. On the other hand, these divisions, these social positions are not regarded as absolute, and are not hereditary. The position of the individual is essentially as changeable as the incessant movement of the tents, and with them the demons of the desert (*kel esuf*, the spirits of solitude). Admittedly, social status only changes posthumously, on the scale of several stages of life. In brief, in a soft and mobile architecture of this sort, distinct kinds of interactions are established between the sexes and the generations, and between people and animals (the domestic animals are an integrated part of the human collective, whose lives depend on them); distinct imaginaries of 'identity' develop.

Figure 1: Tuareg leather tent, ca. 2000 CE (credit: http://arlit.free.fr/images/tente2.jpg)

Nomadic architectures like the tents give the collective not only a distinct 'structure' with distinct kinds of interaction and conduct. They also generate a specific, vivid, and physical *form*. Thus the Tuareg are divided architecturally into different groups. The Tuareg tribes of the tents of goatskins (the northern Tuareg – *Kel Ajjer*, *Kel Ahaggar*) contrast with those that use tents made from mats of interwoven palm fronds (the southern Tuareg, *Kel Ferwan*).[10] The architectural form not only divides two different groups of Tuareg; It also has effects on the imagination and divisions within society. Thus the northern Taureg tribes institute their collective organization – a tribal confederation comprising tribes with equal rights – by conceiving this society in terms of the tent: no part of the tribal confederation is superior to the other, their behavior to one another resembles the tent supports which are all of the same length and all carry the same load (Claudot-Hawad 2004; see also the portrayals of the Tuareg in Delitz 2010a; Delitz 2018).

As well as these morphological characteristics of the tent, the movement of the entire collective – including all the artifacts, living creatures, and other non-humans – is socially paramount.

The nomad has a territory; he follows customary paths; he goes from one point to another; he is not ignorant of points (water points, dwelling points, assembly points, etc.). But the question is what in nomad life is a principle and what is only a consequence. To begin with, although the points determine paths, they are strictly subordinated to the paths they determine, the reverse of what happens with the sedentary. The water point is reached only in order to be left behind; every point is a relay and exists only as a relay. A path is always between two points, but the in-between has taken on all the consistency and enjoys both an autonomy and a direction of its own. The life of the nomad is the intermezzo. Even the elements of his dwelling are conceived in terms of the trajectory that is forever mobilizing them. (Deleuze/Guattari 1987: 380)

Such a society, such a mode of collective organization, is dependent on mobile architecture – it does not express itself in this architecture but emerges within it. In contrast to what accompanies monumental architecture (a 'striated space'), the low, small, weaved, or sewn architectures create a "smooth space" (Deleuze/Guattari 1987: 410)[11] that does not distribute and dispose individuals across the territory in a fixed and temporally constant fashion. It is rather the case that the territory that each tribe uses changes incessantly – it moves too. This is revealed, for instance, in the way that maps are drawn – with movement instead of taking a bird's eye view (Bernus 1988). The centre of the political or accumulations of power are therefore not urban concentrations. On the contrary, it is the – not-fixed – borders that are politically central. The goal in a 'culture of war' (Klute 2010), like that of the Tuareg, is the permanent expansion of these borders. Positions of status are not decided according to fixed center-periphery divisions here. The decisive points are rather who may first choose a site for their tent, and how far

---

10 On these two Tuareg cultures see esp. Bernus (1981) and Casajus (1987).

11 "The primary determination of nomads is to occupy and hold a smooth space: it is this aspect that determines them as nomad (essence). On their own account, they will be transhumants, or itinerants, only by virtue of the imperatives imposed by the smooth spaces."

and how quickly is movement away from the tent possible – thanks to the mounts. Given all this, the Tuareg actually do have towns (such as Timbuktu), which were constructed by Muslim traders. These towns have an economic and – in a culture of war – servicing function. They hold no privileged position in the collective imaginaries or the history of the Taureg. Over the centuries they will be simply forgotten (de Moraes Farias 2010).

In brief: it is not the size of the architecture but rather the intensity of the movement that is paramount here. Precisely because of this, in all attempts to contain the nomads, to hinder their movements, architecture becomes a political instrument. This calls to mind the Great Wall of China, built to halt the flood of Mongolian nomads; or colonial territorial policy and the dispersal of the Taureg across different nations where they form national minorities instead of holding a hegemonic position.[12]

2.2 Residential atomism – dispersed and transient, instead of concentrated and permanent

There are other societies that demonstrate no monumental architecture. This is true, for instance, of certain cultures in the South-American rainforests. The northern, historical Maya and other 'prehistoric' cultures of the Andes exhibit monumental architecture that impresses with both the size of the individual constructions and the number and expanse of buildings. But in contrast the Peruvian Achuar have a "residential atomism" (Descola 1994: 8). They scatter themselves in the mode of architecture and settlement patterns. They institute a "zero-degree" of social integration (Descola 1994: 9). Small villages are repeatedly constructed with a prescribed (small) number of houses and prescribed walking distances between the villages thus created. The materials are such that the architecture survives for about 15 years before a new house must be constructed on a new site – in the surroundings of the tropical rainforest the posts begin to rot after just seven years (Descola 1994: 116 f.). All traces of the architectures fade after only a few years. Archaeologically speaking, such societies are just as difficult to research as nomadic ones. The plant-based materials to be used for each building element are prescribed ('customary'). The dimensions and methods of construction are similarly set in tradition and convention (Descola 1994: 116–117). It is also instructive that the houses are conceived as organisistic. They lead an autonomous life and are thought of as analogous to the human placenta. They are also closely linked to origin myths; they form the terrestrial place that connects the heavenly world and the chthonic world underground (Descola 1994: 120–121). It is the owner of the

---

12 On the dispersal of the Tuareg in national states – their 'ethnicization' – see Claudot-Hawad (2014).

house that defines its continuity – not the longevity of the house itself (Descola 1994: 121). In contrast to what was reported about the Tuareg (where, incidentally, the tent is the property of the woman), the size of the house is decisive for status – the more guests the head of the house can host, the more esteemed he is. Rather than measuring about 15 by 12 m and 5–6 m in height, a house can then reach a size of about 23 by 12 m and 7 m in height (Descola 1994: 114). The differences are nonetheless moderate – there is no architecture that can be described as 'monumental' in comparison to the rest; the materials also remain the same, as do the forms and constructions used. In this architecture the collective is organized (on the village scale) into different families, and (within the house) into male and female individuals.

Figure 2: Achuar house, 1980s (Descola 1986: Cover)

The collectives maintain their small size through the relations of the villages to one another and the stipulations governing obligatory walking distances and the maximum number of houses. As Pierre Clastres wrote in the context of other South-American Indians – like the Guayaki in Paraguay – and other institutions – war and the symbolic and weak function of the chief – this has a political function. The accumulation of power is averted in the mode of dispersal, the state is refuted – this is a 'society against the state' (Clastres 2010a). A 'centrifugal' form of collective existence such as that provided by residential atomism, architectural scattering, means a genuine political mode of refutation of the state, of a 'centripetal force'. Architecture of this sort is thus in many ways opposed to a monumental, urban, and concentrated architecture that renders individuals unequal – not least in the question of the distribution or accumulation of power. For:

> What about the State? It is, in essence, a putting into play of centripetal force, which, when circumstances demand it, tends toward crushing the opposite centrifugal forces. The State considers itself and proclaims itself the center of society, the whole of the social body, the absolute master of this body's various organs. Thus we discover at the very heart of the State's substance the active power of One, the inclination to refuse the multiple, the fear and horror of difference. (Clastres 2010b: 107)

'Monumental' architecture only occurs here in the case of intertribal war. And it then primarily has a protective function, not that of generating inequality between the individuals within the society of the tribe. Here too there is a culture of war; in addition to the architectural dispersal this collective scatters itself through violence, through ritual war. During the wars, which last up to four years, the houses are enlarged so that they encompass the whole village, namely up to 70 persons (Descola 1994: 110). Descola describes the households (and thus the architectures) as the *central social principle*: the house determines the household, and the household constitutes the basic group or the "only effective principle of enclosure" (Descola 1994: 108). The families are set against one another and instituted in the houses, only held together by the superordinate tribes.

2.3 Monumental, fixed architecture: the example of the medieval cathedrals

As far as fixed, infrastructure societies with large buildings and urban concentrations are concerned, it is possible, firstly, to cite the many archaeological cases of classical antiquity that have always fascinated 'us' (subjects of European societies with fabled origins in Ancient Greece and Rome). Secondly, it is equally possible to turn to modern, present-day Western societies – for instance the current global competition about the highest skyscraper; the invention of high-rise buildings in Chicago in the 1890s; the monumental plans of the French 'revolutionary architects' and their historical precedents and contexts; or indeed the big architecture of the National Socialists, Soviets and fascists.[13] The medieval religious architec-

---

13 On a few of these architectures see the following, explicitly exemplary, sociological analyses: firstly Foucault (1977) on disciplinary architectures (even if the focus here is not literally on monumentality, Foucault's insight into the subjecting, addressing, and controlling effects of architecture is indispensible); for the competition between 'landmark buildings' (Jones 2009; 2011; also Jones 2016 on the state of the English-language sociology of architecture; and also Löw/ Steets 2014); on colonial architecture which must – at least in its concentration and with the

tures of between 1000 and 1250 CE also formed large buildings. The "fundamental phenomenon" of central Europe from 1000 to 1250 CE was the "numerous large church buildings, whose dimensions were seldom exceeded in the following centuries" (Warnke 1984: 27). Substantial resources were invested in the large cathedrals, and materials and workers brought in from great distances. They developed their own particular effect. And they amazed even contemporary observers: why the enormous investment and why now?

In 1030 CE the Burgundian monk Rudolf Glaber looked back and commented that in 1003 CE almost everywhere on earth, but especially in Italy and France, people started to renovate church buildings; without there being any real need, every Christian community was eager to confront the others with a worthier church: *"It was as though the world had given itself a good shake, discarded the old and all around donned a shiny gown of churches."* (Warnke 1984: 20)

Warnke suggests there was a new "supra-regional level of aspiration", which, in the case of church buildings, was subject to a compulsion for "prestige". The enormous dimensions, the discrepancy between the large building and its surroundings, may be explained by a new pressure to demonstrate legitimacy that emanated from within the (estate-based) society. Those instigating the building work feel compelled to shore up their power by building in a way that is "superior to any comparison, thus inwardly dominating" (Warnke 1984: 21). At the same time there is a new "reference to the outside", new competition with positions beyond the territorial dominion. The sources reveal a supra-regional "differentiated comparative optic" (Warnke 1984: 21). There are new hegemonic constellations, hegemonic struggles between secular and ecclesiastical positions, and those of the citizens. In confronting them, the established rulers found themselves in the midst of a legitimacy crisis – regionally with those of lower formal status who had to be repeatedly stabilized in this position, and supra-regionally with actors of the same sovereign rank. Established rulers were thus forced to surpass themselves. This was not about expressing existing power, because the buildings would not have been necessary if the social and political position of authority had still been sufficiently secured through a system of established norms (Warnke 1984: 24). It is rather the case that the medium of the large buildings was necessary in order to maintain the "gap to competing power holders". This involved not only the building's size "but also its swift realisation" (Warnke 1984: 23).

What are the effects, what is the social meaning or impact? The 'growing large buildings' did not just express the hegemonic positions, nor did they consolidate them. Indeed, the end result was that such positions were rather 'withdrawn' and

---

new infrastructures – be viewed as comparatively monumental (King 2007); and generally on the theories and perspectives of the sociology of architecture e. g. the papers in Delitz/Fischer (2009); for classical and newer approaches also Delitz (2009).

'softened' by the necessity to involve more and more parties in the financing. The institutions of letters of indulgence and holy relics are paradigmatic illustrations of this development – as more people became involved in the endowment of the church, they claimed the right to be heard and the building had to become more public and generally accessible. In the form of God a 'fictive mandate' was invoked for the big architecture – the building was in his honor (not for the king's splendor). In this way the enormous expenditure could undoubtedly be justified. However, precisely because the architectures constructed by the bishops and territorial princes obscure their particular will, their "special rights" lapsed and the building served the *collective as a whole*: it created a fiction of a unified society (Warnke 1984: 66). The big architecture became necessary because of new social positions with hegemonic demands. The cathedrals did not just express an existing potential for power, they were to re-stabilize it. And the more thoroughly the costs of the building overran, the more individuals needed to be enlisted. This forced everyone to curb their own interests, at least to the extent "that they did not render one another incapable of action" (Warnke 1984: 153). In brief, in medieval big architecture "conflicting social forces" found a mode of cooperation – the productive binding of conflicts. There may have been other institutions involved. But none of them "required to the same extent the long-term amalgamation of all material, technological and intellectual abilities". In this sense the medieval sacred big architecture involved society "overcoming itself" – overcoming its estate-based divisions (Warnke 1984: 153).[14] This medieval society constituted itself as *one*; and it could do so (argues Warnke) *only in this non-linguistic mode*. In the buildings this society imagined itself as a collective unit, in the architecture it gave itself an unprecedented, visual form in which it transformed itself.

At this point it is possible to refer to much that we have previously touched upon – the generation of social disparities, the fiction of a collective identity, and the basis of an ultimate foundation (God); also the establishment of new elites such as master builders and architects as opposed to craftsmen (Warnke 1984: 128–145). Equally important were appropriate building materials, load-bearing homogenous stones, which could now – thanks to the monetization of the building trade – be acquired from long distances rather than a continuing reliance on local materials and labor (Warnke 1984: 94–95). Finally, also of note was the centralization of the building trade, the establishment of a public building industry. On the other hand, a number of points should be added – the subject-forming power of these religious big architectures, the daily physical generation of religious affects, and the practicing of specific body techniques in the

---

14 Warnke also construes worldly big architecture – the fortresses and princely residences – not just as instruments of a unilaterally adjudicating power, but as the result of a need for legitimization (see, for the example of the royal palaces [Warnke 1984: 83–92]).

interior[15], just like the impressiveness of the exterior. Later, anger was also relevant, directed against church architecture – the iconoclasm of the Reformation was an assault on the churches, on the interior architecture (see e. g. Schnitzler 1996).

2.4 Monumental religious and political buildings: the cultic topography of Uruk

In the High Middle Ages there was a differentiation between political and religious (church, institutionalized) power, including a built differentiation between different building types, the cathedral being only one of these (see Seidl 2006). However, in the society of Uruk there was a religious-political form of power division. Similar to the late medieval doctrine of the divine right of the king (Kantorowicz 1957), the hegemonic power here was clearly theologically formulated and legitimated, and the social structure was religiously based, sanctioned, and stabilized.[16] In the context of a society of this sort where the hegemonic division of power takes the form of an elite of priests around the 'man in the net skirt' (the priest-king), it is just as interesting to inquire into the meaning of religious architecture as into that of fortifications (city walls) and the architectural domination of the province from the centre. At least in these three respects – the construction of 'landmark buildings' (ziqqurats), of the city wall, and of infrastructure across the territory and its colonization – large buildings and building techniques are of immense significance – a mode of existence of this first urban and maybe imperial society.

Of the various aspects of the structuring of society engendered in big architecture (all of which would be equally interesting), the following focuses only on the architectural restructuring of the *principal sanctuaries* and thus also the *urban structure* of Uruk in the Seleucid era (312–63 BCE).[17] This development had already begun in the Achaemenid period with the transformation of the Uruk pantheon and the relocation of the principal sanctuary from the Eanna district and the Anu Ziqqurat to the Rēš Temple and the Irigal Temple. This Achaemenian restructuring cannot, however, be archeologically verified. It seems certain that the old Eanna Temple, which in the Ur-III period (2112–2004 BCE) was found on the so-called Eanna Ziqqurat, was destroyed under Darius I (521–486 BCE) or, at the latest,

---

15 Here it would be appropriate to adopt the perspective of Foucault (1977) and the concept of 'pastoral power' which is concerned with 'inner truth' – the individualization of the soul (Foucault 1988; 2005). In historical, medieval church building it is also about – a specific – disciplining and individualization. See on present-day religious architectures Karstein/Schmidt-Lux (2017).

16 On the sociological interpretation of the imaginary God or the Gods, see – in addition to the aforementioned Castoriadis (founding outside) – especially Durkheim (2008).

17 On the development of infrastructure across the territory and the significance of the imperial artifact-culture of Uruk, esp. in the Uruk period see Algaze (2005; 2008).

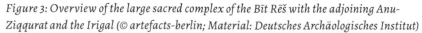

Figure 3: Overview of the large sacred complex of the Bīt Rēš with the adjoining Anu-Ziqqurat and the Irigal (© artefacts-berlin; Material: Deutsches Archäologisches Institut)

under Xerxes I (486–465 BCE). Thereafter, the cult of the Eanna was only continued to "a very limited extent" (Kleber 2008: 344; Kose 1998: 187).[18] Consequently, in the late Achaemenid period (c. 375–300 BCE), the pantheon of Uruk was restructured. Anu now took on the function of the principal deity of Uruk (van Ess 2015: 471). The so-called "skewed tract" from which the Rēš Temple later emerged also dates from this time (Kose 1998: 12). The Seleucid governors Anu-uballit-Nikarchos and Anu-uballit-Kephalon permanently moved the cultic centre of Uruk from the Eanna district in a south-easterly direction in the second half of the 1st millennium BCE. Subsequently and in a very short space of time, enormous urban restructuring occurred in Uruk, which involved not only the relocation of the cultic centers. The 'old' Eanna Ziqqurat was also given a 'make-over'. The Irigal or Ešgal[19] Temple erected in the Seleucid period under Anu-uballit-Kephalos (the governor of Uruk under Antiochus III around 200 BCE) replaced the Inanna or Ištar Temple on the Ziqqurat in the Eanna district as the seat of the goddess Inanna/Ištar. Simultaneously the archaic Anu Ziqqurat was extended to form a vast temple complex,

---

18 There is, however, discussion about the extent of the destruction of the Eanna Temple under Xerxes, and whether the descriptions are perhaps not largely a symbolic 'rendering'. See here Baker (2014: 192) and Kose (1998: 273).

19 Space constraints prevent a detailed discussion of the name here, relevant references can be found in Kose (1998: 197, footnote 1282).

the so-called Bīt Rēš; the new principal deity Anu then moved here. In addition to the building of the Rēš Temple, the archaic Anu Ziqqurat was renovated and enlarged (Figure 3).[20] The Eanna district, which had been the most important temple precincts of the city since the Uruk period (c. 4000–3100 BCE) was, however, not forgotten. At the same time as the two temple complexes (Irigal and Bīt Reš) were constructed, covering 77.700 m², the Eanna Ziqqurat of the Eanna district was also renovated and considerably enlarged (Kose 1998: 157–168).

In the context of this discussion (addressing the social significance of big artifacts and architectures), the individual steps of the renovation and restructuring of the religious landscape of Uruk are of less interest than the presumed intention and, more precisely, the collective, social *function* of this large-scale renewal project.[21] Particularly interesting is the social function or positivity of the architectural reconstruction: what were the *collective* reasons that motivated the renovation and enlargement of the old, partially destroyed ziggurat – and this although it clearly no longer fulfilled a cultic function? (And which political was favored by a 'relocation of the Gods' of this sort?[22])

The transformation of the urban system of Uruk began in the Achaemenid period in the time after Darius I, thus from the middle of the 5th millennium BCE, although there is little archaeological indication of this – most of the remains of this building layer had to give way to later Seleucid building (Baker 2014: 197–198).[23] Nonetheless, no fundamental change in the urban structure of Uruk can be detected for the Seleucid period (drawing on Kose's work on Uruk). There was rather extended, continued restructuring. This was associated with shifts in power and changes in the Uruk pantheon in the late Achaemenid period, supporting these changes and, first and foremost, rendering them visible and tangible, bringing them to 'power' (Baker 2014: 191, 197). Other effects include a change in the ritual processional ways, claimed by the 'Gods' for special occasions.[24] Subsequent to the relocation of the religious centre, a political identification of the population with the temple may have emerged (as Baker supposes). "It appears that in the second half of the 1st millennium BC we witness in Uruk an increased

---

20 However, it can be assumed that the Irigal and Bīt Rēš formed one larger unit together (Baker 2014: 200).

21 For a detailed analysis see again Baker (2014) and also Kleber (2008). On the distinction between individual motives or intentions and collective functions see, e. g., Durkheim (2002) and secondarily e. g. Delitz (2013).

22 On the social importance of a 'relocation of the Gods' for the – very different – case of post-Reformation, European societies see Eßbach (2014).

23 Although there is also evidence for late Achaemenid predecessors of the skewed tract, see Kose (1998).

24 Incidentally, Baker refers here to the need for a revision of Falkenstein's topography of Uruk (see Falkenstein 1941: esp. 45–49). These were also used by Kose (1998: 14, Figure14).

self-identification of the urban community with the temple itself." (Baker 2014: 204) Nevertheless, it does not seem possible to completely replace the old cultic principle with the new – the old Gods remained, collective identities and their religious sanctioning seem to have continued to exist. Generally, it seems necessary to recall the function served by creating a collective memory: tradition and collective memory establish themselves on the monumentality of the place and buildings, and thus on their perpetuity.[25] In the face of the relocation of the cult, the Eanna district remained the *lieu de mémoire* – a monument that established the collective. And even though the cultic architectures of Bit Rēš and Irigal were of considerable perpetuity, these buildings clearly did not achieve the significance of Eanna. It could therefore be argued that the hegemonic project of the architectural relocation of the Gods, the construction of a 'new place of power'[26] and thus a new political domination, was actually a failure – because of the architectural permanence, the continued social function of the Eanna district, because of its entanglement with the old elite and their regulation and division of this society.

Conclusion: The various social functions of big architectures – and the social function of a 'society against big architectures'

Of course the cathedrals of the High Middle Ages are a special case, less because of their enormous dimensions and more due to the specific social effects. This is not just about an overly generalized and repressive understanding of the exercise of 'power'. Not all big architecture, not every monumental building, generates the negative affects of anxiety, shock, and fear with which this paper opened. The cathedrals at least *also* had other positive affects – such as fostering unity (according to Warnke's interpretation). Furthermore, these medieval big buildings (including the comparatively small houses that stand in relation to them) certainly generate a 'territorialization' of individuals, situating them in a territory and ensuring their individualizing distribution. The corresponding large-scale infrastructure also carves up and centralizes the social space. In other words: the cathedrals are part of a general architectural mode of collective existence – the mode of fixed architecture of hard, mineral materials with firm foundations, which has its own distinctive social effects. There are many interesting examples of a *society with monumental architecture* beyond those mentioned here (including

---

25 On this concept see esp. the study on the 'permanently identical' holy places of Christianity (despite their actual incessant relocation) by Halbwachs (2008).

26 On the political philosophy of the representation of society in the person of the king as the central place of power – and its institutional emptying in the case of modern democracy – see Lefort (2006).

the Great Wall of China or the Fascist architecture of the 1930s). This is particularly true for the archaeological context (thinking of Babylon, Rome, or the menhirs of France, but also the 'rest' of Europe, etc.).

In none of the examples is it the case that social differences constituted in other ways are simply 'expressed' in architecture and big architecture. It is rather that these differences are incessantly created also through the artifacts – visually, tactually, in the movement and physical posture that the buildings compel or at least enable. This actually holds particularly true for non-monumental architecture – and for collectives that do not have big architecture. These should, in our view, be addressed as *societies against big architectures* rather than as societies 'without' big architecture. An instructive archaeological case in this context is that of Çatalhöyük – the architectural structuring of an egalitarian society where all the houses were built close together without infrastructure, all with the same dimensions and the same functions (Hodder 2006; Hodder/Pels 2010). Or we can think of the Göbekli Tepe, where an enormous collaborative effort was undertaken to erect the special buildings.[27] This achievement could only be accomplished by a mass of workers, many times the size of the local population, thus necessitating a combined effort by a number of settlements or even a trans-societal undertaking to construct the buildings. Perhaps the real 'Neolithic Revolution' lay in such collaborative activities – which in archaeological terms is too often associated with the path to sedentary life, along an evolutionary imaginary of social development that always progresses from nomadic to sedentary, architecturally fixed collectives, never the other way round (Childe 1936; Helwing/Aliyev 2014; Watkins 2010).[28] If this argument is pursued it is possible to conclude that the real purpose of the whole process of constructing large complexes was to create identity, independent of the ultimate function of the buildings. In contrast, we are dealing here with two different, mutually exclusive modes of collective existence. Sociologically, it is not only possible to identify different collective functions of big architectures – the absence of such architecture also comprises a social rationality. The refutation of the infrastructural development of a territory, the refutation of a power centre and of an affective, impressive, and awe-inspiring architecture, institutes a different, specific form of collective existence, of the categorization of individuals, of the relationing of nature and culture, of the narrative of origin and collective identity.

---

27 On these interpretations as a collectively utilized temple see Schmidt (2006); and on the function of collective building rituals the aforementioned Maunier (1926). For other interpretations of the special buildings of the Göbekli Tepe see Banning (2011).

28 See also Levenson (in this volume). Ian Hodder conceives the term Neolithic Revolution differently (2006) – as an increasing entanglement, quantitatively and qualitatively, of people, animals, and things; and as domestication, which was linked to the cult of wild animals.

Bibliography

Algaze, G. (2005): The Uruk World System (2nd ed.), Chicago: University of Chicago Press.

Algaze, G. (2008): Ancient Mesopotamia at the Dawn of Civilization: The Evolution of an Urban Landscape, Chicago: Chicago University Press.

Baker, H. D. (2014): "Temple and City in Hellenistic Uruk: Sacred Space and the Transformation of Late Babylonian Society." In: E. Frood/R. Raja (eds.), Redefining the Sacred: Religious Architecture and Text in the Near East and Egypt 1000 BC – AD 300. Contextualizing the Sacred 1, Turnhout: Brepols, pp. 183–208.

Balibar, E. (2003): "Structuralism: A Destitution of the Subject?" In: differences: A Journal of Feminist Culture Studies, 14/1, pp. 1–21.

Banning, E. B. (2011): "So Fair a House – Göbekli Tepe and the Identification of Temples in the Pre-Pottery Neolithic of the Near East." In: Current Anthropology, 52/5, pp. 619–660.

Bataille, G./Leiris, M./Griaule, M./Einstein, C./Desnos, R./Baron, J./Reich, Z./Dandieu, A. (1970): Dictionnaire critique, Paris: Gallimard.

Bernbeck, R. (2010): "The Neolithic Pottery." In: S. Pollock/R. Bernbeck/K. Abdi (eds.), The 2003 Excavations at Tol-e Baši, Iran – Social Life in a Neolithc Village. Archäologie in Iran und Turan 10, Mainz: Philipp von Zabern, pp. 65–151.

Bernus, E. (1981): Touaregs nigériens. Unité culturelle et diversité régionale d'un peuple pasteur, Paris: ORSTOM.

Bernus, E. (1988): "La représentation de l'espace chez des Touaregs du Sahel." In: Mappemonde, 3, pp. 1–5.

Bradley, R. (1998): The Significance of Monuments. On the Shaping of Human Experience in Neolithic and Bronze Age Europe, London: Routledge.

Cache, B. (1995): Earth Moves. The Furnishing of Territories, Cambridge: MIT Press.

Casajus, D. (1987): La tente dans la solitude. La société et les morts chez les Touaregs Kel-Ferwan, Paris: Éditions de la Maison des sciences de l'homme.

Castoriadis, C. (1987): The Imaginary Institution of Society, Cambridge: MIT Press.

Childe, G. (1936): Man makes himself, London: Watts.

Clastres, P. (1989): Society Against the State Society Against the State. Essays in Political Anthropology, New York: Zone books, pp. 189–218.

Clastres, P. (2010a): "Archaeology of Violence." In: Archeology of Violence. War in Primitive Societies, Los Angeles: Semiotext(e), pp. 237–278.

Clastres, P. (2010b): "Of Ethnocide." In: Archeology of Violence. War in Primitive Societies, Los Angeles: Semiotext(e), pp. 101–112.

Claudot-Hawad, H. (2004): "Neither Segmentary, nor Centralized: the Sociopolitical Organization of a Nomadic Society (Tuaregs) beyond Categories." In: Orientwissenschaftliche Hefte 14, pp. 57–69.

Claudot-Hawad, H. (2014): "Nomadic Societies in the Middle East and North Africa Entering the 21st Century." In: B. Badie/D. Vidal (eds.), Puissances d'hier et de demain. L'Etat du Monde. Paris: La Déouverte, pp. 198–205.

Corbusier, L. (1987): Journey to the East, Cambridge: MIT Press.

de Moraes Farias, P. (2010): "Local Landscapes and Constructions of World Space: Medieval Inscriptions, Cognitive Dissonance, and the Course of the Niger." In: Afriques 02: Histoires de territoires. Vestiges et territoire. doi:10.4000/afriques.896.

Deleuze, G./Guattari, F. (1987): A Thousand Plateaus: Capitalism and Schizophrenia 2, Minneapolis: University of Minesota Press.

Delitz, H. (2009): Architektursoziologie, Bielefeld: transcript.

Delitz, H. (2010a): "'Die zweite Haut des Nomaden'. Zur sozialen Effektivität nichtmoderner Architekturen." In: P. Trebsche/N. Müller-Scheeßel/S. Reinhold (eds.), Der gebaute Raum. Bausteine einer Soziologie vormoderner Architekturen, Münster: Waxmann, pp. 83–106.

Delitz, H. (2010b): Gebaute Gesellschaft. Architektur als Medium des Sozialen, Frankfurt a. M.: Campus.

Delitz, H. (2013): Émile Durkheim zur Einführung, Hamburg: Junius.

Delitz, H. (2018): "Architectural Modes of Collective Existence: Architectural Sociology as a Comparative Social Theory." In: Cultural Sociology 12/1, pp. 37–57.

Delitz, H./Fischer, J. (eds.). (2009): Die Architektur der Gesellschaft. Theorien für die Architektursoziologie, Bielefeld: transcript.

Delitz, H./Maneval, S. (2017): "The 'Hidden Kings', or Hegemonic Imaginaries. Analytical Perspectives of Postfoundational Social Thought." In: Im@go. Journal of the Social Imaginary 10, pp. 33–49.

Descola, P. (1986): La nature domestique. Symbolisme et praxis dans l'écologie des Achuar, Paris: Éditions de la Maison des sciences de l'homme.

Descola, P. (1994): In the Society of Nature: A Native Ecology in Amazonia, Cambridge: Cambridge University Press.

Durkheim, É. (2002): Suicide. A Study in Sociology, London: Routledge.

Durkheim, É. (2008): The Elementary Forms of Religious Life, Oxford: Oxford University Press.

Eßbach, W. (2014): Religionssoziologie 1. Glaubenskrieg und Revolution als Wiege neuer Religionen, München: Fink.

Falkenstein, A. (1941): Topographie von Uruk I: Uruk zur Seleukidenzeit, Ausgrabungen der Deutschen Forschungsgemeinschaft in Uruk-Warka 3, Leipzig: Harrassowitz.

Foucault, M. (1977): Discipline and Punish: The Birth of the Prison, New York: Vintage Books.

Foucault, M. (1988): The History of Sexuality, Vol. 3: The Care of the Self, New York: Pantheon Books.

Foucault, M. (2005): The Hermeneutics of the Subject: Lectures at the College de France 1981–1982, New York: Palgrave McMillan.

Gauchet, M. (1994): "Primitive Religion and the Origins of the State." In: M. Lilla (ed.), New French Thought. Political Philosophy. Princeton: Princeton University Press, pp. 116–122.

Gauchet, M. (1999): The disenchantment of the world: a political history of religion, Princeton: Princeton University Press.

Halbwachs, M. (2008): La topographie légendaire des évangiles en terre sainte: Etude de mémoire collective, Paris: Puf.

Helwing, B./Aliyev, T. (2014): "A Monumental Neolithic? New Results of the Ongoing Azerbaijanian-German Investigations in the Mil Steppe, Azerbaijan." In: P. Bieliński/M. Gawlikowski/R. Koliński/D. Ławecka/A. Sołtysiak/Z. Wygnańska (eds.), Proceedings of the 8th ICAANE (Vol. 2), Wiesbaden: Harrassowitz, pp. 247–258.

Hodder, I. (2006): The Leopard's tale: Revealing the Mysteries of Çatalhöyük, New York: Thames and Hudson.

Hodder, I./Pels, P. (2010): "History houses: A new interpretation of architectural elaboration at Catalhöyük." In: I. Hodder (ed.), Religion in the emergence of civilization: Çatalhöyük as a case study, Cambridge: Cambridge University Press, pp. 163–186.

Jones, P. (2009): "Putting Architecture in its Social Place: A Cultural Political Economy of Architecture." In: Urban Studies, 46/12, pp. 2519–2536.

Jones, P. (2011): The Sociology of Architecture: Constructing Identities, Liverpool: Liverpool University Press.

Jones, P. (2016): "(Cultural) Sociologies of Architecture." In: D. Inglis (ed.), The Sage Handbook of Cultural Sociology, London: Sage, pp. 465–480.

Kantorowicz, E. (1957): The King's Two Bodies. A Study in Mediaeval Political Theology, Princeton: Princeton University Press.

Karstein, U./Schmidt-Lux, T. (eds.) (2017): Architekturen und Artefakte. Zur Materialität des Religiösen, Wiebaden: VS.

King, A. (2007): Colonial Urban Development: Culture, Social Power, and Environment, Abington: Routledge.

Kleber, K. (2008): Colonial Urban Development: Culture, Social Power, and Environment, Alter Orient und Altes Testament 358, Münster: Ugarit Verlag.

Klute, G. (2010): "Kleinkrieg in der Wüste: Nomadische Kriegsführung und die 'Kultur des Krieges' bei den Tuareg." In: T. Jäger (ed.), Die Komplexität der Kriege, Wiesbaden: VS, pp. 188–220.

Kose, A. (1998): Uruk: Architektur IV, von der Seleukiden- bis zur Sasanidenzeit (Vol. 1–2), Ausgrabungen in Uruk-Warka Endberichte, Vol. 17, Mainz: Zabern.

Laclau, E./Chantal, M. (1985): Hegemony and Socialist Strategy: Towards a Radical Democratic Politics, London: Verso.

Lefort, C. (2006): "Permanence of the Theologico-Political?" In: H. d. Vries/L. E. Sullivan (eds.), Political Theologies: Public Religions in a Post-secular World, Fordham: Fordham University Press, pp. 148–187.

Lévi-Strauss, C. (1966): The Savage Mind, London: Weidenfeld & Nicholson.

Lévi-Strauss, C. (1969): The Elementary Structures of Kinship, Boston: Beacon Press.

Lévi-Strauss, C. (1987): Introduction to the work of Marcel Mauss, London: Routledge & Kegan Paul.

Leys, R. (2011): "The Turn to Affect: A Critique." In: Critical Inquiry 37, pp. 434–472.

Löw, M./Steets, S. (2014): "The Spatial Turn and the Built Environment." In: A. A. Kyrtsis/S. Koniordos (eds.), Routledge Handbook of European Sociology, London: Routledge.

Maran, J. (2006): "Mycenaean Citadels as Performative Space." In: J. Maran/C. Juwig/H. Schwengel/U. Thaler (eds.), Constructing Power. Architecture, Ideology and Social Practice, Frankfurt a. M.: Lang, pp. 75–92.

Maran, J. (2012): "Architektonischer Raum und soziale Kommunikation auf der Oberburg von Tiryns – Der Wandel von der mykenischen Palastzeit." In: F. Arnold/A. Busch/R. Haensch/U. Wulf-Rheidt (eds.), Orte der Herrschaft. Charakteristika von antiken Machtzentren, Rahden/Westf.: Leidorf, pp. 149–162.

Marchard, O. (2010): Post-Foundational Political Thought: Political Difference in Nancy, Lefort, Badiou and Laclau, Edinburgh: Edinburgh University Press.

Markus, T. A. (1993): Buildings and Power. Freedom and Control in the Origin of Modern Building Types, London: Routledge.

Maunier, R. (1926): La construction collective de la maison en Kabylie. Étude sur la coopération économique chez les Berbères du Djurjura, Paris: Institut d'Ethnologie.

Popitz, H. (1995): Der Aufbruch zur artifiziellen Gesellschaft. Zur Anthropologie der Technik, Tübingen: Mohr.

Schmidt, K. (2006): Sie bauten die ersten Tempel. Das rätselhafte Heiligtum der Steinzeitjäger. Die archäologische Entdeckung am Göbekli Tepe, München: Beck.

Schnitzler, N. (1996): Ikonoklasmus – Bildersturm. Theologischer Bilderstreit und ikonoklastisches Handeln während des 15. und 16. Jahrhunderts, München: Fink.

Seidl, E. (2006): Lexikon der Bautypen, Stuttgart: Reclam.

Seyfert, R. (2011): Das Leben der Institutionen. Zu einer Allgemeinen Theorie der Institutionalisierung, Weilerswist: Velbrück.

Simondon, G. (2017): On the Mode of Existence of Technical Objects, Washington: Univocal Publishing.

Tilley, C. (1994): A phenomenology of landscape: places, paths and monuments, Oxford: Berg.

van Ess, M. (2015): "Lemma 'Uruk. B. Archäologisch'." In: M. Streck (ed.), Reallexikon der Assyriologie und Vorderasiatischen Archäologie 14, Berlin: de Gruyter, pp. 457–587.

Warnke, M. (1984): Bau und Überbau. Soziologie der mittelalterlichen Architektur nach den Schriftquellen, Frankfurt a. M.: Suhrkamp.

Watkins, T. (2010): "New Light on Neolithic Revolution in south-west Asia." In: Antiquity 84, pp. 621–634.

Monumental Negligence:
the Difference between Working and Alienated Labor

Reinhard Bernbeck

Nothing is more obvious and at the same time hidden than the link between monumentality and labor. Bertolt Brecht's oft-cited poem is right on the mark when it comes to monumentality in the ancient Near East:

> "Who built Thebes of the seven gates?
> In the books you will read the names of kings.
> Did the kings haul up the lumps of rock?
> And Babylon, many times demolished,
> Who raised it up so many times?"
> (Brecht 2012: 13)

It seems that we have never really tried to answer these "questions from a worker who reads".

An outward answer to Brecht's worker consists in taking the sources literally: yes, Hammurabi and Nebuchadnezzar built the walls of Babylon. Didn't ancient Western Asian kings depict themselves as laborers with baskets of mud on their heads (Figure 1)? Why should we assume *a priori* that they were lying? Let us take the sources seriously unless proven otherwise.

Uncounted and uncountable citations of historians and archaeologists are at our disposal to show that, indeed, this is the current opinion. I abstain from direct citations, as it would be unjust to single out specific scholars for their literal interpretation of such pictorial and textual sources. A five-minute search turned up fine sentences such as: "Assurnasirpal II baute seinen großartigen Königspalast auf der Zitadelle", "Nebuchadnezzar set out to rebuild Babylon", "the Apadana complex was completed by Xerxes" and others. At least outwardly, both ancient depictions and modern scholarly texts converge on an implicit belief in the heroic deeds of the ancient rulers and a concurrent silencing of laborers.

The reader may object that it is obvious that the language of history serves as a shorthand for 'King X was responsible for the planning and realization of

*Figure 1: Stela depicting Assurbanipal rebuilding the temple of ESAGILA in Babylon,
excavated by Hormuzd Rassam in 1871 in Babylon (© Trustees of the British Museum)*

building Y', that the metaphorical use of image and text is obvious.[1] However, the
mechanism behind such reductive imagery is ideology *par excellence*, as it depicts

---

1   We encounter the same effect in another main activity node, namely the leading of wars. Here we
     find exactly the same metaphorical use of 'ruler X led a war against ruler Y'. This can be traced into

the particular as the general. More importantly, I submit that this careless language has had a long-lasting deleterious effect on the whole historiography of ancient Western Asia: forgetting not just labor, but more specifically, laborers.

It is therefore appropriate for any discussion of monumentality to not just reflect on the issue of the 'size' of buildings, and thus the perception of them as monumental, but also on the *production of size*. Beyond the ruler-builder, we do indeed find investigations of the relationship between labor and monumentality. However, such research remains one-sided, as the main interest is geared towards the amount of work that goes into a single monument, calculated mainly in terms of person hours. Calculations of this kind have been made for European megaliths (Müller 1990; Bartelt 2007), the pyramids of ancient Egypt (Arnold 1997; Stadelmann 1997: 217–228; Müller-Römer 2011), ancient Mesopotamian monumental projects (Schmid 1995; Sauvage 1998; Wäfler 2003; discussed in Sievertsen 2014), in a different way for the Mississippian mound of Cahokia (Schilling 2012), and on a comparative scale (Brunke et al. 2016). Some of these works are based on a whole school of archaeological thought that has its origin in Elliott Abrams' 'architectural energetics' (Abrams 1994; Abrams/Bolland 1999) where labor is reduced to energy plus organization. Maude Devolder (2017), while using the approach herself, provides a substantial and well-argued critique that, however, leaves one element out: labor from the perspective of laborers themselves. This glaring lacuna is detectable in most other accounts of the relation between monumentality and labor that I know of, even those that critique research in this realm (e. g. Richardson 2015). This tells us a lot about archaeology's position in relation to the powers that be, whether ancient or modern. The discourse amounts to a laborious attempt at objectivity in questions of large-scale, mostly governmental projects, which has led to serious distortions in the reconstruction of ancient political economic mechanisms. Worse, it constructs a top-down view of history where the actual contributions of most people – and even more their aspirations – are left out and silenced. These are the narratives Walter Benjamin (1992) so much derided in his last and desperate reflections on history.

Why should the calculation of work hours be biased? If there is such a bias, what are its mechanisms of misrepresentation? And how can it be avoided? I have argued in other contexts that the historical questions we ask are driven by an eagerness to know, but a knowledge that is not objective (Bernbeck 2009). Knowledge is always constructed from a specific perspective; it is never 'neutral'. Feminist histories are a good case of showing that the supposedly 'objective' androcentric historical narratives exclude one half of humanity (Wylie 2011). Decolonial histories reveal similar problems in the realm of modern international history

the history of more recent times where one may sometimes get the impression that World War II was a conflict between individuals such as Hitler, Stalin, Churchill, and Roosevelt.

(Trouillot 1995). The main issue is a paradox: the attempt to avoid perspectivism actually leads straight into it. A direct parallel between the historian/archaeologist's view and that of anyone in the past was supposed to be avoided by taking an omniscient position, a 'bird's eye' (or 'god's eye') view. To continue the metaphor, such a view is not and cannot be taken by anyone 'on the ground'. However, such a view from above is already an approximation of positions in past societies. The view from 'above' asks questions akin to those of past rulers, scribes, and others with management functions. Why not develop questions that focus on other standpoints, following the advice of Georg Lukács (1971) or Sandra Harding (1993)?

To relate this historiographical problem back to the case of labor in ancient times: calculations of the amount of labor that went into the construction of a ziggurat, a temple, a pyramid, or palace need to be assessed for how they impinge on their own objective, which I presume to be the history of the region in question. History itself as a discourse about past times can be written from many positions, even if there is a tendency among historians to claim that an ideal position is an omniscient and presumedly objective one. The historian's reflections about the question "How much labor was needed?" merge easily into the past scribe's question of "How many laborers are needed?" Both questions entail a move, that of an abstraction of concrete practical work and the consideration of work as a commodity independent of the individual laborer's experience of it.

What is alienated labor?

In my further discussion, I take my inspiration from some of Marx's writings. In his well-known late works such as *Das Kapital*, he distinguishes 'abstract labor' from 'concrete labor'. Concrete labor is the making of something, a creative, skilful energy that is needed in the crafting of directly usable objects, in Marx's terminology a 'use value' or *Gebrauchswert*. In both the first volume of *Das Kapital* (Marx 1979) as well as *Zur Kritik der politischen Ökonomie* (Marx 1974), Marx binds abstract labor firmly to the production of exchange value, and an exchange value that has no real purpose other than increasing profits. In this specific sense, abstract labor did not exist in ancient Mesopotamia and related cultures as it is tied to capitalist forms of economy. However, in other writings, at a time when he was still trying to derive the development of capitalism from earlier historical forms of political economy, Marx used a third term, alienated labor. Some scholars have rightly pointed out that the distinction between alienated and abstract labor is crucial; however, most of them deride alienated labor as a notion connected to Marx' early, and therefore idealistic, writings.

My sense is that it is exactly the interest in different historical forms of labor that led Marx to describe 'alienated labor' as a widespread condition for working people in pre-capitalist societies. He attached four characteristics to alienated labor (Marx 1966: 77–87). First, workers do not work for goals they set for themselves, but rather fulfill the labor demands of others. Second, as a consequence, laboring is not tied to a perspective of usefulness for those who carry it out. The workers' praxis appears to them an externality, uncoupled from their own interests. "It is activity as suffering, strength as weakness" (Marx 1966: 80). They will therefore stop working immediately whenever there is an opportunity to do so. Third, workers as human beings are alienated from their own constitutive, specifically human foundation. Marx compares structures of insects and animals such as bees and beavers with those of human beings, and argues that humans can set themselves generalized productive goals independently of their own physical-biological reproduction. The basis for this is the specifically human relation between labor and consciousness (Balibar 1995: 27–28). Human beings are potentially free to labor or not to do so. However, this fundamental freedom is lost in alienated labor. Finally, laborers are not just alienated from their product, their work, and themselves under such conditions, but also from other workers.

Alienated labor is easily transformed into abstract labor, an entity in a chain that is driven by capitalist profit only (but see Elbe 2014). For workers and an emerging working class, alienated and abstract labor may not differ much subjectively. For those who command labor, the main place where alienated and abstract labor differ from each other is in the generalized objectivation of labor *as well as its products*. Abstract labor is to be distinguished from alienated labor because it is, according to Marx, interested neither in the products and their use value after sale, nor in the quality and amount of labor that go into their production. These issues are of relevance only because they shape the possibilities of making an abstract profit via the appropriation of means of production and a surplus that can be derived from all dependent labor, in order to increase the capital that is behind the whole process. And both kinds of labor must be distinguished from a primordial productive praxis that was 'living labor' (Marx 1983: 592–594), free from private property and the possibilities for an expropriation of means of production. Both alienated and abstract labor imply that bodily (and in our times at least, intellectual) activity can be distinguished from the particular person who performs it, in order to be exchanged against something else, whether for payment or for specific goods. It furthermore means – something we are automatically accustomed to today – that it is possible to conceive of quantities of labor independently of the specific work processes performed and of particular tasks that must be carried out independently of the person who conducts them.[2] Briefly, both alienated and abstract labor can be quantified and packaged into discrete

---

2 In our days, the representatives of workers, the 'unions', and their counterparts, the 'employers', converge on this understanding of human production.

blocks that are parceled out to laborers. Furthermore, it is assumed that there are people who will carry out these tasks for the sake of their own survival, whether they are interested in the product of this specific labor or not.

So far, these reflections include subjectivist perspectives, the point of view of potential laborers. However, in the later writings of Marx himself and especially in the exegesis of his followers, we find an insistence that such subjective and therefore individualizing concerns are bourgeois and inappropriate for a political economic analysis. The dispute between the late 19th century *Grenznutzenschule* (marginal utility theory) around Carl Menger and Eugen von Böhm-Bawerk (e. g. Böhm-Bawerk 1974) on the one hand and early Marxists such as Nikolai Bucharin on the other is important for my further argumentation. Böhm-Bawerk strongly criticized Marx's theory of labor value from the perspective of the diminishing utility of products in an economic landscape driven by supply-demand mechanisms. In return, Marxists such as Rudolf Hilferding, Bucharin and later Paul Sweezy attacked that narrow and individualizing perspective on political economy and the specific form of labor in the genesis of product value (Hilferding 1904: 11).

> Die Arbeitswerttheorie von A. Smith [...] ist eine *subjektivistische Arbeitswerttheorie*. Umgekehrt ist die Werttheorie von Marx ein objektives, d. i. gesellschaftliches Preisgesetz, seine Theorie ist demnach eine *objektivistische Arbeitswerttheorie* [...] (Bucharin 1926: 37, emphasis in the original)

I think that the marginalists around Menger and Böhm-Bawerk and the Marxists missed a further issue in their dispute, one that insists on a different aspect of the value of labor beyond consumption. It is interesting that the subjectivist dimension of the laborers themselves and especially their influence on performance 'on the job' were unimportant issues for both the Vienna *Grenznutzenschule* and Marxist theoreticians.[3] They both assumed that laborers would carry out labor as an assigned task in the way conceptualized by capitalists, 'employers', the state. Steadiness of labor across time and space, independent of the quality and kind of labor and of the people who carry it out, is the precondition for all the further economic modeling of these staunchly antagonistic schools. This is also an unspoken assumption that often links us as historians/archaeologists with the organizers and/or theoreticians of labor past and present, whether Roman, Mesopotamian, or others.

---

3 This dimension certainly occupies an important place in present-day theoretical considerations of labor, especially in post-operaist thinking (e. g. Virno 2004).

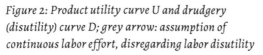

Figure 2: Product utility curve U and drudgery (disutility) curve D; grey arrow: assumption of continuous labor effort, disregarding labor disutility

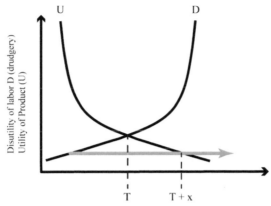

The steadiness of labor performance is entirely unrealistic, as clearly demonstrated by Soviet economist Alexander Chayanov who investigated the logic of non-market peasant production. In economic terms, peasant households can be defined as units producing to an overwhelming extent what they consume; furthermore, the internal distribution of goods amongst individual members is characterized by unconditional reciprocity (Tschajanow 1987). Such households do not conceive of labor as a linear function where the more they work the more they produce up to a point of diminishing product utility $T+x$, but rather as a function of drudgery (or 'disutility of labor') as exponentially related to the product of labor (Figure 2). Simply put, the first hour of work in a day is easy and therefore the product of such an hour has a relatively high value compared to input. The willingness to labor, compared to the value of the product, decreases as the day goes on. And this is also true for longer-term stretches of labor such as a month-long harvest. Thus, the assumed linear relationship of labor to the value of a product from the laborer's point of view does not hold, because workers see their work and its product in the eyes of concrete, living labor. The consequence is that after a specific point of laboring T (Figure 2), a discrepancy between linear labor requirements and drudgery is reached, marking a point at which physical exhaustion is experienced as outweighing the gains of that effort. According to Chayanov, kinship-based households stop producing at that threshold (see also Durrenberger 1984; Tannenbaum 1984).

Between this state of working in a kin-based and largely self-subsistent household and the abstract labor of capitalist production, we find the third type of labor: Marx' alienated labor. Under conditions of institutions such as the early temple households, palaces, or other large-scale institutions in ancient Mesopotamia, workers toil not for themselves but for those who decide what kinds of products they have to produce. The four conditions of alienated labor listed above all apply to such a situation. Since the drudgery curve as a subjective perspective of laborers still obtains, those who organize the labor will have to be careful not to reach a crisis point where major conflicts ensue because of too large a discrepancy between drudgery and the gains obtained through submission to large-scale productive units. Public households of early states had to develop specific mechanisms if they wanted to maximize gains from production. In the ancient world we find several different solutions to this problem of transcending what I call the 'utility-drudgery threshold' (hereafter UDT). I outline these mechanisms here briefly in the abstract before discussing a specific case.

(1) Willingness to continue to work can be increased vastly through what Michael Dietler and Ingrid Herbich (2001) call 'labor feasts', the promise of drink and food after the completion of a laborious collective task. This method of mobilizing labor is very widespread in ethnographically documented agrarian societies, mainly those where production occurs in kin-based households. The many circumstances under which such labor feasts happen have recently caught attention, especially in Western Asian archaeology (cf. contributions in Pollock 2015).

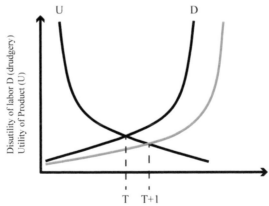

Figure 3: Decreasing disutility of labor through the promise of feasting (T + 1)

In terms of the disutility-utility relation, labor feasts effectively lower the rate at which feelings of drudgery grow with the duration of labor because of a reasonable expectation of an enjoyable reward in the form of a social and commensal event that often includes the consumption of alcohol (Dietler 2006). Consequently, the drudgery curve is lowered and the critical point of exhaustion (UDT) shifts from T to T +1 (Figure 3).

(2) The second solution to increase output in the face of the adversity of laborers to drudgery is sheer repression. In my view, many of the manifestations of violence in early states need to be seen in states' (or other institutions') efforts to enforce continued production through threats to physical integrity. This happened in situations where any personal gains beyond payment, such as competition for better status positions, were simply not to be expected. Such mechanisms for increasing the labor output from a subjectively bearable point T to T+2 (Figure 4) work only punctually and increase tensions to the point of evasion, emigration, or even violent disruption. In the long term, these are not sustainable conditions.

Figure 4: Possibilities of producing temporarily beyond the equilibrium point of labor disutility (drudgery) and product utility (T+2)

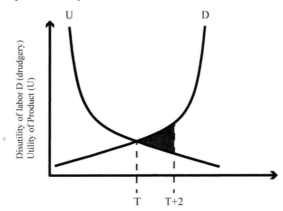

(3) Repression is not the only means to force people to labor more than they would, could they choose. Another means consists of the mobilization of various mechanisms in what Louis Althusser called 'ideological state apparatuses' (1971; cf. also Charim 2009). Particularly effective are those that work through a mix of spectacle, awe, and fear of future retaliation, such as institutionalized religions; the development of social relations that include punishment for debt are another powerful means in this realm. Again, such mechanisms do not lead to any change in the utility of product/disutility of labor curves but uphold its original intersection point. The attraction of spectacles and belief in ideological schemes that suggest a duty to produce beyond the interests of one's own closely-knit social group often end up in a vague sense of obligation coupled with widespread cynical attitudes towards the powerful. Relatively stable political-economic conditions may ensue, but they are no more than a thin veneer under which resentment runs deep (Scott 1990; 2017). Working to rule

while full of contempt and scorn about the work situation is a serious issue we have difficulties grasping historically (but see Lüdtke 1993) and even more archaeologically.

(4) There are several other, more benign possibilities to deal with the discrepancy between alienated labor and drudgery. One is to divide the labor process into smaller temporal stretches, stopping at the point where drudgery is so high that grumbling and complaints become dangerous. Timothy Pauketat (2000) has shown that the huge 'Monks Mound' at the Mississippian site of Cahokia was built incrementally, not in one extended labor process. To mention a different example, the completion of Cologne Cathedral took 632 years (Back/ Höltken 2008). Stretching the time it takes to complete a monument may not always be intentional, but the long breaks of building inactivity are often at least partly due to the reaching of the UDT. To pick up the Brechtian question cited at the beginning of this paper, it is important not only to ask who built the monuments, but also 'How long did it take them?'

(5) A fifth possibility is that the labor force is organized into alternately working groups. The realization of this possibility requires an extremely large labor force and produces potentially very large numbers of non-working people who must be fed in addition to those who are working. In this case, the utility of the labor curve could be significantly changed since the decrease of each single unit produced is much lower than in the cases described above (Figure 5). However, how this plays out at the level of laborers is another, less predictable issue.

Figure 5: The effects of an increase in the work force on the utility of labor-curve

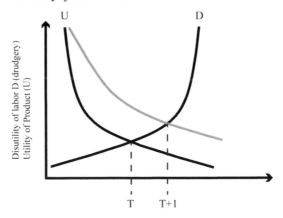

(6) Finally, a solution to this problem consists in the development of new means of production that lower the drudgery curve, often considerably, so that the point of stopping because of physical or psychological exhaustion is signifi-

cantly postponed. This solution is based on technological innovation with the goal of lowering the drudgery curve (similar to Figure 3). Current studies of ancient innovations show attempts at technological change in many facets of life (Flohr 2016; Burmeister/Bernbeck 2017), but also reveal a striking lack of interest in improving labor conditions. While we find some instances in ancient times where such a strategy was followed, for example in the invention of windmills in eastern Iran (e. g. Mishmastnehi/Bernbeck 2015), this mechanism came into full force only with modernity and the invention of the steam machine. From that time on, working people came increasingly under pressure to increase their labor efficiency to keep up with the new technological devices. Thus working people were regularly losing out on work opportunities, meaning that they were no longer threatened by the drudgery of work because they faced the greater danger of losing their subsistence base altogether. Mimicking machines, this forgotten side of a basic mechanism of capitalist production has led humanity to try desperately to adapt to the machinery it has created, an effect Günter Anders (1956) calls a 'Promethean slope' (cf. also Rosa 2013).

Obviously, one of the questions for concrete historical cases is whether this problem of a clash between alienated and concrete labor arose, and if so, which of the possible roads was taken to solve it. It is obviously highly unlikely that in any specific case one single mechanism was mobilized at the expense of all others. Realistically, we have to assume the employment of a mix of these and other possibilities wherever political-economic conditions led to the emergence of abstract labor.

Alienated labor in Ancient Mesopotamia

A systematic search for how archaeological texts deal with the issue of ancient alienated labor and its organization is beyond the scope of this paper but would contribute an important chapter to the intellectual history of archaeology. Even well-known Marxist archaeologists such as Gordon Childe were of the opinion that enslavement was a great step forward in human history as it allowed the erection of monumental buildings (Childe 1941: 134). Such crude assessments have become less frequent or at least less explicit. Mostly, accounts concerned with economic issues assume laborers to just have been there. Apparently, they could be easily duped into toiling for the rulers and elites of the past. Two main arguments prevail in the literature. One is the idea that ideological means simply sufficed to convince people that adhering to a status of submission was in their own best interests. A second uses the vocabulary of 'mobilizing' labor, suggesting a constant effort at attracting people to work for a larger system and measuring the success of such endeavors in terms of the 'prestige' of a ruler or an elite (see below).

The most important source concerning alienated labor in the past consists of documents of payment for work. Where textual evidence is available, it is possible to calculate labor payments and their changes over time. In ancient Mesopotamia, they were mostly calculated in person-days, as rations handed out to workers (but see Steinkeller 2015: 27). Here, I will refer to a very early period where texts are only partly readable, but where we are in the comfortable position of disposing of a massive amount of archaeological remains for labor payment. This is the mid-4th to early 3rd millennium, when so-called beveled rim bowls have been found at many sites in extremely large numbers (Figure 6). Hans Nissen (1970) has suggested, based on a parallel between a proto-cuneiform pictorial sign for 'eating' and similarities to a head eating/drinking out of a bowl, that the sign designates beveled rim bowls as containers for the distribution of food. A long list of alternative interpretations is available, none of which is able to include so many of the most basic characteristics of this strange mass artifact (for a useful history of interpretations cf. Potts 2009; cf. also Goulder 2010; Sanjurjo-Sánchez et al. 2016). So far, attempts at specifying their function via the analysis of food remains have not been very successful (but see Sanjurjo-Sánchez et al. 2018).

Figure 6: Beveled rim bowls (Photo by bpk/Staatliche Museen zu Berlin, Vorderasiatisches Museum/Olaf M. Teßmer)

Without going into great detail here, these bowls are distributed over a huge geographical expanse, reaching from western Pakistan to southeastern Turkey. Remarkable is the very high density at which they occur at many sites, as well as the fact that they were often thrown away while still complete and useable. This underscores their role as a cheap means of labor compensation in early historical periods in Western Asia.

I consider the time during which the bowls were used as a period when structures of political economy did not change fundamentally. Thus, I shall take the liberty to pull different facets of an overarching political economy from various places and sub-periods together under the presumption of a coherent system that existed for some time. The bowls themselves are an early manifestation of alienated labor, of dependency and institutions that had an interest in keeping this system running (Nissen et al. 1993). Consequently, it is important to identify potential measures that may have served to negotiate reaching the UDT in one or several of the ways outlined above. Before going into more detail, I might add that this paper will not try to differentiate the kinds of labor carried out by different genders, a lacuna to be filled by taking into account the problems of the gender/labor nexus in the period in question (cf. Pollock/Bernbeck 2000; Asher-Greve 2008).

I include a number of indicators that do not necessarily co-occur everywhere or along the whole duration of the existence of these bowls. In the late 4th millennium BCE there are so far no traces of unhierarchized labor feasts as described by Dietler and as postulated for a precursor of the bevelled rim bowls, the 'Coba Bowls' in late 5th millennium northern Mesopotamia (Kennedy 2015). In the 4th millennium, different, hierarchized kinds of feasting certainly played an important role and are documented for Arslantepe's public buildings as well as the TW sector at Tell Brak (Emberling/McDonald 2003; Helwing 2003; Frangipane 2012).

Who were the laborers? In several papers, Robert Englund (1998; 2009) has shown that textual evidence from this period depicts laborers on a par with working animals. It is important to integrate this insight into any labor history, as the various possibilities of manipulating the utility-drudgery threshold are based on this mind set among the elite. It is therefore perhaps not astonishing to find the first depictions of brutal violence in these times of the earliest states, i. e. in the Late Uruk and Jamdat Nasr periods. Such scenes, particularly sealings from the excavations in Uruk itself, have sometimes been connected to inter-polity wars.[4] Traditional art historical interpretations leave open the question of the kind of violence and cast the representations as 'prisoner' or 'torture scenes' (Figure 7; Englund 1998; Boehmer 1999).

---

4 There is indeed potential evidence for collective violence from the northern Mesopotamian site of Hamoukar (Reichel 2011) and extensive evidence for violence resulting in mass graves at Tell Brak/Majnuna, also located in northeastern Syria. At least for Tell Brak/Majnuna, the analyses point to violence on a local level (McMahon et al. 2007: 163).

Figure 7: 'Prisoner scene' depicting brutal violence against unknown adversaries by a power holder and his adherents (from Boehmer 1999, Tafel 17, Nr. 4 I-L)

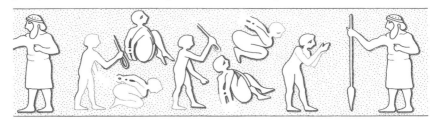

The actual seals with the beating of bound and shackled naked people have not been found, only their impressions on clay sealings. However, the importance of this imagery is obvious. Boehmer's analysis leads him to recognize 27 different seals that were used for the Late Uruk corpus he analyzed from the Eanna precinct at Uruk. Among these he identified six different types of scenes, from offering bearers to temple scenes, a hero and animals, various kinds of animals, and a mysterious 'oil jug and fraying cloth'. The scene with the largest number of different seals was the prisoner imagery, with seven out of the 27 seals used for the production of the sealings recovered (Boehmer 1999).

It was exactly the seals with these depictions that were used particularly frequently, and such sealings need to be understood in their full effect. They are first of all a 'witness for a contact', namely between the seal and the object on which it was impressed, and thus for a present absence: the person or institution who owned the seal (Didi-Huberman 2008). Breaking the seal was either an act of power or one of deceit, and the violent imagery refers to the potential consequences of actions against the rules. The 'prisoner' seals can be read as an early rendering of the pretension to monopolize the use of violence. Second, sealings were the only way to reliably multiply imagery in ancient times: they were a kind of ancient Instagram device. Since seals were part of a dispositive of control, we can infer that the frequency and ubiquity of a seal image were driven by a political will to impart a message, in the case of the prison/war scenes that of fear. I read the documentation of the late 4th to early 3rd millennium sealings from Uruk itself as a threat of violence, a sign that violence was part of the repertoire used to enforce labor, should it not be performed according to requirements. This is underscored by the finds of small limestone figurines of bound and shackled persons in Uruk (Feller 2013: fig. 24.5). As mentioned above, such acts could not turn into continuous practices in a political-economic system but likely remained the dramatic climax of mounting tensions that frequent depiction integrated firmly into collective memory.

Public feasts were another element that replaced the above-mentioned labor feasts. The famous 'Warka Vase' has been subject to numerous interpretations, the most thoroughgoing of recent times by Zainab Bahrani (2002). In the uppermost register, it depicts a scene that can be amended to have been the meeting between a woman, the goddess Inanna or her priestess, and a broken away figure that can be reconstructed as the 'En' or ruler who appears on seals and other imagery. Between the two is a tribute bringer, behind the 'En' an attendant, while the Inanna/priestess figure is accompanied by cult materials such as statues of adorants, but also two further vases of the kind on which the whole scene is depicted. Bahrani discusses the complex message of this constellation of figures, first in terms of the old and worn question of who the woman is, later arguing that her *performance* as goddess in the meeting with the ruler matters, not whether she *is* a goddess or a priestess.

The complex cosmology of the vase has been commented on sufficiently. I will focus instead on the naked tribute bringers of the second register. They are all men who carry huge baskets or vessels overflowing with products, enacting through ritual "an order that may not be fully itself without such celebration. In joyfully reaffirming order and legitimacy, rulers and elites use wealth to counter fragility, especially in celebrations and ceremonies that involve much of the wider society" (Yoffee 2005: 40). Such a reading renders the common understanding of the message of this vase, of religious systems, elaborate temples, palaces, and other material manifestations of ancient states: they have the function of producing the awe that makes people stay part of a system where they are the losers. But were these ideological means really powerful enough to increase the willingness of laborers to toil for others at the expense of their own interests? The instability of ancient political systems tells a different story, and political instability may well have been to the advantage of those at the lower end of the social ladder (Scott 2017). Small-scale and mostly failed uprisings, it should be remembered, have not been a focus of archaeology, whether in Western Asia or elsewhere. But direct resistance is not the only possibility to deal with unbearable labor conditions. Evasion is another, perhaps more often chosen, option and consisted mainly of 'voting with the feet', leaving the realm of the sedentary cities and villages to take up a mobile way of life (Nissen 1980; see also Sallaberger 2007).

As mentioned, another potential way for the elites to deal with the problem of the utility-drudgery threshold is the increase of the labor force so that one part of the workers can dispense with working for some time. Such a situation is extremely difficult to trace, whether through textual or archaeological evidence. And in addition, this attempt at finding a solution to avoid reaching the utility-drudgery threshold (UDT) could lead to an ancillary problem of unrest among the non-working parts of a dependent population. Gregory Johnson (1987) has proposed that major building projects can be traced back to measures aimed at preventing such secondary social problems by starting public work efforts that were not directly connected to subsistence labor. The construction of large monuments could have been part of such make-work projects. He coined the term 'piling behavior' for these mechanisms and linked them to the massive buildings observable in Mesoamerica, Egypt, and Mesopotamia. Monumentality, if one follows that argument, would be a secondary effect of other large-scale public projects that were situated in the subsistence realm, such as harvesting and the construction and upkeep of canals (Richardson 2015).

It is indeed remarkable that the time when we witness the first massive appearance of alienated labor produces a highly unusual effort at erecting a variety of monumental buildings whose shapes were hitherto completely unknown. The vast ensemble of the Eanna complex in the city of Uruk still does not reveal to us the specific functions of most of these buildings (Eichmann 2007; Butterlin 2015), not to speak of functional relations between these structures. Because of their multiplicity and the close sequence of various structures with quite different plans, they almost give the impression of having been constructed for the sake of constructing. Remarkably, many of the types of buildings in the Eanna precinct, such as the 'Pfeilerhalle' or the 'Steingebäude', remain unique in Mesopotamian history. Thus, the suspicion voiced by Johnson that such monuments in all their complexity were the result of keeping a vastly increased labor force occupied is not an outlandish speculation. One caveat must be added: recent analyses about the building process itself show that the variety of skills needed for transport, preparation, and construction of such buildings was considerable – this was not simply a scheme to occupy masses of unskilled laborers (Hageneuer/Levenson 2018), even though plenty of them were likely drawn into such projects.

The initial need for the upkeep of major irrigation works would have led to the demand for a significant labor force and the structural problem of reaching the utility-drudgery threshold. Attracting people from the surroundings, that is, rural-urban migration (Pollock 1999), would have enabled a labor organization that was based on alternating work gangs. In turn, this might have produced the need for 'make-work' jobs, the materialization of which is seen in the inscrutable monuments of Eanna in Uruk. However, such a solution had a paradox effect, since a positive feedback cycle set in that led to even greater demand for labor and in the long run to an untenable situation. Paradoxically, the political solution to a problem aggravated it, as the erection of monuments increased drudgery instead of diminishing it. Linking such conditions to David Graeber's (2018) catchy expression of patently useless jobs in the digital age, we can claim that toiling to erect massive public buildings was not only the first case of 'bullshit jobs' in history, but that such jobs emerged almost simultaneously with alienated labor itself.

A final solution for the utility-drudgery threshold could be the introduction of technologies that could decrease drudgery during work, a transfer of bodily spent energy to machines. Susan Pollock (2017) has recently shown that innovations in the realm of labor in the Uruk period were meant to speed up work processes, such as pottery making on a fast wheel. However, those innovations that would alleviate drudgery are few and far between. One of them likely was the domestication of equids, which probably occurred in northwestern Africa some-time in the 5th to 4th millennia BCE (Rossel et al. 2008). Their earliest appearance in imagery, however, depicts them as draught animals for the wagons of the elite, not as animals destined for the lowering of human drudgery. Strangely, another machine-like device, the newly introduced potter's wheel, was employed for the production of all kinds of vessel shapes, but *not* for the mass-produced beveled rim bowls, which continued to be shaped by hand through pressing them in molds. Only at the very end of the era considered here, in the Jemdet Nasr period, do we find mass-produced wheel-turned vessels. Technological innovations apparently served aesthetic, ideological, and specific functional purposes, but the lowering of the utility-drudgery threshold was not among them.

Conclusion

Labor is a precondition for ancient monumentality. However, calculations of the amount of labor that went into a particular building need to take into account sub-jective aspects of labor, and particularly those on the part of the laborers them-selves. Requirements for massive construction efforts cannot be assumed to sim-ply meet approval from laborers because workers see their toil in relation to their own living conditions. While this would seem to be self-evident, archaeological literature shows that this statement merits repeating. A host of different mech-anisms were used in ancient societies to force and cajole people into carrying out unappealingly dull, laborious, backbreaking tasks or to lure them into finding the rewards attractive. In the event, new temporalities – scheduling mechanisms for work – may have been invented, and the solutions to the issue likely produced their own set of unintended consequences. Only rarely can we identify technolog-ical solutions that would have alleviated drudgery, and if so, they tend to be sec-ondary applications of an innovation in another sphere of life. We need to consider more closely the perspective of those who dug foundation trenches, who plucked sheep wool, who made bricks, who wove cloth, and who carried baskets of clay on their heads. Then we might better understand who raised up Babylon so many times after it was demolished.

Acknowledgements

Many thanks to Susan Pollock for critical discussion and advice, as well as to partici-pants in a seminar on labor, held together with Philipp Lepenies in the winter of 2018, where parts of this paper were discussed. I also thank the editors for their invitation to contribute to this volume and two anonymous reviewers for their helpful critiques.

Bibliography

Abrams, E. M. (1994): How the Maya Built Their World. Energetics and Ancient Architecture, Austin: University of Texas Press.

Abrams, E. M./Bolland, T. W. (1999): "Architectural Energetics, Ancient Monuments, and Operations Management." In: Journal of Archaeological Method and Theory 6/4, pp. 263–291.

Althusser, L. (1971): Lenin and Philosophy and Other Essays. Ben Brewster transl., New York: Monthly Review Press.

Anders, G. (1956): Die Antiquiertheit des Menschen. Über die Seele im Zeitalter der zweiten industriellen Revolution, Vol. I, München: C. H. Beck.

Arnold, D. (1997): Building in Egypt: Pharaonic Stone Masonry, Oxford: Oxford University Press.

Asher-Greve, J. (2008): "Images of Men, Gender Regimes, and Social Stratification in the Late Uruk Period." In: D. Bolger (ed.), Gender Through Time in the Ancient Near East, Lanham: AltaMira Press, pp. 119–172.

Back, U./Höltken, T. (2008): Die Baugeschichte des Kölner Domes nach archäologischen Quellen. Befunde und Funde aus der gotischen Bauzeit, Köln: Verlag Kölner Dom.

Bahrani, Z. (2002): "Performativity and the Image: Narrative, Representation, and the Uruk Vase." In: E. Ehrenberg (ed.), Leaving No Stones Unturned: Essays on the Ancient Near East and Egypt in Honor of Donald P. Hansen, Winona Lake: Eisenbrauns, pp. 15–22.

Balibar, E. (1995): The Philosophy of Marx. Chris Turner transl., London: Verso.

Bartelt, U. (2007): "RiesenWerk. Wieviel Arbeit macht ein Großsteingrab?" In: Archäologie in Niedersachsen 10, pp. 22–26.

Benjamin, W. (1992): "Über den Begriff der Geschichte." In: R. Tiedemann (ed.), Walter Benjamin. Sprache und Geschichte. Philosophische Essays, Stuttgart: Reclam, pp. 141–154.

Bernbeck, R. (2009): "Class Conflict in Ancient Mesopotamia. Between Knowledge of History and Historicising Knowledge." In: Anthropology of the Middle East 4/1, pp. 33–64.

Boehmer, R. M. (1999): Uruk – Früheste Siegelabrollungen, Ausgrabungen in Uruk-Warka: Endberichte, Vol. 24, Mainz: Philipp von Zabern.

Böhm-Bawerk, E. von (1974): "Zum Abschluß des Marxschen Systems." In: H. Meixner/M. Turban (eds.), Etappen bürgerlicher Marx-Kritik, Giessen: Achenbach, pp. 47–132.

Brecht, B. (2012): Poems, Poemhunter.com – The World's Poetry Archive, https://www.poemhunter.com/i/ebooks/pdf/bertolt_brecht_2012_3.pdf (last accessed April 16, 2019).

Brunke, H./Bukowiecki, E./Cancik-Kirschbaum, E./Eichmann, R./van Ess, M./ Gass, A./Gussone, M./Hageneuer, S./Hansen, S./Kogge, W./May, J./Parzinger, H./Pedersén, O./Sack, D./Schopper, F./Wulf-Rheidt, U. (2016): "Thinking Big. Research in Monumental Constructions in Antiquity." In: eTopoi. Journal for Ancient Studies 6, pp. 250–305.

Bucharin, N. (1926): Die politische Ökonomie des Rentners. Die Wert- und Profit-lehre der Österreichischen Schule, Berlin: Verlag für Literatur und Politik.

Burmeister, S./Bernbeck, R. (eds.) (2017): The Interplay of People and Technologies. Archaeological Case Studies on Innovations, Berlin: Edition Topoi.

Butterlin, P. (2015): "Late Chalcolithic Mesopotamia: Towards a Definition of Sa-cred Space and Its Evolution." In: N. Laneri (ed.), Defining the Sacred: Ap-proaches to the Archaeology of Religion in the Near East, London: Oxbow Books, pp. 60–72.

Charim, I. (2009): Der Althusser-Effekt. Entwurf einer Ideologietheorie, Wien: Passagen Verlag.

Childe, V. G. (1941): Man Makes Himself, London: Watts & Co.

Devolder, M. (2017): "Architectural Energetics and Late Bronze Age Cretan Archi-tecture: Measuring the Scale of Minoan Building Projects." In: Q. Letesson/C. Knappett (eds.), Minoan Architecture and Urbanism: New Perspectives on an Ancient Built Environment, Oxford: Oxford University Press, pp. 57–79.

Didi-Huberman, G. (2008): La ressemblance par contact. Archéologie, anachro-nisme et modernité de l'empreinte, Paris: Éditions de Minuit.

Dietler, M. (2006): "Alcohol: Anthropological/Archaeological Perspectives." In: Annual Review of Anthropology 35, pp. 229–249.

Dietler, M./Herbich, I. (2001): "Feasts and Labor Mobilization: Dissecting a Fun-damental Economic Practice." In: M. Dietler/B. Hayden (eds.), Feasts: Archae-ological and Ethnographic Perspectives on Food, Politics, and Power, Wash-ington, D. C.: Smithsonian Institution Press, pp. 240–264.

Durrenberger, E. P. (1984): "Operationalizing Chayanov." In: E. P. Durrenberger (ed.), Chayanov, Peasants, and Economic Anthropology, San Diego: Academic Press, pp. 39–50.

Eichmann, R. (2007): Uruk. Architektur I. Von den Anfängen bis zur Frühdynas-tischen Zeit, Ausgrabungen in Uruk-Warka: Endberichte, Vol. 14, Rahden: Marie Leidorf.

Elbe, I. (2014): "Entfremdete und abstrakte Arbeit. Marx' ökonomisch-philoso-phische Manuskripte im Vergleich zu seiner späteren Kritik der politischen Ökonomie." In: I. Elbe/P. Hogh/Ch. Zunke (eds.), Oldenburger Jahrbuch für Philosophie 2012, Oldenburg: BIS-Verlag, pp. 7–69.

Emberling, G./McDonald, H. (2003): "Excavations at Tell Brak 2001–2002: Prelim-inary Report." In: Iraq 65, pp. 1–75.

Englund, R. K. (1998): "Texts from the Late Uruk Period." In: P. Attinger/M. Wäfler (eds.), Mesopotamien. Späturuk-Zeit und frühdynastische Zeit, Göttingen: Vandenhoeck & Ruprecht, pp. 15–236.

Englund, R. K. (2009): "The Smell of the Cage." In: Cuneiform Digital Library Journal 2009/4, https://cdli.ucla.edu/pubs/cdlj/2009/cdlj2009_004.html (last accessed December 23, 2018).

Feller, B. (2013): "Die Anfänge der Bürokratie. Funktion und Einsatz von Siegeln im 4. und 3. Jahrtausend v. Chr." In: N. Crüsemann/M. van Ess/M. Hilgert/B. Salje (eds.), Uruk. 5000 Jahre Megacity, Petersberg: Michael Imhof, pp. 159–165.

Flohr, M. (2016): Innovation and Society in the Roman World, Oxford Handbooks Online. DOI: 10.1093/oxfordhb/9780199935390.013.85 (last accessed December 23, 2018).

Frangipane, M. (2012): "Fourth Millennium Arslantepe: The Development of a Centralised Society without Urbanisation." In: Origini XXXIV, pp. 29–40.

Goulder, J. (2010): "Administrators' Bread: An Experiment-Based Re-Assessment of the Functional and Cultural Role of the Uruk Bevel-Rim Bowl." In: Antiquity 84, pp. 351–362.

Graeber, D: (2018): Bullshit Jobs. A Theory, New York: Simon & Schuster.

Hageneuer, S./Levenson, F. (2018): "Das Steinstiftgebäude in Uruk – Ein gescheitertes Experiment?" In: K. Rheidt/W. Lorenz (eds.), Groß Bauen – Großbaustellen als kulturgeschichtliches Phänomen, Basel: Birkhäuser, pp. 109–122.

Harding, S. (1993): "Rethinking Standpoint Epistemology: What Is 'Strong Objectivity'?" In: L. Alcoff/E. Potter (eds.), Feminist Epistemologies, London: Routledge, pp. 49–82.

Helwing, B. (2003): "Feasts as a Social Dynamic in Prehistoric Western Asia: Three Case Studies From Syria and Anatolia." In: Paléorient 29/2, pp. 63–86.

Hilferding, R. (1904): "Böhm-Bawerks Marxkritik." In: M. Adler/R. Hilferding (eds.), Marxismusstudien, Wien: I. Brand, pp. 1–61.

Johnson, G. A. (1987): "The Changing Organization of Uruk Administration on the Susiana Plain." In: F. Hole (ed.), The Archaeology of Western Iran, Washington, D. C.: Smithsonian Institution Press, pp. 107–139.

Kennedy, J. R. (2015): "Commensality and Labor in Terminal Ubaid Northern Mesopotamia." In: S. Pollock (ed.), Between Feasts and Daily Meals. Towards an Archaeology of Commensal Spaces, Berlin: Edition Topoi, pp. 143–180.

Lüdtke, A. (1993): Eigen-Sinn. Fabrikalltag, Arbeitererfahrungen und Politik vom Kaiserreich bis in den Faschismus, Hamburg: Ergebnisse-Verlag.

Lukács, G. (1971): History and Class Consciousness: Studies in Marxist Dialectics, Cambridge: MIT Press.

Marx, K. (1966): "Ökonomisch-Philosophische Manuskripte (1844)." In: I. Fetscher (ed.), Marx – Engels Studienausgabe II. Politische Ökonomie, Frankfurt a. M.: Fischer, pp. 38–129.

Marx, K. (1974): "Zur Kritik der Politischen Ökonomie." In: Karl Marx – Friedrich Engels – Werke, Berlin: Dietz-Verlag, pp. 3–160.

Marx, K. (1979): Das Kapital, Vol. 1, Berlin: Dietz-Verlag.

Marx, K. (1983): "Grundrisse der Kritik der politischen Ökonomie." In: Ökonomische Manuskripte 1857/1858, Berlin: Dietz-Verlag, pp. 47–770.

McMahon, A./Oates, J./Al-Quntar, S./Charles, M./Colantoni, C./Hald, M. M./ Kaarsgard, P./ Khalidi, L./Soltysiak, A./Stone, A./Weber, J. (2007): "Excavations at Tell Brak 2006–2007." In: Iraq 69, pp. 145–171.

Mishmastnehi, M./Bernbeck, R. (2015): "Die Nutzung erneuerbarer Energien im alten Iran. Geschichte und Technik der persischen Windmühlen." In: Das Altertum 60, pp. 81–100.

Müller, J. (1990): "Die Arbeitsleistung für das Großsteingrab Kleinenkneten 1." In: M. Fansa (ed.), Experimentelle Archäologie in Deutschland, pp. 210–219.

Müller-Römer, F. (2011): Der Bau der Pyramiden im alten Ägypten, München: Herbert Utz.

Nissen, H. J. (1970): "Grabung in den Quadraten K/L XII in Uruk-Warka." In: Baghdader Mitteilungen 5, pp. 102–191.

Nissen, H. J. (1980): "The Mobility between Settled and Non-Settled in Early Babylonia: Theory and Evidence." In: M.-T. Barrelet (ed.) L'archéologie de l'Iraq: Perspectives et limites de l'interprétation anthropologique des documents, Paris: Éditions du CNRS, pp. 285–290.

Nissen, H. J./Damerow, P./Englund, R. K. (1993): Archaic Bookkeeping: Early Writing and Techniques of Economic Administration in the Ancient Near East, Chicago: University of Chicago Press.

Pauketat, T. R. (2000): "The Tragedy of the Commoners." In: M.-A. Dobres/J. Robb (eds.), Agency in Archaeology, London: Routledge, pp. 113–129.

Pollock, S. (1999): Ancient Mesopotamia. The Eden that Never Was, Cambridge: Cambridge University Press.

Pollock, S. (ed.) (2015): Between Feasts and Daily Meals. Towards an Archaeology of Commensal Spaces, Berlin: Edition Topoi.

Pollock, S. (2017): "Working Lives in an Age of Mechanical Reproduction: Uruk-Period Mesopotamia." In: S. Burmeister/R. Bernbeck (eds.), The Interplay of People and Technologies. Archaeological Case Studies on Innovations, Berlin: Edition Topoi, pp. 205–224.

Pollock, S./Bernbeck, R. (2000): "And They Said, Let Us Make Gods in Our Image: Gendered Ideologies in Ancient Mesopotamia." In: A. Rautman (ed.), Reading the Body. Representations and Remains in the Archaeological Record, Philadelphia: University of Pennsylvania Press, pp. 150–164.

Potts, D. T. (2009): "Bevel-Rim Bowls and Bakeries: Evidence and Explanations from Iran and the Indo-Iranian Borderlands." In: Journal of Cuneiform Studies 61, pp. 1–23.

Reichel, C. (2011): "Hamoukar 2005–2010. Revisiting the Origins of Urbanism in Syria." In: The Oriental Institute News & Notes 211, pp. 3–9.

Richardson, S. (2015): "Building Larsa: Labor-Value, Scale and Scope-of-Economy in Ancient Mesopotamia." In: P. Steinkeller /M. Hudson (eds.), Labor in the Ancient World, Dresden: Islet, pp. 237–328.

Rosa, H. (2013): Beschleunigung und Entfremdung, Berlin: Suhrkamp.

Rossel, S./Marshall, F./Peters, J./Pilgram, T./Adams, M. D./O'Connor, D. (2008): "Domestication of the Donkey: Timing, Processes, and Indicators." In: Proceedings of the National Academy of Sciences 105/10, pp. 3715–3720.

Sallaberger, W. (2007): "From Urban Culture to Nomadism: A History of Upper Mesopotamia in the Late Third Millennium." In: C. Kuzucuoğlu/C. Marro (eds.), Sociétés humaines et changement climatique à la fin du troisième millénaire: Une crise a-t-elle eu lieu en Haute Mésopotamie ?, Varia Anatolica. Lyon: Institut Français d'Études Anatoliennes, pp. 417–456.

Sanjurjo-Sánchez, J./Fenollós, J.-L./Prudêncio, Maria I./Dias, M. I. (2016): "Geochemical Study of Beveled Rim Bowls from the Middle Syrian Euphrates Sites." In: Journal of Archaeological Science: Reports 7, pp. 808–818.

Sanjurjo-Sánchez, J./Kaal, J./Fenollós, J.-L. (2018): "Organic Matter from Bevelled Rim Bowls of the Middle Euphrates: Results From Molecular Characterization Using Pyrolysis-GC-MS." In: Microchemical Journal, pp. 1–6.

Sauvage, M. (1998): La brique et sa mise en œuvre en Mésopotamie, Paris: Éditions Recherche sur les Civilisations.

Schilling, T. (2012): "Building Monks Mound, Cahokia, Illinois, A. D. 800–1400." In: Journal of Field Archaeology 37/4, pp. 302–313.

Schmid, H. (1995): Der Tempelturm Etemenanki in Babylon, Mainz: Philipp von Zabern.

Scott, J. C. (1990): Domination and the Arts of Resistance: Hidden Transcripts, New Haven: Yale University Press.

Scott, J. C. (2017): Against the Grain. A Deep History of the Earliest States, New Haven: Yale University Press.

Sievertsen, U. (2014): "Bauwissen im alten Orient." In: J. Renn/W. Osthues/H. Schlimme (eds.), Wissensgeschichte der Architektur, Berlin: Max Planck Institute for the History of Science, Edition Open Access, pp. 131–180.

Stadelmann, R. (1997): Die ägyptischen Pyramiden. Vom Ziegelbau zum Weltwunder. 3. Auflage, Mainz: Philipp von Zabern.

Steinkeller, P. (2015). "Introduction. Labor in the Early States: An Early Mesopotamian Perspective." In: P. Steinkeller/M. Hudson (eds.), Labor in the Ancient World, Dresden: Islet, pp. 1–36.

Tannenbaum, N. (1984): "Chayanov and Economic Anthropology." In: E. P. Durrenberger (ed.), Chayanov, Peasants, and Economic Anthropology, San Diego: Academic Press, pp. 27–38.

Trouillot, M.-R. (1995): Silencing the Past: Power and the Production of History, Boston: Beacon Press.

Tschajanow, A. (1987): Die Lehre von der bäuerlichen Wirtschaft, Frankfurt a. M.: Campus.

Virno, P. (2004): A Grammar of the Multitude: For an Analysis of Contemporary Forms of Life, New York: Semiotext(e).

Wäfler, M. (2003): Tall Al-Hamidiya 4. Vorbericht 1988–2001, Göttingen: Vandenhoeck & Ruprecht.

Wylie, A. (2011): "What Knowers Know Well: Women, Work, and the Academy." In: H. E. Grasswick (ed.), Feminist Epistemology and Philosophy of Science: Power in Knowledge, Springer: Dordrecht, pp. 157–179.

Yoffee, N. (2005): Myths of the Archaic State. Evolution of the Earliest Cities, States, and Civilizations, Cambridge: Cambridge University Press.

Zerstörungswut – The Deliberate Destruction of MonuMentality in Ancient and Modern Times

Sabrina N. Autenrieth & Dieuwertje van Boekel

1. Introduction

Monuments were not only built collectively, they were also abandoned and some-times even destroyed collectively by specific groups. This aspect is often omitted from archaeological research. A number of examples suggest that the destruction of monumental structures took even more effort and time than the building pro-cess itself.[1] Monumental buildings are expected to last. They are, in contrast to their architects or initiators, permanent, or at least constructed as permanent architectural features (Fisher 2017: 42).

Monumental architecture usually serves as a communal place, where people meet, exchange materialistic and non-materialistic goods, and celebrate special events. It is a place which is easy to find within an urban setting or within the land-scape, it is also a place that people come back to on a regular basis for different rea-sons. The main difference between 'regular' and monumental architecture is the perception of people towards the architecture itself. The people, without any words or deeper thoughts, will know whether a specific building is monumental or has a monumental meaning. This is why such buildings draw people towards them and why they are important, even beyond their own understanding and beyond their own time. Similar arguments can be made for figurative works, like statues, stelae, and iconographic monuments. These structures hold meaning for the people that created them and the people that behold them. Their value is often bound to a cer-tain ideology or past event, and, as with architecture, this value is known without needing words. As Bevan (2016: 26) puts it, "[...] buildings gather meanings to them by their everyday function, by their presence in the townscape, and by their form. They can have meaning attached to them as structures or, sometimes, simply act as containers of meaning and history." As such containers, monuments (both architec-tural and figurative) are also a storage medium of elapsed memory and information, a bulky and stationary version of a floppy disk to all intents and purposes.

---

1 See structure 10 of the Neolithic site of Ness of Brodgar, Orkney.

This paper compares the deliberate destruction of monuments such as the 'temple' of Ness of Brodgar and the Olmec statues, which were destroyed or altered in ancient times, with monuments like the Temple of Baal in Palmyra and the Berlin Wall. These structures were deliberately destroyed and set in scene in the last decades. With this comparison we want to demonstrate how destructive behavior is part of ancient and modern societies and to what extent this behavior underlies the mechanisms of economic implications and shared ideology.

First, the destruction of monumental architecture within an urban setting will be discussed, including the Neolithic site of Ness of Brodgar (United Kingdom), the ancient Temple of Baal in Palmyra (Syria), and the more recent Berlin Wall (Germany). Secondly, we will compare the monumental statues of the formative period of Olmec culture (Mesoamerica), the Bamiyan Buddhas (Afghanistan), and a Lenin statue from Berlin (Germany).

2. Monumental architecture

The majority of destruction can be found in buildings that are of great value to a society. The following section therefore discusses the alteration and destruction of monumental architecture in an urban setting. Three case studies are presented in order to examine different types of destruction and to analyze the intentions and approaches of the violators. First the Neolithic site 'Ness of Brodgar' in Scotland is discussed. Subsequently the temple of Baal in Syria and the Berlin wall are examined, whereupon the three cases are compared and analyzed.

2.1 Ness of Brodgar, United Kingdom

The Neolithic site Ness of Brodgar is situated on the Orkney Islands, which are 3.4 km away from the Scottish mainland, separated from it by the Pentland Firth (*Land Use Consultant* 1998). Due to the lack of trees, material other than wood had to be used to build architectural structures, such as domestic houses or monuments. Luckily, Orkney has a great variety of geology and a vast amount of suitable stones to construct enduring architecture, which allows archaeologists to get a glimpse of Neolithic architecture. The Ness of Brodgar is a complex of architectural structures within a ritual landscape (Stones of Stenness, Ring of Brodgar, Maes Howe, etc.) that is surrounded by a fresh- and a saltwater loch as well as a hilly landscape (ibid. 1998).

The last major structure, the so-called temple (Structure 10) was built around 2900 BCE by deconstructing and replacing the prior Structures 1, 8, and 12 which were demolished after a few centuries of use. Structure 10 is 25 m long and 20 m wide, with walls 4–5 m thick, including a standing stone that was integrated in the walls. The structure, which distinguishes itself from prior structures in size and style, was covered by a walkway and the inside is cross-shaped, similar to House 1 of Skara Brae (*Current Archaeology* 2018). This example is the largest Neolithic structure currently known in Northern Britain. "In some ways, this mirrors a general trend towards monumentality – the birth of what we call 'big houses' – in the later Neolithic period" (*Current Archaeology* 2018). We can assume that this structure within the whole Ness of Brodgar complex dominated the ritual landscape of the peninsula with its appearance and size. It is possible that the development of big buildings like Ness of Brodgar's Structure 10 reflects the evolution of more complex social systems, which could be originally hierarchical, while the earlier buildings might have represented communities operating on an individual level (*Current Archaeology* 2018: 25). Structure 10 was rebuilt in around 2800 BCE. Its use ended around 2300 BCE with one single event which included a feast of at least 400 individual cattle.[2] The cattle bones were prepared for food consumption,[3] and afterwards they were placed in the surrounding covered passageway of Structure 10. This event is the end of the complex (*Current Archaeology* 2018: 25). The whole building was deliberately destroyed and filled with midden material after it was leveled. It is assumed that the effort of destroying this structure was the same as the effort put into the construction of Structure 10.

What could have been the reason for rebuilding and demolishing this specific structure? Was there a change in belief, politics, or ideology for the people who were using the Ness of Brodgar? Or did a foreign group take over this temple complex? What was the common idea(ology)? The cause of this event is thus far unproven, but we can assume that this process must have been a symbolic transition, since it took as much time and effort to destruct this structure as to construct it. It is worth mentioning that the transition from the Neolithic to the Bronze Age took place at around the same time (2300 BCE). But while the British mainland experienced an influx of new technical knowledge, values, and material from the European continent, Orkney's inhabitants seem to have been reluctant to embrace this new Bronze Age mindset. Further, it is noteworthy that while the structures of Ness of Brodgar were destroyed and abandoned, the henges and cairns are still standing.

2.2 The Temple of Baal, Syria

The destruction inflicted on the Temple of Baal in Palmyra (Syria) was differently motivated. This temple was one of the most important religious architectural structures in the 1st century CE, located in the Middle East. According to Paul Veyne, the Temple of Baal was not a shrine or monumental reliquary (2017: 8),

---

2 It is estimated that one cow can feed more than 200 persons.
3 Including the extraction of bone marrow.

unlike the Greek or Roman temples: "[The temple] was the home where Bel lived and where his statue sat on a throne as the saint of all saints" (Veyne 2017: 8). The temple itself was placed in the centre of a rectangular 200 m long enclosure which featured porticoes. Paul Veyne emphasizes that neither the enclosure nor the size was outstanding for that time period. If there was enough space available, the Palmyrenes used it to enclose their temple buildings. The porticoes were used by merchants who sold religious objects; objects which were then brought to the Temple of Baal as *ex-votos* (Veyne 2017: 9). Pilgrims not only left offerings to the god, but also engravings[4] of their "I was here" on the back wall of the temple, to mark and prove their visit (Veyne 2017: 9).

Unlike the temple of Ness of Brodgar, this temple structure was not destroyed in ancient times. It stood as cultural heritage until it was demolished in 2015 by the terrorist organization Daesh (ISIS). This staged act of destruction not only shocked the people in the surrounding area, but also the more remote Western world. Sadly, this was not the first or last act of destroying culturally and historically significant sites.[5] The destruction of cultural sites that are important to a great majority of people is a powerful tool of terror and propaganda (Bevan 2016: 9). It is also more viewer-friendly to show the demolition of a monument on the evening news than a beheading. This destruction was intentionally directed to demonstrate power and to intimidate, scare, and hurt the world.

2.3 The Berlin Wall, Germany

The Berlin Wall is probably the most famous example mentioned in this paper; not much needs to be said about its history. The Wall was "designed to secure peace" (Bevan 2016: 206) and to stop people from leaving the new concept of the GDR. It quickly evolved as a symbol of division, dependence, sovereignty, and confinement. The day it was taken down was a day of celebration for people on both sides of the wall (with few exceptions). After years of fear and oppression, people climbed on top of the wall and started dancing, while others could not wait to erase this piece of German history with their hammers or other utensils: "There was an eagerness among people to be part of its destruction using their own hands" (Bevan 2016: 209). But not only the bricks of the Wall fell, statues of previous heads of governments (see: Lenin's head) were also toppled over.[6] In the case of the Berlin Wall, destruction was seen and experienced as an act of liberation, which is why most of the Wall fell quite quickly. But even though people wanted to raze the Wall to

---

4   Graffiti and engravings were also part of the architectural structures of Ness of Brodgar and the Berlin Wall.

5   See also the case study of the Bamiyan Buddhas which were destroyed by the Taliban in 2001.

6   See also Göttke 2010.

the ground and erase it from their daily life, they were still looking for ways to remember this architectural monument and its attached meaning. Some pieces of the Wall have been 'saved' as a memorial, to experience and tell German history. The invisible part of the Wall can nowadays be followed by a line which is marked on the ground in some locations. It is even possible to buy certified fragments of the Berlin Wall as souvenirs. The ones with colorful graffiti are the ones which sell best. But although most of the physical reminders of the Wall have vanished, some people still experience a *Mauer im Kopf* (wall in the mind) and can't really let go of the past. They look back sentimentally to what they experienced as a better system, a term which is called *Ostalgie* (Banchelli 2008).

2.4 Analysis – monumental architecture

The previous three examples show how deliberate destruction can be perceived differently by the affected societies. Structure 10 of Ness of Brodgar shows how three existing architectural structures were demolished and re-used to build an even bigger building on the same location. The material used and the location remained constant, but the structure and therefore the underlying meaning and idea changed by transitioning the three smaller structures into only one big building. But then the ideology of the society is assumed to have changed again, since the bigger structure 10 was also demolished and filled with midden material while celebrating this special event with a huge feast. The ancient Temple of Baal in Palmyra was demolished in more recent times by a terror organization. In this case, a group of people intentionally attacked the ideology and values of another group, who not only mourn the loss of this, but also of other historical monuments and the loss of human lives.[7] Hurting a society by slaughtering their monuments as well as erasing their history, culture and values is nothing new, as can be seen in iconoclasm (Section 3). The Berlin Wall experienced a different type of treatment. It was destroyed by the people who were being suppressed by the wall and the underlying system. Similar to Structure 10 of Ness of Brodgar, this event of destruction was also celebrated; this did not include a feast of 400 cows, but it did involve dancing, singing, and champagne. Nowadays the Wall serves as a memorial, as an open-air museum, to give people the chance to experience the vastness and meaning of this structure. Unlike the previous two examples, the fragmented remains of the Wall are being sold as souvenirs.

---

7 It must be noted that even before the destruction of the Temple of Baal, the site was often subjected to illegal excavation and looting. In a way this can also be perceived as acts of destruction, since such disregard for Syrian cultural heritage causes a loss of information that could have otherwise been gained by proper excavation and research. The purpose of this type of destruction however is mainly economic.

3. Iconic destruction

The following section focuses on the mutilation and destruction of monuments and figurative art in ancient Mexico, the Netherlands, Afghanistan, and present-day Germany. Several case studies are examined and various kinds of destruction are analyzed in order to establish the underlying reasons for the specific acts of violence that occurred in these places. First the mutilation of Olmec iconographic monuments will be discussed as an example of destruction in ancient times. After this the Iconoclastic Fury is examined, followed by the destruction of the Bamiyan Buddhas, and the beheading and burial of the Lenin statue.

3.1 Olmec monuments, Mesoamerica

The Olmec culture consisted of a number of ancient societies in Mesoamerica, who shared a certain belief system and an accompanying monumental style. The most well-known part of the Olmec region is situated in the Isthmus of Tehuantepec in Mexico; an area forming the thin stretched boundary between the Gulf of Mexico and the Pacific Ocean. The exchange network of the Olmec style and ideology, however, is much larger, spreading as far as Honduras (Joyce/Henderson 2010). The Olmec style can be positioned in the Early and Middle Formative period, lasting from approximately 1500 to 400 BCE (Pool 2007: 6). In contrast with many other Mesoamerican cultures, Olmec art is not incorporated into the architecture. In the Isthmus region stone is not readily available, which made it a costly material. Most buildings were therefore made from clay (Bernal 1969: 55). Stone was used for the construction of sculptures and monuments, such as the so-called 'throne-altars'. These large stone altars, decorated with high- and bas-relief, depict figures and scenes from the Olmec ideology. The Olmec are also known to construct stelae, statues, and colossal stone heads, all of which were richly decorated with iconographic scenes and/or features.

Among the stone monuments of the Olmec culture, many were found to be deliberately mutilated or destroyed. The mutilations occurred in all types of artwork, but throne-altars seem to have been subjected most to the violence. The mutilations take many forms, including the making of pits or grooves, and the removal of facial features. Anthropomorphic figures are often beheaded and stelae broken or fractured (Grove 1981: 49). The Olmec colossal heads are frequently found buried beneath the surface, accompanied by other monuments (Grove 1981: 65). This type of destruction is especially visible at the site of San Lorenzo, located in the north of the Isthmus, close to the Gulf of Mexico. Around 1200 BCE, complex settlements and large monumental structures arose, along with more elaborate social stratification (Bernal 1969: 111). The settlement of San Lorenzo was at its prime between 1150 and 900 BCE, after which the population receded and many monuments were destroyed. Around 600 BCE the population was partially restored; this lasted 200 years before the settlement came to a definite end (Flannery/Marcus 2000: 3).

The reason behind the destruction of the San Lorenzo monuments has not yet been agreed upon. Some scholars ascribe the mutilations to the performance of rituals related to the end of a period or site (Grove 1981: 49). Michael Coe (1968: 86) states that the mutilated statues of San Lorenzo point to a period of chaos, starting around 900 BCE. Diehl (2004: 58) suggests, on the other hand, that the monuments in San Lorenzo were regularly reused, and that the inhabitants of the site were simply in the middle of this process when the city was abandoned. This theory, however, does not explain why some monuments were specifically beheaded or completely broken. Neither is it certain why the giant stone heads were buried. The mutilation of the monuments seems to have been very deliberately and carefully executed. David Grove (1981: 62–63) therefore believes the destruction to be part of a ceremony relating to the change or death of a leader. Grove bases his theory on ethnographic comparisons with the *Canelos Quichua* from the lowlands of Ecuador, and other cultures from the tropical rainforest. These people have a belief system in which the spiritual leaders possess a 'seat of power' that has to be neutralized once the owner has passed. The seat of power is destroyed in order to prevent the uncontrolled release of supernatural powers after the death of the leader. According to Grove (1981: 63–64), the Olmec ideology is consistent with the beliefs of the *Canelos Quicha*. In this analogy, the throne-altars would be the 'seats of power' that have to be destroyed after the death of the ruler.

These are only a few of the theories that exist about the Olmec mutilations. To this day the exact nature of the destructive acts is still unknown. Destruction and mutilation are easy to recognize in the archaeological record, but the events preceding such acts can only be guessed at. The manner of the Olmec mutilations seems to be consistent with an iconoclastic act. 'Iconoclasm' can be defined as "the action of attacking or assertively rejecting cherished beliefs and institutions or established values and practices" (*Oxford Dictionary*). By decapitating anthropomorphic figures, it seems that the mutilators intended to destroy the identity of the monument (whether as ritual or otherwise). The same argument can be made for the removal of facial features and the breaking of scenery on stelae and throne-altars. These monuments are believed to depict important people and events in Olmec culture. The destruction can therefore be seen as a way of destroying the history and/or belief system of the people that created them.

3.2 Iconoclastic Fury, Northwest Europe

Similar types of destruction can be seen in more recent historical events, like the Iconoclastic Fury that took place in the Low Countries from August to October 1566. During this period a great number of Catholic churches and statues were destroyed by a Calvinistic movement, which advocated against the depiction of the sacred and the worship of idols. The revolt was preceded by several iconoclastic events throughout a large part of northwestern Europe, ultimately resulting in a wave of destruction through present-day Flanders and the Netherlands (Cools 2011). Geeraert Brandt wrote in *The History of the Reformation and Other Ecclesiastical Transactions in and about the Low Countries* (1720),

> [...] they attacked the Crosses and Images that had been erected in the great Roads of the Country; next, those in Villages; and lastly, those in the Towns and Cities: All the Chapels, Churches, and Convents which they found shut, they forced open, breaking, tearing, and destroying all the Images, Pictures, Shrines, and other consecrated things they met with: nay, some did not scruple to lay their hands upon Libraries, Books, Writings, Monuments, and even the dead bodies in Churches and Churchyards. Swift as lightning the evil diffused itself, insomuch that in the space of three days above four hundred Churches were plundered.

Even though the iconoclasm was clearly an act fuelled by ideological ideas, the revolt itself was the result of a combination of economic and political stress, which had been building up for years before the mutilations started. A war with France caused a significant increase in tax rates and food prices, resulting in a general state of unease. Although in 1559 a peace treaty was signed, the sudden death of King Henry II caused the tension between the Catholics and Calvinists to escalate, as both religious parties tried to seize power. The first iconoclastic movements occurred in the South of France, and continued north during the civil war that broke out in 1562. In the Netherlands the Calvinistic parties were still being suppressed and heavily persecuted. People accused of heresy were burnt at the stake. In 1565 a petition was signed by the noblemen to cease these prosecutions. This allowed Calvinistic exiles to return and openly proclaim their religious ideals, which in 1566 resulted in the Iconoclastic Fury (Cools 2011; Petegree 1992).

3.3 The Bamiyan Buddhas, Afghanistan

In more recent times we have also seen the destruction of many figurative works, like statues, pots, and paintings, during the Taliban movement in Afghanistan. The explosive elimination of the Bamiyan Buddhas is considered to be the 'nadir of their cultural policy' (Bevan 2006: 163). At the beginning of March 2001 the statues were attacked with guns, rockets, and tank shells, after months of fighting in the surrounding regions (Harding 2001).

The Buddha statues are located in the Bamiyan valley in the Hindu Kush Mountain range, about 250 km northwest of Kabul. The site is found in the broadest part of the valley, stretching out for 1.5 km, and comprises thousands of caves that were constructed between the 3rd and 8th centuries CE (Toubekis et al. 2009: 185). The two giant Buddhas were a product of the Gandhara school of Buddhist art and are known as the largest standing depictions of Buddha. The smaller statue was 38 m high and dated from the second half of the 6th century. The largest Buddha was constructed some time later, at the beginning of the 7th century, and measured 55 m in height (Toubekis et al. 2017: 271). In between the two figures, several seated depictions of Buddha were located, which were also destroyed during the Taliban attack.

The destruction of the monuments is evidently an act of iconoclasm, driven by the Taliban's proscription of idols and their unwillingness to accept any representation of non-Islamic belief systems. According to Bevan (2006: 163), however, the Taliban's reason for the destruction of the Buddhas was more elaborate than is usually assumed. For the local inhabitants of the Bamiyan region the Buddhas had become a symbol of permanence and continuity (Bevan 2006: 163). This minority Muslim group, named the Shi'a Hazara, had resisted Taliban rule for several years. The Bamiyan region was continuously attacked as part of a political and military conquest, in which eventually the town of Bamiyan was destroyed, its people killed or driven out, and the symbols of their infidelity destroyed (Bevan 2006: 163). The destruction of the monuments can therefore be seen as a demonstration of power, as much as a religious act.

3.4 Lenin's head, Germany

In April 2016, a new exhibition with the title "Enthüllt, Berlin und seine Denkmäler" opened in Berlin. German newspapers (Reich et al. 2016) reported this event with a provocative image at the top of each article: Lenin's granite head. Lenin's statue had been erected on a square in Eastern Berlin in April 1970 during Germany's shaken history and after being buried in a pile of sand, he was now being raised from the earth.

While planning the exhibition, many problems occurred. First, is it acceptable to display one of the most controversial figures of East Germany's history in the city of Berlin? Second, where is the exact location of Lenin's head? After removing the statue from the former Leninplatz in East Berlin many years ago, its components had been buried underneath a 10 m long and 2 m high mound in the forest of Köpenick, covered with debris to protect the pieces from being found. According to the Mayor of Berlin, no documents about the exact location of Lenin's head exist. The explanation of this circumstance is simple: the whole purpose of Lenin's deposition was to make him disappear, anonymously to be specific (Reich et al. 2016). "At least removing the visible reminder makes it easier for a community to heal and forget" (Hood 2010: 6). Now, Lenin is back, at least his head is being displayed on a platform in Berlin Spandau, with all the visible damage to his ear and beard which was caused many years ago. But Lenin's head is not alone in the exhibition. Numerous other famous but out-of-favor monumental statues are on display as well, like Prussian electors and statues from the Nazi era. Most of the monuments show clear signs of deliberate destruction, like decapitation or cut off hands, which might bring the concept of iconoclasm to mind. In a nutshell, the exhibition shows how a society treats remains from a painful and bitter past, now and then.

3.5 Analysis - iconic destruction

As can be seen from these case studies, iconoclasm may not be the sole reason for the mutilation or destruction of ideological monuments. The causes for such acts are often much more complex, and developed from years of conflict and/or disagreement. In the case of the Iconoclastic Fury the continuous oppression of the Calvinists and economic pressure during times of war caused the people to revolt. The destruction of the Bamiyan Bhuddas was part of a military conquest, in which a resisting group of people was targeted and vanquished. Lastly, Lenin's statue was beheaded and buried to erase his memory from the face of the earth (quite literally). Unfortunately these underlying reasons are near impossible to retrieve archaeologically, unless there are clear signs of war or periods of chaos. What can be distinguished, however, is the manner of destruction and how this might have affected the society the images belonged to. In the case of the Calvinistic revolt, the Taliban destruction, and the beheading of Lenin, it is evident that the actions were symbolic; by destroying specific icons the iconoclasts meant to shock society, and show both their disagreement and their strength.

Although these cases cannot be compared directly, the manner of destruction is similar to the mutilations found in San Lorenzo. Whether the mutilation of the Olmec monuments was caused by a change in leadership or the violent intervention of a different group, it remains clear that the act of destruction was (at least partly) symbolic as well. Specific iconographic elements were targeted, while others were ignored. The creation of pits and grooves, and the beheading of anthropomorphic figures (like the example of Lenin's statue), indicate carefully planned action that held great significance to both the destructors and 'destructees'.

Another aspect that is evident from these examples is that the meaning of monuments changes for different periods of time and different groups of people. The example of the Bamiyan Buddhas is illustrative. Originally, the statues were created as part of a cave site where Buddhist monks practiced their religion. Even though the current Shi'a Hazara inhabitants are Muslim, the ancient statues were of great value to them as symbols of permanence and continuity. However, their acceptance of the Buddhas was seen by the Taliban as heresy and idolism. For them the Buddhas were a symbol of the Shi'a Hazara resistance; a stain on the Islamic belief system. Similarly, the statue of Lenin was built by supporters of the Soviet regime, as an emblem of Lenin's power and his ideals. After Lenin's fall the statue became a reminder of the suffering that was endured during his reign. Years later however, when the memories had receded, the statue was resurrected as a commemoration of historic events, once again adopting a different meaning for the people that behold it.

These examples show that differences in the perception of a monument are ultimately the reason for its destruction. Not only the act of destruction is symbolic, the monuments themselves are symbols as well; icons that need to be eliminated in order to resolve the conflict.

Conclusion

The examples of Structure 10 of Ness of Brodgar and the Olmec statues are illustrations of ancient sites with contemporary destruction. The Temple of Baal in Palmyra and the Bamiyan Buddhas represent how ancient sites were destroyed in modern times. Lastly the Berlin Wall and the head of Lenin demonstrate the more recent destruction and re-use of recent architectural monuments.

As has been shown in the previous examples, the deliberate destruction of monuments happened throughout time and space. This destructive practice is not limited to specific time periods or regions, but is rather limited to certain events and meaningful locations. Of course, in comparison to all the monuments which have not been deliberately destroyed, the monuments that have undergone destruction represent a rather small percentage. The deliberate destruction of monuments might involve small-scale events which happen on rare occasions, but the impact on the society is extremely high. This impact can be perceived as either positive or negative, or both simultaneously by different groups of people. Destruction can be perceived as an act of intended hurt, insult, a demonstration of power, or indeed as freedom. Freedom from prior restrictions. Freedom from old and meaningless traditions. And freedom from unwanted knowledge and memory. Freedom is a desideratum people have been pursuing for aeons.

For ancient monuments it is difficult to say if the act and result of deliberate destruction were perceived as positive or negative by the contemporary society. There are so many different levels of destruction, ranging from the deliberate alteration and deposition of small objects, which is a very old idea (e. g. in Bronze

Age societies[8]) to the eventful demolition of oversized monuments. An important aspect of analyzing the destruction of monuments is time. If the alteration and destruction of a monument requires a considerable amount of time, which was apparently unnecessary if the end goal was the simple erasure of the monument, then it appears that the event itself had special meaning. In this case not only the erasure itself but also the process mattered. But again, it is difficult to say if this process and its result were perceived as good or bad by the group of people affected.

From the case studies about iconoclasm it has become evident that the meaning of a monument is subject to change, and that differences in perceptions are often (part of) the reason for its destruction. Architectural destruction and iconoclastic events are often preceded by a long period of conflict. Figurative works are mutilated or destroyed to show disagreement and strength, and to give meaning to acts of violence. The destruction of a monument can be caused by a transitional change, or it can be a symbolic act demonstrating power or emphasizing conflict. With the destruction of monuments not only the building or object itself is being annihilated, but also the connection of people with the monument and their meaning respectively. Attacking and erasing monumental architecture equally attacks (and tries to erase) human culture, history, and being. It further attacks the ideologies of a society, trying to crush their mentality, forcing a *tabula rasa*. The reasoning behind iconoclastic acts is often similar to the destruction of architecture, but incorporates a highly symbolic element. Figurative works can be seen as an embodiment of the conflict. Their destruction is therefore a symbol of change; a way to show disagreement with a society's MonuMentality.

Bibliography

Banchelli, E. (2008): "Ostalgie: eine vorläufige Bilanz." In: F. Cambi (ed.), Gedächtnis und Identität. Die deutsche Literatur der Wiedervereinigung, Würzburg: Königshausen & Neumann, pp. 57–68.

Benson, E. P. (1981): The Olmec and their Neighbors: Essays in Memory of Matthew W. Stirling, Washington D. C: Dumbarton Oaks, Trustees for Harvard University.

Bernal, I. (1969): The Olmec world, Berkeley: University of California Press.

Bevan, R. (2016): The Destruction of Memory: Architecture at War, Glasgow: Reaktion Books Ltd.

Brandt, G. (1720): The History of the Reformation and Other Ecclesiastical Transactions in and about the Low-Countries, 4 vols., London: Timothy Childe.

---

8 See Economies of Destruction.

Cambi, F. (2018): Gedächtnis und Identität. Die deutsche Literatur der Wiedervereinigung, Würzburg: Königshausen & Neumann.

Coe, M. D. (1968): America's First Civilization, New York: American Heritage Publishing Co., Inc.

Cools, H. (2011): "De Beeldenstorm in de Lage Landen." In: https://dutchrevolt. leiden.edu/dutch/begrippen/Pages/beeldenstorm.aspx (last accessed April 10, 2019).

Diehl, R. A. (2004): The Olmecs: America's First Civilization, London: Thames and Hudson Ltd.

Fisher, H. J. (2017): Violence Against Architecture: The Lost Cultural Heritage of Syria and Iraq, MA thesis, New York, NY: The City University of New York.

Flannery, K. V./Marcus, J. (2000): "Formative Mexican Chiefdoms and the Myth of the Mother-culture." In: Journal of Anthropological Archaeology 19, pp. 1–37.

Göttke, F. (2010): Toppled: A Book, Rotterdam: Post Editions.

Grove, D. C. (1981): "Olmec Monuments: Mutilation as a Clue to Meaning." In: E. P. Benson (ed.), The Olmec and their Neighbors: Essays in Memory of Matthew W. Stirling, Washington D. C.: Dumbarton Oaks, Trustees for Harvard University, pp. 49–68.

Harding, T. (2001): "Taliban blow apart 2000 years of Buddhist history." In: The Guardian, March 3, https://www.theguardian.com/world/2001/mar/03/afghan istan.lukeharding (last accessed April 10, 2019).

Hood, B. M. (2010): The Science of Superstition: How the Developing Brain Creates Supernatural Beliefs, New York: Harper Collins.

Joyce, R. A./Henderson, J. S. (2010): "Being 'Olmec' in early Formative period Honduras." In: Ancient Mesoamerica 21, pp. 187–200.

Land Use Consultant (1998): "Orkney landscape character assessment." In: Scottish National Heritage Review No. 100, https://www.nature.scot/snh-review-100-orkney-landscape-character-assessment (last accessed April 12, 2019).

Petegree, A. (1992): Emden and the Dutch revolt: exile and the development of reformed Protestantism, Oxford: Oxford University Press.

Pool, C. A. (2007): Olmec Archaeology and Early Mesoamerica, Cambridge: Cambridge University Press.

Reich, A./Perdoni, S./Plaga, C. (2015): "Kopf hoch, Lenin!" In: https://berlinerver lag.atavist.com/lenin (last accessed April 10, 2019).

Toubekis, G./Mayer, I./Döring-Williams, M./Maeda, K./Yamauchi, K./Taniguchi, Y./Morimoto, S./Petzet, M./Jarkef, M./Jansen, M. (2009): "Preservation and Management of the UNESCO World Heritage Site of Bamiyan: Laser Scan Documentation and Virtual Reconstruction of the Destroyed Buddha Figures and the Archaeological Remains." In: 22nd CIPA Symposium, Kyoto, Japan, pp. 185–192.

Toubekis, G./Jansen, M./Jarke, M. (2017): "Long-Term Preservation of the Physical Remains of the Destroyed Buddha Figures in Bamiyan (Afghanistan) Using

Virtual Reality Technologies for Preparation and Evaluation of Restoration Measures." In: ISPRS Annals of the Photogrammetry, Remote Sensing and Spatial Information Sciences 4/2, pp. 271–278.

Veyne, P. (2017): Palmyra: An Irreplaceable Treasure, Chicago: The University of Chicago Press.

Other Sources

https://en.oxforddictionaries.com/definition/iconoclasm (last accessed April 7, 2018)

https://economiesofdestruction.wordpress.com (last accessed April 10, 2018)

"The Ness of Brodgar, Uncovering Orkney's Neolithic heart." In: Current Archaeology 335, pp. 20–28, https://www.archaeology.co.uk/articles/the-ness-of-brodgar.htm (last accessed January 4, 2019).

The operation of monumentality in low occupation-density settlements in prehistory: a regional scale view

Kirrily White & Rachel Lane

Introduction

Monuments are multi-functional, operate on multiple scales, and can be envisaged in general and abstract terms, as well as in particular terms. The prevalence of monument construction globally and over deep time indicates that it represents a successful human behavior. However, it is difficult to compare monuments on a global scale given the extraordinary diversity of construction contexts, cultures, and material outcomes in the archaeological record. One way to address the issue of comparison is to contextualize the analysis of monuments within a broader settlement and landscape approach. Such a framework, however, requires a reappraisal of the implicit philosophical understanding of monuments as 'ontologically isolated' which is arguably a limiting factor in the creation of a viable theoretical framework. The 'ontological turn' is a recent trend in the philosophy and theory of archaeology, offering a critical reflection on the materiality of objects (Caraher 2016: 326). Instead of an isolationist view, the role of monuments can be conceptualized within landscapes as stabilizing operators carrying slow-changing spatial messages across broad temporal and areal scales. An expanded view provides the opportunity to observe monuments as active components of regional order and large group formation. They appear to have been an important structuring principle of very large, low-density settlement in prehistory where we would expect dispersed occupation patterns to be a significant challenge to group coherence.

In his work on *The Limits of Settlement Growth*, Fletcher (1995) identified three trajectories of human settlement behavior from high to very low occupation density at different population scales over time. The low-occupation-density settlement outcomes of the first trajectory to areal extents beyond 100 ha are the subject of current research and more than 190 examples have been identified across the world (White n.d.). Of these sites, more than 75 per cent have monumental structures. While their local conditions of development were diverse, these settlements typically appeared in regions with stable long-term settlement building traditions including traditions of building monuments and well-established regional and supra-regional interaction networks. In most regions, there are multiple contemporaneous examples and many smaller examples with the same morphology. This suggests that their emergence might be usefully considered in terms of regional rather than local operational parameters. The issue of monumentality and the extensive deployment of monument building across regions which produced these settlements highlights the importance of considering other types of regional cohesion than centrality. In the context of these settlements, monuments operated not only as focal components of place, but expanders of relational space and stabilizers of regional populations.

An operational view of monuments – theoretical context

Monuments are a long-term staple of archaeological studies (Osborne 2017: 163). Over time, archaeological approaches to studying monuments have raised several high-stakes epistemological issues. One of the greatest concerns has been to formulate a coherent framework within which to analyze monuments and monumentality in the past. Osborne (2014: 3) would ultimately like to see a unifying cross-disciplinary discourse for monumentality, but there are strong challenges to be overcome in the diversity of approaches and myriad of definitions. In the late 1980s, Bradley and Chambers (1988: 271) claimed that the study of monuments had been largely particularist and that "there has been less willingness to generalize about the nature of monuments and the monumental". If a general theory is not viable due to epistemological and definitional issues, it might be possible to address the problematic binary of particularist/generalist through the behaviors of monuments at regional and settlement scales of operation within the context of these large, low-occupation-density settlements. This view does not preclude other questions about monuments at different scales of analysis, but it proposes that the operation of monuments as objects can be decoupled from culturally specific meanings for comparative purposes. This broader operational view is contingent upon shifts in the ontological understanding of monuments.

In Aristotelian metaphysics, ontology refers to the study of the substances or essences of physical entities or being. More than forty years ago, David Clarke envisaged that archaeology in the future would enter into an era critical of self-consciousness by means of metaphysical study, suggesting that "[a]rchaeological metaphysics is the study and evaluation of the most general categories and concepts within which archaeologists think; a task long overdue" (Clarke 1973: 12). Clarke was prophetic in this sense, as ontology is perhaps the latest buzzword in archaeology, made explicit and popularized by Olsen (2010) in his work *In Defense of Things: Archaeology and the Ontology of Objects*. Olsen (2010) reconfigures material 'things' as important in their own right and not merely as epiphenomena of the social world. Ontological studies concerning the human individual in the past had already been taken up in the overtly humanistic phase of archaeological theory in the late 1980s (eg. Hodder 1992; Shanks/Tilley 1987). Postprocessual theorists critiqued the understanding of humans in the past as rational, universal, and autonomous (Silliman 2001: 192), ultimately attempting to de-essentialize the human category. In the context of this paper, the nature of monuments requires reorientation whereby the category is not viewed as fixed or universally understood. It is possible to have a definition of monument that is de-essentialized, meaning it is applicable to a broader scale and more generalized view without allegiance to the universal properties of monuments such as 'size'.

The term 'monument' normally implies qualities of massive size and longevity due to the frequent use of highly durable materials in construction. While acknowledging that monumentality as a quality is not predicated on specific types of materials, in terms of research, the archaeological record has a historical bias towards features which are materially substantial, evocative, and awesome. As monuments are typically anomalous or exceptional in their mediums and contexts, this has meant such features have had a strong influence on theorizing about the social world. There is a broad assumption that size and saliency correlates to complex social mechanisms within which labor and supporting resources could be organized. The idea that there is an indexical relationship between monument size and social complexity stems back to Renfrew's (1973) work on Neolithic Wessex (Thomas 1999: 34). It can be argued, however, that treating the material as an epiphenomenon of the social world by drawing causal connections between 'elite' power, labor, and monument building has contributed to the subordination of materiality to social concerns in archaeology and produced knowledge about the past that is regionally particularist and difficult to use in cross comparison. This epistemological problem in archaeology partially accounts for Bradley and Chambers (1988: 271) claim of the lack of willingness to generalize about monuments in the discipline.

The particularist view of monuments in archaeology is arguably part of a wider set of modern cultural perceptions of the past whereby the disjunction of implied past grandeur and accomplishment of monuments and present degraded materiality is the subject of a romanticized and somewhat nostalgic view. This is also a reminder that monuments continue to have meaning into the present because of their materiality. On Salisbury Plain in southern England, the author of *Tess of the D'Urbervilles*, Thomas Hardy (1891: 501–504), creates of Stonehenge a "monstrous place". Hardy's phenomenological treatment of monument, allowing his characters to encounter it as an unknown presence in the dark, reminds us that the material bulk of monuments has meaning even though non-verbal. The image of

Figure 1: Global distribution of large, low-occupation-density settlements with monumentality

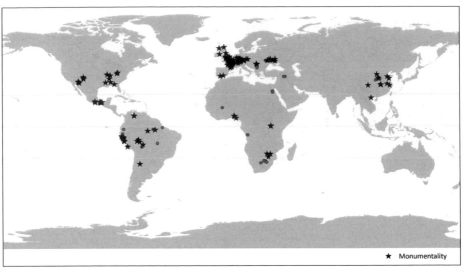

the monument as a fixed and isolated presence in the landscape is important intuitively because it resonates with our sense of connection with the past and past experience. The experiential and perceptual domains of interaction with monuments are of course important subjects for analysis at different temporal scales but these types of concerns are situationally unique, and it is difficult to form from them a generalist view.

As a mechanism for expanding an analytic view beyond ontological isolation, monuments are reconsidered here as non-verbal regulators of interaction on multiple scales. Within this view and in the specific context of the low-density sites examined in this paper, a monument can be defined as a highly salient material entity with a slow rate of change, signaling a temporally specific, culturally agreed-upon value which, given its specific magnitude and location, can constrain behavior on multiple spatial scales. Defining monument as signal acknowledges that, given slow rates of change in durable materials, and while the verbal meanings of monuments are context specific, the endurance of monuments as physical forms in the landscape perpetrates a non-verbal message. This material behavior impacts the formation, maintenance and endurance of interaction and occupation patterns in a region over long periods of time (Fletcher 1995: 31) even as the active landscape system within which the monument was constructed collapses. In a profound way, monument construction can be allied to the kinds of regional stability which allowed large population aggregates to form coherent and viable settlements with dispersed occupation patterns in prehistory.

Monumentality in large, low-occupation-density settlements

Low-occupation-density settlements of less than or equal to around ten people per hectare on average and more than 100 ha in areal extent (see Fletcher 1995 for the theoretical basis of the threshold density) began to appear from as early as 5000 BCE in southeast Europe. One of the earliest forms was possibly the Vinča culture site of Belovode in eastern Serbia (Radivojević et al 2010). They appeared periodically across the world into the early 19th century CE in southern Africa with late examples in the largest stone-built Tswana settlements such as Molokwane in North West Province, South Africa (Steyn 2011; Morton 2013) (Figure 1). The significance of these settlements is that they were able to be sustained without the enormous amount and diversity of material and technological infrastructure usually associated with compact settlements of a similar areal extent (Fletcher 1995: 134–151). Moreover, compact settlements and small low-density settlements can be expected to scale in areal extent in predictable ways with population growth (Ortman et al. 2014), but these very large settlements formed and grew in diverse ways, not always by increasing population at their margins and not by uniformly densifying. Their formation and development processes were locally unique but, as Moore (2012: 413) suggests for the polyfocal complexes of the British Iron Age, they were typically integrated into broader regional economic and social systems and formed focal points for regional interaction. With two exceptions, all the settlements over 1000 ha in areal extent operated with monument construction (Figure 2). Moreover, while individual settlement durations and sizes could vary according to local conditions, across most regions this was a stable recurring settlement form. In Neolithic China, Iron Age Europe, the Amazon basin, and the western desert of the USA amongst other regions, the form only collapsed with region-scale catastrophic change. This would suggest that the stability of large, low-occupation-density settlement forms was intricately linked to operational stability on a regional scale, enacted in common regional traditions of which monument building was an important component.

Figure 2: Percent distribution of monumental elements across three size classes of low-density settlement

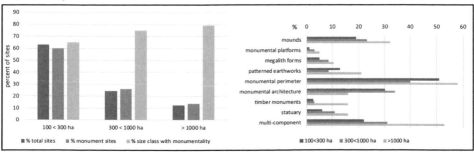

Types of monument

The types of monument and monumental construction and the spatial config-uration of monuments in these settlements were varied and culturally specific. Burial mounds and mounds which included burials as incidental to their pri-mary construction were common to most regions and integrated in settlements in various ways. At some of these settlements such as at the Alamito culture Campo del Pucará in Catamarca, northwest Argentina (ca. 200–500 CE), houses were grouped in replicated units with a mound and plaza configuration and platforms associated with stone heads and figures (Nunez Regueiro 1970: 137) (Figure 3). In other regions, such as at the linear Camutins mound complex on Marajó Island in the mouth of the Amazon, large ceremonial or 'elite' mounds were clustered at the southern and northern ends of the site with habitation mounds predominantly clustered around the centre (Schaan 2004: 157–158). House monuments, architectural monuments, or great houses appeared first perhaps in the Trypillia culture of the Chalcolithic forest steppe zone in east-ern Europe in ca. 3900 BCE with the mega-structures at Nebelivka (Chapman et al. 2014) and in the 3rd millennium BCE at sites such as Taosi in Neolithic China (He 2004; 2009). The first associations between these very large settle-ments and monumental architectural complexes appeared in the Norte Chico region of Peru, also in the 3rd millennium BCE (Figure 4). In southwest USA great houses appeared in the Ancestral Puebloan, Hohokam, and Mogollon cultures in ca. 900–1400 CE, and in southern Africa a version of enclosure households developed to monumental proportions at sites such as Mapungubwe and Great Zimbabwe in the 13th century CE (Manyanga/Pikirayi/Chirikure 2010: 577). Geo-metric enclosure monuments like Atlantic European Neolithic henges were also common to other cultures such as the geometric earthworks builders in Acre state, Brazil and in the Bolivian *Llanos de Moxos*. Stone statuary and other forms of megalithic monument were features of many time periods and regions including Neolithic, Bronze Age, and Iron Age Europe and the Olmec sites in Mesoamerica. Monumental-scale perimeter and areal features such as walls and ditches in earth and stone appeared in Europe, Africa, and Asia across multiple time periods and cultures.

Figure 3: Supra-household scale monument and house clusters, Campo del Pucará (5 m contour lines generated from ASTER GDEM VOO2, NASA LP DAAC, 2015; house cluster after Nunez Regueiro [1970: Figure 2]; site plan after Gianfrancisco and Fernández [2016: 26])

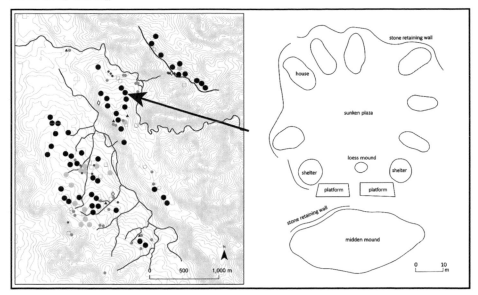

Monument building traditions

The tradition of constructing monuments typically preceded the formation of a large settlement, sometimes by more than a thousand years. The Mississippian culture site of Cahokia (ca. 1050–1350 CE), for example, was a more than 1200 ha agglomeration of mounds and plazas in a tradition of mound clustering and potential settlement formation that dated back to 3900–3300 BCE at sites like Watson Brake in the Lower Mississippi region (Morgan 1999: 35) (Figure 5). Cahokia was embedded in a landscape of broadly contemporaneous multiple and single mound sites extending across the central Mississippian and lower Ohio river valleys into the mid-south, with related cultures and trade connections extending further still. Locally, the site was connected by a road to a contemporaneous mound and shrine complex, the 'Emerald Acropolis' around 24 km to the east (Pauketat/Alt/Kruchten 2017: 207) and the Pulcher region mound sites around 25 km to the south (Kelly 2002: 136). In the middle Huanghe region of Neolithic China, the 280 ha Longshan culture site of Taosi (ca. 2300–1900 BCE) with its rammed earth enclosure walls, platforms and monumental ritual building (He 2004) was constructed in a building tradition which dated back to the Late Pengtoushan settlement of Bashidang (ca. 5540–5100 BCE) (Yang 2004: 43). It was one of at least four contemporaneous walled sites of over 100 ha in the local region of the Linfen and Yuncheng river basins (He 2013: 257–259). Preceding and contemporaneous with the development of Taosi, rammed earth settlement walling and platform construction also reached monumental proportions at large and small settlements in the upper, middle, and lower Yangzi river regions. The territorial site of Liangzhu (5000 ha, ca. 2600–2200 BCE) in the Yangzi delta featured a rammed earth platform (Moji-aoshan) which covered around 30 ha and an enclosure wall around 7 km long and 40–60 m wide at the base (Qin 2013: 589). In the middle Yangzi river valley, the settlement complex of Shijiahe (800 ha, ca. 2600–2100 BCE) had a walled area with a surrounding moat 4.8 km long and 80–100 m wide. This site was the largest of around 17 walled and moated sites in close proximity on the Jianghan-Dongting plain (Zhang 2013: 511).

Figure 4: Caral, Norte Chico region, Peru. Monumental building sectors C and E (Image: Google Earth, DigitalGlobe 2018)

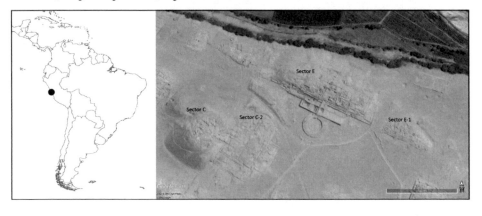

Figure 5: (a.) The territorial sites of Liangzhu and (b.) Cahokia at the same scale as (c.) the bounded site of Taosi (5 m contour lines generated from ALOS PALSAR RTC high res DEM; Liangzhu after Liu and Chen [2012: Figure 7.12.]; Cahokia after Fowler [1989: Figure 2.7]; Taosi after Liu [2004: Figure 4.19])

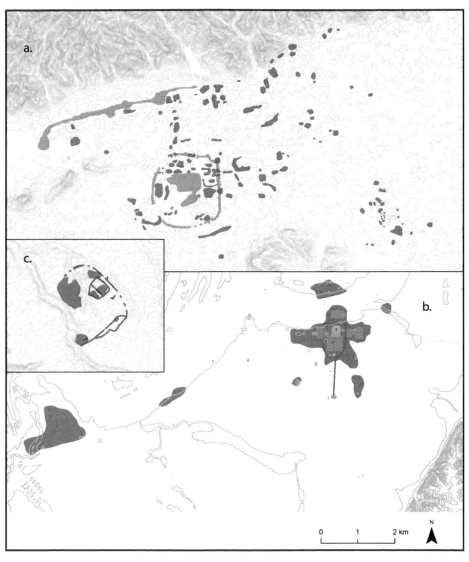

Monumentality of perimeter infrastructure

The extraordinary size of perimeter infrastructure in enclosed forms of low-occupation-density settlement presents the possibility that these settlements themselves, taking a broader scale view, could also be regarded as monuments. They
were typically highly salient, materially permanent, large in scale, and required
a significant investment of resources and labor for construction and maintenance (cf. Brunke et al. 2016: 255). Moreover, with one exception, the site of Co Loa
(Dongson culture ca. 300 BCE-100 CE) in northern Vietnam, they did not occur
in isolation within their regions, but were embedded in extensive regional and
supra-regional networks of interaction. In Europe, the enclosure of settlements,
particularly in elevated positions like hilltops, appeared at intervals from the
Neolithic period onwards (Fernández-Götz 2014: 386). However, the behavior of
enclosing and monumentalizing even very large settlements such as the extraordinary Corneşti-Iarcuri (1780 ha ca. 1400–1000 BCE) in the Banat region of modern
Romania appears to date from the middle Bronze Age (Heeb et al. 2017). During
the Iron Age, this type of settlement construction proliferated with the Scythian
gorodishche to the east (ca. 700–300 BCE) and the Hallstatt (ca. 600–300 BCE)
Fuerstensitz in the centre and west. By the late La Tène period (ca. 200 BCE-30 CE),
construction of oppida as a monumental settlement form (Fernández-Götz 2014)
was a frequent behavior across central and western Europe. While acknowledging that the local socio-economic and political functions of these settlements and
their internal materiality was diverse (Woolf 1993; Moore 2017), the formation processes of many of these enclosed settlements suggest that the significant non-verbal component of their regional operation was monumentality. Many of the largest, such as the oppidum of Heidengraben bei Grabenstetten (1660 ha) in southern
Germany or the Scythian gorodishche of Belsk (4020 ha) were plateau enclosures
with extensive amounts of open space. For the European oppida in particular, this
close relationship between site position, topography, and enclosed extent was an
integral characteristic of their morphology at all sizes (Fichtl/Pierrevelcin 2012:
17). Their distribution across central and western Europe typically followed major
rivers (Figure 6). Punctuating these river highways, they were highly circumscrib-
ing of approach and egress behaviors. The effect of enclosure and saliency of these
settlements as monuments was to potentially change the pace of movement and
order interaction, regardless of other verbalized meaning, on a regional scale, and
this ordering principle was replicated settlement by settlement across vast territories.

Figure 6: Linear cluster distribution patterns of Iron Age European oppida (Hot spot, Getis-Ord GI* analysis for clustering conducted in ArcGIS 10.5; rivers from Andreadis et al. [2013])

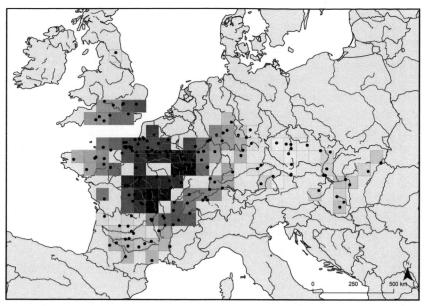

Extending monumentality across regions

By extension, in some regions, such as the Iron Age Scythian territories in Eastern Europe, or across the European Atlantic Neolithic, multiple types and scales of regional monument construction were not only componential to settlement development but extended across larger areas of landscape. Scythian kurgan (mound) burials dated to between around 800 and 300 BCE are an enduring feature from the eastern Eurasian steppe to the Danube river (van Geel et al. 2004). These monuments are frequently distributed in linear patterns along watersheds and ridges (Sulimirski et al. 1992: 550), but in a similar spatial pattern to the Hallstatt Fuerstensitz, they were also concentrated around Gorodishche in vast cemeteries. At the settlement of Belsk between the Suchaja-Grunt and Vorskla rivers in modern Ukraine, cemeteries of kurgans extended the monumental walled settlement which was already around 4020 ha out to around 8000 ha of occupied territory. These integrated regional monument and settlement systems were also a feature of Atlantic European Neolithic and early Bronze Age complexes such as at Brodgar/Stenness on Mainland Island, Orkney, greater Stonehenge in southern Britain and Brú na Bóinne in County Meath, Ireland. In the British Iron Age, under different political and economic conditions, territorial oppida such as Camulodunum (2000 ha) segregated large expanses of agricultural land and habitation by the construction of many kilometers of linear ramparts and ditches across landscape on a monumental scale (Hawkes/Crummy 1995).

This pattern of nesting extensive zones of occupation into landscapes of monuments is also a feature of regions in the tropical world. Operating within continuously modified landscapes, these settlement forms challenge our notions of what constitute settlement boundaries. An extreme example is that of the landscapes of the Llanos de Moxos in Bolivia where mounds, anthropogenic forest islands, and raised field complexes are connected to each other through canals and pathways constituting a richly networked fabric of which monumentality is a significant part (Lombardo/Prümers 2010: 1883). A similar pattern of landscape integration including monument is a feature of the Barinas region of the Venezuelan llanos with extensively integrated mound sites including the causewayed enclosure settlement of El Cedral (E33) at around 150 ha (Redmond/Spencer 2007) embedded in a network of causeways extending over roughly 448 km^2 (Redmond/Gassón/Spencer 1999: 121–122). These integrated landscape-scale operations are also evident at the Hertenrits Mound complex in coastal French Guiana where mounds and their associated raised field and aquaculture complexes are also connected over a hierarchical system of pathways and canals extending out over many kilometers (Rostain 2008: 288–289). In eastern Acre state, Brazil, in southwestern Amazonia, clusters of geometric earthwork enclosures often connected by roadways have been revealed by forest clearance over a region of some 47,000 km^2 between the Acre and Abunã rivers (Figure 7). The construction and use of these earthworks appears to have continued over a long period of time between around 1000 BCE to 1400 CE (Saunaluoma/Schaan 2012: 1). These earthworks do not enclose material evidence of occupation but there are possible habitation mounds and raised field systems in association, suggesting that they were elements of settlement, although the contemporaneity of these features is yet to be understood (Saunaluoma 2012: 575).

These types of landscape-scale, connective features in tropical zones are distinctly related to water management and access (Erickson 2008: 172–173) but there are examples of unbounded patterns of continuous distribution of features on a monumental scale in other types of environments. Late Archaic occupation patterns in the Supe Valley in the coastal desert zones of western Peru, during the late Archaic period (ca. 3000–1800 BCE) suggest that this valley may be considered a single settlement with continuous agricultural zones on the narrow strips either side of the river and dispersed zones of habitation and monuments on the terraces above. A large concentration of architectural mounds, plazas, and aggregated domiciles at the site of Caral towards the eastern extent of occupation indicates that this area was a focal point for the settlement (Shady 2006: 64), but the distribution of sites down the valley towards the ocean can be compared to the spatial

Figure 7: Distribution of geometric monuments in Acre State, Brazil (Location data from Jacobs [2017] with configurations potentially indicating settlement sites greater than 100 ha, identified through near neighbor analysis [Near neighbor and kernel density analyses conducted using ArcGIS 10.5.])

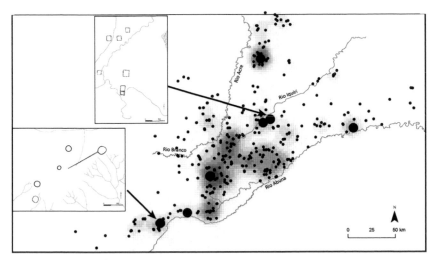

pattern of monumental great houses at the settlement of Chaco Canyon (ca. 850–1150 CE) in southwest USA. Furthermore, the distribution of contemporaneous occupation and monument building in the wider adjacent valleys of Fortaleza and Pativilca shows a far more dispersed pattern as well as several low-density-occupation settlements extending over more than 100 ha in themselves (Creamer et al. 2013; Creamer/Ruiz/Haas 2007).

On the Isle of Lewis in the Western Hebrides of Scotland (Figure 8), Late Neolithic (ca. 3000–2500 BCE) stone circle building on ridges overlooking east-west valleys across the island may be related to routeways from the east coast to the major monument complex of Callanish on Loch Roag (Richards/Challands/Welham 2013). Two potential overland and two Atlantic routeways into the complex have been identified by fieldwork and it would appear that the circles were placed for maximum visibility from the valley floors (Richards et al. 2013).

The Callanish monument group is comprised of nine separate stone circles and the unusual cruciform shaped monument at Callanish I with a small chambered tomb dated to slightly later (Armit 1996: 83). To the north of the site, a distribution of stone circles in elevated positions less than 3 km from the Atlantic coast supports other evidence of extensive interaction networks along the Atlantic façade dating from the Early Neolithic (ca. 4000/3700 BCE) (Cummings 2017: 40, 160) and particularly an "island centered geography" focused on sea travel proposed by Armit (1996: 6–7).

Figure 8: Distribution of stone circles and chambered cairns across Scotland and on the Island of Lewis. The circle indicates a 10 km radius around the site of Callanish I. (Data from Historic Environment Scotland, 2018).

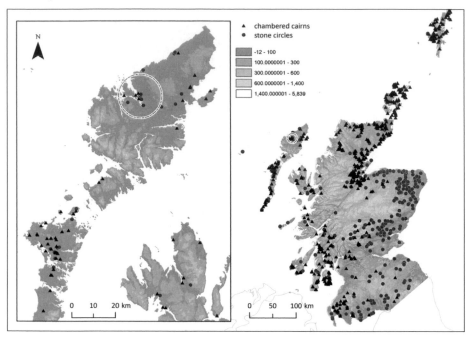

Overview of monument operation

From a non-particularist perspective the material forms of monument- and landscape-scale features in these regions had low morphological diversity. There were, of course, local variations, but the large, low-density settlements formed within long trajectories of settlement building traditions and material cultures which had had time to locally diversify but remained strongly interconnected. As slow changing components of these landscapes, monuments appear to have been highly successful as faciliatory mechanisms for repeated region-scale interaction, creating and maintaining highly stable locational systems within which large groups had time and space to form. Local diversity in material outcomes was bounded by a regionally shared set of architectural and spatial values (Armit 1996). These types of non-verbal messages encoded in monumental-scale building operated over longer periods of time than local change (Bradley 1993: 91). The replication of this non-verbal component of a signal perhaps could be characterized as some form of "normative pressure" (DiMaggio/Powell 1983: 152) in the language of institutional isomorphism, acknowledging a shared cognitive base for the iteration of specific spatial and material patterns in generationally perpetuated skill sets. Clark Erickson (2008: 161), working with communities in the Andes and Amazon, expressed this stability in an experiential way, noting that people in these areas spent more time out in the landscape than in their domestic zones and that these investments in 'landscape capital' forged strong intergenerational systems of material and knowledge which ordered the interactions and behaviors of populations over long periods of time.

As an operational characteristic of settlement and regions, this kind of isomorphism does not require or indicate any particular form of economic or social structure. Shared spatial and material principles are essentially carried with verbal messaging of any type because they represent a "basal grammar" (Fletcher 1995: 31) for behavior. While many of these settlements had agrarian economic bases, for example, there are sites such as Poverty Point in the Mississippi delta dating to the Late Archaic period (ca. 1600–1250/900 BCE) which were associated with a hunting-gathering economic system and high population mobility (Kidder 2011: 118). The required energetic input for the rapid construction of the largest of the mounds, Mound A, with a total volume of around 238,500 m³ of earth (Kidder et al. 2009: 116), is comparable to almost any of the more sedentary agrarian sites. In other parts of the world, such as Late Neolithic China, monumental architecture is associated with 'elite' residence and burial, but not exclusively. There is no evidence that the organization of labor at these sites was coercive. Rather, the construction of platform and rampart structures were the outcomes of locally patterned behaviors which continued, in the case of Taosi, with the abandonment and destruction of the 'elite' residence forms (He 2013: 269–270). Some of the most striking examples of monumental architecture in this set of sites are the stone-built enclosures at Great Zimbabwe. The energetic requirements for constructing the hill complex were potentially between 32,400 and more than 200,000 person hours, depending on how granite blocks from quarries up to 4.8 km away (Hall 1905) were transported to the site. The bulk of this expenditure, however, was distributed over around 100 years in additions and modifications between 1200 and 1310 CE (Chipunza 1994). With very low permanent populations (Chirikure et al. 2017), this mode of construction does not imply complex mechanisms for organizing labor, but ongoing expressions of a basal grammar for settlement construction over hundreds of years.

Monumental structures and iterative construction elements have the potential to foster material and spatial coherence at multiple scales, ordering settlement and cultural territories across vast landscape. This is not to say that each monument construction was not a unique process with its own meaning, but that the cumulative effect of these large-scale constructions was the creation of landscapes and settlements with predictable constraints on behavior which were perpetuated over hundreds of years. While the formation processes of monuments were varied from single events to palimpsests of addition and modification over time, the effect of repeated interaction with them was to stabilize specific places in landscape and by visibility or memory of visibility, to interconnect these stabilization points. The issue of monumental perimeter walling is somewhat different. In many cases, the enclosing of a settlement with monumental walling effectively monumentalized the settlement itself within the landscape. These distributions of monuments across broader landscapes suggest that some regional mobility was a frequent condition of these settlements. Moving beyond the understanding of monuments as ontologically isolated and epiphenomena of the social world, the problematic binary of particularist/generalist can be addressed by observing monuments in operational terms.

Acknowledgements

We would like to thank the Excellence Cluster Topoi (B-2) XXL for the opportunity to participate in the discussion forum "Size Matters". Our especial thanks to Eva Cancik-Kirschbaum and Felix Levenson. Thanks also to the Carlyle Greenwell bequest, the Postgraduate Award scheme of the Australian Federal Government and the University of Sydney for providing facilities and support for research. Finally, thanks to Professor Roland Fletcher for his generous help and advice, and Dr Rosemary Whitecross, Dr Bernhard Heeb, Dr Natalie Blake and Mr Ben Dharmendra for suggestions, friendship and great discussions on this work.

Bibliography

Andreadis, K./Schumann, G./Pavelsky, T. (2013): "A Simple Global River Bankfull Width & Depth Database", http://gaia.geosci.unc.edu/rivers/ (last accessed January 3, 2016).

Armit, I. (1996): The Archaeology of Skye and the Western Isles, Edinburgh: Edinburgh University Press.

Bradley, R. (1993): Altering the Earth. The Origins of Monuments in Britain and Continental Europe, Monographs of the Society of Antiquaries of Scotland, Edinburgh: Society of Antiquaries of Scotland.

Bradley, R./Chambers, R. (1988): "A new study of the cursus complex at Dorchester on Thames." In: Oxford Journal of Archaeology 7/3, pp. 271–289.

Brunke, H./Bukowiecki, E./Cancik-Kirschbaum, E./Eichmann, R./van Ess, M./ Gass, A./Gussone, M./Hageneuer, S./Hansen, S./Kogge, W./May, J./Parzinger, H./Pedersén, O./Sack, D./Schopper, F./Wulf-Rheidt, U./Ziemssen, H. (2016): "Thinking Big. Research in Monumental Constructions in Antiquity." In: G.

Graßhoff/M. Meyer (eds.), Space and Knowledge. Topoi Research Group Articles, eTopoi. Journal for Ancient Studies, Special Volume 6, Berlin: Edition Topoi, pp. 250–305.

Caraher, W. (2016): "Ontology, World Archaeology, and the Recent Past." In: American Journal of Archaeology 120/2, pp. 325–331.

Chapman, J./Videiko, M. Y./Gaydarska, B./Burdo, N./Hale, D. (2014): "Architectural differentiation on a Trypillia mega-site: preliminary report on the excavation of a mega-structure at Nebelivka, Ukraine." In: Journal of Neolithic Archaeology 4, pp. 135–157.

Chipunza, K. T. (1994): A diachronic analysis of the architecture of the Hill Complex at Great Zimbabwe, Uppsala: Societas Archaeologica Upsaliensis.

Chirikure, S./Moultrie, T./Bandama, F./Dandara, C./Manyanga, M. (2017): "What was the population of Great Zimbabwe (CE 1000–1800)?" In: PLoS One doi:10.1371/journal.pone.0178335.

Clarke, D. L. (1973): "Archaeology: the loss of innocence." In: Antiquity 47/185, pp. 6–18.

Creamer, W./Rubio, A. R./Perales Munguia, M. F./Haas, J. (2013): "The Fortaleza Valley, Peru: archaeological investigation of Late Archaic sites (3000–1800 BC)." In: Fieldiana Anthropology N. S. 44, pp. 1–108.

Creamer, W./Ruiz, A./Haas, J. (2007): "Archaeological investigation of Late Archaic sites (3000–1800 B. C.) in the Pativilca Valley, Peru." In: Fieldiana Anthropology N. S. 40, pp. 1–79.

Cummings, V. (2017): The Neolithic of Britain and Ireland, London; New York: Routledge.

DiMaggio, P. J./Powell, W. W. (1983): "The Iron Cage Revisited: Institutional Isomorphism and Collective Rationality in Organizational Fields." In: American Sociological Review 48/2, pp. 147–160.

Erickson, C. L. (2008): "Amazonia: The historical ecology of a domesticated landscape." In: H. Silverman/W. Isbell (eds.), The Handbook of South American Archaeology, Berlin: Springer Science + Business Media, LL, pp. 157–183.

Fernández-Götz, M. (2014): "Reassessing the Oppida: The Role of Power and Religion." In: Oxford Journal of Archaeology 33/4, pp. 379–394.

Fichtl, S./Pierrevelcin, G. (2012): Les Premières Villes de Gaule: Le temps des oppida celtiques, Lacapelle-Marival: Editions Archéologie Nouvelle.

Fletcher, R. (1995): The Limits of Settlement Growth: A Theoretical Outline, Cambridge: Cambridge University Press.

Hall, R. N. (1905): "Ancient Architecture at Great Zimbabwe (Rhodesia)." In: The British Architect 63/15, pp. 265–267.

Hardy, T. (1891): Tess of the D'Urbervilles, London: Macmillan.

Hawkes, C. F. C./Crummy, P. (1995): Colchester Archaeological Report 11: Camulodunum 2. Colchester: Colchester Archaeological Trust Ltd.

He, N. (2004): "Monumental Structure from Ceremonial Precinct at Taosi Walled-town in 2003 (Summary of original report from Kaogu 考古 2004, 7, 9-24 by Shanxi Fieldwork Team of the Institute of Archaeology, Chinese Academy of Social Sciences, Shanxi Provincial Institute of Archaeology and Linfen Municipal Administrative Bureau of Cultural Relics)." In: Chinese Archaeology 5, pp. 51–58.

He, N. (2009): "Large-sized Rammed-earth Building Foundations of the Middle Taosi Culture Discovered on the Taosi City-site in Xiangfen County, Shanxi (summary from original report in考古2008, 3: 3-6 by He, N., Gao, J. & Wang, X.)." In: Chinese Archaeology 9, pp. 86–89.

He, N. (2013): "The Longshan period site of Taosi in southern Shanxi province." In: A. P. Underhill (ed.), A Companion to Chinese Archaeology, Chichester: Blackwell Publishing Ltd, pp. 255–277.

Heeb, B. S./Szentmiklosi, A./Bǎlǎrie, A./Lehmpuhl, R./Krause, R. (2017): "Corneşti-Iarcuri – 10 years of research (2007–2016). Some important preliminary results." In: B. S. Heeb/A. Szentmiklosi/R. Krause/M. Wemhoff (eds.), Fortifications: The Rise and Fall of Defended Sites in Late Bronze and Early Iron Age of South-East Europe, Berlin: Staatliche Museen zu Berlin, pp. 217–228.

Historic Environment Scotland (2018): "Canmore database", https://www.historic environment.scot/archives-and-research/archives-and-collections/canmore-database/ (last accessed March 1, 2018).

Hodder, I. (1992): Theory and Practice in Archaeology, London; New York: Routledge.

Jacobs, J. Q. (2017): "Hundreds of Geoglyphs Discovered in the Amazon", http://www.jqjacobs.net/archaeology/geoglyph.html (last accessed September 25, 2017).

Kelly, J. E. (2002): "The Pulcher Tradition and the Ritualization of Cahokia: A Perspective from Cahokia's Southern Neighbor." In: Southeastern Archaeology 21/2, pp. 136–148.

Kidder, T. R. (2011): "Transforming Hunter-Gatherer History at Poverty Point." In: K. E. Sassaman/D. H. Holly (eds.), Hunter-Gatherer Archaeology as Historical Process, Tucson: The University of Arizona Press.

Kidder, T. R./Arco, L. J./Ortmann, A. L./Schilling, T./Boeke, C./Bielitz, R./Adelsberger, K. A. (2009): Poverty Point Mound A: Final Report of the 2005 and 2006 Field Seasons, Baton Rouge: Louisiana Division of Archaeology and the Louisiana Archaeological Survey and Antiquities Commission.

Lombardo, U./Prümers, H. (2010): "Pre-Columbian human occupation patterns in the eastern plains of the Llanos de Moxos, Bolivian Amazonia." In: Journal of Archaeological Science 37/8, pp. 1875–1885.

Manyanga, M./Pikirayi, I./Chirikure, S. (2010): "Conceptualising the Urban Mind in Pre-European Southern Africa: Rethinking Mapungubwe and Great Zimbabwe." In: P. J. J. Sinclair/G. Nordquist/F. Herschend/C. Isendahl (eds.), The

Urban Mind: Cultural and Environmental Dynamics, Uppsala: African and Comparative Archaeology, Department of Archaeology and Ancient History, Uppsala University.

Moore, T. (2012): "Beyond the Oppida: Polyfocal Complexes and Late Iron Age Societies in Southern Britain." In: Oxford Journal of Archaeology 31/4, pp. 391–417.

Moore, T. (2017): "Beyond Iron Age 'Towns': Examining Oppida as Examples of Low Density Urbanism." In: Oxford Journal of Archaeology 36/3, pp. 287–305.

Morgan, W. N. (1999): Precolumbian Architecture in Eastern North America, Gainesville: University Press of Florida.

Morton, F. (2013): "Settlements, landscapes and identities among the Tswana of the western Transvaal and eastern Kalahari before 1820." In: The South African Archaeological Bulletin 68/197, pp. 15–26.

Nunez Regueiro, V. A. (1970): "The Alamito Culture of Northwestern Argentina." In: American Antiquity 35/2, pp. 133–140.

Olsen, B. (2010): In Defense of Things: Archaeology and the Ontology of Objects, Lanham, New York, Toronto; Plymouth: Altamira Press.

Ortman, S. G./Cabaniss, A. H./Sturm, J. O./Bettencourt, L. M. (2014): "The pre-history of urban scaling." In: PLoS One 9/2, doi:10.1371/journal.pone.0087902.

Osborne, J. F. (ed.) (2014): Approaching Monumentality in Archaeology, IEMA Proceedings, Albany: State University of New York Press.

Osborne, J. F. (2017): "Counter-monumentality and the vulnerability of memory." In: Journal of Social Archaeology 17/2, pp. 163–187.

Pauketat, T. R./Alt, S. M./Kruchten, J. D. (2017): "The Emerald Acropolis: elevating the moon and water in the rise of Cahokia." In: Antiquity 91/355, pp. 207–222.

Qin, L. (2013): "The Liangzhu Culture." In: A. P. Underhill (ed.), A Companion to Chinese Archaeology, Chichester: Wiley Blackwell.

Radivojević, M./Rehren, T./Pernicka, E./Šljivar, D./Brauns, M./Borić, D. (2010): "On the origins of extractive metallurgy: new evidence from Europe." In: Journal of Archaeological Science 37/11, pp. 2775–2787.

Redmond, E. M./Gassón, R. A./Spencer, C. S. (1999): "A Macroregional View of Cycling Chiefdoms in the Western Venezuelan Llanos." In: Archeological Papers of the American Anthropological Association 9/1, pp. 109–129.

Redmond, E. M./Spencer, C. S. (2007): Archaeological Survey in the High Llanos and Andean Piedmont of Barinas, Venezuela, New York: American Museum of Natural History.

Renfrew, C. (1973): "Monuments, mobilisation and social organisation in Neolithic Wessex." In: C. Renfrew (ed.), The explanation of culture change: models in prehistory: proceedings of a meeting of the Research Seminar in Archaeology and Related Subjects held at the University of Sheffield, London: Duckworth, pp. 539–558.

Richards, C./Challands, A./Welham, K. (2013): "Erecting stone circles in a Hebridean landscape." In: C. Richards (ed.), Building the Great Stone Circles of the North, Oxford: Oxbow Books, pp. 201–223.

Richards, C./Demetri, G./French, C./Nunn, R./Rennell, R./Robertson, M./Wellerman, L./Wright, J. (2013): "Expedient monumentality: Na Dromannan and the high stone circles of Calanais, Lewis." In: C. Richards (ed.), Building the Great Stone Circles of the North, Oxford: Oxbow Books, pp. 224–253.

Rostain, S. (2008): "The archaeology of the Guianas: an overview." In: H. Silverman/W. Isbell (eds.), Handbook of South American Archaeology, New York: Springer, pp. 279–302.

Saunaluoma, S. (2012): "Geometric earthworks in the state of Acre, Brazil: excavations at the Fazenda Atlântica and Quinauá Sites." In: Latin American Antiquity 23/4, pp. 565–583.

Saunaluoma, S./Schaan, D. (2012): "Monumentality in western Amazonian formative societies: geometric ditched enclosures in the Brazilian state of Acre." In: Antiqua 2/e1, pp. 1–11.

Schaan, D. (2004): "The Camutins Chiefdom: Rise and Development of Social Complexity on Marajó Island, Brazilian Amazon." Ph. D. Thesis, Pittsburgh, Pennsylvania: University of Pittsburgh.

Shady, R. (2006): "La civilización Caral: sistema social y manejo del territorio y sus recursos. Su transcendencia en el proceso cultural andino." In: Boletín de Arqueología PUCP 10, pp. 59–89.

Shanks, M./Tilley, C. (1987): Re-Constructing Archaeology: Theory and Practice, Cambridge: Cambridge University Press.

Silliman, S. (2001): "Agency, practical politics and the archaeology of culture contact." In: Journal of Social Archaeology 1/2, pp. 190–209.

Steyn, G. (2011): "The spatial patterns of Tswana stone-walled towns in perspective." In: South African Journal of Art History 26/2, pp. 101–125.

Sulimirski, T./Taylor, T./Boardman, J. (1992): "The Scythians." In: I. E. S. Edwards/ E. Sollberger/N. G. L. Hammond (eds.), The Cambridge Ancient History, Cambridge: Cambridge University Press, pp. 547–590.

Thomas, J. (1999): Understanding the Neolithic, London: Routledge.

van Geel, B./Bokovenko, N. A./Burova, N. D./Chugunov, K. V./Dergachev, V. A./Dirksen, V. G./Kulkova, M./Nagler, A./Parzinger, H./van der Plicht, J./Vasiliev, S. S./ Zaitseva, G. I. (2004): "Climate change and the expansion of the Scythian culture after 850 BC: a hypothesis." In: Journal of Archaeological Science 31/12, pp. 1735–1742.

White, K. M. (n. d.): "A global comparison of low occupation density settlement behaviour in prehistory" (working title) Ph. D. thesis in preparation, Sydney: The University of Sydney.

Woolf, G. (1993): "Rethinking the Oppida." In: Oxford Journal of Archaeology 12/2, pp. 223–234.

Yang, X. (2004): New Perspectives on China's Past: Chinese Archaeology in the Twentieth Century, 2 vols, vol. 2, New Haven; London: Yale University Press.

Zhang, C. (2013): "The Qujialing-Shijiahe Culture in the Middle Yangzi River Valley." In: A. P. Underhill (ed.), A Companion to Chinese Archaeology, Chichester; Malden: Wiley-Blackwell, pp. 510–534.

The Massif Rouge and Early Dynastic high terraces: Dynamics of monumentality in Mesopotamia during the 3rd millennium BCE

Pascal Butterlin

High terraces and ziqqurats have always fascinated Near Eastern archaeologists, not least because of the Babel tale. It is precisely because of its gigantic proportions that the Tower of Babel became a problem and an expression of a kind of human *hybris* against the gods (Parrot 1949). More than 27 of this kind of monument have been excavated in the Near East (Figure 1) and it is usually thought that the development of the classical Mesopotamian ziqqurats from the Ur-III period on was preceded by a long period in which high terraces played a similar role, especially in proto-urban settlements (Butterlin 2013) and thereafter during the so-called Early Dynastic period (2900–2300 BCE). Many studies have been devoted to these buildings and they are usually compared to other gigantic monuments, for instance pyramids or massive towers all over the world (Quenet 2016: 49, Figure 4).

Conceived as mega-buildings from the start, such terraces dominated the Mesopotamian cities with their mass and their height. It is interesting to figure out more precisely what this meant, first through the actual dimensions of the monuments and secondly through their insertion in the cities. The size of the monuments under consideration has always been a challenge for archaeologists: excavating a ziqqurat is a painful and difficult task, requiring an enormous amount of work and involving huge problems. Badly exposed to erosion, the later levels are usually difficult to understand and in rare instances has it been possible to cut deeply into the masonry to uncover the earlier levels, which are sometimes well preserved. A second challenge is to understand the environment of buildings which during the later phases of the history of Mesopotamia stood isolated in a walled *temenos*. For earlier phases, either we know nothing of what was happening around the monument or it appears that they were set up in a dense and compact urban environment, so that it is necessary to be very careful when assessing how far the monuments were visible from a distance, crowning the Mesopotamian city skyline.

From the start this has been our aim in excavating the monumental center in Mari and especially the so-called 'Massif Rouge', between 2006 and 2010. Here we present briefly the results of our excavations at the Massif Rouge, thereafter comparing it with other monumental buildings of the time, both in the general layout of the building and its urban setting.

Figure 1: Distribution map of known ziqqurats and high terraces (author's map)

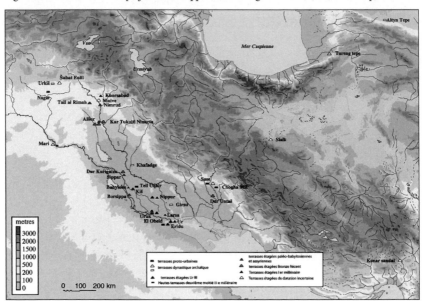

Back to the Massif Rouge

We have presented elsewhere the results of the Massif Rouge excavation projects (Butterlin 2014; 2015b; 2016b). Here we just concentrate upon the question of scale and the way we have figured out the main layout of this very peculiar monument. This building was first identified by Parrot and recognized thanks to its red core already during the first campaign in Mari. Before World War II, Parrot identified a very peculiar concentration of religious buildings on more than 10.000 m². Among these buildings, he identified the so-called 'Lion Temple', and to the north a first terrace which he named 'ziqqurat' and is now just named the 'High Terrace'. West of the 'Lion Temple', he excavated the so-called 'esplanade', which he thought to be limited by a *temenos*, and to the north a beautiful recessed façade, which appeared later to be the southern façade of the Massif Rouge.

The monument itself was only excavated during the seventh and the eighth campaigns in 1952 and 1953, and never published apart from preliminary reports

(Parrot 1953; 1954). Parrot identified a two-level recessed façade to the west. To the north, he excavated three rooms which were directly connected to the Massif itself, with one altar. To the east, he encountered a complicated situation: the Massif was heavily eroded and he discovered a monumental façade made up of roughly cut gypsum blocks. The whole eastern façade was cleared and presented this kind of wall, rendering understanding of the building quite difficult. Parrot thought initially that the building could have been a massive grave and decided to proceed towards the south where he was quickly completely absorbed by the discovery of the Inanna-Zaza temple (Parrot 1967).

Until 1999, no excavation occurred at this spot of the tell. The southern façade was briefly studied by Dominique Beyer during his excavations at Chantier G.[1] To the south of the Massif he identified a massive brick wall which was clearly linked to the inner structure of the Massif with a heavily burnt wash. This meant that the whole structure of the Massif was composite and that, as in the north, it included a lot of satellite buildings. We decided to resume in full the excavations upon that mysterious monument which was still standing as a huge mass on the top of the tell just beside the 'High Terrace'. The 'High Terrace' itself had been studied by Parrot and thereafter by Margueron (2004) but the Massif Rouge had remained untouched and unpublished (Figure 2).

Figure 2: Mari, Massif Rouge in 2005, before resuming excavation, mission archéologique française de Mari (Photo by Pascal Butterlin)

---

1 Beyer 2014 for the preliminary results of excavations at Chantier G from 1990 to 2010.

It quickly became apparent that the Massif itself was still there – exactly as it was during the last days of Parrot's excavations. Using unpublished data from the Parrot archives, we could easily resume the study of the building. The excavations proceeded in a threefold fashion. First, the four façades of the terrace were cleaned and precisely studied. Next, the top of the terrace was excavated in order to record the extent of the red mud-brick structure and see if some details could be recorded about the layout of the core of the terrace. And thirdly, we made some soundings to understand the relationship between the building and its environment.

The full results of the excavation are not presented here. Our main conclusions were the following. As stated, Parrot had recognized two phases. The study of the monuments established that there existed at least five phases, three assigned to *ville II* (2500–2300 BCE) and two to the *ville III* of Mari (2250–1759 BCE). In its initial stage (phase 1), the Massif Rouge was a stepped terrace, made up of red semi-baked bricks; the façade was red washed with white plastering for the first level floor (Figure 3). It is impossible to know the original height of the second level of the building, which was still 1 m high. The first step had a façade of at least 5 m and presented niches and recesses with a general slope of 75°.

Figure 3: Mari, Massif Rouge, northern façade, double-recessed, red-washed façade, mission archéologique française de Mari (Photo by Pascal Butterlin)

It is still difficult to figure out the complete plan of this first terrace which is hidden by later development, but a general estimation for the ground level suggests a surface of up to 800 m² and for the second level of around 400 m². No trace of an upper

Figure 4: Mari, Massif Rouge, northeastern angle gypsum blocks massive, mission archéologique française de Mari (Photo by Pascal Butterlin)

building has been observed but that clearly does not mean that one did not exist. Looking through the dimensions of other high temples of this type may reveal such a temple. During the excavations of the Great Trench, Parrot discovered a foundation deposit typical of the early second city and this first stage of the massif is dated to the beginning of the *ville II*, that is around 2500 BCE (Butterlin/Gallet 2016).

This monument was enlarged twice during the history of the *ville II* as it was established in a trench in the northern part of the Massif itself. The last enlargement probably occurred after major destruction, and the Massif was enlarged towards the north and the east, acquiring its typical trapezoidal shape at this time. Its dimensions were then as follows: eastern façade: 40.7 m, western façade: 36.7 m, southern façade: 28.1 m, and northern façade: 28.1 m with an estimated surface area of 1232 m².

The massive gypsum blocks of masonry were erected at this time and it appears after our excavations that this operation did not just create a protecting wall but in fact involved the building of a massive terrace of gypsum stones, up to 2 m long and 4 m high (Figure 4). This huge construction was not visible: at the southwestern corner where Parrot had not excavated, we found that the stone walling was covered by a heavy red wash of earth, 10 cm deep. It covered the upper part of the masonry, while the lower part was in foundations, under the level of the so-called *voie sacrée* which runs along the eastern façade of the building. At this stage, the Massif occupied a surface of more than 1200 m². This monument, like the rest of the city, suffered major damage at the fall of the *ville II* and was exposed for a long time to erosion which cut especially deeply into the eastern part of the monument, damaging even the structure of the first stage of the monument which therefore cannot be safely reconstructed in its entirety.

After the sack of the city, the monument remained abandoned until the reign of Apil Kin, ca. 2100 BCE. This Shakkanakku of Mari is well known since his reign constitutes one of the links between the U kings, namely Ur-Nammu, and the Mari Kings. Interestingly, he decided to rebuild the monument and at the southwestern corner of the building we discovered a foundation deposit well known in Mari, indicating that Apil Kin rebuilt the *sahuru* monument. Besides its chronological interest, this discovery gives us the name of the monument itself, a much-debated term used much later to designate the temple on the Babylon Etemenanki ziqqurat. It appears that it was this Shakkanakku who packed the red buildings and their remains in a huge grey brick massif (Figure 5), so the old stepped terrace became a high terrace next to the High Terrace built during the 23rd century by the so-called *shakkanakkû restaurateurs*, especially Ishtup El and successors (Butterlin 2007a). The building therefore offers an interesting case study: it is the only case where a stepped terrace is replaced by a high terrace precisely at a time when the Ur-III kings identify the classical layout of the ziqqurats at Ur, Uruk, Eridu, and Nippur.

Figure 5: Mari, general plan of ville II, mission archéologique française de Mari (Plan by Pascal Butterlin)

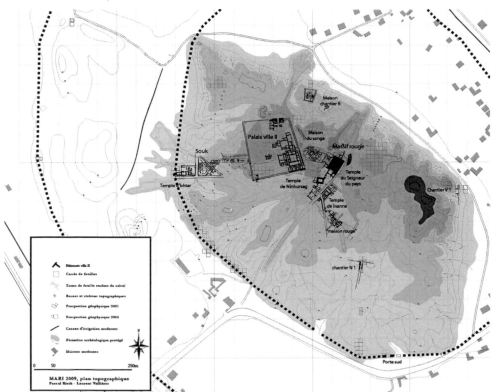

A second curious feature of the Massif Rouge is its urban setting (Figure 5). In contrast to the contemporary monuments excavated in southern Mesopotamia, the Massif Rouge is not isolated in an oval compound. It was structurally linked to the north and the south to two temples (Figure 6). We have already mentioned the northern altar which was part of a huge building situated to the north. To the south, our excavations showed that the Massif was linked to another building identified as the temple of the lord of the land (Figure 7). This multilayered building had a very complex history. Its *cella* was partly embedded in the Massif itself. It was square during the first phase of the massif and was later reduced. To the east, as previously stated, is the *voie sacrée* and to the west we discovered the remains of a sacred alley made up of white plaster which ran along the façade towards the northern building.

The southern temple was clearly the lower temple of a complex combining lower temple and terrace, as was later the case in Assyria for example. This southern temple was destroyed at the fall of the city but later rebuilt by the Akkad kings.

It had been identified by Parrot as the 'Temple Anonymes'. But at that stage the terrace remained in ruins and, as far as we can determine, the temple had lost its link to the terrace.

Figure 6: Mari, general outline of the monumental center, mission archéologique française de Mari (Plan by Pascal Butterlin)

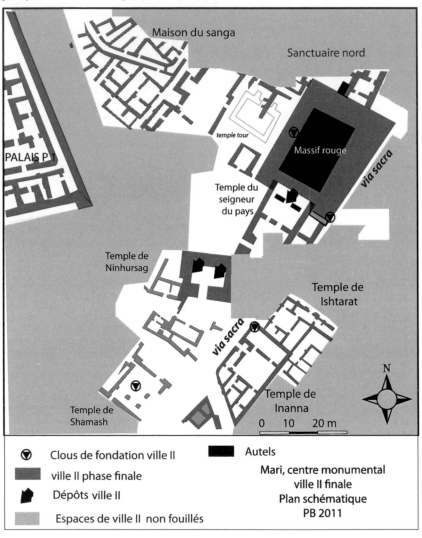

The Massif Rouge and the contemporary oval temples and high terraces of Early Dynastic Mesopotamia

It is interesting to compare the Massif Rouge complex as we know it now and other gigantic complexes of Early Dynastic Mesopotamia (Figure 8). Five main complexes have been identified: the Ninhursag sanctuary at Adab (Wilson 2012), the Eninnu of Ningirsu at Girsu (Parrot 1948; Forest 1999), the Ibgal of Inanna at Lagash (Crawford 1972; Hansen 1980–1983), the Ningirsu oval at Al 'Ubaid (Hall 1930; Hall/Woolley 1927), and the famous Oval temple at Khafadjah (Delougaz 1940). These buildings have been reviewed recently by Quenet and it is interesting to compare them to the Massif Rouge complex as it appeared around 2300 BCE just before its destruction (Quenet 2016: 143–147).

The Adab terrace was a composite building, with two adjoining terraces, one with the temple (21 by 20 m) and the other designed as a southern terrace (20 by 13,5 m), Quenet (2016: 143) estimates that its surface was more or less 700 m², because the limits to the north have not been defined for the second terrace. This layout could be the result of the enlargement of an initial square terrace. At Girsu, it is extremely difficult to assess the exact extent of the terrace supporting the famous Ur Nina construction. Forest (1999) proposed a reconstruction of a huge terrace up to 33,75 by 41,25 m, that is 1393 m². We have no information about a possible terrace at Lagash. The most well-known terraces are those of the Ninhursag temple at 'Ubaid/Nutur and of the oval at Khafadjah. The 'Ubaid terrace was 33 by 26 m, that is 858 m², and the oval temple terrace was 30 by 25 m, that is 750 m². One building complex is peculiar: the supposed oval precinct at Tell Mozan (Pfälzner 2008). With a surface of up to 2475 m², it is (as we will see below) another kind of high terrace. When we compare these results to our own findings at the Massif Rouge it is obvious from the start that the surface-areas of the Early Dynastic terraces were remarkably stable, around 800 m². We can consider this case as a typical standard for the high terraces of the time of the great city states of Sumer and Akkad. The Eninnu of Lagash is much bigger and can only be compared to stage 3 of the Massif Rouge. These two buildings could be considered as a new step in the general monumentalization of the high terraces, which probably occurred during the proto-imperial and imperial phases of the Akkad empire time.

We have little information about the general layout of these Early Dynastic terraces. At Adab and Girsu, we know that temples were erected upon what seem to be high terraces. At 'Ubaid, the temple has disappeared, but reconstructions have been produced using the material discovered at the bottom of the terrace. As for Khafadjah, the terrace is a high terrace and it has been proposed that a mono-cellular temple was on top of it. Considering the discoveries at the Massif Rouge, Quenet (2016: 150) has proposed recently that a second storey could be a possibility, but we have no definitive clue about the upper temple, as in Mari itself.

From this first set of observations we can conclude that the initial stage of the Massif Rouge was a typical terrace as built in Early Dynastic Mesopotamia during the middle of the 3rd millennium. But it is distinguished by its two storeys, a feature that at present seems to be specific to Mari. This is not to say that stepped terraces were invented in Mari; we have previous examples, at least partially, in 4th millennium Mesopotamia. This feature could have been specific to central Mesopotamia if Khafadgé also presented this kind of building.

Anyway, the Mari case is much more specific when discussing the general layout of the monumental center. Obviously, at Mari we cannot identify the typical high terrace with its oval as in 'Ubaid, Khafadjah, Lagash, or even Girsu. With its two adjoining northern and southern temples, the Massif Rouge complex is a very peculiar case and it could in some ways be compared to the Adab complex. At Adab, an enclosure wall existed but the terraces were closely linked to other buildings mainly to the north. The relationship is not clear and we may recall that a high temple was situated on the top. In Mari, the question remains unresolved, especially since we discovered the low temple which might have been the main sanctuary.

This quick review leaves a lot of questions about the general layout of these monumental centers. It is difficult to assess their global scale: 93 by 130 m at Lagash, 80 by 100 at Girsu, at 'Ubaid and 100 by 70 m at Khafadjah. This means that these monumental centers occupied roughly between 7000 m² and 12.000 m². At Mari, we estimate that the whole complex of the Massif Rouge occupied roughly 130 by 80 m, that is almost 10.000 m². This is only an estimate since the limits of the Massif remain uncertain. There is no *temenos* wall at that time in Mari and these figures do not include the palace with its *enceinte sacrée* (more than 24.000 m²). Included are, however, the terrace with its two temples as we know them and the Ninhursag temple to the south, but also the *dépendances de Dagan* and the recessed building identified by Parrot under the 'High Terrace'.

Anyway, we now have good insights into the layout and the scale achieved by this kind of monument around 2400 BCE. This is but one step along the history of these buildings. If we compare the figures we obtained for these terraces to the earlier and later monuments, we can gain an insight into the development of the monuments.

The Early Dynastic terraces are much smaller in size than the great proto-urban terraces from Susiana or Mesopotamia: 1500 m² is the average during the 4th millennium (Butterlin 2015a), with the exception of Susa (6400 m²) and only 800 m² during the Early Dynastic. In between these periods, we have little information. At Uruk, the first high terraces built in the Eanna, above the protopalatial complex at the beginning of the 3rd millennium, are interesting cases (Eichmann 2007). Two terraces whose surface is respectively 600 and 800 m² were built up and at a later stage were connected to each other, creating a L-shaped structure (Figure 7). This type of building could be the missing link between the two types of terraces.

Figure 7: Mari, general plan of the Massif Rouge excavations, mission archéologique française de Mari, l (Plan by Lorraine Sartorius)

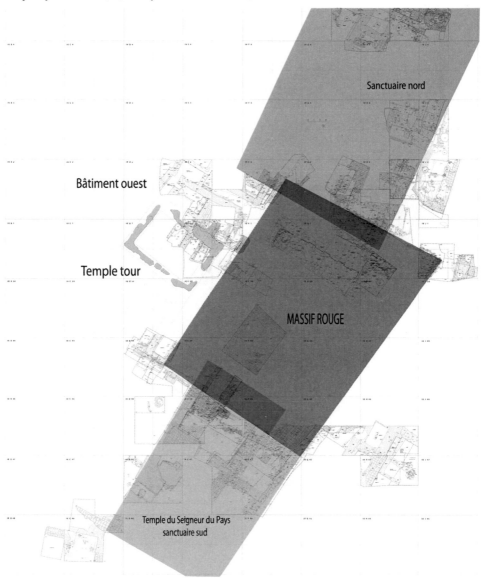

With a surface up to 1.232 m², the last stage of the Massif Rouge constitutes a clear break and the next stage (up to 2.400 m²) was achieved during the Ur III period. The four ziqqurats built by the Ur III king are rectangular buildings, Ur (62,5 × 43 m, 2.687 m²), Uruk (56 × 52 m, 2.912 m²), Eridu (61 × 46 m, 2.806 m²), and

Figure 8: High terraces and oval temples, comparison at same scale (after Quenet 2016; Butterlin 2016, author's composite plate)

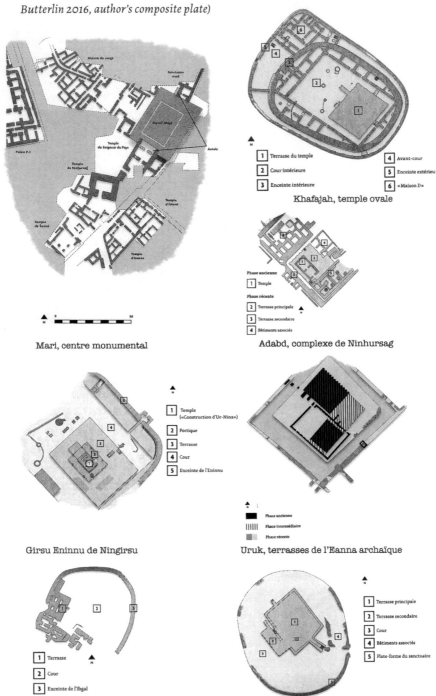

Mari, centre monumental

Khafajah, temple ovale

Adabd, complexe de Ninhursag

Girsu Eninnu de Ningirsu

Uruk, terrasses de l'Eanna archaïque

Lagash, complexe ovale

El Obeid, temple de Ninhursag

Nippur (53 × 38 m, 2.014 m²). The only comparable earlier terrace is the high terrace at Mozan, as we have seen previously.

I would suggest that these three steps constitute three different generations of terraces, defined by their scale but also by the number of storeys. Usually, the development of the multiple storey ziqqurats during the Ur-III period has been considered a major step. However, our observations in Mari show that while this might be the case for southern Mesopotamia it is not the case in central Mesopotamia, at least on the Middle Euphrates.

Conclusion

Were high terraces a question of scale? This short paper provides a preliminary answer to this question: there was definitely an idea of the scale to be achieved to create an urban landscape during the Early Dynastic period, shaped by those definite markers that were the high houses of the main god of the city. The high terraces were certainly landmarks, even if we still do not know precisely what happened on their tops. The standard size of this kind of terrace seems to have been 800 m², and the terraces were usually quadrilateral in shape, but they were not as standardized as the Ur-III ziqqurats became with their famous layout. As might be expected in the polycentric world of the cities of the middle of the 3rd millennium, every terrace was part of a local religious topography, whose roots are not easy to understand. Looking through the data, we observe different cases, even in the way the terraces were linked to the nearby temples and sacred precincts.

Bibliography

Beyer, D. (2014): "Les temples de Mari, Bilan de 20 ans de travaux au chantier G (1990–2010)." In: P. Butterlin/J. Margueron/B. Muller/M. Maqdissi/D. Beyer/A. (eds.), Mari – ni est ni ouest. Actes du colloque international 'Mari, ni est ni ouest', Damas, Syrie, 20–22 octobre 2010, Syria Supplementum 2, Beyrouth: Presses de l'Ifpo, pp. 34–54.

Butterlin, P. (2007a): "Mari, les Shakkanakkû et la crise de la fin du III e millénaire." In: C. Kuzugluoglu/C. Marro (eds.), Sociétés humaines et changement climatique à la fin du III e millénaire: une crise a t'elle eu lie en Haute Mésopotamie? Actes du colloque de Lyon, 5–8 décembre 2005, Institut français d'études anatoliennes Georges Dumézil-Istanbul: de Boccard, pp. 227–247.

Butterlin, P. (2007b): "Les nouvelles recherches archéologiques françaises à Mari, un premier bilan (2005–2006)." In: Orient Express 2007/1, pp. 5–13.

Butterlin, P. (2013): "Les terrasses monumentales proto-urbaines et les centres proto-urbains de Suse à Uruk, étude proto-urbaine 1." In: J. L. Montero-Fenollos (ed.), Du village néolithique à la ville mésopotamienne, Bibliotheca Euphratica, vol. I, pp. 117–132.

Butterlin, P. (2014): "Recherches au massif rouge, données nouvelles sur le centre monumental de Mari et son histoire." In: P. Butterlin/J. Margueron/B. Muller/M. Maqdissi/D. Beyer/A. (eds.), Mari – ni est ni ouest. Actes du colloque international 'Mari, ni est ni ouest', Damas, Syrie, 20–22 octobre 2010, Syria Supplementum 2, Beyrouth: Presses de l'Ifpo, pp. 81–111.

Butterlin, P. (2015a): "Late Chalcolithic Mesopotamia, towards a definition of sacred space and its evolution," In: N. Laneri (ed.), Defining the sacred. Approaches to the Archaeology of Religion in the Ancient Near East, London: Oxbow Books, pp. 60–72.

Butterlin, P. (2015b): "Au cœur du pouvoir à Mari. Le 'massif rouge' et le temple du 'Seigneur du Pays', enjeux et résultats des nouvelles recherches conduites à Mari 2006–2010." In: C. Michel (ed.), De la maison à la ville dans l'orient ancien: bâtiments publics et lieux de pouvoir, Cahiers des thèmes transversaux d'ArScAn 12, Nanterre: ArScAn, pp. 119–130.

Butterlin, P. (2016a): "Le phénomène des temples sur haute terrasse de la période urukéenne." In: P. Quenet (ed.), Ana ziqquratim. Sur la piste de Babel, Strasbourg: Presses Universitaires de Strasbourg, pp. 96–102.

Butterlin, P. (2016b): "Le massif rouge de Mari, une terrasse étagée aux marges du Sud mésopotamien." In: P. Quenet (ed.), Ana ziqquratim. Sur la piste de Babel, Strasbourg: Presses Universitaires de Strasbourg, pp. 137–143.

Butterlin, P./Gallet, Y. (2014): "Archaeological and Geomagnetic Implications of New Arcaheomagnetic intensity data from the Early Bronze High Terrace Massif Rouge at Mari (Tell Hariri Syria)." In: Archaeometry 180, pp. 1–15.

Crawford, V. E. (1972): "Excavations in the swamps of Sumer." In: Expedition 14, pp. 12–20.

Delougaz, P. (1940): The Temple Oval at Khafajah, Oriental Institute Publications 53, Chicago: The University of Chicago Press.

Eichmann, R. (2007): Uruk, Architektur I, Ausgrabungen in Uruk-Warka Endberichte 14, Rahden/Westf.: Marie Leidorf.

Forest, J.-D. (1999): Les premiers temples de Mésopotamie (4 ème et 3 ème millénaires), BAR International Series 765, Oxford: Archaeopress.

Hall, H. R. (1930): A Season's work at Ur, al-Ubaid, Abu Sharain (Eridu) and elsewhere. Being an Unofficial Account of the British Museum Archaeological Mission to Babylonia, 1919, London: Metheun.

Hall, H. R./Woolley, L. (1927): Al Ubaid, Ur excavations 1, Oxford: University Press.

Hansen D. P. (1980–1983): "Lagash. B. Archäologisch." In: Reallexikon der Assyriologie 55/4, pp. 422–430.

Margueron, J. (2004): Mari, Métropole de l'Euphrate au IIIe et au début du IIe mil-
    lénaire, Paris: Picard/ERC.

Parrot, A. (1948): Telloh, vingt campagnes de fouilles (1877–1933), Paris: Geuthner.

Parrot, A. (1949): Ziggurat et tour de Babel, Paris: Albin Michel.

Parrot, A. (1953): "Les fouilles de Mari, huitième campagne (Automne 1952)." In:
    Syria XXX, pp. 196–221.

Parrot, A. (1954): "Les fouilles de Mari, neuvième campagne (Automne 1953)." In:
    Syria XXXI, pp. 151–171.

Parrot, A. (1956): Le Temple d'Ishtar, Mission archéologique de Mari, tome I, Paris:
    Geuthner.

Parrot, A. (1967): Les temples d'Ishtarat et de Ninni zaza, Mission archéologique de
    Mari, tome III, Paris: Geuthner.

Pfälzner, P. (2008): " Das Tempeloval von Urkeš. Betrachtungen zur Typologie und
    Entwicklungsgeschichte der mesopotamischen Ziqqurrat im 3. Jt. v. Chr." In:
    Zeitschrift für Orient-Archäologie 1, pp. 396–433.

Quenet, P. (ed.) (2016): Ana Ziqquratim. Sur la piste de Babel, Strasbourg: Presses
    Universitaires de Strasbourg.

Wilson, K. (2012): Bismaya. Recovering the Lost City of Adab, Oriental Institute
    Publications 138, Chicago: The Oriental Institute of the University of Chicago.

La grandeur de Babylone: étude des inscriptions royales

Laura Cousin

"L'Assyrie contient plusieurs grandes villes, mais Babylone est la plus célèbre et la plus forte. C'était là que les rois du pays faisaient leur résidence depuis la destruction de Ninive. Cette ville, située dans une grande plaine, est de forme carrée; chacun de ses côtés a cent-vingt stades de long, ce qui fait pour l'enceinte de la place quatre-cent-quatre-vingts stades. Elle est si magnifique que nous n'en connaissons pas une qu'on puisse lui comparer"
Hérodote, Histoires I.178[1].

Au premier millénaire av. notre ère, Babylone est la plus grande ville de Mésopotamie, la capitale politique et religieuse de la Babylonie. Elle s'étend sur près de 1000 hectares à son apogée sous le règne de Nabuchodonosor II (604–562) au VIe siècle. La ville est traversée par l'Euphrate et se compose de dix quartiers (voir figure 1). Elle est protégée par une double muraille et compte 43 sanctuaires, d'après une liste de textes topographiques composée à la fin du XIIe siècle av. notre ère et dédiée à l'urbanisme sacré de Babylone (George 1992). Elle présente la particularité d'abriter le sanctuaire du dieu principal du panthéon babylonien, Marduk, et le palais royal. Le temple de Marduk, l'Esagil ("Temple dont le sommet est élevé"), se trouve au cœur de la ville et forme avec la ziggurat Etemenanki ("Temple qui relie le ciel et la terre") un grand complexe sacré de près de 20 hectares. Au nord de la cité, le complexe palatial est constitué de deux édifices, appelés Palais Sud et Palais Nord[2]. Le Palais Sud est le palais original de Babylone, où se situe la salle du trône, et il s'étend sur six hectares. Le Palais Nord, plus vaste encore, fut édi-

---

1 Citation consultée sur le site Web http://remacle.org/bloodwolf/historiens/herodote/clio.htm (le 5 janvier 2019).
2 Sur les plans établis par R. Koldewey, le Palais Sud correspond au Südburg et le Palais Nord à l'Hauptburg.

fié sous le règne de Nabuchodonosor II et présente la singularité de se situer à l'extérieur de la muraille. Babylone apparaît donc à la fois comme une ville sacrée prééminente et comme la principale ville du pouvoir royal temporel.

Figure 1: Plan de Babylone (George 1992: 24)

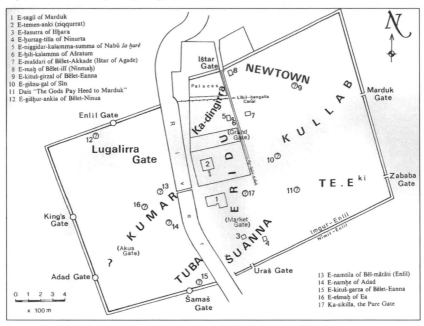

La localisation de Babylone ne fut jamais complètement perdue. On doit les premières fouilles à l'architecte et archéologue allemand R. Koldewey, qui œuvra sur le site entre 1899 et 1917 (Koldewey 1925). Babylone est à nouveau fouillée entre 1962 et 1973 sous la direction de H. Schmid et de J. Schmidt (Schmid 1995; Marzahn 2008: 525), puis par une équipe italienne sous la direction de G. Bergamini (1974–1989). La mission italienne a surtout permis de reconsidérer les niveaux de Babylone et d'en revoir la stratigraphie (Bergamini 1977). Enfin des fouilles irakiennes, menées entre la fin des années 1970 et le début des années 1980, ont permis d'identifier certains sanctuaires – comme le temple de Nabû *ša harê* – et de découvrir un certain nombre de textes provenant de la Voie Processionnelle (voir les volumes 35, 37, 41, 45 de la revue Sumer). L'archéologie a permis de dégager la ville de Babylone du premier millénaire, notamment celle restaurée et fortifiée sous le règne de Nabuchodonosor II. Les niveaux plus anciens, en particulier ceux du deuxième millénaire, n'ont pu être atteints que dans certaines parties de Babylone, dans le quartier du Merkes ("centre-ville", voir Reuther 1926) et dans le secteur as-Sahn, non loin du centre cultuel de la ville (Pedersén 2005: 17–65 et Marzahn 2008: 522).

Babylone apparaît comme une ville antique monumentale, à la fois grâce aux travaux menés par les archéologues, mais aussi dans la documentation textuelle, et plus particulièrement dans les inscriptions royales qui lui sont consacrées. Ces textes produisent des discours officiels sur la grandeur et la majesté de la ville et sont un outil précieux afin de déterminer l'idéologie qui se déploie dans la ville de Babylone. Ces inscriptions sont le plus souvent elles-mêmes monumentales, commandées par un souverain afin de célébrer l'un de ses hauts faits (une victoire militaire), ou l'un de ses actes de piété (la restauration d'un temple). La fonction de tels documents est de garantir la postérité du nom du monarque; c'est pour cette raison qu'elles s'adressent aux dieux éternels ainsi qu'aux futurs rois, mais aussi à un auditoire plus contemporain, occupant de hautes positions sociales (Da Riva 2008: 26). Les cylindres, supports de prédilection des inscriptions royales néo-babyloniennes, sont considérés comme des documents de fondation et sont donc enterrés à leurs côtés, tandis que les briques – autre support des inscriptions royales – sont recouvertes d'enduit (Charpin 2006: 153–154). La question de la réception des inscriptions, et celle de leur possible lecture[3], doit aussi être prise en compte, puisque ces documents sont d'importants moyens pour le roi de s'exprimer.

La majesté de Babylone dans la documentation antérieure au premier millénaire

Dans les sources du troisième millénaire

Le premier document mentionnant Babylone est une inscription votive (YOS 9, 2), composée vers 2500 av. notre ère:

> "[Le début est cassé] gouverneur de BAR.KI.BAR, fils d'Ahu-ilum, homme d'Ilumbelī, homme d'Ur-kubi, bâtisseur du temple de Marduk, a mis en place [cassure]" (Sommerfeld 1982: 20).

La localité, appelée BAR.KI.BAR, pourrait être lue Babbal ou Babbar et serait le nom originel de Babylone (Lambert 1984: 8–9; 2011: 73). Il est, par ailleurs, remarquable que cette première mention de Babylone soit en lien avec la construction d'un temple dédié à Marduk, le dieu poliade de la cité. Babylone joue, en outre, un rôle en Babylonie depuis le troisième millénaire: sous la troisième dynastie d'Ur

---

3 Au sujet de la lecture à haute voix des inscriptions royales, voir Grayson 1981: 43 et Nevling Porter 1993: 112–114.

au XXIᵉ siècle, elle apparaît dans la documentation économique comme centre administratif secondaire, placé sous la domination d'un gouverneur ENSI (Lambert 2011: 71).

Dans les sources paléo-babyloniennes

Si la monumentalité de Babylone apparaît de façon éclatante au premier millénaire, la grandeur de la ville est déjà évoquée dans les noms d'année des rois de la première dynastie de Babylone (1880–1595). Dès le règne de Sûmû-la-El (1880–1845), le fondateur de la première dynastie de Babylone (Charpin 2004: 81–86), il est question d'une "grande muraille" érigée dans la ville (année Sûmû-la-El 5[4]). C'est sous son règne, vers 1877, que l'enceinte a probablement été édifiée – il est à noter que le second mur d'enceinte, appelé Nimitti-Enlil, n'est évoqué qu'à partir du règne de Sargon II (721–705) (George 1992: 344). La muraille de Babylone apparaît ensuite dans le nom d'année Apil-Sîn 2 sous la formulation de "nouveau grand mur de Babylone" (Horsnell 1999: 76–77).

Dès le deuxième millénaire, on voit toutefois émerger un autre sens à la monumentalité. Elle ne semble pas uniquement être provoquée par la grandeur physique des édifices, mais aussi par la forte charge symbolique qu'ils détiennent. Les souverains insistent sur l'aspect sacré de Babylone: l'année Hammurabi 3 met ainsi l'accent sur la réalisation d'un grand dais dans l'Ekišnugal de Babylone, temple dédié au dieu Lune Sîn (Horsnell 1999: 107–109), tandis que Samsu-iluna 7 nous renseigne sur la réalisation d'un emblème dans le temple de Marduk (Horsnell 1999: 189–190).

La grandeur de Babylone dans les sources du premier millénaire

Dans les inscriptions royales néo-assyriennes

Au premier millénaire, la monumentalité de Babylone est surtout célébrée à partir du règne d'Assarhaddon (680–669), qui procède à la reconstruction de la ville après sa destruction par son père, le roi assyrien Sennachérib (704–681). Le Prisme A de Babylone, composé pendant le règne d'Assarhaddon, apporte des détails significatifs quant à la restauration de la muraille Imgur-Enlil:

---

4   Charpin 2003. On a longtemps admis que l'enceinte de Babylone était l'œuvre de Sûmû-abum, ce que suggérait le nom de sa première année de règne. Cette interprétation a été remise en question par D. Charpin qui a montré la ressemblance exacte entre les noms d'années Sûmû-abum 1 et Sûmû-la-El 5. Il en a ensuite conclu que si Sûmû-abum était placé avant Sûmû-la-El dans les listes de noms d'années, il devait s'agir d'une reconstitution opérée a posteriori par les scribes.

"Avec une corde-aš[lu], j'ai mesuré les dimensions d'[Imgur-Enlil, la grande muraille].
Chaque [longueur] (et chaque) largeur faisaient 30 aš/u (±1800 mètres). Je (l')ai
bâtie comme elle était avant et j'ai élevé (son sommet) haut comme une montagne.
J'ai construit (et) achevé Nimitti-Enlil, le mur extérieur, et l'ai rempli de splendeur
(en faisant) un objet d'émerveillement pour l'ensemble des gens" (Leichty 2011:
texte Esarhaddon 104, col. v. l. 1–9).

Assarhaddon décrit l'enceinte de Babylone et, par extension, la ville elle-même
comme un carré parfait d'un périmètre de 7,2 kilomètres. Cette présentation
d'Imgur-Enlil a participé à l'édification de son mythe et fut reprise par Hérodote,
qui donne des dimensions encore plus colossales pour le mur d'enceinte (88,8 km)
(*Histoires*, I.178), et plus tard par Pline l'Ancien[5]. On peut également remarquer l'expression "haut comme une montagne" *(huršaniš)*, qui devient, à partir des inscriptions d'Assarhaddon, l'un des moyens privilégiés de rendre compte de la monumentalité d'un édifice.

Dans les inscriptions royales néo-babyloniennes

Après la disparition du roi assyrien Assurbanipal en 627, Nabopolassar prend le
pouvoir en Babylonie en 626 avec l'aide des Mèdes[6]. Son règne marque le com-
mencement d'une nouvelle ère, l'époque néo-babylonienne (626–539 av. notre
ère). Les souverains qui se succèdent en Babylonie ont tous réalisé d'importants
travaux dans leur capitale, mais celui qui l'a modelée pour qu'elle devienne une
cité monumentale est Nabuchodonosor II, le fils et successeur de Nabopolassar.
Dans plusieurs inscriptions royales, il détaille les réalisations qu'il a commandi-
tées dans Babylone. L'inscription rupestre du Wadi Brisa, rééditée par R. Da Riva
(2012), présente ainsi l'ensemble des travaux réalisés par Nabuchodonosor II dans
la capitale de son empire. Le premier chantier se concentre autour de la défense
de la capitale: le roi fait en sorte que la ville soit protégée par un système complexe
de murailles. Ces travaux étaient devenus essentiels et constituaient un préalable
aux autres restaurations.

Il renforce ensuite l'enceinte de Babylone, bâtit deux bastions sur l'Euphrate
et réalise une enceinte extérieure (un *dūru dannu*, "mur fort"), depuis l'Euphrate

---

5 *Naturalis Historia*, vi, xxx: "Babylone, capitale des nations chaldéennes, a joui longtemps de la plus
grande célébrité dans tout l'univers; c'est d'elle que tout le reste de la Mésopotamie et de l'Assyrie
a été appelé Babylonie. Elle avait 60.000 pas de tour, des murs hauts de 200 pieds, larges de 50
(et le pied babylonien a trois doigts de plus que le nôtre), traversée par l'Euphrate, que bordaient
des quais aussi admirables que l'enceinte. Le temple de Jupiter Bélus y subsiste encore; Bélus fut
l'inventeur de l'astronomie" (voir la traduction sur http://remacle.org/bloodwolf/erudits/plinean
cien/livre6.htm, consultée le 5 janvier 2019).

6 Sur les origines de Nabopolassar et son lien avec la ville d'Uruk, voir Jursa 2007.

jusqu'au Tell Babil au nord de la ville où se tient le "Palais d'été" (le Sommerpalast, selon la dénomination de R. Koldewey). Outre les restaurations de nombreux sanctuaires, le souverain mène des travaux de consolidation et de rehaussement, comme les fouilles archéologiques l'ont mis en évidence dans le quartier de la Porte d'Ištar et de la Voie Processionnelle (Margueron 2008). Les ouvriers ont alors recours à une nouvelle technique de construction, alliant briques cuites et bitume. La brique cuite est un matériau plus solide que la brique crue, rendant les constructions sont plus durables. L'hydrologie explique également cette nouveauté dans l'urbanisme, car les briques cuites permettraient de lutter contre la remontée des eaux de l'Euphrate, particulièrement dans le quartier du palais royal (Margueron 2008).

Étude de cas: les constructions monumentales dans Babylone

Le complexe palatial

En tant que capitale politique et religieuse du pays, Babylone accueille deux pôles majeurs: le complexe palatial, situé au nord de la ville, et le complexe sacré, érigé au centre de la cité. Le complexe palatial de Babylone se situe dans le quartier de ká.dingir.ra, la "Porte des Dieux". Il est composé de deux édifices, appelés Palais Sud et Palais Nord par l'archéologue R. Koldewey (Koldewey 1931 sur le Palais Sud; 1932 sur le Palais Nord). Le Palais Sud est le palais originel de Babylone; il est ensuite agrandi et complété par le Palais Nord, construit sous le règne de Nabuchodonosor II (Cousin 2015: 210–211).

Le Palais Sud (voir figure 3) doit se situer à cet emplacement précis au moins depuis la composition de la liste topographique *Tintir = Bābilu* à la fin du XIIᵉ siècle[7]. La strate paléo-babylonienne du palais n'a pas été explorée, à cause du niveau trop élevé de la nappe phréatique et du difficile démantèlement des couches néo-babyloniennes de cet édifice colossal.

Il est à noter que le palais royal de Babylone est peu évoqué dans les inscriptions royales. Sennachérib décrit tout de même au VIIIᵉ siècle celui de Mérodach-Baladan II, mais c'est surtout l'accumulation de richesses qui est soulignée, preuve tangible de la conquête réalisée par le souverain assyrien (Grayson/Novotny 2012: 34, texte Sennacherib 1, l. 30–33).

Les inscriptions royales néo-assyriennes n'évoquent plus le palais royal de Babylone, même parmi les édifices restaurés par Assarhaddon, suite à la destruction de la ville par Sennachérib en 689 (Cousin 2015: 2010). C'est véritablement sous Nabuchodonosor II que le complexe palatial devient un sujet à part entière

---

7 Pour les palais à l'époque paléo-babylonienne, voir Charpin 1991.

Figure 2: Le complexe palatial de Babylone (Koldewey 1931: pl. 1)

Figure 3: Le Palais Sud (Koldewey 1931: pl. 2)

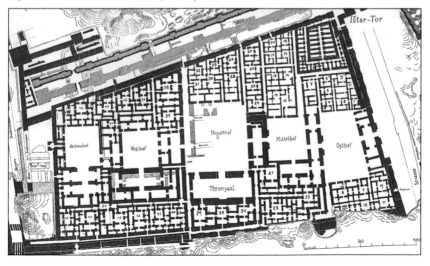

des inscriptions royales, ce qui correspond à l'apogée du pouvoir royal dans la ville du roi des dieux, Marduk[8]. Les descriptions présentées dans le *Cylindre du Palais Sud* et le *Cylindre du Palais Nord* – composés sous Nabuchodonosor II – apportent de précieuses informations quant à la manière dont le roi envisage sa résidence. La monumentalité du Palais Sud est suggérée par des expressions telles que "j'ai établi ses fondations face aux eaux, je les ai bâties hautes comme des montagnes", ou par l'utilisation de matériaux de construction précieux et majestueux, comme du bois de cèdre, dont les troncs sont utilisés pour la toiture du palais, ou pour réaliser les vantaux. Le roi babylonien ajoute par ailleurs:

> "En argent, en or et en pierres précieuses, parmi tout ce qui est précieux et abondant, j'ai empilé à l'intérieur les biens, les possessions, le symbole de la gloire; j'ai amassé en son sein l'héroïsme, la glorification, le trésor royal" (Langdon 1912: Nbk 14, col. ii, l. 1–21).

Ce passage résume bien ce qui semble participer de la monumentalité pour les souverains: le palais, grand édifice, est aussi vecteur d'une certaine idée du pouvoir[9]. La grandeur se traduit aussi dans le nom donné au Palais Sud. Son nom cérémoniel demeure inconnu (George 2001/02), mais il est pourvu d'épithètes renvoyant à sa majesté:

- dans le *Cylindre du Palais Sud*, il est qualifié par Nabuchodonosor II de "résidence de ma royauté, de lien avec mon vaste peuple, la résidence de la joie et de l'allégresse, le lieu des orgueilleux que j'ai soumis" (Langdon 1912: Nbk 9, col. iii, l. 27–30).
- dans le *Cylindre du Palais Nord*, il est qualifié par le roi de "palais, maison de l'étonnement du peuple, le lien entre les pays, la demeure pure, la résidence de ma royauté" (Langdon 1912: Nbk 14, col. ii, l. 2–3).

Durant son règne, Nabuchodonosor II bâtit, au nord du Palais Sud, un autre palais plus vaste encore, le Palais Nord (voir figure 3). Cependant, ce nouvel édifice n'a été que partiellement fouillé et les informations à son propos demeurent incomplètes. Nabuchodonosor II évoque sa construction dans *l'Inscription de la East India Company*:

---

8 Voir par exemple le *Cylindre du Palais Sud* (Langdon 1912: Nbk 9) et le *Cylindre du Palais Nord* (Langdon 1912: Nbk 14), composés sous le règne de Nabuchodonosor II, ainsi que le *Cylindre du Palais Royal* (Da Riva 2013: C23) composé sous le règne de Nériglissar (560–556).

9 Sur la question de la réprésentation du pouvoir royal dans Babylone, voir Joannès 2011.

"Dans Babylone, l'espace de ma résidence ne convenait plus à la qualité de ma royauté: comme mon cœur était plein de respect envers mon seigneur Marduk, dans Babylone, sa place-forte, pour agrandir ma résidence royale, je n'ai pas bouché le moindre de ses canaux. J'ai cherché tout alentour (un espace disponible pour) ma résidence" (Langdon: 1912, Nbk 15, col. viii, l. 27–41).

Le souvenir du Palais Nord a été entretenu par le prêtre de Bēl, Bérose, dans ses *Babyloniaca*, composées au IIIe siècle av. notre ère Il a définitivement contribué à mythifier le palais de Nabuchodonosor II en évoquant une durée de construction de quinze jours seulement[10]. Le Palais Nord n'apparaît, dans l'état actuel des sources, que dans la documentation issue du règne de Nabuchodonosor II, notamment dans le *Cylindre du Palais Nord*, dans lequel sa construction est relatée:

"Sur 490 coudées de terre aux alentours de Nimitti-Enlil, le mur d'enceinte à l'extérieur de Babylone, j'ai réalisé deux quais solides en bitume et briques cuites. J'ai créé un mur d'enceinte haut comme une montagne, une ouverture en briques cuites dans leurs constructions. À leur sommet, j'ai réalisé le grand palais, pour demeure de ma royauté, en bitume et en briques cuites. Je l'ai relié avec le palais de mon père et j'ai doté la demeure de ma domination. J'ai mis pour sa toiture des cèdres puissants, originaires des montagnes pures, des pins solides, des cyprès de grande qualité, sélectionnés. J'ai fixé sur ses portes des vantaux en bois de *musukkanu*, en cèdre, en cyprès, en diorite et en ivoire, des montures en argent et en or, couverts de cuivre, des coins en argent, et des montants en cuivre [...]. J'ai fait faire cette résidence pour l'étonnement, je l'ai faite remplir pour que le peuple entier voie la splendeur. Son extérieur était enveloppé de fierté, de fureur, de la terreur causée par le rayonnement de la royauté" (Langdon 1912: Nbk 14, col. ii, l. 31–54).

De la même façon que l'on méconnaît la structure du Palais Nord, ainsi qu'une grande partie des fonctions qui lui étaient attribuées, son nom cérémoniel n'est pas attesté. Dans les documents de la pratique issus du temple de l'Eanna d'Uruk, le palais est appelé *ekallu ša pāni abul Ištar*, "le palais situé devant la porte d'Ištar", soit une indication d'ordre strictement topographique (Beaulieu 2005: 48). En outre, dans l'archive de Marduk-nāṣir-apli, chef de la famille Egibi de Babylone sous le règne de Darius Ier, plusieurs textes renseignent sur les probables noms usuels des Palais Nord (le "Nouveau Palais" *ekallu eššu*) et Palais Sud (le "Grand Palais" *ekallu rabu*) (Abraham 2004: textes 15, 18 et 54).

---

10 Voir l'édition des *Babyloniaca* de Bérose dans Burstein 1978: 27, 2a.

Le complexe cultuel

De 1899 à 1917, les fouilles allemandes ont permis de mettre au jour, en partie, le temple de l'Esagil sur le tell Amran Ibn Ali, ainsi que les vestiges de la ziggurat Etemenanki dans le quartier as-Sahn. Comme pour l'ensemble de Babylone, les fouilles du complexe sacré demeurent partielles et inachevées. Cependant, d'après la *Tablette de l'Esagil*, le sanctuaire à lui seul devait s'étendre sur deux hectares (George 1992: 109–119). La *Stèle Schøyen* offre, quant à elle, la seule représentation connue de la ziggurat, formée de six étages auxquels s'ajoute un temple sommital, constituant un septième niveau[11]. La *Tablette de l'Esagil* détaille l'architecture interne du temple sommital, qui abritait plusieurs chapelles consacrées aux dieux principaux, ainsi qu'une chambre à coucher destinée au dieu Marduk et à son épouse divine Şarpanitu (George 1992: 109–119).

Selon la *Tablette de l'Esagil*, la ziggurat devait s'élever à 90 mètres de haut. L'archéologie a confirmé que, pour la dernière phase du bâtiment, la base du monument équivalait à un carré de 90 mètres de côté, véhiculant l'idée d'un édifice aux dimensions égales et parfaites (Schmid 1995: 79–94). Cependant, seul le plan au sol de la ziggurat a été mis au jour, le monument étant presque complètement détruit. De fait, l'hypothèse d'une tour haute de 90 mètres a été remise en question par J. L. Montero Fenollós, qui propose de revoir sa hauteur à 60 mètres (Montero Fenollós 2008). Les autres ziggurats dégagées au Proche-Orient, comme celle d'Ur dans le sud de l'Irak actuel, sont d'ailleurs généralement plus larges que hautes, pour apporter une meilleure stabilité à la construction.

Enfin, les symboles divins apposés sur les murs et portes des sanctuaires contribuent à leur monumentalité et à la grandeur de la ville. Par exemple, le principal marqueur de l'Etemenanki est une décoration de cornes, comme pour les autres ziggurats (André-Salvini 2008: 167), tandis que les portes du temple de l'Esagil étaient ornées de dragons-*mušhuššu*, également animal attribut du dieu Marduk (Da Riva 2013: C23, col., l. 21–32). L'implantation divine s'exprime, en outre, par la décoration de points névralgiques dans Babylone, comme la Voie Processionnelle et la Porte d'Ištar, qui portent des représentations d'animaux fantastiques et apotropaïques (lions, taureaux et dragons-*mušhuššu*), destinés à protéger la ville des dangers (Watanabe 2015).

---

11 George 2011: 156 et pl. LVIII et LIX. Voir également https://www.schoyencollection.com/history-collection-introduction/babylonian-history-collection/tower-babel-stele-ms-2063 (consulté le 5 janvier 2019).

Conclusion

L'aspect monumental de Babylone ne s'exprime pas simplement au travers de la grandeur physique de ses monuments. La monumentalité est, bien sûr, synonyme de bâtiments colossaux, démesurés, mais qui véhiculent dans le même temps des qualités grandioses et puissantes, destinées à étonner et à subjuguer. Par conséquent, pour être considérés comme monumentaux, une ville ou un édifice doivent aussi détenir une forte charge symbolique. Babylone apparaît comme une ville immense, polarisée entre un grand complexe palatial et un immense centre religieux. L'une de ses principales caractéristiques est d'être une ville sacrée, garante d'un certain nombre de privilèges pour ses habitants, comme le résume bien la lettre SAA 18 158 issue de la correspondance des rois assyriens:

> "'Babylone est le lien entre les pays'. Quiconque entre en son sein voit ses statuts privilégiés assurés. De plus, Babylone est le bol du chien d'Enlil. Son nom établit la protection. Même un chien qui entre dans la ville n'est pas tué" (Reynolds 2003: texte 158).

La singularité de Babylone s'exprime au sein des inscriptions royales, commandées par les souverains afin de louer la majesté et la grandeur de leur capitale et ce, particulièrement, pendant la période néo-babylonienne. Si cela est éclatant pendant le règne de Nabuchodonosor II, cette expression d'une ville sacrée grandiose était déjà en germe dans une inscription royale du roi assyrien Tiglath-Phalazar III (745–727), qui évoquait Babylone comme une "ville sacrée sans rivale", au même titre que Sippar, Nippur ou Borsippa (Tadmor et Yamada 2011: texte Tiglath-Phalazar III 47, l. 11).

Bibliographie

Abraham, K. (2004): Business and Politics under the Persian Empire. The Financial Dealings of Marduk-nāṣir-apli of the House of Egibi (521–487 B.C.E.), Bethesda: CDL Press.

André-Salvini, B. (2008): "La ville au temps de Nabuchodonosor II: plans et monuments." In: B. André-Salvini (ed.), Babylone, Paris: Musée du Louvre Éditions, pp. 161–168.

Beaulieu, P.-A. (2005): "Eanna's contribution to the construction of the North Palace at Babylon." In: H. D. Baker/M. Jursa (eds.), Approaching the Babylonian Economy. Proceedings of the START Project Symposium Held in Vienna, 1–3 July 2004, Alter Orient und Altes Testament 330, Münster: Ugarit-Verlag, pp. 45–73.

Bergamini, G. (1977): "Levels of Babylon Reconsidered." In: Mesopotamia 12, pp. 111–152.

Burstein, S. M. (1978): The Babyloniaca of Berossus, Sources from the Ancient Near East 1/5, Malibu: Undena.

Charpin, D. (1991): "Les deux palais de Babylone." In: Nouvelles Assyriologiques Brèves et Utilitaires 1991/02, pp. 39–40.

Charpin, D. (2003): "La date de la construction de la muraille de Babylone." In: Nouvelles Assyriologiques Brèves et Utilitaires 2003/01, pp. 3.

Charpin, D. (2004): "Histoire politique du Proche-Orient ancien (2002–1595)." In: P. Attinger/W. Sallaberger/M. Wäfler (eds.), Mesopotamien. Die altbabylonische Zeit, Orbis Biblicus et Orientalis 160/4, Freiburg; Göttingen: Vandenhoeck & Ruprecht, pp. 25–480.

Charpin, D. (2006): "Chroniques bibliographiques. 7. Les inscriptions royales suméro-akkadiennes d'époque paléo-babylonienne." In: Revue d'Assyriologie et d'Archéologie Orientale 100, pp. 131–160.

Cousin, L. (2015): "Construction, destruction et rénovation: le palais de Babylone au Ier millénaire." In: C. Michel (ed.), De la maison à la ville dans l'orient ancien: bâtiments publics et lieux de pouvoir, Cahiers des thèmes transversaux d'ArScAn 12, Nanterre: ArScAn, pp. 209–216.

Da Riva, R. (2008): The Neo-Babylonian Royal Inscriptions. An Introduction, Guides to the Mesopotamian Textual Records 4, Münster: Ugarit-Verlag.

Da Riva, R. (2012): The Twin Inscriptions of Nebuchadnezzar at Brisa (Wadi esh-Sharbin, Lebanon). A Historical and Philological Study, AfO Beiheft 32, Vienna: Institut für Orientalistik der Universität Wien.

Da Riva, R. (2013): The Inscriptions of Nabopolassar, Amēl-Marduk and Neriglissar, Studies in Ancient Near Eastern Records 3, Boston; Berlin: De Gruyter.

George, A. R. (1992): Babylonian Topographical Texts, Orientalia Lovaniensia Analecta 40, Leuven: Peeters.

George, A. R. (2001/02): "Palace names and Epithets, and the Vaulted Building." In: Sumer 51, pp. 38–42.

George, A. R. (2011): Cuneiform Royal Inscriptions and Related Texts in the Schøyen Collection, Cornell University Studies in Assyriology and Sumerology 17, Bethesda: CDL Press.

Grayson, A. K. (1981): "Assyrian Royal Inscriptions: Literary Characteristics." In: F. M. Fales (ed.), Assyrian Royal Inscriptions: New Horizons in literary, ideological, and historical analysis. Papers of a symposium held in Cetona (Siena) June 26–28, 1980, Orientis Antiqui Collection 17, Rome: Istituto per l'Oriente, Centro per le antichità e la storia dell'arte del Vicino Oriente, pp. 35–47.

Grayson, A. K./Novotny, J. R. (2012): The Royal Inscriptions of Sennacherib, King of Assyria, 704–681 BC. Part 1, The Royal Inscriptions of the Neo-Assyrian Period 3/1, Winona Lake: Eisenbrauns.

Hérodote, Histoires I.178, http://remacle.org/bloodwolf/historiens/herodote/clio. htm (last accessed January 5, 2019).

Horsnell, M. J. A. (1999): The Year-Names of the First Dynasty of Babylon. Volume II, Hamilton: McMaster University Press.

Joannès, F. (2011): "L'écriture publique du pouvoir à Babylone sous Nabuchodonosor II." In: E. Cancik-Kirschbaum/M. van Ess/J. Marzahn (eds.), Babylon: Wissenskultur in Orient und Okzident, Topoi 1, Berlin; New York: De Gruyter, pp. 113–120.

Jursa, M. (2007): "Die Söhne Kudurrus und die Herkunft der neubabylonischen Dynastie." In: Revue d'Assyriologie et d'Archéologie Orientale 101, pp. 125–136.

Koldewey, R. (1925): Das wieder erstehende Babylon: die bisherigen Ergebnisse der deutschen Ausgrabungen, Leipzig: J. C. Hinrichs.

Koldewey, R. (1931): Die Königsburgen von Babylon. 1. Teil: die Südburg, Wissenschaftliche Veröffentlichung der Deutschen Orient-Gesellschaft 54, Leipzig: J. C. Hinrichs.

Koldewey, R. (1932): Die Königsburgen von Babylon. 2. Teil: die Hauptburg und der Sommerpalast Nebukadnezars im Hügel Babil, Wissenschaftliche Veröffentlichung der Deutschen Orient-Gesellschaft 55, Leipzig: J. C. Hinrichs.

Lambert, W. G. (1984): "Studies in Marduk." In: Bulletin of the School of Oriental and African Studies 47, pp. 1–9.

Lambert, W. G. (2011): "Babylon: Origins." In: E. Cancik-Kirschbaum/M. van Ess/J. Marzahn (eds.), Babylon: Wissenskultur in Orient und Okzident, Topoi 1, Berlin; New York: De Gruyter, pp. 77–89.

Langdon, S. (1912): Die neubabylonischen Königsinschriften, Vorderasiatische Bibliothek 4, Leipzig: J. C. Hinrichs.

Leichty, E. (2011): The Royal Inscriptions of Esarhaddon, King of Assyria (680–669 BC), The Royal Inscriptions of the Neo-Assyrian Period 4, Winona Lake: Eisenbrauns.

Margueron, J.-C. (2008): "Considérations sur le palais de Babylone." In: B. André-Salvini (ed.), Babylone, Paris: Musée du Louvre Éditions, pp. 228.

Marzahn, J. (2008): "Les fouilles archéologiques allemandes." In: B. André-Salvini (ed.), Babylone, Paris: Musée du Louvre Éditions, pp. 516–525.

Montero Fenollós, J. L. (2008): "La tour de Babylone repensée." In: B. André-Salvini (ed.), Babylone, Paris: Musée du Louvre Éditions, pp. 229–230.

Nevling Porter, B. (1993): Images, Power, and Politics: Figurative Aspects of Esarhaddon's Babylonian Policy, Philadelphia: American Philosophical Society.

Pedersén, O. (2005): Archive und Bibliotheken in Babylon. Die Tontafeln der Grabung Robert Koldeweys 1899–1917, Abhandlungen der Deutschen Orient-Gesellschaft 25, Berlin: Saarländische Druckerei und Verlag.

Pline l'Ancien, Naturalis Historia VI. XXX, http://remacle.org/bloodwolf/erudits/ plineancien/livre6.htm (last accessed January 5, 2019).

Reuther, O. (1926): Die Innenstadt von Babylon (Merkes), Wissenschaftliche Veröffentlichung der Deutschen Orient-Gesellschaft 47, Leipzig: J. C. Hinrichs.

Reynolds, F. S. (2003): The Babylonian Correspondence of Esarhaddon and Letters
to Assurbanipal and Sin-šarra-iškun from northern and central Babylonia,
State Archive of Assyria 18, Helsinki: Helsinki University Press.

Schmid, H. (1995): Der Tempelturm Etemenanki in Babylon, Baghdader Forschungen 17, Mainz am Rhein: P. von Zabern.

Sommerfeld, W. (1982): Die Aufstieg Marduks. Die Stellung Marduks in der neubabylonischen Religion des zweitens Jahrtausends v. Chr., Alter Orient und
Altes Testament 213, Kevelaer; Neukirchen-Vluyn: Butzon & Bercker; Neukir-
chener Verlag.

Tadmor H./Yamada, S. (2011): The Royal Inscriptions of Tiglath-pileser III (744–
727 BC) and Shalmaneser V (726–722 BC), Kings of Assyria, The Royal Inscriptions of the Neo-Assyrian Period 1, Winona Lake: Eisenbrauns.

Watanabe, C. E. (2015): "The Symbolic Role of Animals in Babylon: A Contextual
Approach to the Lion, the Bull and the *mušḫuššu*." In: Iraq 77, pp. 215–244.

Other Sources

Stèle Schøyen, 5 Janvier 2019 (https://www.schoyencollection.com/history-collec
tion-introduction/babylonian-history-collection/tower-babel-stele-ms-2063).

The monumental Late Antique cisterns of Resafa, Syria as refined capacity and water-quality regulation system[1]

Catharine Hof

Although Resafa's four large cisterns were built consecutively, they constitute an associated sophisticated system. This monumental system contributed not only to the amount of storage capacity but also divided the various basic needs by quality, thereby avoiding any waste. This approach was an outstanding hygienic measure to cope with the poor quality of the run-off wadi water.

This paper analyses the hydraulic system and hints at the efforts exerted by the local community to deal with life in a basically uninhabitable place.

Conditions and town development

Two conditions dictated settlement activities in Resafa. First and foremost was the climate of the desert-steppe with its meager average annual rainfall of 100–200 ml (Wirth 1971: 92–93 maps 3–4; Jaubert et al. 1999: 15 map 3). The environmental conditions have changed little since antiquity, so that modern weather data are used in hydrological modeling for ancient Resafa (Beckers 2013: 34–84, 46). Additionally, the lime-gypsum earths between the Euphrates and the Jabal Abu Rajmayn, as part of the Palmyra folds, determined the quality of the groundwater. It is brackish in the entire region and of exceptionally poor quality, and thus non-potable near Resafa where groundwater salinity is 3000–6500 mg/l TDS (Wagner 2011: 168, 175; cf. Al-Charideh/Hasan 2013: 74, Tab. 1). Resafa had no fresh groundwater (contra Wagner 2011: 144) and, accordingly, the seasonal rainwater had to be collected in cisterns and this supply had to last over the year.

---

1 Work on the Great Cistern of Resafa is part of the general Resafa Project 2006–2012, led by Dorothée Sack of the Berlin University of Technology. With the support of a fellowship from the Free University of Berlin (Topoi Excellence Cluster 264) in 2016, I have been able to explore the raw data of the laser scans and establish the plans of the cistern presented here. The laser scans were performed in 2010 by Ingo Neumann and Hansbert Heister and their team from the Bundeswehr University Munich.

Figure 1: Situation plan (C. Hof)

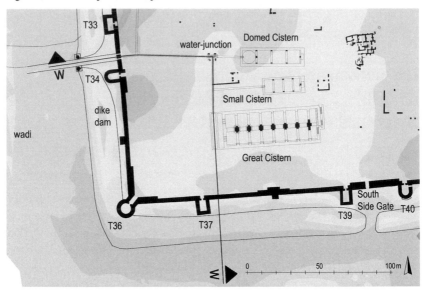

Figure 2: Resafa, southwestern city area (C. Hof)

Resafa started off as a military fort and in the early stages of settlement (approximately from the 4th to the late 5th century CE), the fresh water was collected in individual, small, and usually pear-shaped cisterns (Brinker 1991: 123–124, 132–137).

Despite the unfavorable conditions of water provision, Resafa experienced exceptional development because it was on the crossing of long-distance trade routes, and more so, because it turned into the pilgrimage center of Saint Sergius. Both aspects were attractive to visitors, who were the main source of the city's growing wealth.

The need for expansion led to a large-scale urban development project. This enterprise was launched at the turn of the 5th to the 6th century CE, comprising a new extended town wall, several churches, and a monumental hydraulic system (Hof 2016: 399–404). The provision of this first cistern must have been a basic requirement for running the large-scale city expansion building site in the desert steppe (Hof 2017: 68–69 with Figure 2).

The water catchment structure in its final stage comprised dikes, partly embanking the wadi as-Sayla, a transversal earthen barrier damming the wadi-floods, a canal leading the water into the city, and four capacious cisterns.[2]

The smallest of these tanks lies isolated in the northwestern city area, while the three others, the Domed, the Small, and the Great Cisterns, form a group near the southwest corner of the city wall (Figures 1–2).

Short description

The Great Cistern (Figure 3) rises over a rectangular plan with internal dimensions of 64.56 m in length and 19.58 m in width (Figure 4) (cf. Spanner/Guyer 1926: 45–46, 69; Brinker 1991: 126–127; Brinker/Garbrecht 2007: 132–133). Seven massive, cruciform pillars (I-VII) form an arcade dividing the chamber into two naves and eight bays.

The easternmost pillar (I) marks the intersection of the arcade wall with a transversal wall. This transversal wall divides the seven-bayed main reservoir from a double-chamber with a flight of stairs along the east wall. This entrance bay is narrower than the other seven bays, lower, and covered by a transverse barrel vault made of brick ('mitre-pattern vaults', Hof 2018) rather than the gypsum and limestone vaults of the main naves (Figure 4). On the western end of the cistern, two inlets are placed slightly higher (288.73 m AMSL) than the springing of the main vaults.

---

2 The barrage-canal system damming the wadi is presented in Brinker 1991; Garbrecht 1991; Brinker/Garbrecht 2007. For the dike structures running alongside the flow direction to the south of the city's enclosure, cf. Beckers 2013: 55–56, 67–68, 76–77. The western rampart of the city wall and its original sole function also as a dike is discussed in Hof (forthcoming). Major studies on Resafa's cisterns are Brinker (1991) and Westphalen/Knötzele (2004).

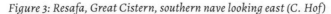

Figure 3: Resafa, Great Cistern, southern nave looking east (C. Hof)

Figure 4: Resafa, Great Cistern, ground plan and sections (C. Hof)

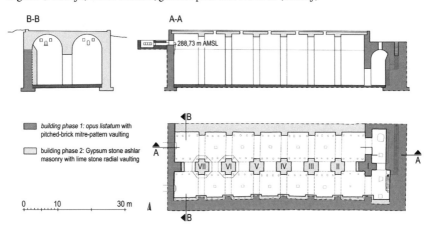

The highest possible filling height was 12.20 m. Former works have estimated the volume to 15–16,000 m³ (Spanner 1926: 45) or to 14,600 m³ (Brinker 1991: 126 and Garbrecht 1991: 246 Figure 9). Yet, cistern capacity figures are often too high because the volumes of pillars and walls within the body of the tank are not subtracted in the estimation. According to the volume properties of our 3D CAD model based on the laser scans, the maximum water capacity up to the inlet level was 12,600 m³ (Figure 5).

Figure 5: Resafa, Great Cistern, 3D model of maximum water capacity (C. Hof)

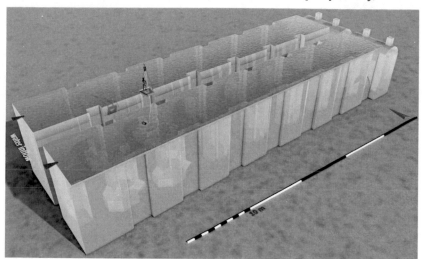

This volume is equivalent to the amount of water that the renowned Piscina Mirabilis near Naples, Italy was able to hold (De Feo et al. 2010). For a provincial structure, this is truly large – although the roughly contemporary Yerebatan Sarnıcı in Constantinople is nearly six times larger. Table 1 provides some reference data.

Table 1: Examples of Late Antique large cisterns

Cistern	Capacity	Date
Cistern of La Malga (Carthage)	~55,000 m³ *	approximately 1st century BCE to 2nd century CE
Yerebatan Sarnıcı (Constantinople)	~80,000 m³ *	approximately 540 CE
Piscina Mirabilis (Bascoli)	10,700 m³ * 12,600 m³ **	approximately 30 BCE
Great Cistern (Resafa)	12,600 m³	late 5th/early 6th century CE
All four cisterns in Resafa	ca. 18,800 m³ ***	late 5th to approximately 8th century CE

* After Döring 2007: 12, Table 1.
** After De Feo et al. 2010: 351, 354.
*** Sum: (Small Cistern 2050 m³ + Domed Cistern 3400 m³ + Northwest Cistern 770 m³ after Brinker 1991) + Great Cistern 12,600 (laser scanning 2010) = 18,820 m³

The Great Cistern of Resafa already held two-thirds of the total capacity of all four large cisterns of Resafa taken together. According to the typology by Mathias Döring, Resafa's Great Cistern represents "perfection in [Roman] cistern building"

i. e. his 'Typus IV' with several longitudinal and transversal aisles or naves (Döring 2007: 13–14; Döring 2014: 218; cf. Riera 1994: 313–386). Nevertheless, what makes the Great Cistern of Resafa highly significant is not so much its absolute capacity as its role within the overall hydraulic system of the city.

Building phases

According to our present knowledge, the water infrastructure in Resafa seems to have developed as follows (Sack Resafa 8 forthcoming, for former deviating estimates cf. Brinker 1991; Westphalen/Knötzele 2004). In the last quarter of the 5th century CE, the large church building of Basilica A was under construction. The brackish groundwater might have been sufficient, albeit not ideal, for construction needs, but the first cistern, called the Domed Cistern, had probably been built to meet the needs of the workmen (Hof 2017: 68–69). In the next phase of the urban building project, which expanded from approximately 500 CE onwards, the monumental new town wall came under construction. Therefore, far larger amounts of water had to be provided and with some certainty the Great Cistern was built next. Still in the course of the earlier 6th century, the Small Cistern seems to have been added and the Great Cistern was almost completely rebuilt, again meeting the needs of a thriving town and its further development projects.[3] The entire system was maintained in the second quarter of the 8th century and from then on appears to have fallen into disrepair.

Hydraulic concept and strategy of provision

The terrain section (Figure 6) follows an angled line from the axis of the water canal *extra muros* in the west to the four-pillared canal junction where one branch turns sharply south, passing the intake canals of the Domed and Small Cisterns, continuing through the settling tank in front of the Great Cistern, and ending at the terrain to the south of the city wall.

In the profile exaggerated vertically by 2:1, the subtle inclination changes of the bottom line of the canal are hardly apprehensible. Thus, a second, more schematic graph of the same section but with a vertical exaggeration of 100:1 further illustrates the situation (Figure 7).

Coming from the wadi to the west, the floodwater passes a shallow settling basin (288.70 m) at the two pillars roughly 30 m outside of the city wall. From there,

---

3 The construction or rebuilding of an unspecified cistern is known due to an inscription dated to the time after 528 CE (Gatier 1998: 237–240; Chaniotis et al. 1998).

Figure 6: Resafa, Terrain section w-w, vertically exaggerated 2:1 (C. Hof)

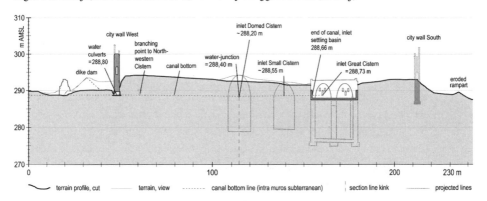

Figure 7: Schematic profile w-w, vertically exaggerated 100:1 (C. Hof). The red line indicates the bed of the canal. The blue line is the gradient between the bed of the water culvert through the city wall and the inlet of the Great Cistern. The colored area simulates a floodwater level at 288.82 m AMSL, thus 2 cm above the canal bed within the culvert

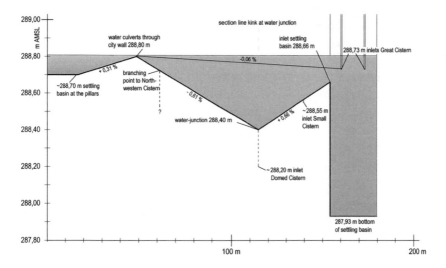

the canal suddenly has a positive slope (+0.31 per cent) until it reaches the culverts in the city wall (288.80 m). With again a negative slope, now of –0.61 per cent, the canal continues to the junction (a four-pillared building structure) with its bed at 288.40 m. The original old branch of the canal continues straight to the Domed Cistern, the inlet of which lies at approximately 288.20 m. The presumably younger branch bends south to feed the Small and Great Cisterns. The surprising finding is that this branch of the canal has an ascending slope (+0.66 per cent, the steepest) until it reaches the inlet (at 288.66 m) of the settling tank in front of the Great Cistern. After roughly half the reach, the canal again splits and a branch turns east to feed the Small Cistern.

The uphill gradient was not an accident but was achieved deliberately. Both measures, the positive slope of the canal and the settling tank resulted in inlet throttling and thus, particle settling. The overall slope of the system from the culverts through the city wall to the inlets of the Great Cistern (blue line) is extremely small. Over a length of 112 m, the height difference is only 7 cm, which is equivalent to 0.06 per cent, an angle of 0.04°.[4] This slope may seem very small, as a modern-day architect would certainly suggest a 1–3 per cent drainage slope for a water run-off device or structure such as a rain gutter or flat roof. Nevertheless, the value is by no means unusual, as comparison shows.

For example, in the vicinity of Androna (al-Andarīn), not far west of Resafa, the *qanat* (Lightfoot 1996; Jaubert et al. 1999: 32–35) system supplying the so-called Northwest Reservoir has been surveyed (Mundell Mango 2011: 104–107, esp. Figure 10 from which the gradient can be calculated). Its mean gradient is 0.08 per cent with a maximum slope of 0.17 per cent. The system of Valens aqueduct, which directs water from the northwestern hinterland to Constantinople, has almost the same total gradient, i. e. 0.07 per cent, as those in Resafa and Androna (Crow et al. 2008: 121). The complete hydraulic system comprising the famous Aqueduct of Nimes in France has an average slope of only 0.034 per cent, which seems to mark the minimum for Roman systems (Hodge 1992: 186).[5] The mean gradient of Roman aqueducts ranges between 0.15 per cent and 0.3 per cent (Hodge 1992: 218).

Altogether, the hydraulic system in Resafa shows several measures aimed at flow throttling. We can assume that during seasons of heavy rain, large amounts of floodwater rushed through the system and had to be tamed. The measures taken show the need to address not only the incoming water but also the refuse and solvents it brought along.

---

4   This clearly contradicts Garbrecht's statement that the inlet of the Great Cistern lies 0.60 m below the bed of the canal near the pillars *extra muros* (Garbrecht 1991: 245). Garbrecht provides no level measurements, but the same difference can be derived with some transformation from Brinker's (1991) levels given in his Figure 11 (canal between the pillars) and Figure 12 (culverts through the city wall). According to present knowledge, the heights presented in Figure 11 must be wrong. A complete discussion will be presented in Sack Resafa 8 (forthcoming).

5   Hodge's dimensions for slope are meter per kilometer; thus, he speaks of a gradient of 0.34 which is equivalent to 0.034 per cent.

Cisterns in serial connection

The question arises as to why the three large cisterns in the southwest of Resafa form a group. If we look, for example, at Constantinople or Dara, the cisterns are built as close as possible to the neighborhood where there is an actual demand for water. One reason for the series connection can be deduced from a recommendation by Vitruvius in approximately 20 BCE:[6]

> If such constructions [cisterns] are in two compartments or in three so as to insure clearing by changing from one to another, they will make the water much more wholesome and sweeter to use. For it will become more limpid, and keep its taste without any smell, if the mud has somewhere to settle; otherwise it will be necessary to clear it by adding salt. (Vitruvius 1914: 8. 6. 15).

The salt mentioned probably refers to potassium alum, which was used in antiquity for purifying water (Syvänne 2007: 71–74).

Vitruvius describes the purpose of two to three tanks in series to improve water quality. In theory, an arrangement in series allows the water to seep between the partitions of the cisterns thereby filtering it. Although the statement by Vitruvius is not clear on structural details, the key message is that a series of cisterns can be used to improve water quality. Vitruvius seems to describe two phenomena as one: on the one hand, the filter effect of the soil or rock and, on the other hand, the problem of pollution by suspended solids.

The general objective of Vitruvius' book 8 on water is a three-part, hierarchical distribution; the highest priority is given to public basins and fountains, then to public baths, and finally to households that pay for private supplies (Vitruvius 1914: 8. 6. 1-2; cf. Evans 1997: 7). Archaeological evidence has not been provided to demonstrate this strict division in the form of practical implementation, but the hypothetical approach illustrates the importance of a general water supply policy in communities.

A filtering effect of the spaces between the cisterns could not have been intended in Resafa because each cistern is sealed by hydraulic plaster. In addition, they are too far apart to achieve a communication system by leachate. However, sophisticated water purification could have been intended otherwise, as indicated by the fact that the supply line rises along the cisterns and that only the Great Cistern has its own settling basin. With this arrangement, the first flow of unsettled water with high concentrations of turbid substances can be directed into the

---

6 As a starting point for the wider discussion of water treatment in antique scripts cf. Vuorinen 2007a.

Domed Cistern. This water of inferior quality was suitable as process water and was not dispensable as in other sites with abundant water.

The Domed Cistern was not necessarily filled to the brim; rather the canal to the Great Cistern was opened as soon as possible. Beyond the canal junction, the flow speed was reduced and particles settled out before entering the Great Cistern. There, the inlet was kept open as long as water of sufficient quality arrived, preferably until the Great Cistern was full. The water in the Great Cistern was purified and primarily served as drinking water. Thereafter, the final weakening flow of the precious water could be redirected to further fill the Domed Cistern. The Small Cistern between the two others could have served as a buffer for both demands with medium-quality water.

A good 120 years after Vitruvius, Sextus Iulius Frontinus wrote his work, which deals with the water supply of Rome and emphasizes the improvements in this area made by Emperor Nerva (r. 96–98 CE) (Frontinus *Aquaeductu*: 87–93 quoted after Evans 1997: 37–39). Rome hardly had any problems with water availability, but its blessed inhabitants would at times complain about the presence of turbid water. Frontinus describes the problems regarding the fluctuating water quality in the collection plants. A situation that pleased the residents of Resafa, namely, rainy weather, was a nuisance to the consumers in Rome. Precipitation and surface run-off water in aqueducts that were fed from open-water plants contaminated the water at the source of the aqueduct, the external collection points (Frontinus *Aquaeductu*: 89 quoted after Evans 1997: 38; for Frontinus on water quality cf. Rodgers 2004: 23–24). Settling tanks were not sufficient to clear the water enough to satisfy consumer's taste. Some aqueducts, such as the Aqua Claudia named by Frontinus, and especially the Aqua Marcia, were appreciated for their cold and pure water even in bad weather conditions. Promoting the same high quality of all aqueducts was not possible, so Frontinus makes the theoretically understandable, but in practice hardly feasible, proposal to use the reservoirs according to their water quality: pure water such as that from Aqua Marcia as drinking water, other conduits with medium-quality water for other purposes, and finally polluted water, such as from the Anio Vetus, for garden irrigation (Frontinus *Aquaeductu*: 92 quoted after Evans 1997: 39) and probably livestock (Evans 1997: 81; Rodgers 2004: 255). In practice, this approach would have meant that three lines would have had to arrive in every water-supply quarter.

Neither the technical design according to Frontinus (separate supply lines for separate quality levels) nor the older Vitruvian approach (filtering according to a leakage principle) can be found in Resafa exactly as outlined in the sources. Nevertheless, the basic ideas of quality improvement and quality separation are reflected in Resafa's hydraulic system. Unlike Rome's, Resafa's collection system relied completely on rainfall. However, the alluvial muddy run-off water from the dusty, naturally polluted environment was hardly suitable for drinking. This condition seems to have been recognized only after having experienced water-quality issues with the Domed Cistern as the sole reservoir. The hydraulic system was extended and redesigned to become the subtle and sophisticated operating mechanism described above.

Resafa's cistern system under hygienic considerations

The crucial difference between Resafa's water collection system and most of the other localities that also sourced water from the surrounding area was that the water of Resafa did not come from smooth, rocky plains but from the sandy, dusty soils of extensive pastureland near the confluence of several small wadis with the wide funnel of Wadi as-Sayla. This water was not only clouded by inert soil particles but was contaminated by organic and thus hazardous substances such as animal faeces, insects, plants, and small animal carcasses.

The sanitary problems associated with such so-called surface-water run-off cisterns, which are primarily fed from surface water from unsealed areas, were examined in the early 20th century in two extensive studies on Jerusalem, Palestine, and Syria.[7] The groundwater in Jerusalem is like that in Resafa, i. e. unusually brackish, and thus fresh water was collected in cisterns and consumed until the modern age. Anastasius I (r. 491–518 CE) held such conditions to be appalling and initiated the construction of an aqueduct supply system (Procopius of Gaza 1986: 18).[8] Two aqueducts brought clean water to the so-called Solomonic ponds near Bethlehem and from there to Jerusalem's upper city, but the other urban areas remained completely dependent on locally collected rainwater (Masterman 1918: 57–58).

Until the 19th century, the microbial causes of diseases due to aquatic pathogens were unknown, but the basic causal relationships between water quality and health were well understood in previous times. Clear and cool water was considered not only the best in taste but also the most wholesome. Covered drinking water cisterns were viewed as extremely important, whereas open reservoirs usually served as process water supply (Hellmann 1994; Vuorinen 2007a: 48–49, 53–54, 64; Vuorinen 2007b: 110; van Tilburg 2013; Fahlbusch 2014: 11–14).

In its last stage of development, the water supply and the proposed elementary hygienic concept seemed to have worked satisfactorily. Otherwise, the ancient

---

7 Mühlens 1913; Masterman 1918. On the problems of surface-water runoff cisterns, cf. Mühlens 1913: 57–58; Mühlens' early work as an engaged physician in Jerusalem, Aleppo, and Constantinople and his later change to become a compliant servant of the regime in the Third Reich are described in Wulf 2005.

8 On the discussion about whether the passage refers to Jerusalem, or Hierapolis in Phrygia, or Hierapolis in Cilicia cf. Pickett 2018: 119 n. 127.

authors Procopius (2002[1954]: 2, 9, 3–9), Yāqūt ar-Rūmī (Kellner-Heinkele 1996: 146) and Ḥamza ibn Ḥasan al-Iṣfahānī (Musil 1928: 267; Kellner-Heinkele 1996: 150–151 as cited in Ibn al-ʿAdīm and Ibn Šaddād) would hardly have claimed authorship for the named builders, respectively rulers, Emperor Justinian I (r. 527–565) or al-Munḏir ibn al-Ḥāriṯ (r. 569–582).[9] Just recently Jordan Pickett has demonstrated how Procopius elevated the technical structures of inconspicuous reservoirs and cisterns to the league of commonly praiseworthy targets of imperial patronage, such as aqueducts and baths (Pickett 2018: 99, 118–122).

Fortuna or luminary?

Resafa's sizeable hydraulic system required the highest engineering competencies for execution. Developing and implementing the purifying concept and the additional separation by water quality to the primal basic collecting installation clearly followed a sophisticated plan. This finding not only added further tanks in a row but also refined the methods of settling suspended particles through throttling the feed rate of the cisterns, particularly the Great Cistern. What traces of acknowledged expertise do we know of, whose influence or even direct participation would have been possible?

The most probable authority is known to have been responsible for the hydraulic structures at Dara-Anastasiupolis, which were built around 507 CE under Anastasius I (r. 491–518). That fortified border city dates to the same time as the advancing project of city expansion in Resafa. A short time after Dara had been built, with its enclosure wall encompassing a section of the Cordes stream, a devastating seasonal flash flood damaged the city wall and parts of the town (Procopius 2002[1954]: 2, 2, 13–15). The same luminary who had planned the original system, Chryses of Alexandria, was now consulted to achieve a safer system of dams, canalization, and water storage.[10] The exact dating of the flood event and the following redesign of the hydraulic system in Dara remains unclear but can be estimated to the

---

9   The sources mention an-Nuʿmān ibn al-Ḥāriṯ ibn al-Ayham, who ruled 434–453, which is too early; thus, a naming error might have occurred. If this mistake effects the given name and the patronising ibn al-Ḥāriṯ is correct, then the name should have been al-Munḏir ibn al-Ḥāriṯ (r. 569–582), the builder of the so-called al-Munḏir-Building just outside the walls of Resafa (Kellner-Heinkele 1996: 146, n. 114 – she also regards the Father, al-Ḥāriṯ ibn Ǧabala r. 529–569 as a candidate; Shahîd 2002: 122–129, esp. n. 194).

10   For the twisted story of Chryses' divine inspiration through a dream, leaving the Emperor Justinian as the true designer of the plan cf. Procopius (2002[1954]): 2, 3, 3–15; for the paradox of the events, cf. Turquois 2015: 228–230. The full description of the rebuilding is covered by Procopius (2002[1954]): 2, 3, 1–26. For Dara's role within the topic of water management in Procopius' Buildings cf. Pickett 2018: 105–110.

first third of the 6th century CE.[11] Chryses was a contemporary of the renowned architects of the Hagia Sophia (532–537) at Constantinople, Isidore of Miletus and Anthemius of Tralles, and according to the descriptions of Procopius, he was responsible not only for the hydraulic structures in Dara but also for those "in the rest of the country" (Procopius 2002[1954]: 2, 3, 2). Chryses must have visited Dara twice, before and after the flood, and his journey may have led him over Resafa which lies on one of the possible routes between Alexandria and Dara. At the later G. Garbrecht finds considerable similarities between the description by Procopius and the still existing remains of the dam, even if the dam wall is polygonal and not crescent shaped (Garbrecht 2004: 117, 119–120). There is no reason to assume that the building developers in Resafa would not have made use of the expertise of Chryses, coming from the "City of Cisterns", Alexandria (Empereur 1998: 125–144).

The traces concerning the motivation to expand the infrastructural facilities of the former military post in Resafa do not indicate the involvement of the emperor or any military personality but hint at a local client (Ulbert 2000: 144–145; Mundell Mango 2008: 78–79). One cistern (as yet unspecified) is attested by inscription and connected to John, the deacon of Antioch, with a terminus *post quem* of 528 CE (Chaniotis et al. 1998; Gatier 1998: 237–240). The civil authorities in Resafa at the time probably made an extra large-scale investment in what was becoming the main economic factor of their community: the well-being of pilgrims and merchants.

Literature

Al-Charideh, A./Hasan, A. (2013): "Use of Isotopic Tracers to Characterize the Interaction of Water Components and Nitrate Contamination in the Arid Rasafeh Area (Syria)." In: Environmental Earth Sciences 70/1, pp. 71–82.

Beckers, B. (2014): "Ancient Food and Water Supply in Drylands. Geoarchaeological Perspectives on the Water Harvesting Systems of the Two Ancient Cities Resafa, Syria and Petra, Jordan." Ph. D. Thesis, Berlin: Freie Universität Berlin.

Brinker, W. (1991): "Zur Wasserversorgung von Resafa-Sergiupolis." In: Damaszener Mitteilungen 5, pp. 119–146.

Brinker, W./Garbrecht, G. (2007): "Die Zisternen-Wasserversorgung von Resafa-Sergiupolis." In: C. Ohlig (ed.) Antike Zisternen, Schriften der Deutschen Wasserhistorischen Gesellschaft 9, Siegburg: Deutschen Wasserhistorischen Gesellschaft, pp. 117–144.

---

11 The building of the dam still within the reign of Anastasius I (r. 491–518) is suggested by Croke/ Crow 1983: 158. M. Whitby (1986: 768) holds the 520s more probable, thus during the reign of Justin I (r. 518–527) or the early Justinian I (527–565), thus following Procopius. The 530s are also mentioned as an extended option (Zanini 1990: 250).

Chaniotis, A./Pleket, H. W./Stroud, R. S./Strubbe, J. H. M. ([First published online:] 1998): "SEG 48-1867-1868. Sergioupolis-Resafa. Two inscriptions, after 518/528 A. D." In: A. Chaniotis/T. Corsten/N. Papazarkadas/R. A. Tybout (eds.), Supplementum Epigraphicum Graecum, http://dx-1doi-1org-1oo7e65xz022f.erf.sbb. spk-berlin.de/10.1163/1874-6772_seg_a48_1867_1868 (last accessed December 29, 2018).

Croke, B./Crow, J. (1983): "Procopius and Dara." In: The Journal of Roman Studies 73, pp. 143–159.

Crow, J./Bardill, J./Bayliss, R./Bono, P. (2008): The Water Supply of Byzantine Constantinople, The Journal of Roman Studies Monograph 11, London: Society for the Promotion of Roman Studies.

De Feo, G./De Gisi, S./Malvano, C./De Biase, O. (2010): "The Greatest Water Reservoirs in the Ancient Roman World and the 'Piscina Mirabilis' in Misenum." In: Water Science & Technology Water Supply 1, pp. 350–358.

Döring, M. (2007): "Römische Aquädukte und Großzisternen der Phlegraeischen Felder." In: C. Ohlig (ed.), Antike Zisternen, Schriften der Deutschen Wasserhistorischen Gesellschaft 9, Siegburg: Deutschen Wasserhistorischen Gesellschaft, pp. 3–87.

Döring, M. (2014): "Römische Grosszisternen der Phlegraeischen Felder." In: T. Schäfer/F. Schön/A. Gerdes/J. Heinrichs (eds.), Antike und moderne Wasserspeicherung, Internationaler Workshop vom 11.–15. Mai 2011 in Pantelleria (Italien), Tübinger archäologische Forschungen 12, Rahden/Westf.: Leidorf, pp. 215–245, 307.

Empereur, J.-Y. (1998): Alexandria rediscovered, New York: George Braziller.

Evans, H. B. (1997): Water Distribution in Ancient Rome: The Evidence of Frontinus, Ann Arbor: University of Michigan Press.

Fahlbusch, H. (2014): "Konstruktionsunterschiede von antiken Trink- und Brauchwasserspeichern. Vorüberlegungen zur Speicherung von Wasser in Zisternen." In: T. Schäfer/F. Schön/A. Gerdes/J. Heinrichs (eds.), Antike und moderne Wasserspeicherung, Internationaler Workshop vom 11.–15. Mai 2011 in Pantelleria (Italien), Tübinger archäologische Forschungen 12, Rahden/Westf.: Leidorf, pp. 11–18.

Garbrecht, G. (1991): "Der Staudamm von Resafa-Sergiupolis." In: Deutscher Verband für Wasserwirtschaft und Kulturbau (ed.), Historische Talsperren 2, Stuttgart: Wittwer. pp. 237–248.

Garbrecht, G. (2004): "Procopius und die Wasserbauten von Dara." In: C. Ohlig (ed.), Wasserbauten im Königreich Urartu und weitere Beiträge zur Hydrotechnik in der Antike, Schriften der Deutschen Wasserhistorischen Gesellschaft 5, Norderstedt: Books on Demand GmbH, pp. 105–132.

Gatier, P.-L. (1998): "Inscriptions grecques de Résafa." In: Damaszener Mitteilungen 10, pp. 237–241.

Hellmann, M.-C. (1994): "L'eau des citernes et la salubrité. Textes et archéologie." In: R. Ginouvès (ed.), L'eau, la santé et la maladie dans le monde grec, Actes du colloque organisé à Paris (CNRS et Fondation Singer-Polignac) du 25 au 27 novembre 1992 par le Centre de Recherche 'Archéologie et Systèmes d'Information' et par l'URA 1255 'Médecine grecque', Athen: École Francaise d'Athènes, pp. 273–282.

Hodge, A. T. (1992): Roman Aqueducts and Water Supply, London: Duckworth.

Hof, C. (2016): "The Late Roman City Wall of Resafa/Sergiupolis (Syria). Its Evolution and Functional Transition from Representative over Protective to Concealing." In: R. Frederiksen/S. Müth/P. Schneider/M. Schnelle (eds.), Focus on Fortification. New Research on Fortification in the Ancient Mediterranean and the Near East. Conference 6–9 December 2012 at the Danish Institute at Athens, Monographs of the Danish Institute at Athens 18, Oxford: Oxbow Books, pp. 397–412.

Hof, C. (2017): "Baulos, Werkgruppe und Pensum. Zur Baustellenorganisation an der Stadtmauer von Resafa." In: K. Rheidt/W. Lorenz (eds.), Groß Bauen – Großbaustellen als kulturgeschichtliches Phänomen, Basel: Birkhäuser. pp. 63–75, 294–295.

Hof, C. (2018): "Late Antique Vaults in the Cisterns of Resafa with 'Bricks Set in Squares'." In: I. Wouters/S. van de Voorde/I. Bertels/B. Espion/K. de Jonge (eds.), Proceedings of the Sixth International Congress on Construction History, Brussels, July 9–13 2018, vol. 2, Boca Raton: CRC Press. pp. 755–763.

Hof, C. (forthcoming) "The Revivification of Earthen Outworks in the Eastern and Southern Empire by the Example of Resafa/Syria." In: S. Barker/C. Courault/E. Intagliata (eds.), Constructing City Walls in Late Antiquity. An Empire-Wide Perspective. Conference 20–21 June 2018 at the British School at Rome and Swedish Institute of Classical Studies.

Jaubert, R./Debaine, F./Besançon, J./al-Dbyiat, M./Geyer, B./Gintzburger, G./Traboulsi, M. (1999): The Arid Margins of Syria. Land Use and Vegetation Cover. Semi-arid and Arid Areas of Aleppo and Hama Provinces (Syria). Cahiers de recherché, Lyon: Groupe de recherches et d'études sur la Méditerranée et le Moyen-Orient.

Kellner-Heinkele, B. (1996): "Rusafa in den arabischen Quellen." In: D. Sack, Die große Moschee von Resafa – Rusāfat Hišām, Resafa 4, Mainz: Philipp von Zabern, pp. 133–154.

Kollwitz, J./Wirth, W./Karnapp, W. (1958/1959): "Die Grabungen in Resafa Herbst 1954 und 1956." In: Les annales archéologiques arabes syriennes 8/9, pp. 21–54.

Lightfoot, D. R. (1996): "Syrian Qanat Romani. History, Ecology, Abandonment." In: Journal of Arid Environments 33, pp. 321–336.

Masterman, E. W. G. (1918): "Hygiene and Disease in Palestine in Modern and in Biblical Times." In: Quarterly Statement. Palestine Exploration Fund (Palestine Exploration Quarterly) 50, pp. 15–20, 56–71, 112–119.

Mühlens, P. (1913): "Bericht über eine Malariaexpedition nach Jerusalem." In: Centralblatt für Bakteriologie, Parasitenkunde und Infektionskrankheiten, Abt. 1. Medizinisch-hygienische Bakteriologie, Virusforschung und tierische Parasitologie, pp. 41–85.

Mundell Mango, M. (2011): "Byzantine Settlement Expansion in North Central Syria. The Case of Androna/Andarin." In: A. Borrut/M. Debie/A. Papaconstantinou (eds.), Le Proche-Orient de Justinien aux Abbassides. Peuplement et dynamiques spatiales. Actes du colloque «Continuités de l'Occupation entre les Périodes Byzantine et Abbasside au Proche-Orient, VIIe-IXe Siècles», Paris, octobre 18–20, 2007, Bibliothèque de l'Antiquité Tardive 19, Turnhout: Brepols, pp. 93–122.

Musil, A. (1928): Palmyrena. A Topographical Itinerary. American Geographical Society, Oriental Explorations and Studies 4, New York: American Geographical Society.

Pickett, J. (2018): "Water and Empire in the De aedificiis of Procopius." In: Dumbarton Oaks Papers 71, pp. 95–125.

Procopius (2002[1954]): On Buildings, ed. and translated by H. B. Dewing/G. Downey, Loeb Classical Library 343, Cambridge: Harvard University Press.

Procopius of Gaza (1986): Procope de Gaza. Priscien de Césarée. Panégyriques de l'empereur Anastase Ier, translated and commented by A. Chauvot, Antiquitas 1, Abhandlungen zur alten Geschichte 35, Bonn: R. Habelt.

Riera, I. (1994): "Le testimonianze archeologiche." In: G. Bodon/I. Riera/P. Zanovello (eds.), Utilitas necessaria. Sistemi idraulici nell'Italia romana, Milano: Progetto Quarta Dimensione, pp. 163–466.

Rodgers, R. H. (ed.) (2004): Frontinus. De aquaeductu urbis Romae, ed. with introduction and commentary, Cambridge Classical Texts and Commentaries 42, Cambridge: Cambridge University Press.

Sack, D. et al. (forthcoming), Resafa – Sergiupolis /Rusafat Hisham. Stadt und Umland, Resafa 8.

Shahîd, I. (2002): Byzantium and the Arabs in the Sixth Century, vol. 2, Toponymy, Monuments, Historical Geography, and Frontier Studies, Washington: Dumbarton Oaks Research Library and Collection.

Spanner, H./Guyer, S. (1926): Rusafa. Die Wallfahrtsstadt des heiligen Sergios, Forschungen zur islamischen Kunst 4, Berlin: Reimer.

Syvänne, I. (2007): "Water Supply in the Late Roman Army." In: P. S. Juuti/T. S. Katko/H. S. Vuorinen (eds.), Environmental History of Water, London: IWA Publishing, pp. 69–91.

Turquois, E. (2015): "Technical Writing, Genre and Aesthetic in Procopius." In: G. Greatrex/H. Elton (eds.), Shifting Genres in Late Antiquity, New York: Routledge, pp. 219–232.

Ulbert, T. (2000): "Procopius, De aedificiis. Einige Überlegungen zu Buch II, Syrien." In: J.-M. Carrié/N. Duval/C. Roueché (eds.), De aedificiis. Le texte de Procope et les réalités. Actes du colloque de Londres 25–26 septembre 1998, Antiquité tardive, Revue internationale d'histoire et d'archéologie 8, pp. 137–147.

van Tilburg, C. (2013): "Greek and Roman Ideas about Healthy Drinking-Water in Theory and Practice." In: Eä. Revista de humanidades médicas & estudios sociales de la ciencia y la tecnología 5, pp. 1–30.

Vitruvius (1914): "De Architectura." In: Vitruvius, The ten books on architecture, translated by M. H. Morgan, Cambridge: Harvard University Press.

Vuorinen, H. S. (2007a): "Water and Health in Antiquity: Europe's Legacy." In: P. S. Juuti/T. S. Katko/H. S. Vuorinen (eds.), Environmental History of Water, London: IWA Publishing, pp. 45–67.

Vuorinen, H. S. (2007b): "The emergence of the Idea of Water-Borne Diseases." In: Water Science and Technology, Water Supply 7.1, pp. 103–115.

Wagner, W. (2011): Groundwater in the Arab Middle East, Heidelberg: Springer.

Westphalen, S./Knötzele, P. (2004): "Water Supply of Resafa, Syria – Remarks on the Chronology of the Big Cisterns." In: H.-D. Bienert/J. Häser (eds.), Men of Dikes and Canals: The Archaeology of Water in the Middle East. International Symposium Held at Petra, Wadi Musa (H. K. of Jordan) 15–20 June, 1999, Orient-Archäologie 13, Rahden/Westf.: Leidorf, pp. 345–354.

Whitby, M. (1986): "Procopius' Description of Dara. Buildings II 1-3." In: P. Freeman/D. Kennedy (eds.), The Defence of the Roman and Byzantine East. Proceedings of a Colloquium Held at the University of Sheffield in April 1986, British Archaeological Reports, International Series 297, Oxford: B. A. R., pp. 737–783.

Wirth, E. (1971): Syrien. Eine geographische Landeskunde, Wissenschaftliche Länderkunde 4/5, Darmstadt: Wissenschaftliche Buchgesellschaft.

Wulf, S. (2005): Jerusalem – Aleppo – Konstantinopel: der Hamburger Tropenmediziner Peter Mühlens im Osmanischen Reich am Vorabend und zu Beginn des Ersten Weltkriegs, Münster: Lit.

Zanini, E. (1990): "La cinta muraria di Dara. Materiali per un'analisi stratigrafica." In: F. de' Maffei/A. G. Guidobaldi/C. Barsanti (eds.), Costantinopoli e l'arte delle province orientali, Milion, Studi e ricerche d'arte bizantina 2, Rom: Campisano, pp. 229–264.

Monumentality, Building Techniques, and Identity Construction in Roman Italy: The Remaking of Cosa, post-197 BCE

Marcello Mogetta

Introduction

Although certainly not the grandest with its 13 ha., the Latin colony of Cosa (founded in 273 BCE) provides detailed archaeological evidence to study the tempo and dynamics of mass-construction projects in higher-order settlements of the Roman Republican period (cf. Dyson 2013; Fentress/Perkins 2016; for the bigger picture: Sewell 2010; 2016). A closer look at both the chronological sequence and process of construction of Cosa's public architecture reveals meaningful patterns that can help us characterize the cultural component of the technological choices underlying large-scale building programs in Roman colonial contexts.

In this study, then, the specific focus is on mortared-rubble architecture (for which the term *opus caementicium* or Roman concrete is used interchangeably; cf. Lancaster 2015: 21–23). As we see, at Cosa the technology was implemented for the renovation of the main civic symbols (namely the Comitium, the center of all political activity; and the so-called Capitolium, the largest temple at the site), most likely after the colonial resettlement of 197 BCE. Expanding the shelf of available techniques (i. e., costly limestone polygonal masonry; vernacular earthen architecture), the new building medium required significant logistical innovations, including water-supply (which was particularly problematic at a site lacking water sources; De Giorgi 2018: 6–10), and quarrying and transportation of reworked volcanic sands from the coastal plain. It also allowed, however, for the involvement of unskilled manpower in the actual construction process.

Thus, in what follows I locate Cosa's phenomenon at the particular nexus between monumentality, materiality, and collective action, linking technological change with the creation of a new communal identity, precisely at a time when a contingent of 1000 new colonists was reportedly sent to the colony. Questioning previous interpretations based on the idea that the technology was simply imported as part of a package from Rome, I argue for a more active role of the locals, concluding that early experiments with concrete construction, while still relying on the local geology and economy, are brought about primarily by social and cultural needs.

Roman colonization, monumentality, and the origins of Roman concrete

Architectural features employing mortared masonry are known from several Mid-Republican colonies, most notably Ostia, Alba Fucens, and Cosa, and are commonly assigned to the earliest levels of the settlements (e. g., Giuliani 2006: 217–218). Using colonial foundation dates as fixed points, and combining them with ideas of progressive evolution of facing styles (from irregular to regular) and composition of the binder (from clay-based to lime-based), the spread of the building technique in Italy has been dated no later than the 3rd century BCE, though mostly on circumstantial grounds (for the typological approach see Tombrägel 2012: 39–102; on the development of mortars in Pompeii, see Peterse 1999; cf. Mogetta 2016, highlighting the methodological problems with the conventional dating framework). In previous studies, therefore, the variant seen at Cosa has been described as the precursor of standardized Roman concrete (*opus caementicium*), reflecting an experimental phase for which there would be indirect evidence in the literary sources (e. g., Cato, *Agr.* 14.1–2: walls made *calce et caementis*; Vitruvius 2.8.1, *genus antiquum*; Blake 1947: 324–327; Lugli 1957, 1: 374; cf. Von Gerkan 1958). On the false assumption that Roman colonies were miniature copies of Rome in their institutional framework as well as in their physical aspect, the conclusion was that the technological innovation originated in or around the metropolis, and that it was exported from core to periphery (cf. Fentress 2000 with reference to Cosa; Stek/Pelgrom 2014 for a critique of the traditional model of Roman colonies; on the implications: Mogetta 2015: 2–7; Mogetta 2016, 43–44).

The interpretation of mortared-rubble architecture as a marker of Roman identity or influence rests also on the idea that Roman magistrates were directly involved in the urbanization programs affecting the colonies. There is evidence that this was probably the case from around the mid-2nd century BCE onwards. A fragmentary testimony in Livy (41.27-28) suggests that one of the Roman censors of 174 BCE, Q. Fulvius Flaccus, used allotted funds to carry out re-planning projects at the Roman colonies of Sinuessa, Pisaurum, and Potentia. Furthermore, an inscription referring to the resettlement of Aquileia in 169 BCE (*AE* 1996, Nr. 685) demonstrates that the *triumviri* (commission of three) sent from Rome were also responsible for physically configuring the urban landscape of colonies of Latin right (Sewell 2010: 84). Contemporary literary sources hint at an increasingly intensive use of contractors (known as *publicani* or *redemptores*) who carried out public construction works throughout Italy (Polybius 6.17.2-5;

see the discussion in Sewell 2010: 110–111; but Anderson [1997: 99–100] notes how Polybius may exaggerate the extent of censorial contracting, since the passage refers to the industry as it existed at the start of the Second Punic War). In this perspective, architects and skilled craftsmen coming from Rome would have been responsible for the introduction of Roman building types and building techniques in state-sponsored construction projects (Lugli 1957, 1: 445–446 for the class of concrete walls known as *opus incertum*; Torelli 1980: 153–154 for *opus reticulatum*). While there is no explicit reference of that sort for the 4th and 3rd centuries BCE, the expectation has nonetheless been that, at the very least, Roman masonry styles were transferred to Mid-Republican colonial sites like Cosa by the Roman colonists, who would have brought with them practices learned in their place of origin (Brown 1951: 109–110, emphasizing parallels with sites in Latium).

The distribution map of the earliest reliable examples of mortared masonry in central Italy (Figure 1) includes Cosa alongside other major urban sites where the archaeological evidence, however, points to a later date than previously thought (from the 2nd century BCE onwards; for a broad survey in Latium and Campania see Cifarelli 2013). Most notable in the sample are Pompeii, Cumae, and Teanum (Mogetta 2013: 264–281), to which we may add colonial Liternum (De Vincenzo 2018) and Puteoli (though with less confidence, due to limited stratigraphic excavations: Paternoster et al. 2007). Signature aspects of the techniques attested at some of these sites (e. g., the ashlar limestone framework at Pompeii; the use of poured concrete foundations at Teanum; the selection of head-to-fist size wall-facing tesserae at Puteoli) are entirely missing at Cosa. The lack of any standardized pattern emerging from this seems to suggests that the switch to mortar-and-rubble construction was not necessarily a centrally regulated phenomenon, but rather one betraying a great deal of local adaptation. For the same reason, the possibility that the same group of builders moved from site to site can be excluded.

Instead of characterizing the spread of the technology as a symptom of cultural diffusion in Roman Italy, I propose a different approach, using the Cosan material as a test-bed. While acknowledging the important role that private contractors hired by the colonists might have played in building Cosa, precisely because of the link between architectural development and colonial encounters at the site, my goal is to investigate what social identities and interpersonal relations could have been expressed and enacted within the arena of technological practice (which includes construction works), focusing on the cultural component (or technological style) of the innovation within the local context.

Figure 1: Map of Italy with main sites mentioned in the text (courtesy of Antiquity À-la carte; CC BY 4.0)

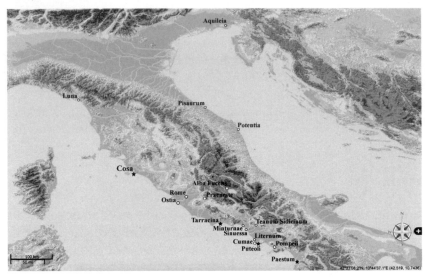

Roman building techniques and technological style

The literary evidence mentioned above actually provides a useful starting point for reorienting the discussion around issues of identity construction, because it also demonstrates how building methods could become caught up in contemporary social discourse. Cato the Elder, the source closer to the period under discussion, construed early Roman concrete as a discursive category primarily to express concerns about Roman identity and morals, and thus score political goals. In his *De Agricultura*, he singled out lime-based mortared rubble as the proper medium to build the foundations of Roman farms, alongside beaten earth for floors and dung plaster for coatings, contrasting his idealized view of traditional domestic architecture against the excesses seen in the *villae expolitae*, the "villas embellished to the most impressive degree" owned by his political rivals. In other rhetorical fragments, he in fact describes his own habitation, like his other personal effects, as utterly modest (*ORF*[4] 8.174, after 164 BCE?), denouncing greedy (public?) building as a form of political corruption (*ORF*[4] 8.133, ca. 183 BCE) (Nichols 2010; Nichols 2017: 83–129).

Of course, Cato's precepts are not to be taken at face value. His examples are at odds with archaeological realities, which seems normal considering that we are dealing with excerpts from works that were mainly literary in scope (Terrenato 2012). To be sure, known rural buildings in the region of Rome are either older, larger and richer, or much smaller but more nicely-appointed than Cato's *villae* and none of them features rubble construction, ashlar masonry being the norm (Mogetta 2015: 23–24, Table 4). On the whole, however, texts like Cato's (and more extensively Vitruvius's *De Architectura*; Nichols 2017, especially pp. 42–82) suggest that construction methods and processes could be charged with social meaning. The main implication is that building technology itself can be described as a form of material culture. Thus, just as in other spheres of artifact production (pottery, metallurgy, textiles etc.), concentrating on the role of specific technological choices behind the introduction of mortared-rubble architecture at colonial sites across Roman Italy may reveal more complex components of social agency than Roman influence. During technical activities people are rarely constrained to a single operational chain, and opportunities and alternatives constantly arise, affecting the decision-making process. These choices are indeed capable of acquiring communicative potential, since technological gestures can be witnessed by others in the community, thus suggesting that technological practice and performance can help express and manipulate salient identities, and construct more than mere material objects (cf. Lechtman 1977 on the ability to identify cultural decisions and choices in the technologies behind object production; see Hoffman/Dobres 1999 for archaeological examples of how identities can be 'manufactured' through technological practice).

The relevance of Cosa for the study of early concrete architecture

The archaeological evidence from Cosa presents itself as an ideal testing ground for exploring the relationship between technological innovation, stylistic behavior, and the construction of social identity in the context of Roman Republican urbanism. Cosa is not only one of the most extensively researched Mid-Republican Latin colonies (with Alba Fucens, Fregellae, Paestum), but also one for which the publication record is relatively complete. This is why the site figures prominently in studies of early Roman architecture, making dealing with its legacy data almost inevitable (Figure 2).

The results of F. Brown's excavations in 1948–1954 and 1967–1972 have been disseminated through a series of monographs covering specific areas of the site primarily by building types: the fortifications (Brown 1951), the temples on the Arx (Brown et al. 1960), the port (McCann 1987), the Forum and its dependencies (Brown et al. 1993), and the houses (Bruno/Scott 1993). Each of these studies includes specific information on the relevant building methods. Adequate publication of the finds associated with these architectural remains, however, lagged generally behind, as it relied significantly on the final dissemination of Brown's stratigraphic analysis (the main publication for the dating of the Republican contexts is

Scott 2008; for the coins Buttrey 1980). While the early works sketched the image of a fully developed Mid-Republican city, the results of more recent fieldwork projects carried out in 1991–1997 (Fentress et al. 2003) and from 2013 onwards (Scott et al. 2015) have seriously questioned the existence of a substantial settlement within the fortification circuit of the colony for most if not all of the 3rd century BCE (Fentress et al. 2003: 14–28; Sewell 2005; Sewell 2010: 25–33).

Figure 2: State plan of Cosa (De Giorgi 2018: 7, Figure 2; used by permission of the author)

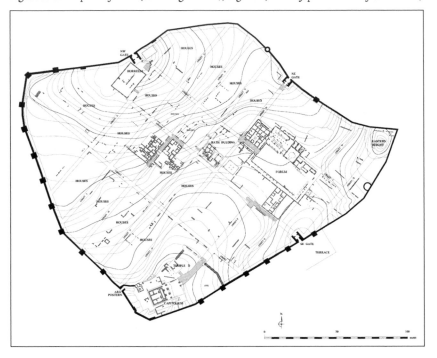

Besides providing a critical mass of archaeological data, Cosa can also contribute significantly to our understanding of the relationship between early concrete architecture and local geology, especially because of the town's proximity to sources of both limestone and volcanic sands (i. e. the key ingredients for high-quality mortars). The spatial distribution of sites where the switch to mortar-and-rubble architecture has been dated with some confidence within the first half of the 2nd century BCE suggests a possible correlation in this sense, given that these are located at the interface between the limestone and volcanic regions of central Italy (think of Praeneste). The link between locally available resources and building techniques seems to have been a constant in the architectural history of these sites, since they also fall within the area of diffusion of the so-called polygonal masonry, a class of walls made of massive blocks of polygonal shape laid without mortar in a

Figure 3: Geological deposits in the region of Cosa. Key: Limestone and marls;
Cretaceous marls and limestone; Jurassic limestone; Dolomitic limestone (adapted from
Perkins 1999: 6, Figure 1.1.3; used by permission of the author)

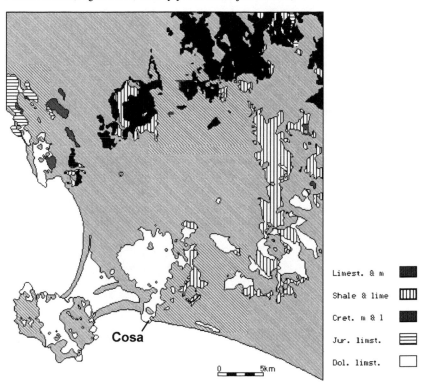

random pattern. Crosscutting cultural boundaries, polygonal masonry is almost
exclusively found in areas where hard stones outcrop: marine limestones in the
Apennine foothills of ancient Samnium, South Latium, the Sabinum, and parts
of Umbria, and other sandstones and conglomerates in parts of coastal Etruria
and North Etruria (cf. Helas 2016). At Cosa, polygonal masonry is the only form
of monumental construction attested for the period pre-dating the urban reno-
vations, as shown primarily by the fortifications (where it is found in combination with fills of dry rubble) and the cisterns located at the Northwestern Gate,
the Northeastern Gate, and at the intersection of Streets 4 and K, and 5 and O (De
Giorgi 2018: 9). Other structures securely dated to the initial phase of the colony of
273 BCE consist of rock-cut features (e. g., the so-called Auguraculum on the Arx;
Brown et al. 1960: 11–13).

The innovation of mortared-rubble architecture at Cosa probably emerged as
the result of the interplay between different regional traditions (thus Von Gerkan
1958: 151–152, interpreting mortared masonry at Cosa as an evolution of polygonal

Figure 4: Geological deposits in the region of Cosa. Key: Pleistocene deposits; Lacustrine limestone (adapted from Perkins 1999: 4, Figure 1.1.1; used by permission of the author)

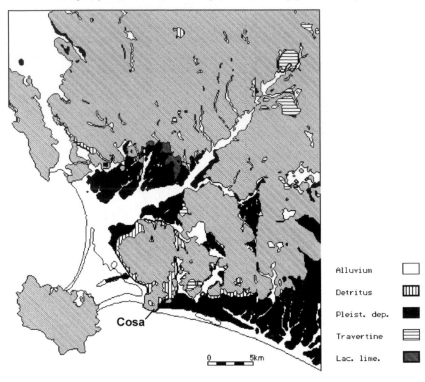

masonry), the economy of construction (but see Torelli 1980: 156–157, comparing the skills required to finish individual elements in walls with *opus incertum* facings with the dressing of blocks in polygonal masonry at the building site), and the supply of locally available building materials.

The promontory on top of which the town sits is composed of a variety of grey Dolomitic limestone conventionally defined as *calcare cavernoso*, which in places is well layered, but elsewhere highly brecciated (Figure 3). Quarries of polygonal blocks have been reported near the harbor, just east of the promontory (where there are deposits of finer quality than those available from the hill outcrop; Gazda 1987: 87–88), though blocks for the fortification walls came from multiple quarry faces very close to the walls themselves. Smaller blocks and rubble could be obtained right at the building sites, particularly during preparation works (i. e., by regularizing the bedrock). Sandstone and clayey schists occur in association with the *calcare cavernoso*, outcropping in petrified dunes running parallel to the coast, about 1 km inland east of Cosa (Perkins 1999: 3–6. On the sourcing of the calcareous sandstone see Brown 1951: 59; Brown et al. 1960: 31, n.15).

The main source of sediments on the hill is the *terre rosse*, a silty clay rich in ferrous oxides that results from the weathering of the local limestone. Pockets of this material fill depressions in the bedrock topography. Other important materials for building purposes came from the dune beach and offshore sands south and east of the promontory (Figure 4). These sands are rich in heavy minerals, which take up to half or more of their composition, and vary in color from light to dark gray depending on the percentage of the minerals (Bourgeois 1987: 50–53). They originated from the mountains 60–80 km to the north-east of Cosa, in the area of Lake Bolsena, which consisted of volcanic rocks and sediments, including tuffs and pozzolan (Marra/D'Ambrosio 2013). Scientific evidence has been reported to support the idea that there was long-distance trade of pyroclastic rocks from the Vulsini district in the Republican period. Cosa was located not far from the mouth of the Fiora river, which would have represented the main transportation route for the material, but the 4th–2nd century BCE date for the establishment of the trade (Marra/D'Ambrosio 2013: 1019) is questionable (it is based on material recovered from the Pisa shipwreck B, which has been assigned to the Augustan period).

The planning of the Forum ensemble of Cosa

The early development of mortared-rubble architecture at Cosa occurred in parallel with the emergence of civic infrastructure. There is a general consensus that the final aspect of the Forum of Cosa materialized only in a piecemeal fashion. The earliest activity would be represented by the digging of four open oblong cisterns, two on the NE side, parallel to the main square, two perpendicular to its SW side, and of a series of pits lining the SE half of the square. Construction of the free-standing structure of the Comitium, with its axial covered hall (identified as the Curia, or town council building) on the NE side, in the area between the two cisterns, would have soon followed. While the excavators assigned these buildings to the first phase of occupation of the colony (between 273–241 BCE, according to Brown et al. 1993: 26), Fentress/Perkins (2016: 381) recently revised the dating to the third quarter of the 3rd century BCE (between 240–220 BCE). The fixed point for this is based on the ceramic materials and coins contained in the fills that put out of use a neighboring structure, an enclosure with catchment area around the cistern SE of the Comitium, to be transformed into a sacred precinct (Templum Beta; Brown et al. 1993: 51–56). Another building on the NE side of the square has been assigned to the same sub-phase, and its vaulted basement identified with a Carcer (prison: Brown et al. 1993: 38–39). Significantly, the voting structures with annexed ritual spaces and jail are all located on one of the long sides of the open square. The progressive infilling and beautification of the remaining sides is more securely dated to the 2nd century BCE: first the construction of the so-called

Atrium Buildings (four on the long SW side of the square, two on each of the short sides, best understood as élite *domus*; Sewell 2010: 137–165), and the Southwest Annex (an open-plan structure centered on the axis of the Comitium and Street P) (Brown et al. 1993: 57–106) (Figure 5); then the colonnaded triporticus and a monumental gateway (Brown et al. 1993: 107–138.); a small prostyle temple (Temple B, replacing Templum Beta: Brown et al. 1993: 142–153); and finally, a basilica on the N corner, built in the second half of the 2ⁿᵈ century BCE (Brown et al. 1993: 207–227) (cf. Figure 7).

Figure 5: Reconstruction of the Forum area around 180 BCE (after Fentress et al. 2003: 22, Figure 9; used by author's permission). Key: 1 = Comitium and Curia; 2 = Templum Beta; 3 = Forecourt; 4 = Carcer; 5 = Southwest Annex; 6 = House of Diana. The hatched area indicates the extent of excavations

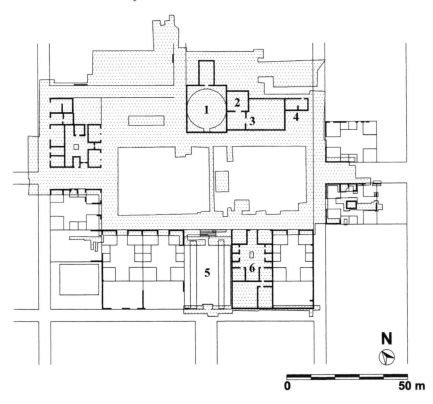

The picture of gradual development has been challenged quite convincingly by Sewell, who has brought to our attention a series of anomalies in the planning of the excavated Forum: the fact that the open square has no streets along its edges, as is normally the case for contemporary Mid-Republican colonial layouts;

Figure 6: Composite plan showing the overlap of the 2ⁿᵈ-century BCE state (gray) on Sewell's ideal layout of Cosa in the 3ʳᵈ century BCE (red) (adapted from Sewell 2010: 27 Figure 8, and 29, Figure 10). Note especially the shifting and reorientation of Street P from its reconstructed position in the original plan, which effected the trapezoidal, irregular shape of the city-block delimited by Streets P, Q and 5

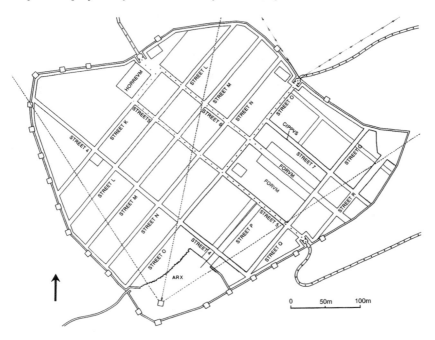

the irregular shape of the city-blocks on its NW and SE sides; the positioning of the Comitium/Curia complex in a city-block that was not nearly wide enough, causing it to block Street 7 and encroach upon part of the adjoining plot (Sewell 2005; Sewell 2010: 27–32). Despite the lack of direct archaeological evidence, an attractive explanation to account for these irregularities is to consider the existing forum as a later insertion (Figure 6). Whether the original 3ʳᵈ-century plan was ever completed remains debatable, because of the significant difference in height that exists between Streets 5 and 7 (2 m according to Sewell 2010: 29; up to 3 m according to Fentress/Perkins 2016: 380). A steep cut in the bedrock is still visible at the back of the House of Diana (one of the 2ⁿᵈ-century BCE *domus* facing onto the SE side of the square), i. e. where the SW half of the original piazza would have stood, meaning that part of its surface would have remained unfinished until the creation of the domestic structure.

The main implication is that none of the buildings lining the NE side of the excavated Forum can be assigned to the early phase of the colony of 273 BCE, with

Figure 7: Actual state of Cosa's Forum. Key: 1 = Comitium; 2 = Triple Arch (gateway); 3 = Temple B; 4 = Carcer; 5 = Basilica (from Sewell 2010: 28, Figure 9; used by permission of the author). Note the slightly skewed alignment of the buildings located on the north side of the Forum (red dashed line) and their relationship to the axis of Street P (yellow dashed line)

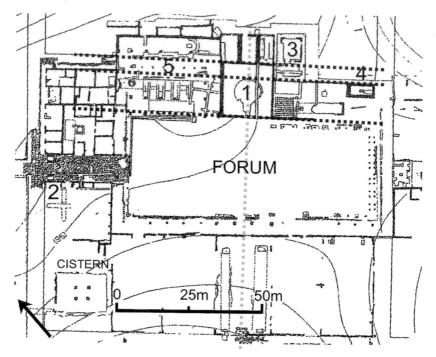

the possible exception of the Carcer, whose extent would seem to respect the width of the resulting narrow city-block delimited by the continuation of Street 6 and Street 7, north of the original Forum. It must be noted, however, that the Carcer, Templum Beta, and the back wall of the Comitium all share the same slightly skewed alignment with respect to the urban grid (Figure 7). The odd angle seems generated by the axis of Street P, which also stands out for having a different orientation to all other streets running from SW to NE (cf. Figure 6). Since Street P enters the redesigned Forum exactly at its center, Sewell considers it as part of the 2nd-century BCE redevelopment (incidentally, the final stretch of Street P explains both the siting of the cisterns and the function of the Southwest Annex as a monumental entrance). Assigning the Carcer to the later building phase, therefore, does not pose problems. Brown et al. (1993: 40) dated it to the period between the First and Second Punic Wars (241–220 BCE) primarily on account of the odd alignment of the wall running from the S corner of Temple B to the N corner of the Carcer, contrasting the random rubblework and rusticated quoins of the Carcer's superstructure with the well-dressed and coursed facings of Temple B to confirm the earlier date of the former building (i. e., assuming that there was a progressive evolution of the facing style). Its unfaced concrete barrel vault, however, would have no parallels in the mid-3rd century BCE (Mogetta 2015: 8, Table 2).

Sewell's proposal agrees well with the general state of underdevelopment of Cosa in the 3rd century BCE, meaning that there would have been space available to relocate the square. No private buildings have been found to predate the 2nd century BCE (Fentress et al. 2003: 14; Fentress/Perkins 2016: 380).[1] Given its axial position, there is little doubt that the Comitium/Curia complex was the first element to be built. No datable material comes from the excavation of the deposits from the enclosure itself to support its 3rd-century BCE dating (Brown et al. 1993: 26. See also the discussion in Sewell 2005: 109–110). As already mentioned, indirect evidence comes from the construction sequence of the adjoining buildings to the E (Figure 8). In particular, the tile-floored catchment area adjacent to the SE corner of the Comitium has been taken to postdate the voting enclosure, because its NW wall partly abuts the circuit wall of the Comitium near its S corner (the short stretch in question, however, is clearly a later plug). What is certain is that the two structures coexisted for some time. The single fragment of Black Gloss from the construction level of the catchment area (Scott 2008: 115, Deposit TBa) can at best provide a *terminus post quem*, but should not be used as a *terminus ante quem* for the Comitium. The finds from the shallow layer of sediments deposited on top of the tile floor include coins from within the range 340–220 BCE (the majority of them from after the mid-3rd century BCE), all in a very worn state (implying that they circulated for a long time before entering the stratigraphy; Buttrey 1980, coins CF 2224, 2227-31, 2233-7; cf. Sewell 2005: 109–110). In addition to 3rd-century BCE types, the few diagnostic Black Gloss fragments from the same level also include a form uncommon at Cosa and dated elsewhere to the 2nd century BCE, suggesting that the assemblage consists mostly of residues (e. g., Scott 2008: 117, Deposit TBb, form Morel 1281, taking the smaller size of the Cosan example as evidence of an early experiment to confirm the last quarter/end of the 3rd-century BCE date originally suggested by Brown et al. [1993: 37–38] for the use period of the catchment). A date of 190 BCE has been proposed for the podium fills of Templum Beta, a structure built on top of the catchment area and which clearly abuts the Comitium, but the possibility of a later date cannot be ruled out.[2]

---

1 Casarotto et al. 2016 show that site density in the territory of Mid-Republican colonies is not compatible with the expected number of sites based on ancient demographic accounts. At Cosa, small areas with high site-density are found in the vicinity of the urban center, but the overall evidence suggests that a nucleated settlement strategy in villages farther away from the colony may have had an important role in early colonial societal organization.

2 Among the finds are also Campana A kylikes of the Anses en Oreille type, commonly dated to the second quarter of the 2nd century BCE (cf. Scott 2008: 134–135, Deposit TB, form Morel 4111). This

Figure 8: Detailed plan of the buildings located E of the Comitium (modified from Brown et al. 1993: 32, Plan IV)

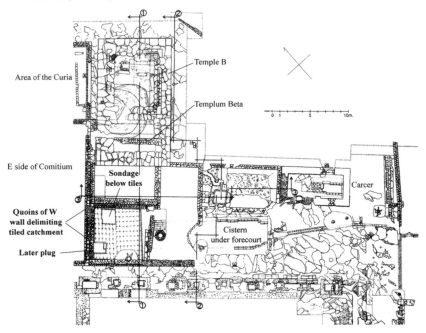

In sum, the combined evidence of planning and stratigraphy seems to support the idea that the excavated Forum at Cosa was substantially redeveloped in the 2nd century BCE, which we know represented a time of renewal for the town. Livy (33.24.8-9) records that in 197 BCE a contingent of 1000 colonists was sent out to Cosa, an event that could have just as well resulted in the upheaval of the urban fabric (cf. Lackner 2008 for an overview of contemporary practice). Not by chance, both the paving of the streets and the first intense phase of house construction can also be dated to within the first half of the century (on the chronology of the street paving see Scott 2008: 109, Deposit F, whose *terminus ante quem* of 180 BCE should be taken as a *terminus post quem*; on the dating of the houses to 190 BCE and onwards see Scott 2008: 163–167, on the assumption that the Forum project took priority).

---

assemblage would provide the *terminus post quem* for Templum Beta, not the *terminus ante quem* for the Comitium (Scott notes that the pottery from the layers that seal Templum Beta is contaminated due to the continued maintenance of its monumental successor, Temple B, preventing a more precise dating of the actual use of the platform). Fentress et al. (2003: 30) place the construction of Temple B around the end of the second quarter of the 2nd century BCE.

The making of the Forum ensemble at Cosa

If we accept the new reconstruction, the series of building activities that produced the redevelopment and beautification of the Forum must be compressed in a shorter period of time than posited before. The notable irregularities in the spacing of the columns of the Forum portico as reconstructed by Brown, and the fact that the SE stretch of the colonnade encroaches upon Street Q speak for a project that was the result of successive interventions. Brown's date of 175 BCE for the NW gateway, which he assigns to either "before or right after construction of the portico" (Brown et al. 1993: 128) appears based primarily on comparanda known from literary sources for which we have no material correlate (i. e., the *ianos tris* built by Q. Fulvius Flaccus in the aforementioned passage by Livy). The same *opus incertum* technique of the gateway, which features fist- to head-sized facing blocks in a random pattern, is employed for the Basilica, dated to 150–140 BCE (Brown et al. 1993: 207–213; on typological grounds, however, Gros 2011: 240 prefers a date of ca. 120 BCE).

The burst of construction post-197 BCE may have provided the impetus for experimentation with, and implementation of, new building methods employing lime mortar. For all we know, the introduction of this building medium represents a clean break from previous architectural practice at the site. The town-walls, the only feature securely datable to the 3rd-century BCE occupation phase, do not employ mortared rubble in their original configuration, since they were built making exclusive use of massive polygonal masonry (Benvenuti 2002; Poggesi/Pallecchi 2012 report the use of lime mortar for the single round tower inserted in the north stretch of the circuit; according to Von Gerkan 1958b: 152, similar mortared-rubble additions on top of the projecting towers are to be understood as later restorations). The technological shift is even more significant because lime mortar is only found in public architecture. All the domestic buildings in Republican Cosa were in *pisé de terre*, i. e. rammed earth laid on dry-stone footings or directly onto the cut bedrock (as exemplified by the House of Diana; cf. Fentress et al. 2003: 19–21), a technique that might have been in use already in the 3rd century BCE (a possible candidate for a superstructure of this kind is the square building under the cella of the so-called Capitolium on the Arx, of which the rock-cut footings and possible architectural decoration survive; cf. Brown 1960: 11; Taylor 2002: 78). Whereas clay-based architecture (e. g., the first phase of the Curia; the water catchment E of the Comitium) or even polygonal masonry of smaller module (e. g., Temple B podium; later modifications of the Curia) can be found in combination with each other, all the components of the new Forum ensemble feature exclusively one variant of mortared-rubble architecture.

The building methods employed for the construction of the Comitium, i. e. the first monument in the sequence of development of the square, demonstrate which specific technological choices were made by local builders to switch, thus providing important clues for interpreting the economic and social context of the innovation. A sounding on the NE side near the N corner showed that the walls of the enclosure are laid on a foundation consisting of a single course of unworked limestone boulders placed directly on the bedrock, and leveled with rammed earth. On the SW side was found a 0.35 m-deep socle of mortared-rubble masonry resting directly on the crests of the bedrock (Brown et al. 1993: 14). It is unlikely that the latter was a restoration, because it, too, was found leveled by a layer of rammed clay, so the creation of a uniform foundation does not seem to have been a primary concern (the loads were not very heavy, since the Comitium was unroofed). The main structural function of the enclosure walls was to respond to the lateral thrusts from the fills it retained.

The mortar used for both the SW foundation and the superstructure of the Comitium contains a high proportion of local volcanic sands, but the early development of the recipe has little to do with selective use in an airtight environment (unlike in Rome, where pozzolanic mortars were developed for use in foundations; cf. Mogetta 2015: 32). Because of their alteration from weathering, the volcanic rock inclusions in these sands have inferior pozzolanic properties in comparison with the pyroclastic-flow and pyroclastic-fall deposits of the Vulsini district from which they originate. In fact, hydraulic mortars attested at the site always include ground terracotta as a reactive agent, but are utilized primarily for revetments (Gazda 2008 discusses the practice of mixing ceramic fragments as aggregates with mortars of lime and local sands with relation to the superstructures of the port and fishery of Cosa, where imported pozzolan was selectively employed only for the submerged parts).

In the retaining walls of the Comitium, the medium is employed primarily for the bedding of brick-like slabs of the local calcareous sandstone, varying from 22 to 44 cm in length and 3.5 to 6.5 cm in thickness (at the corners are larger slabs or blocks of the same stone). These slabs are stacked in sub-horizontal courses on top of thick mortar beds of 2.5 to 3 cm, to form 60-cm-thick walls with uniform faces and a core of smaller limestone rubble and tile fragments (Figure 9) (Brown et al. 1993: 15). The use of lime mortar was clearly meant to facilitate the construction process: the walls were built up using stone elements that could be handled by individual workmen without the need of complex lifting devices, and whose relatively flat dimensions allowed even the unskilled to stagger them in sections without much supervision (the layers and joints could be regularized by adjusting the thickness of the mortar beds; only one leveling course has been identified across the four sides, 1.1 m from the reconstructed top of the precinct wall).

Figure 9: Cosa, Comitium Curia. Building C. SE Room. Level I. SW wall (Photo by American Academy in Rome, Photo Archive: AAR.COSA.1954.16; used by permission)

While bringing significant savings in labor costs due to ease of construction in comparison with ashlar masonry (further discussed below), the technology developed for the Comitium required other forms of investment for the large-scale production of the building medium. First, the procurement of lime for the mortar had to be organized *ex novo*, establishing a lime industry or trade network. Second, as part of the new building process, the quarrying and transportation of sands from the coastal dunes to the hilltop had to be arranged. Third, access to water supply from the storage system available on site needed to be regulated (there were no springs on the promontory so the water collected in the rock-cut cisterns had to be shared for construction purposes). The latter point explains the close spatial relationship between the Comitium and the annex at its SE corner: the water catchment area next to the rock-cut cistern was formally delimited to be probably used while the Comitium was under construction, only to be completely backfilled once the enclosure wall was completed. Brown et al. (1993: 37–38) describe the building technique of the catchment feature (crude brick walls; no *opus signinum* revetment; lack of any drainage) as being dictated by economy and haste, suggesting that durability was not a concern. Significantly, the SW and SE walls of the annex were rebuilt to form the forecourt of Templum Beta, and extended to resemble the façade of the Comitium (Figure 10).

Figure 10: Cosa, Temple B. Forecourt. SW wall full stretch (Photo by American Academy in Rome, Photo Archive: AAR.COSA.1953.46; used by permission)

Discussion: Constructing civic identity at Republican Cosa

The type of construction just described for the Comitium is found at another major landmark at Cosa, the so-called Capitolium on the Arx. With the refoundation of the colony in the early 2nd century BCE, the citadel, too, became the focus of monumentalization, and was the object of a new phase of temple building, which has been taken to be roughly contemporary with the construction activities in the Forum (ca. second quarter of the 2nd century BCE; cf. Taylor 2002, presenting the current simplified chronology of the temples of the Arx based on the typology of their terracotta roof decorations and related stratigraphic evidence). The Capitolium stands out not only for its plan and size (at 23.2 x 31.7 m, it is the largest temple of Cosa and the only one with tripartite cella), but also for its siting: the temple dominates the height and the front of its podium is at the end point of Street P, which created a direct line of sight from the Comitium. Brown's original interpretation of it as a temple to the Capitoline triad (1980: 53–56) has been rightly challenged: Bispham (2006: 99–101) has pointed out that the evidence for it to be a Capitolium is negligble (in citizen colonies like Ostia, Tarracina, Minturnae, and Luna such a structure is located along the *decumanus* and near the Forum).

The very same idea of the ideological link between Capitolia and colonial status has been called into question (Quinn and Wilson 2013: 118–128, with reference to Cosa). However, it is likely that the cult activities relating to that temple had a prominent status in the colony's religious and cultural identity, especially if we consider that the first and only 3rd-century BCE temple on the Arx was intentionally demolished to make room for an entirely new building (Bispham 2006: 104.). Thus, we might suspect that the temple was dedicated to Cosa's tutelary deity (cf. Boos 2011: 27–28), which expands the argument for its civic function despite the rejection of Brown's identification.

Figure 11: Cosa, Capitolium. Cella N.1 W. Rear wall interior, excavated to bedrock (Photo by American Academy in Rome, Photo Archive: AAR.COSA.1949.27; used by permission)

The building process implemented for the main temple appears more complex than that of the Comitium, betraying an increased level of investment. The same type of mortared masonry featuring sandstone brick-shaped tesserae is used selectively for the foundations and walls of the cella and its projecting antae (Figure 11), but the mortar mix includes ground terracotta as an additive to impart greater pozzolanic properties (Brown et al. 1960: 50–53). Unlike in the Comitium, the technique is combined with high status *opus quadratum*, which is employed for the quoins of the antae (alternating headers and stretchers of brecciated limestone), and for the podium socle. The latter feature was purely formal in function, i. e. a revetment with no structural purpose (except beyond the antae, where it served to retain the fills of the pronaos). It originally consisted of six courses of sandstone blocks, including plinth, base, die, and a crown molding. Only the latter element abutted the walls behind the podium, while the gap between the lower elements and the exterior of the cella, which evidently came first in the sequence of construction, was filled with packed rubble. Brown et al. (1960: 69–70, figs. 46–47) reconstruct the total height based on the traces of discoloration visible on the S side. The curved profile of the crown excludes the possibility that there was an ashlar revetment of the superstructure of the cella (for which see Brown et al. 1960: 71, Figure 48).

In the front part of the long sides of the temple, the socle was founded on the retaining walls that maintained the base level of the pronaos, which, like the column foundations, are made of unfinished limestone blocks laid up in clay (Brown et al. 1960: 59). In its final plan, the complex terminated with a forecourt whose walls were built with polygonal masonry associated with concrete cores, which betrays a later date (Brown et al. 1960: 75–80, Figure 56–57; Fentress [pers. comm.] proposes an Augustan date, whose cultural context would fit well with both the identitaire character of the facing style and its Archaizing flavor).

The mixed features of the Capitolium surely reflect the interplay of economy of construction, structural concerns, and issues of design and decoration. The masonry style of the cella was in all likelihood not visible (Brown suggests that the exterior walls were covered with plaster), so the specific choice has to be explained primarily in terms of construction process. Notably, this differs from the technique used for the only contemporary temple for which the superstructure survives, Temple D, whose cella is built with courses of roughly rectangular blocks whose height diminishes as one moves toward the top (Brown et al. 1960: 28–29). While the similarity between the precinct wall of the Comitium and the cella walls of the Capitolium may indicate a shorter time gap between the two monuments (thus indirectly confirming the later date of the Comitium; Brown et al. 1960: 102–103 proposed 150 BCE for the temple), the correlation with the main communal symbols of Cosa – the place where the assembly of all male citizens met, and the poliadic temple – may reveal some other clues as to the impetus for the technological shift.

One possibility is to consider the impact of the complex social dynamics set in motion with the arrival of the new colonists with the *adscriptio* of 197 BCE (Livy 33.24.8-9). The contingent, which corresponded to one-third of the original colony, probably included participants from Rome and other Roman areas as well as other indigenous groups who would have been given the opportunity to enlist (that colonies founded after the Second Punic War started to include allies has been explained by the suggestion that joining a colony had become undesirable for Romans; cf. Bradley 2006: 171–177). Laffi (2017: 53–54) interprets Livy's specific reference to Cosa as evidence that the new colonists were recruited exclusively among Italian allies. Although colonies at this time were probably founded as hierarchical societies, with different classes of colonists receiving plots of different sizes, both at the urban and rural levels (for the idea that the residential areas of Cosa were allotted in accordance with the property class of the colonist see Sewell 2010: 121–122; 137–141), the long- term success of the enterprise was in part dependent also on the strengthening of inter-group bonds of solidarity and the creation of a shared communal identity, which must have been a concern in light of the demographic crisis of the 3rd-century BCE settlement.

In that respect, the way of doing things introduced for the construction of the Comitium and the Capitolium allowed for the active involvement of the main stakeholders of the colony, even if the colonists hired private contractors to execute the projects. The cooperation of previous inhabitants and/or rural settlers, who had better knowledge of the local environment, must have been a crucial prerequisite for the selection of sources of building materials, especially the volcanic sands and the stratified sandstone. Interestingly, according to Laffi (2017: 54), some of the newly enlisted colonists might just have been recruited from a preexisting group of *immixti* (resident aliens). On the other hand, the implementation of a building method based on the use of reasonably small, stackable elements and facing blocks may have represented a means of including larger pools of civic labor, drawing manpower from the new arrivals even if unskilled.

While production and transportation costs for the materials certainly played a role, for present purposes we can recall DeLaine (2001: 234–245, with Appendix A), who has calculated that tuff ashlar construction at Ostia (which was made with a softer stone than the limestone available at Cosa) is on average two to four times more labor intensive than any form of concrete; furthermore, the labor structure for most operations (e. g., shaping, fine finishing, and squaring of the blocks, dressing of edges) was four skilled to one unskilled laborer. Larger amounts of unskilled labor were of course required for hauling, lifting, and placing blocks (DeLaine's estimate provides a ratio of three skilled to four unskilled for every ton of blocks). While there are no contemporary textual sources for the direct participation of colonists in colonial public construction projects, it is fair to say that at Cosa as elsewhere large amounts of unskilled settlers were involved in the construction of ashlar monuments like the early 3rd-century BCE city walls (Bernard 2018: 108–114 discusses the role of *corvée* citizen labor for the 4th-century BCE fortifications of Rome). However, the introduction of concrete in the 2nd-century BCE probably lowered *both* overall costs and the ratio of skilled to unskilled builders within the workforce (for the laying of concrete wall faces and cores the generally accepted figure is one skilled to one unskilled laborer). In other words, the early form of *opus caementicium* at Cosa would offer broader opportunities than ashlar masonry for unskilled colonial builders to be employed through the finishing stages of the construction process, including the physical raising of walls, while at the same time ensuring an efficient resource management.

Seen in this light, the building process devised for the main architectural components that were necessary for the functioning and self-governing of the town could have been conceptualized and understood as a form of public engagement that gave both the designers and the colonists an opportunity to materially shape the collective civic identity of the colony. Two pieces of evidence might help support the idea that municipal citizens involved themselves directly in public works. Varro (*Ling* 5.179) appears to imply that contributing *munera* formed part of civic identity, whereby he defines the citizens (*municipes*) as those who must jointly perform a *munus* (Bernard 2018: 110–111). The *Lex Ursonensis*, the Flavian copy of a colonial charter dating to the Caesarian period, contains explicit reference to *operae* for construction of *munitiones* (Crawford 1996, 1: 408, Nr. 25, Ch. 98), making it clear that some sort of labor was required from citizens for particular types of monuments (most notably fortifications and perhaps road infrastructure).

The innovative nature of both the building medium and the construction process developed for these communal projects emphasized the important relationship of the structures to Cosa's redefined status. The occurrence of the distinctive technique in monuments that were built in successive stages over the course of a quarter of a century demonstrates that the technological style was deliberately maintained. While restrictions of locally available resources, commercial expediency, the need for structural strength, and fashions in aesthetic appearance probably influenced the pattern, it seems that different variants of mortared architecture were specifically added to the repertoire for use in other structures that were not directly linked with the constitutive civic functions. This contributes to explain the apparently heterogeneous character of the building techniques at the site: from the random rubblework of the Carcer, to the polygonal masonry of smaller module in Temple B and Temple D on the Arx, to the *opus incertum* of the Basilica and the monumental gateway of the Forum. Another possible reason for this variation is that the contracts for these monuments were let out to different firms. In any case, the relationship between the masonry style of the Comitium and of the cella of the Capitolium and the manufacturing of Cosa's communal identity through technological practice could only be appreciated while construction of those monuments was still undergoing, given that the technique in question lacked emblemic value (in contrast with polygonal masonry and *opus quadratum* facings, which were always left visible). Therefore, the process of construction mattered the most, not its finished aspect.

Conclusion

By exploring the materiality of mortared rubble architecture at Cosa, the nexus between the emergence of monumentality and Roman colonization can be revealed in all its complexity, avoiding the traps of cultural diffusionism that have in the past affected the study of the origins of Roman concrete. The approach I advocate for pays greater attention to the local context, and therefore allows for an appreciation of the colonists as active agents that goes beyond impersonal mechanisms of technological transfer from core to periphery. Thus, I question essentialist views about the cultural meaning of Roman concrete architecture and its relationship with Roman identity and ingenuity. The early development of lime-based construction at Cosa is revealed to be mostly implicated with the web of political, social, and economic negotiations that influenced efforts to resuscitate a town that in the previous period of occupation had suffered substantial demographic decline.

This is not to say that broader explanatory frameworks should be dismissed altogether. The first half of the 2nd century BCE was indeed a phase of crucial developments in Roman architecture and urbanism (important building types like the Basilica and the Porticus first materialize in this period). In this sense, the projects that we see reflected in the monumentalization of Cosa were also a response to global trends and ideas about what it meant to be a city in contemporary Roman Italy. The potential for the development and diffusion of technology through *publicani* will also have to be confronted. Yet, archaeological evidence from other colonial sites shows that there was ample variability in the choice of how new towns were built (or rebuilt), suggesting that shared designs could be adapted to local circumstances or preference. The case of Fregellae, another Mid-Republican colony that was completely redeveloped not long after Cosa, is particularly instructive: despite the ready availability of both lime and pozzolan in the immediate surroundings, innovative building types could be crafted using traditional materials and techniques (e. g., fired bricks for vaulting in the baths: Tsiolis 2013; on contemporary houses see Battaglini/Diosono 2011). This suggests that environmental conditions alone were not sufficient to spark technological change. Thus, only the closer investigation of other 2nd-century BCE type-sites in their own social context will enable us to reach firmer conclusions about the processes of invention, innovation, and use of a technology that became inextricably linked with monumentality in Roman Imperial architecture (cf. Lancaster 2005; Van Oyen 2017; Stek 2013 discusses how material culture can be used to elucidate the cultural implications of Roman expansion in Republican Italy).

Acknowledgments

This chapter forms part of a broader ongoing research project on the origins of Roman concrete. Initial work on the material from Cosa and the limestone region of central Italy was carried out in 2014–2015 as part of a DRS COFUND Fellowship at the Insitut für Klassische Archäologie of the Freie Universität Berlin. The Discussion Forum "SIZE Matters" gave me the opportunity to bring the argument and goals into sharper focus. I am grateful to Jamie Sewell, Lisa Fentress, Seth Bernard, and Andrea De Giorgi for their thought-provoking comments on earlier drafts, which greatly improved the final version. Needless to say, any inconsistencies remain my sole responsibility.

Bibliography

Anderson Jr., J. C. (1997): Roman Architecture and Society, Baltimore: Johns Hopkins University Press.

Battaglini, G./Diosono, F. (2011): "Le domus di Fregellae. Case aristocratiche di ambito coloniale." In: M. Bentz/C. Reusser (eds.), Etruskisch-italische und römisch republikanische Häuser, Studien zur Antiken Stadt, 9, Wiesbaden: Reichert, pp. 243–253.

Benvenuti, V. (2002): "The introduction of artillery in the Roman world. Hypothesis for a chronological definition based on the Cosa town wall." In: Memoirs of the American Academy in Rome 47, pp. 199–207.

Bernard, S. (2018): Building Mid-Republican Rome: Labor, Architecture, and the Urban Economy, New York: Oxford University Press.

Bispham, E. (2006): "Coloniam deducere: How Roman was Roman colonization during the Republic?" In: G. Bradley/J.-P. Wilson (eds.), Greek and Roman colonization: Origins, ideologies and interactions, Swansea: University of Wales Press, pp. 73–160.

Blake, M. E. (1947): Ancient Roman Construction in Italy from the Prehistoric Period to Augustus, Washington, D. C.: Carnegie Institution of Washington, William Byrd Press.

Boos, M. (2011): "In excelsissimo loco – An approach to Poliadic Deities in Roman Colonies." In: D. Mladenović/B. Russell (eds.), TRAC 2010: Proceedings of the Twentieth Annual Theoretical Roman Archaeology Conference, Oxford, 25–28 March 2010, Oxford: Oxbow, pp. 18–31.

Bourgeois, J. (1987): "Chapter II. Geography and Geology." In: A. M. McCann (ed.), The Roman Port and Fishery at Cosa, Princeton: Princeton University Press, pp. 44–57.

Bradley, G. (2006): "Colonization and identity in republican Italy." In: G. Bradley/J.-P. Wilson (eds.), Greek and Roman colonization: Origins, ideologies and interactions, Swansea: University of Wales Press, pp. 161–187.

Brown, F. (1951): "Cosa I: History and Topography." In: Memoirs of the American Academy in Rome 20, pp. 5–113.

Brown, F. (1980): Cosa: The Making of a Roman Town, Ann Arbor: University of Michigan Press.

Brown, F./Richardson, E. H./Richardson Jr., L. (1960): "Cosa II. The temples of the Arx." In: Memoirs of the American Academy in Rome 26, pp. 1–380.

Brown, F./Richardson Jr., L./Richardson, E. H. (1993): "Cosa III. The buildings of the forum. Colony, municipium, and village." In: Memoirs of the American Academy in Rome 37, pp. 1–298.

Bruno, V. J./Scott, R. T. (1993): "Cosa IV. The houses." In: Memoirs of the American Academy in Rome 38, pp. 1–211.

Buttrey, T. V. (1980): "Cosa: The Coins." In: Memoirs of the American Academy in Rome 34, pp. 5–153.

Casarotto, A./Pelgrom, J./Stek, T. D. (2016): "Testing settlement models in the early Roman colonial landscape of Venusia (291 B. C.), Cosa (273 B. C.) and Aesernia (263 B. C.)." In: Journal of Field Archaeology 41, pp. 568–586.

Cifarelli, F. M. (ed.) (2013): Tecniche costruttive del tardo-ellenismo nel Lazio e in Campania: atti del Convegno, Segni, 3 dicembre 2011, Rome: Espera.

Crawford, M. (ed.) (1996): Roman Statutes, 2 Vols., Bulletin of the Institute of Classical Studies Supplement 64, London: Institute of Classical Studies.

DeLaine, J. (2001): "Bricks and mortar. Exploring the economics of building techniques at Rome and Ostia." In: D. J. Mattingly/J. B. Salmon (eds.), Economies beyond agriculture in the classical world, London; New York: Routledge, pp. 230–268.

De Vincenzo, S. (2018): "Indagini archeologiche nel foro della colonia romana di Liternum." In: Fastionline 411, pp. 1–25, http://www.fastionline.org/docs/FOL DER-it-2018-411.pdf (last accessed April 12, 2019).

Dyson, S. L. (2013): "Cosa." In: J. DeRose Evans (ed.), A companion to the archaeology of the Roman Republic, Malden: Wiley-Blackwell, pp. 472-484.

Fentress, E. (2000): "Introduction. Frank Brown, Cosa, and the idea of a Roman city." In: E. Fentress (ed.), Romanization and the city. Creation, Transformations, and failures. Proceedings of a conference held at the American Academy in Rome, 14–16 May 1998. JRA Supplementary series 38, Portsmouth: Journal of Roman Archaeology, pp. 11–24.

Fentress, E./Bodel, J./Rabinowitz, A./Taylor, R. (2003): "Cosa in the Republic and Early Empire." In: Memoirs of the American Academy in Rome, Supplementary volume, 2, pp. 13–62.

Fentress, E./Perkins, P. (2016): "Cosa and the ager Cosanus." In: A. E. Cooley (ed.), A companion to Roman Italy, Oxford: Wiley-Blackwell, pp. 378–400.

Gazda, E. K. (1987): "Chapter IV. The Port and Fishery: Description of the Extant Remains and Sequence of Construction." In: A. M. McCann (ed.), The Roman Port and Fishery at Cosa, Princeton: Princeton University Press, pp. 74–97.

Gazda, E. K. (2008): "Cosa's Hydraulic Concrete. Towards a revised chronology." In: R. L. Hohlfelder (ed.), The maritime world of ancient Rome: proceedings of "The Maritime World of Ancient Rome" conference held at the American Academy in Rome, 27–29 March 2003, Memoirs of the American Academy in Rome, Supplementary volume, Ann Arbor: University of Michigan Press, pp. 265–290.

Giuliani, C. F. (2006): L'edilizia nell'antichità, 2nd edition, Rome: Carocci.

Gros, P. (2011): L'Architecture Romaine: du début du IIIe siècle av. J.-C. à la fin du Haut-Empire 1: Les monuments publics, 3rd revised edition, Paris: Picard.

Helas, S. (2016): "Polygonalmauern in Mittelitalien und ihre Rezeption in mittel- und spätrepublikanischer Zeit." In: R. Frederiksen/S. Müth/P. I. Schneider/ M. Schnelle (eds.), Focus on fortification. New research on fortifications in the ancient Mediterranean and the Near East, Fokus Fortifikation Studies, 2, Oxford: Oxbow, pp. 581–594.

Hoffman, C. R./Dobres, M.-A. (1999): "Introduction: A Context for the Present and Future of Technology Studies." In: M.-A. Dobres/C. R. Hoffman (eds.), The Social Dynamics of Technology: Practice, Politics, and World Views, Washington, D. C.: Smithsonian Institution Press, pp. 1–19.

Lackner, E.-M. (2008): Republikanische Fora, München: Biering & Brinkmann.

Laffi, U. (2017): "Italici in colonie Latine e Latini in colonie Romane." In: M. Chelotti/M. Silvestrini/E. Todisco (eds.), Itinerari di storia: In ricordo di Mario Pani, Bari: Edipuglia, pp. 51–61.

Lancaster, L. C. (2005): Concrete Vaulted Construction in Imperial Rome: Innovations in Context, Cambridge; New York: Cambridge University Press.

Lancaster, L. C. (2015): Innovative Vaulting in the Architecture of the Roman Empire: 1st to 4th centuries CE, Cambridge: Cambridge University Press.

Lechtman, H. (1977): "Style in Technology: Some Early Thoughts." In: H. Lechtman/R. S. Merrill (eds.), Material Culture: Styles, Organization, and Dynamics of Technology, Proceedings of the American Ethnological Society, 197, St. Paul: West Pub. Co., pp. 3–20.

Lugli, G. (1957): La Tecnica edilizia romana. Con particolare riguardo a Roma e Lazio, 2 Vols., Rome: Bardi.

Marra, F./D'Ambrosio, E. (2013): "Trace element classification diagrams of pyroclastic rocks from the Volcanic districts of Central Italy. The case study of the ancient Roman ships of Pisa." In: Archaeometry 55, pp. 993–1019.

Mogetta, M. (2013): "The Origins of Concrete in Rome and Pompeii." Ph. D. Thesis, Ann Arbor, Michigan: University of Michigan.

Mogetta, M. (2015): "A New Date for Concrete in Rome." In: Journal of Roman Studies 105, pp. 1–40.

Mogetta, M. (2016): "The early development of concrete in the domestic architecture of pre-Roman Pompeii." In: Journal of Roman Archaeology 29, pp. 43–72.

Nichols, M. F. (2010): "Contemporary perspectives on luxury building in second-century BC Rome." In: Papers of the British School at Rome 78, pp. 39–61.

Nichols, M. F. (2017): Author and audience in Vitruvius' De architectura, Cambridge: Cambridge University Press.

Paternoster, G./Proietti, L. M./Vitale, A. (2007): Malte e tecniche edilizie del Rione Terra di Pozzuoli. L'età Romana, Naples: Giannini Editore.

Perkins, P. (1999): Etruscan settlement, society and material culture in central coastal Etruria, British archaeological reports, International series, 788, Oxford: Hedges.

Peterse, K. (1999): Steinfachwerk in Pompeji. Bautechnik und Architektur, Amsterdam: J. C. Gieben.

Poggesi, G./Pallecchi, P. (2012): "La cinta muraria di Cosa (GR)." In: L. Attenni/D. Baldassarre (eds.), Quarto seminario internazionale di studi sulle mura poligonali, Palazzo Corti Gentili, 7–10 ottobre 2009, Rome: Aracne, pp. 161–168.

Quinn, J. C./Wilson, A. (2013): "Capitolia." In: Journal of Roman Studies 103, pp. 117–173.

Scott, A. R. (2008): Cosa: The Black-Glaze Pottery, 2, Memoirs of the American Academy in Rome, Supplementary volume 5, Ann Arbor: University of Michigan Press.

Scott, R. T./De Giorgi, A. U./Crawford-Brown, S./Glennie A./Smith, A. (2015): "The Cosa Excavations: season 2013." In: Orizzonti 16, pp. 11–22.

Sewell, J. (2005): "Trading places? A reappraisal of the fora at Cosa." In: Ostraka 14, pp. 91–114.

Sewell, J. (2010): The Formation of Roman Urbanism, 338–200 B. C.: Between contemporary foreign influence and Roman tradition, JRA Supplementary series 79, Portsmouth: Journal of Roman Archaeology.

Sewell, J. (2016): "Higher-order settlements in early hellenistic Italy. A quantitative analysis of a new archaeological database." In: American Journal of Archaeology 120, pp. 603–630.

Stek, T. D. (2013): "Material culture, Italic identities and the Romanization of Italy." In: J. DeRose Evans (ed.), A companion to the archaeology of the Roman Republic, Malden: Wiley-Blackwell, pp. 337–353.

Stek, T. D./Pelgrom, J. (eds.) (2014): Roman Republican Colonization: New Perspectives from Archaeology and Ancient History, Rome: Palombi.

Taylor, R. (2002): "Temples and terracottas at Cosa." In: American Journal of Archaeology 106, pp. 59–83.

Terrenato, N. (2012): "The enigma of 'Catonian' villas. The 'De agri cultura' in the context of second-century B. C. Italian architecture." In: J. A. Becker/N. Terrenato (eds.), Roman Republican Villas: Architecture, Context, Ideology, Papers and Monographs of the American Academy in Rome, XXXII, Ann Arbor: University of Michigan Press, pp. 69–93.

Tombrägel, M. (2012): Die republikanischen Otiumvillen von Tivoli, Palilia 25, Wiesbaden: Reichert.

Torelli, M. (1980): "Innovazioni nelle tecniche edilizie romane tra il I sec. a. C. e il I sec. d. C." In: Tecnologia, economia e società nel mondo romano. Atti del convegno di Como 27–29 settembre 1979, Como: Banca Popolare Commercio e Industria, pp. 139–161.

Tsiolis, V. (2013): "The baths at Fregellae and the transition from Balaneion to Balneum." In: S. K. Lucore/M. Trümper (eds.), Greek bath and bathing culture. New discoveries and approaches, Leuven: Brepols, pp. 89–111.

Van Oyen, A. (2017): "Finding the material in 'material culture'. Form and matter in Roman concrete." In: A. Van Oyen/M. Pitts (eds.), Materialising Roman Histories, Oxford: Oxbow, pp. 133–152.

Von Gerkan, A. (1958): "Zur Datierung der Kolonie Cosa." In: Scritti in onore di Guido Libertini, Florence: Olschki, pp. 149–156.

Monumentality of the Landscape: the Coixtlahuaca Valley Archaeology and the Lienzo Seler II[1]

Mónica Pacheco Silva

When we think about Mesoamerican monumentality in Mexico, an image of the archaeological site of Teotihuacan comes to mind, or maybe the popular Mayan site of Chichen Itza, La Venta – also an excellent example of an early monumental site in the Mexican Gulf Coast. Throughout time, monumental buildings have been part of Mesoamerican urban planning. Mesoamerica, a cultural area defined geographically over half a century ago by Paul Kirchhoff (2009), describes a territory extending from northern Mexico to Central America. Mesoamerica covered an area where several cultures developed from the ancient Olmec to the 16th century Aztecs. In Germany, the most popular cultures associated with the area are the Maya and the Aztec, which have proven to be 'blockbusters' at museum exhibitions across the country. However, many of the most popular pyramids or archaeological sites in Mexico, like Teotihuacán or Monte Albán, are neither Aztec nor Maya, since these cultures were not the only ones to have monumental urban planning. Less known internationally are the cultures that developed in Oaxaca, especially in the Mixtec area in the northeastern part of the modern state of Oaxaca in Mexico, although many of the most exquisite examples of their pictographic writing and mapping are found in European collections.[2] Mixteca is a cultural and historical term used in the literature, named after one of the most prominent ethnic groups that inhabited the area: the Mixtecs (Terraciano 2001: 1). The focus of this paper is the Coixtlahuaca Valley (Figure 1) located in the northern part of the Mixtec area, in the Mixteca Alta, and the development of its city-state, known by its *náhuatl* name Coixtlahuaca, from the Late Postclassic through Early Colonial Times (ca. 1200–1600 CE).

1 I would like to thank Dr. Stephen Kowalewski for sharing unpublished material, data, and helping in the elaboration of the present paper.
2 The Codex Becker I and II in the Weltmuseum and Codex Vindobonensis housed in the Österreichische Nationalbibliothek, both in Vienna; the Codex Zouche-Nuttall and the Codex Sánchez Solís or Egerton 2895, both at the British Museum in London; Codex Bodley, Codex Selden, and Selden Roll, all in the Bodleian Library in Oxford, England.

Figure 1: The Coixtlahuaca Valley, white pyramids are important mountains in the landscape, the dotted line delimitates the territory claimed by Lienzo Seler II (modified version of a map by Renate Sander in König 2017b, Map 2)

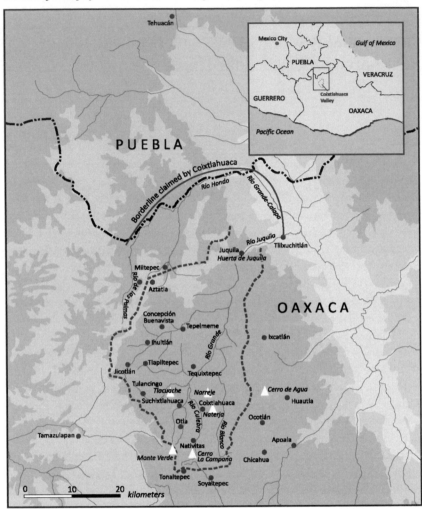

No less than three different documents[3] specifically recount the development of the city-state or *señorío* of Coixtlahuaca, its territory, lineage, and history. These

---

3 Rincón Mautner (2000: 30) enumerates these three *lienzos*: Lienzo Seler or Coixtlahuaca II in the Ethnologisches Museum Berlin; Lienzo de Coixtlahuaca I, Biblioteca del Museo Nacional de Antropología e Historia, Ciudad de México; and the Lienzo A or Meixueiro, a copy of a lost document from the Coixtlahuaca area, in Tulane University, USA. There are other documents con-

documents are made of bands of cotton cloth and are named after their Spanish term *lienzo* (Rincón Mautner 2000: 25). These *lienzos* were fabricated with back-strap looms, which was the indigenous technique of producing textiles. The biggest and most complex of these *lienzos*, the Lienzo Seler/Coixtlahuaca II, measuring a total of about 16 m², is housed today at the Ethnologisches Museum in Berlin, Germany (König 2017a: 45) and is a mythological-historical account of Coixtlahuaca's multiethnic lineages, recording not only events and noble descendant lines but also territory and some architectural features. This paper will address the apparent lack of monumentality in the area during the Late Postclassic (1200–1520 CE) while considering in general the information recorded in the Seler II, in other words, its discourse, and how this contrasts with the archaeological data and certain aspects reflected in the written Mixtec ethnohistorical documents during the first decades of the colonial period (1521–1810 CE). While the archaeological information may seem to contradict the Seler II's discourse, as will be shown, it actually complements it and together with the ethnohistorical sources provides a better picture of the society and its territorial organization.

The Lienzo Seler II discourse

At first glance, the Seler II seems to be a type of geographical map, but on a closer look it becomes apparent that it not only maps a territory but is the historical account of the upper echelons of its city-state and the relationship of its noble lineages to the territory and other *señorios* or communities. Such documents were created under the instruction of the noble lords, registering only the lineages and events relevant to their history so as to exalt and legitimate their royal houses. Nevertheless, as the full discourse of the Seler II is interpreted, several layers of information emerge.

First, along its right side and outside the territory's frontier, the Lienzo depicts a migration or path that connects different city-states and royal houses even beyond the Coixtlahuaca Valley borders. Mythological and historical places are represented along the way, creating a mythical and historical account that ultimately links several city-states to Coixtlahuaca's history (Figure 2). The territorial border is shown by a black dotted and yellow band representing a jaguar skin, a feature associated with royalty in ancient Mesoamerica. Directly on the jaguar band several toponyms mark the boundaries of the territory. Inside the territory, several other toponyms or places are represented together with their ruling couple or founders on top, some lineages extending to several generations. The toponyms

---

sidered to come from Coixtlahuaca too; these form the Coixtlahuaca Group, like the Tlapiltepec Lienzo (Brownstone 2015).

Figure 2: The Lienzo Seler II. Depiction of several paths linking different city-states related to the Coixtlahuaca city-state history (Staatliche Museen zu Berlin, Ethnologisches Museum; Photo by Claudia Obrocki)

Figure 3: The Coatepec (Staatliche Museen zu Berlin, Ethnologisches Museum; Photo by Claudia Obrocki)

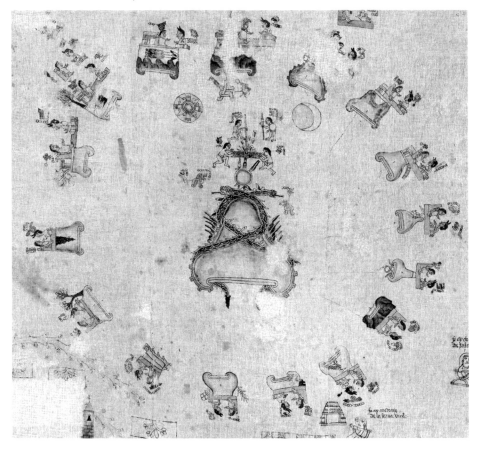

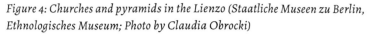

Figure 4: Churches and pyramids in the Lienzo (Staatliche Museen zu Berlin, Ethnologisches Museum; Photo by Claudia Obrocki)

or places are represented by an inverted U-shape that symbolizes a mountain, the depiction of certain objects associated with it give the name of the place.

Continuing with the information recorded, natural features of the landscape are ubiquitous, such as rivers and an impressive mountain surrounded by two serpents (Figure 3) (identified as Coatepec or the Mount of Intertwined Serpents), the latter signifying a geographical and/or a mythical place or mountain (Rincón Mautner 2007; Castañeda de la Paz/Doesburg 2008; Pacheco Silva 2017; König 2017b).

Additionally, architectural elements are represented (Figure 4): two Spanish colonial churches (one in the lower mutilated part of the Lienzo, recognized only by its right bell tower) and two pyramids: one represented in a frontal view while another multicolored structure or pyramid is shown in profile. Along with mythical, historical, architectonical, and topographical features, events are represented: a foundation ritual, a warrior meeting, a war scene, and the hanging of a noble native ruler next to a Spanish *conquistador*. Judging only from the nature, complexity, and the amount of information contained in the Seler II and within the broader cultural and archaeological Mesoamerican context, it could be inferred that the document emerged not only from a stratified society but also from an urbanized culture with monumental architecture, as the two pyramids represented in the Seler II could be taken as good examples of the existence of such monumentality.

The foundation of the city-state of Coixtlahuaca depicted in the Seler II, goes back several generations, possibly to the beginning of the 13th century CE, which would correspond to the Late Postclassic (1200–1520 CE). Coixtlahuaca is depicted with two ruling lineages or houses (Figure 5), one ruling over the 'Heart-Place or Mountain' and the other over the 'Blood-Place', both united under the feather serpent which embodies the Valley of Coixtlahuaca.

Figure 5: Coixtlahuaca's toponym (Staatliche Museen zu Berlin, Ethnologisches Museum; Photo by Claudia Obrocki)

This city-state is known to have been located within the Coixtlahuaca Valley and at least one of its civic-ceremonial centers, known as the archaeological site of Inguiteria, is situated not far from the modern municipal and religious buildings of Coixtlahuaca. With two ancient lineage houses, an impressive colonial church, and at least the representation in the Lienzo of two pyramids within its territory, one could expect monumental architectonical findings. Also, the Aztec interest in controlling the area as portrayed in the Codex Mendoza, an early colonial document, points to Coixtlahuaca's importance within the Mesoamerican economy (Berdan/Anawalt 1997: 105, n.1; Berdan/Anawalt 1992: 102–103).

We could interpret directly just from looking at the Seler II:

1. The Coixtlahuaca Valley was a multiethnic area inhabited by speakers of at least three different languages: *ngiwa* or chocholteco, mixtec, and nahua,[4] which are the languages of the glosses in Latin alphabet around the border.
2. There are two royal lineages whose ancestors came to found and rule the area from outside Coixtlahuaca centuries back. Furthermore, the royal lineages of Coixtlahuaca were not only related to other lineages within the Mixtec area but also outside of it, with links to the Valleys of Mexico and Puebla as other documents, such as the Map of Cuauhtinchan No. 2, indicate (Boone 2007: 30).
3. They utilized architectonical structures as well as natural features, such as mountains, as the setting for their ritual life, as represented by the ritual scene in front of Tulancingo's pyramid and the New Fire Ceremony on the Mount of Intertwined Serpents.
4. Furthermore, it could be implied that Coixtlahuaca ruled throughout the Valley as a hegemonic center with the subject towns under its control represented inside its frontiers, boasting at least one monumental civic-ceremonial site represented by the big plumed serpent with two mounds on its back where the lineage houses were founded and a third house, represented further up the Heart-Place lineage, by a circular element with a palace on top and the multi-colored pyramid associated.

As previously mentioned, the *lienzos* as well as the indigenous Mixtec books known as *códices*, were created by the elites. In them, the elites seek not only to assert their right to power, control, and territory but to recount and preserve their version of history. The Seler II is a document created by the elite, and most probably for the elites, where there is no trace of the commoners or the greater mass of the population, apart from the depiction of architectural features that suggest an important number of laborers at hand. The archaeological record, however, reflects a different picture that does not necessarily contradict the elite discourse displayed in the Seler II but complements it from a different angle.

Archaeology and the ethnohistorical documents

Archaeological evidence reflects a society in its entirety, as the elite and the commoners create their mark on the landscape. Since the commoners were larger in numbers than the elite, the archaeological evidence for this part of the population can overwhelm that of the upper echelons of society, which found expression mainly in public civic-ceremonial architecture and residential palaces. The

---

4 Furthermore, the pictographic nature of the Seler II made its reading possible to people speaking different languages.

archaeological remains complement the elite's discourse of the Seler II, but unlike it reflect a more neutral or unbiased image of the society. Now, we will consider what the most recent research in archaeology and in written ethnohistorical documents of the area has presented about Coixtlahuaca and its social and political organization.

After 1200 CE, the Mixteca Alta region reached its peak in terms of number of settlements and estimated population. It became one of Mesoamerica's largest and wealthiest economies, and it is estimated that during this time Coixtlahuaca occupied an area of at least 30 km² as shown by the latest archaeological surveys of the area (Spores/Balkansky 2013: 91; Kowalewski 2009: 315).

Figure 6: Late Postclassic (1200–1520 CE) settlements found in the Coixtlahuaca Valley by the Recorrido Arqueológico de Coixtlahuaca (used by permission of the project director Stephen A. Kowalewski)

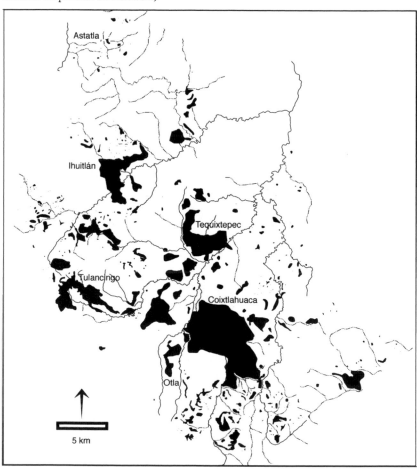

Postclassic (1000–1520 CE) Mixtec society was basically organized in three major hierarchies: the ruling class, a class of nobles, and the commoners. Among the commoners were landless peasants under the control of the ruling class, and slaves, who were not *per se* a social class (Spores/Balkansky 2013: 112; Lind 2000: 570–571). These hierarchies can be partly seen in the archaeological record: the distribution, number, and size of mounds which could be the remains of public architecture or palaces, and the different agricultural and water-drainage systems, which were constructed and maintained around rivers and tributaries by the commoners.

On the other hand, the ethnohistorical documents of the area, as Terraciano (2001) has shown through his work, give a more detailed picture of the socioeconomic organization in the Mixteca. Terraciano (2001: 102–132) identifies different levels of sociopolitical organization. He finds that the Mixtecs referred to any given settlement as *ñuu*, and settlements such as Coixtlahuaca were called *ñuu* in the most general sense. The biggest settlements were named *yuhuitayu* which is translated as 'seat or pair of the reed mat', a direct reference to the pictography of the noble couple sitting atop their city-state or mountain, which is the toponym of place for the seat of rulership (the first ruling couples of Coixtlahuaca can be seen in Figure 5). Following this argument, the representation of the royal couple facing each other seated on a mat would then represent the political level of *yuhuitayu* itself. However, an essential aspect of the *yuhuitayu* is that it united the resources and rulership of at least two *ñuu* or communities without compromising their autonomy and individuality. And while a *yuhuitayu* was considered a *ñuu*, not all *ñuu* were *yuhuitayu*, since only *ñuu* of a considerable size and represented by a royal couple could be considered a *yuhuitayu*. In general, *ñuu* was not utilized for smaller settlements that lacked a "lordly establishment" (Terraciano 2001: 104). This is an interesting aspect when considering which political and territorial level is being represented in the Seler II, which is depicted with at least two noble lineages or *ñuu* (Place of the Blood-Mountain, Place of the Heart and Place of the Palace and Temple where the circular stone element might represent a plaza or open space), who apparently jointly ruled a vast territory that comprised much of the Coixtlahuaca Valley, while incorporating other city-states or *señorios*.[5] These other city-states: Tequixtepec, Aztatla, and Tulancingo, were not ruled by Coixtlahuaca as direct overlords but possibly as adjoining or confederated[6] city-states, or as settlements that together with Coixtlahuaca were part of a cultural tradition that developed within the Coixtlahuaca Valley. This idea might be supported by

---

5 Here the 'smaller' settlements like Tequixtepec and Aztatla were probably not considered *yuhuitayu* but were independent city-states. *Señorío* was the word used by the Spanish for the prehispanic city-states.

6 As Pohl (2010: 61) has suggested that Coixtlahuaca was confederated with states in the Puebla Valley.

the archaeological evidence, since the settlement pattern found by Kowalewski (2017) and his colleagues shows that there are several centers or groups of mounds varying in size and number throughout the area (Figure 7). This type of pattern indicates a rather decentralized political and social organization as we will see later, suggesting cities and towns were mere aggregates of smaller units such as *barrios* (Kowalewski et al. 2017: 364). The units of a *yuhuitayu* as well, which would be considered a community, *ñuu* or *pueblo* in Spanish, could have the same characteristics as the *yuhuitayu*: a noble ruling couple, a temple organization, boundary-shrines, and a political identity of its own (Kowalewski 2017b: 8). This would apply for the cities represented inside the borders of Coixtlahuaca, such as the ones mentioned above, which although they had a lordly establishment were not a *yuhuitayu*.

The communities or *ñuu* are believed to have been divided into smaller units referred to as *siqui*, *siña*, or *dzini* in Mixtec ethnohistorical documents, *sindi* in chocholtec, and translated as *barrio* by the Spanish. These *barrios* and the associated structures would form part of a *ñuu* or directly the *yuhuitayu* of Coixtlahuaca, mainly represented by the two royal lineages.

As aforementioned, the *yuhuitayu* did not compromise the autonomy and independence of the *ñuu* and subsequent *barrios* that formed it, therefore it could co-exist or be imposed upon a more ancient or basic type of socioeconomic organization. Surely, the more stable socioeconomic, territorial, and political organization would lie beyond the *yuhuitayu*.[7] The *barrio* could be this more ancient form of sociopolitical organization, existing before the formation of a *yuhuitayu* and continuing to exist at its dissolution. This corresponds to recent studies that show that community organization existed before the king and the state itself and was powerful enough to even challenge such institutions (Kowalewski et al. 2017: 354, 367). Furthermore, this would also point to the idea that the *yuhuitayu* could be a construct brought and legitimized by elites arriving in the Valley at the dawn of the Postclassic (1000 CE).[8]

The consistent usage of the term for *barrio* in different native languages in the colonial documentation attests to its existence as a distinctly defined sub-entity, and while Terraciano interprets it "as a corporate group unified by ethnic and kinship ties, common origin, and political and economic relations...with ethnicity as one organizing principle of the siqui" (2001: 106), I believe the *siqui* to be organized around territory or, more specifically, a given number of agricultural plots or fields. Ethnicity could be linked to this given territory with language being the central characteristic tied to it.

---

7 Kowalewski (2017b: 4) concludes that investment in agricultural terracing as landesque capital gave the local communities and *barrios* their stability and strength.

8 Thinking of the Seler II's account of the arrival and subsequent foundation of Coixtlahuaca, supported by archaeological evidence by Kowalewski et al. (2017: 361) that might suggest a repopulation of the valley in Early Postclassic times (1000–1200 CE).

Figure 7: Late Postclassic (1200–1520 CE) civic-ceremonial platform distribution by number and size. Size was divided into large, with an area bigger than 200 m², medium: area below 200 m² and small, with dimensions bigger than 10 m² (Kowalewski et al. 2017: 365)

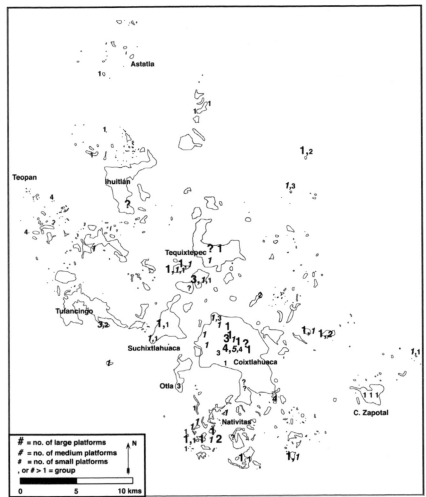

The *barrios*, in turn, were made of smaller units: a group of people working in a field and living within the same household would form the smallest social organizational unit. Check-dams, contour terraces on the hillsides as well as along the streams, were maintained by these household task-groups, who were therefore directly related and tied to the land. The *yuhuitayu*, on the other hand, was rather related and tied to a noble lineage or couple of rulers, which would once more point to the origin of this level of organization being strongly tied to and promoted by the elites.

The interdependent work of several of the task/household groups was essential to manage whole drainage systems and reflects intricate social organization, supporting the existence of the *siqui* or *barrios*. As Kowalewski and his colleagues (2017: 366–367) found in their fieldwork, the lands of these *barrios* coincided with segments of stream drainage, and a community or *ñuu* territory would in turn correspond to a drainage basin. The territories of these *barrios* and communities were marked by shrines or temples, separated by divides, with each being allocated in a different basin. Therefore, the *barrio* and the community is a logical (common-sense) form of organization for administrating not only the land but its water resources. Altogether, the household task-groups, *barrios*, and communities formed economic, territorial, and social organizations that can be identified in the archaeology as the remains of agro-drainage systems of dams and terraces, and formed cohesive groups with attached identities like language, religion, and cultural traits that would link them in turn to a bigger political identity like the *yuhuitayu*.

The ethnohistorical documents register yet another aspect of these subunits: they record some of the names of the *siqui*. These were based on diverse geographical features such as rivers or slopes, while some others were named after a certain animal or insect. The fact that the name of the *siqui* is related to the word 'river' or 'slope' reinforces the evidence found in the archaeology, as the communities and their *barrios* were organized and settled around a segment of stream drainage and/or near mountain slopes as already mentioned. Furthermore, this points to the strong relationship of the settlement and the people with the landscape. In contrast, the names of the *ñuu* or *yuhuitayu* are related to hills or mountains, which might in turn also signalize where the palaces or civic-ceremonial centers might be situated. In summary, 16th-century historic description of *señorios* and *cacicazgos* is similar to the hierarchy and integration of the *ñuu* and/or *yuhuitayu* reconstructed from archaeological data (Terraciano 2001: 107; Kowalewski 2009: 367, 315).

Land Tenure

Another important aspect of the territorial and social organization is the land tenure. The basic Mixtec organization, the household, played a central role in the structure of land tenure and use, as people residing in the same household relied on each other for working the fields and producing goods. And even though lands and properties were owned individually and members of a household could have the right to individual plots, the land was worked jointly by a household so that the produce and tribute was also generated per household. The household was composed of multiple houses organized around a patio and tribute was calculated per household. The nobles had cultivators who worked their lands, plus the tribute they received based on each household's lands and resources. The land where the household and the cultivable land was located was called *ñuhu huahi,* and the best and oldest plot of land was inherited through generations so that it became patrimonial land. For the nobles, their palace or *aniñe* was usually tied to specific lands or arable fields, so that nobles and commoners both had possession or access to patrimonial land (Terraciano 2001: 199, 201, 203–204).

Other properties or land called *ytu* were plots scattered in marginal areas or at the periphery of the community's borders. The holdings of a given household thus consisted of the land where the household was, the cultivable lands associated with it, and plots in other areas (*ytu*) – these lands could be traded, sold, or lost. This system of multiple types of land tenure could have been a way to distribute fertile lands evenly among the community and the different members of a household while promoting agricultural variety in an area with ecological diversity such as the Mixteca. The nobles relied on others to work on their lands and the ownership of land by the commoners and caciques of a *ñuu* was scattered throughout the landscape in a rather fragmented pattern, with one household possibly owning plots in different *barrios,* and maybe even in other *señorios.* The difference between the commoners and lords might have been found not only in the amount of land owned but also in the quality of the land. Furthermore, there were lands that did not belong to specific individuals, a household, or an *aniñe,* and could be considered as corporate lands belonging to a certain *barrio* or *siña.* Even though these *barrios* were part of a certain *ñuu* or *señorio,* their lands belonged to them as a corporate entity or *barrio* and not to the *ñuu* to which they were politically ascribed. These corporate lands owned by a *siña* could be reallocated or reassigned according to their needs and the households working these lands payed tribute to the *siña* directly (Terraciano 2001: 204–205), which would make the *barrio* a powerful entity, even contesting the power of the noble lord or the *ñuu* and his holdings – as previously stated.

In summary, the household or *huahui* was the smallest unit and the foundation of all social and land-tenure organization. Organized intrinsically in *barrios,* the households managed all the drainages and every hillside, creating a terraced landscape that transformed the Coixtlahuaca Valley into a monumental agroecosystem. Their organization as a wider corporate unit, such as *barrios* and communities, might also have been a response to protect their labor investment, *ergo* their land (Kowalewski 2017b: 4). Both smallholders and the elite owned the land, one force contesting the other and keeping a certain balance in the production and distribution of power in the *señorio* or city-state.

Urbanization: Centralization vs. decentralization

The archaeological survey of the Coixtlahuaca Valley made by Kowalewski (2008) and his colleagues showed that in the Late Postclassic (1200–1520 CE) the cities were large but the states were relatively small, reflected in large settlements with rather small and few public civic-ceremonial architectural structures. Intensive rural development was present as the settlement distribution located farmers near their fields, which formed a dispersed settlement pattern. The city of Coixtlahuaca extended continuously over 3000 ha and had a population of approximately 100,000 people. Oaxaca and the Central Mexico regions, in comparison with other regions worldwide, were more urbanized and had more rural development than those in Early Modern Europe (Kowalewski 2017b: 2, 4; Kowalewski et al. 2017: 355, 361, 366).

On one hand, the Seler II portrays two pyramids and the depiction of two colonial churches, which would account for the existence of a settlement and a population of considerable size. This could yield at least one center with monumental architecture, as portrayed by the pyramid[9] (Figure 4) associated with one *barrio* of Coixtlahuaca. On the other hand, the archaeological evidence of the Valley of Coixtlahuaca shows that there were relatively few civic-ceremonial structures, the major site Inguiteria has fewer and smaller platform mounds than smaller settlements in the same region and in the Central Valleys of Oaxaca. The small number of platforms and their size is characteristic for the entire Coixtlahuaca sequence. Therefore, the concentration of public architecture of imposing dimensions is rather weak in the Valley of Coixtlahuaca. The architectural remains seem to be widely distributed rather than concentrated in one place, which suggests that the cities and their public architecture were merely aggregates of the *barrios* rather than centralized and institutionalized places. At Coixtlahuaca, 19 of 32 platforms are located in outlying sectors and only 13 are in a central precinct. The *barrios* of other *ñuu*, such as Tequixtepec, all had civic-ceremonial architecture, but none of it was grouped in one place (Kowalewski et al. 2017: 364).

Considering the discourse of the Seler II, it could be interpreted or expected that the government embodied in the noble couples on top of every city-state toponym would find archaeological expression as a civic-ceremonial center. And it could be expected that such architecture would be found centralized or as a single monumental center governing a rural hinterland. However, the Seler II also illustrates at least two ruling houses for Coixtlahuaca, with two different lineages lines,[10] which

---

9   The multicolored pyramid on the left, which is part of a toponym, forms one of the two lineages of Coixtlahuaca in the Lienzo de Coixtlahuaca I and could be considered as one of the *yuhuitayu barrios* in the Seler II.

10   At least two, because there are in fact three lineages portrayed, as stated before and in my doctoral thesis, Pacheco Silva (2019).

already speaks against a centralization of power and a single architectonical expression of it. The Seler II does portray different architectural features, some even in a monumental fashion (pyramids), but these can be easily accounted as symbolic representations, or better said, as a standardized representation of an idea: a ritual place. In further support of this idea (regardless of the exact date of creation of the Seler II which could be dated to the first or second half of the 16th century[11]), the church construction was not initiated before 1576 so that by the end of that century the church as represented in the Seler II did not exist fully constructed, an indication that it may not be an actual portrayal of the colonial church itself[12] but also a pictographic convention for showing the existence of an ecclesiastical organization in the area. Tulancingo is represented by a pyramid and a ritual scene surrounding it, also within the borders of Coixtlahuaca's territory, but the area of Tulancingo displays little public construction during the Postclassic (1000–1520 CE) apart from five platform mounds atop a mountain which may actually be the pyramid depicted in the Seler II (Kowalewski et al. 2017: 365; Johnson 2015: 111, 121; Doesburg 2004; Kowalewski 2017a: 85). Nonetheless, these mounds are not a single feature with 13 steps, so that it seems we are dealing here with a pictographic convention once more, for a place where important ritual events took place in some sort of architectonical enclosure.

In summary, the architectural representations in the Seler II do not reflect archaeological or historical reality, since there are no archaeological remains of monumental architecture and the ethnohistorical documents of the area and for Coixtlahuaca record a later date for the final construction of its church. From the archaeological point of view, during the Postclassic (1000–1520 CE), urbanization was strongly tied to the best agricultural land and farmers made intensive use of the land; the settlements during this time were associated with *lama-bordos* or terraces and water-drainage systems. During Natividad (1200–1520 CE), corresponding to the Late Postclassic, the sites were spread from valley floors to mountain crests, creating an evenness in site distribution with fewer gaps of uninhabited areas (Kowalewski 2009: 318–319). Thus, the archaeological evidence reflects uninterrupted occupation of the landscape, a strongly dispersed settlement pattern and decentralization, based in the optimal use of agricultural land and water resources. The *barrios* and households with their control of most of the agricultural land, formed the backbone of society while the elite, with their palaces and scant 'urban' architecture made of stone, were mere aggregates to the *barrios* of their city-states.

---

11 There are valid arguments for dating the Lienzo before 1556 and around 1570, see Pacheco Silva (2016); van Doesburg (2017).

12 The actual church has one bell tower on its left and none on its right as portrayed in the Lienzo, and the two adjacent small doors are also missing from the original.

Monumentality in the landscape

Apparently, the archaeological evidence differs from the information in the Lienzo Seler II in regard to the type of political organization, length of power, and monumental architecture. The elite of the Coixtlahuaca *yuhuitayu* wanted to represent a powerful, probably centralized city-state with ultra regional ties, allies, and conquests, one that encompassed a large territory that incorporated most of the Valley as well as the city-states that inhabited it (Figure 1). The archaeological record, however, reflects a highly urbanized state in which the cities were rather aggregates of the rural development, creating a very dispersed settlement pattern. Moreover, evidence of elite power, expressed heavily through monumentality during the Classic (400–800 CE), is rather weak in the Valley during the Late Postclassic (1200–1520 CE).

This apparent discrepancy can be accounted for the moment we change the perspective on the interpretation, not only of the archaeological data but also of the way the landscape and the ethnographical information is understood. Foremost, there is a pervasive element in the Coixtlahuaca Valley: its landscape. It bears the signs of concentrated labor and symbolic meaning through its completely terraced nature and monumental work dating from early prehispanic times (Kowalewski et al. 2017: 364).

Figure 8: The landscape in the Valley of Coixtlahuaca (Photo by Mónica Pacheco Silva 2014)

The Lienzo portrays its most dominating scene in the context of a natural feature: a monumental mountain (Figure 3) as the stage for the New Fire Ceremony considered as the foundational ceremony of the Coixtlahuaca city-state. Moreover, 16 different city-states participate in the ritual, showing not only its importance as a state ceremony of the elites, but the power and legitimation the Coixtlahuaca city-state was to exert. The Mount of Intertwined Serpents as the natural stage for rituals shows the special relation the elite and the state had to the landscape.[13]

From an ethnographic point of view, nowadays the landscape plays an active role in the ritual life of the modern inhabitants of the Valley of Coixtlahuaca, who still have an important relationship with the landscape. Every mountain has a name, and behind it a story which sometimes interconnects with other mountains in the surroundings. Every year, people from the Coixtlahuaca area and adjacent communities come together in a procession to the Cerro de Agua (Water Mountain) requesting rain and a good harvest, a practice well rooted in prehispanic times (Rincón Mautner 2005). This mountain in the Valley of Coixtlahuaca, hosts two emblematic caves (Medina Jaen/Peñaflores Ramírez/Rivera Guzmán 2013). Mixtec religious life did not develop exclusively in architectural ceremonial spaces within the core settlement itself, but also in landscape features such as caves, springs, and mountains (Spores/Balkansky 2013: 93). This points to the fact that such features within the landscape, mountains being especially monumental in size and importance, should be considered as part of the settlement itself, making the settlement an all-encompassing unit of architectural and natural features. Bernal-García (1993: 32, 38) in her work about mythological urban planning in Mesoamerica, points to the significant role certain mountains play in the life of Mesoamerican settlements, a fact recognized since the 1970s. In turn, the impressive double temple of Tenochtitlan was identified as the 'Mountain of the Sustenance', also a mythological mountain. Mountains formed a mound for rituals, while the pyramids emulated sacred mythological mountains.

If the landscape and, more importantly, the mountains surrounding the settlement are taken into account, the sites are suddenly not only a formation of mounds and agricultural plots, but an organism made of architectural and natural features. The landscape plays an active role in the archaeological settlement, it complements and supports it as the stage for rituals and events. The settlement is like an organism with rivers, terraces, mountains, architectural features, and caves constituting its form. Monumentality is expressed through all its variables: the agricultural terraces, the drainage system management, the archaeological mounds, and – above all – the landscape.

Coixtlahuaca with an area of at least 30 km², together with Teposcolula with nearly 25 km², and Yanhuitlán in the Nochixtlán Valley, were among the largest settlements during the Postclassic (1000–1520 CE), rivaling the Aztec capital of Tenochtitlan that caused much amazement among the first *conquistadores* due to

---

13 We have to remember that many of the names of the city-states are related directly to names of mountains, as Terraciano (2001: 107) has pointed out, which seems to reflect the relation between the state and this natural feature of the topography, as mountains may be regarded as pyramids or, even more, are visible symbols of power in the landscape.

its temples and channel systems. However, the critical point is not which site is the biggest or has the most monumental architecture, rather how it is distributed, its relation to the landscape and supported population. The Valley of Oaxaca, for example, had smaller sites and more people living in such sites, as well as a lower urbanization index, so that only 40 per cent of its population lived in settlements of more than 1000 inhabitants, in contrast with 60 per cent from the Central Mixteca Alta (Spores/Balkansky 2013: 92–93; Kowalewski 2009: 321). Nevertheless, the Valley of Oaxaca has several examples of what could be considered monumental architecture and the 'monumentality' of its cultures would never be questioned. Monumental mounds or sites, and architectural features such as pyramids, do not equal urbanization. A highly urbanized society does not necessarily express itself in monumental architectonics when the natural features of the landscape provide such monumentality, just as is the case for the Late Postclassic Mixtec in the Coixtlahuaca area (1200–1520 CE).

Visibility and perception

What can we actually see and perceive in the Valley of Coixtlahuaca? Whether high at the bell tower of the church of Coixtlahuaca or on ground level, one thing is pervasive in the landscape, the completely terraced mountain slopes and the high degree of erosion of the land. On the peak of a mountain next to Cerro del Caracol (Shell Mountain) in Tequixtepec, a small patio and some mounds can be distinguished. The continuity of ceramic sherds indicates an ubiquitous or even occupation of the territory, but there are no high structures. Today, the most impressive feature is the scant population in the almost deserted communities and the highly eroded landscape. It seems as if the history recorded in the Lienzo Seler II speaks not only of another era but of another area. If we only focus our attention on what has been recorded in the *lienzos* and *códices* of the area and the many colonial written documents, the archaeologist and historian would expect to see a landscape full of elements that witness to the development of one of the most important cultures of Postclassic Mesoamerica, bearers of an ancient culture and skilled craftsmen that rivaled the famous Tenochtitlan. But it requires only a shift of perception to recognize that the vast number of 'commoners' in the ancient population were the ones to leave their indelible imprint in the land itself through their work in monumental agricultural terraces and drainage systems, while only a few vestiges of the elite survived in documents, through ceramics, and as exquisite examples of goldsmithery.

In order to reconstruct a more neutral picture of the history of the land and the culture, at least in the first years of the Spanish contact in the 16th century, the archaeological record has to be complemented by the study of ethnohistoric documents, among them written documents from the Spanish administration and, primarily, the oral traditions and modern ethnographic data. Only then can we achieve a less biased interpretation of what we think it was and really is.

Conclusions

A loose image of what happened in the Late Postclassic (1200–1520 CE) until the first years of the contact period could be proposed considering the story told by the Seler II, the archaeology, and the ethnohistory. A group arrived from outside the Valley on the dawn of the Postclassic (1000 CE),[14] as proposed by Kowalewski et al. (2017: 361) and supported by the paths shown on the right side of the Seler II if we interpret them as the migration of a group who eventually founded the city-state of Coixtlahuaca. This newly arrived population gave the already existing communities that had managed the agro-drainage systems since early times (1500 BCE)[15] an additional identity in the form of a political affiliation to a *ñuu*, *yuhuitayu*, or a noble-ruled city-state. By the Late Postclassic (1200–1520 CE), Coixtlahuaca was a member of a wider urban and elite network (Kowalewski 2017: 5) with affiliations and interactions reaching outside its borders into the Central Valleys of Mexico, taking part in the wider Mesoamerican world, as ethnohistoric documents like the Seler II, the Map of Cuauhtinchan, and the *códices* recount. The Lienzo Seler II registers the political foundation and interaction of this city-state under its noble rulership; indeed it is possibly the inauguration into this type of noble-rulership that is portrayed in the ritual of the Mount of the Intertwined Serpents.

On the other hand, the archaeological record mainly shows the organization and interaction of the wider population with the landscape. While these discourses may seem to juxtapose, they complement the overall image of relations within the settlement, between the wider population and the state, coming forward as a balance between the two forces that moved the *señorío*: the household and their management of the agro-drainage system, and the political elite interaction in- and outside the region in the wider Mesoamerican context. The Seler II attests to multiethnicity in Coixtlahuaca, as it records three native languages in

---

14 It cannot be inferred, however, that there were no other groups inhabiting the Valley when the 'newcomers' arrived, there was certainly a population inhabiting the valley from ancient times as the archaeological evidence for the agro-drainage systems goes back centuries. I am, however, inferring that these 'newcomers' who took possession and founded the *ñuu* of Coixtlahuaca brought with them some sort of noble rulership or united a group of *barrios*, smallholder communities, under a noble/lineage type of rule.

15 As Kowalewski et al. (2017: 366, 369) through the archaeological evidence show, investment in long-term material improvements to the land, like terracing and drainage check-dams, began in the Early Formative (1500/1200 BCE).

the glosses around the jaguar-skin frontier. People speaking different languages and with diverse ethnicities not only lived and worked side by side but controlled the area in conjunction. Archaeology can, however, only weakly record such multiethnic interaction, specially of a *nahua*-speaking group (Kowalewski et al. 2010). In contrast, the dispersed settlement pattern seen through the archaeological survey, and the decentralized mound groups scattered through the valley, indicate that no single centralized power ruled throughout the area. This can also be observed in the Seler II as it clearly registers at least two founding lineages for the Valley of the Serpents or Coixtlahuaca. The ethnographic data points to the importance of several landscape features such as caves and mountains as the backdrop of ritual life, signaling the fact that the landscape takes an active role in the settlement itself, which is also clearly identifiable in the Seler II as the biggest and central toponym is a mountain: the Mount of Intertwined Serpents.

Finally, the Seler II depicts at least two lineage houses ruling over the Coixtlahuaca Valley, which supports the decentralized archaeological evidence but also signals shared power. The archaeology reflects that the power of the nobles was rather limited and unstable, as the greater mass of the population controlled not only a large part of the resources but also their landscape.

Bibliography

Berdan, F. F./Anawalt, P. R. (eds.) (1992): The Codex Mendoza: Vol.II: Description of Codex Mendoza, Berkeley: University of California Press.

Berdan, F. F./Anawalt, P. R. (1997): The essential Codex Mendoza, Berkeley: University of California Press.

Bernal-Garcia, M. E. (1993): "Carving mountains in a blue/green bowl: Mythological urban planning in Mesoamerica." Ph. D. Thesis, Austin, Texas: University of Texas.

Brownstone, A. (ed.) (2015): The Lienzo of Tlapiltepec: A painted history from the northern Mixteca, Norman: University of Oklahoma Press.

Castañeda de la Paz, M./van Doesburg, S. (2008): "Coatepec en las fuentes del centro de México y su presencia en el valle de Coixtlahuaca." In: S. van Doesburg (ed.), Pictografía y escritura alfabética en Oaxaca, Oaxaca: Instituto Estatal de Educación Publica de Oaxaca, pp. 161–196.

Johnson, N. (2015): "The Language of Lines on the Lienzo of Tlapiltepec." In: A. Brownstone (ed.), The Lienzo of Tlapiltepec: A painted history from the northern Mixteca, Norman: University of Oklahoma Press, pp. 95–149.

Kirchhoff, P. (2009): Mesoamérica, sus límites geográficos, composición étnica y caracteres culturales, in Suplemento de la revista Tlatoani Núm. 3, ENAH. México D. F., 1960.

König, V. (2017a): "Lienzo Seler II (Coixtlahuaca II): A Biography and History of Research." In: V. König (ed.), On the mount of intertwined serpents: The pictorial history of power, rule, and land on Lienzo Seler II, Petersberg: Michael Imhof, pp. 45–53.

König, V. (2017b): On the mount of intertwined serpents: The pictorial history of power, rule, and land on Lienzo Seler II, Petersberg: Michael Imhof.

Kowalewski, S. A. (2009): Origins of the Ñuu: Archaeology in the Mixteca Alta, Mexico, Boulder: University Press of Colorado.

Kowalewski, S. A. (2017a): "A Human Settlement Context for the Coixtlahuaca Lienzos." In: V. König (ed.), On the mount of intertwined serpents: The pictorial history of power, rule, and land on Lienzo Seler II, Petersberg: Michael Imhof, pp. 79–86.

Kowalewski, S. A. (2017b): Big Cities, Little States: On the Archaeology of City-States, unpublished essay.

Kowalewski, S. A./Barba Pingarrón, L. A./Blancas, J./Cortés Vilchis, M. Y./García Ayala, G./López Zárate, L./Ortiz, A./Pluckhahn, T. J./Steere, B. A./Vilchis Flores, B. (2010): "La presencia azteca en Oaxaca: La provincia de Coixtlahuaca." In: Anales de Antropología 44, pp. 77–103.

Kowalewski, S. A./Brannan, S. P./Cortés Vilchis, M. Y./Diego Luna, L./García Ayala, G./López Zárate, J. L./Méndez Sobel, F./Stiver Walsh, L. R./Turck, E. B./Turck, J. A./Vepretskiy, S. (2017): "Regional Archaeology and Local Interests in Coixtlahuaca, Oaxaca." In: Latin American Antiquity, 28/03, pp. 353–372.

Lind, M. (2000): "Mixtec City-State and Mixtec City-State Culture." In: M. Herman Hansen (ed.), A comparative study of thirty city-state cultures: An investigation conducted by the Copenhagen Polis Centre, Historisk-filosofiske skrifter/Det Kongelige Danske Videnskabernes Selskab 21, Copenhagen: Reitzel, pp. 567–580.

Medina Jaen, M./Peñaflores Ramírez, N. G./Rivera Guzmán, Á. I. (2013): "Rituales de petición en las cuevas de El Calvario y Las Siete Puertas, cuenca de Coixtlahuaca, Oaxaca." In: J. Broda (ed.) Convocar a los dioses: ofrendas mesoamericanas: Estudios antropológicos, históricos y comparativos, México City: Instituto Veracruzano de la Cultura, pp. 465–522.

Pacheco Silva, M. (2016): "El Lienzo Seler II en el Ethnologisches Museum de Berlín, Alemania." In: Cuadernos del Sur 21/40, pp. 28–45.

Pacheco Silva, M. (2017): "Perception and Interpretation of the Sacred Landscape in the Coixtlahuaca Valley and the Actual Geography of the Area." In: V. König (ed.), On the mount of intertwined serpents: The pictorial history of power, rule, and land on Lienzo Seler II, Petersberg: Michael Imhof, pp. 101–108.

Pacheco Silva, M. (2019): "El Lienzo Seler/Coixtlahuaca II en el Ethnologisches Museum Berlín: Correlación del registro topográfico con la realidad geográfica, el registro arqueológico y las fuentes etnohistóricas." Ph. D. Thesis, Berlin: Lateinamerika Institut, Freie Universität Berlin.

Pohl, J. M. D. (2010): "Creation Stories, Hero Cults, and Alliance Building: Confederacies of Central and Southern Mexico." In: M. E. Smith/F. F. Berdan (eds.), The Postclassic Mesoamerican World, Salt Lake City: University of Utah Press, pp. 61–66.

Rincón Mautner, C. (2000): "La reconstrucción cronológica del linaje principal de Coixtlahuaca." In: C. Vega Sosa (ed.), Códices y Documentos sobre México: Tercer simposio internacional, serie historia volúmen 409, México City: INAH, pp. 25–43.

Rincón Mautner, C. (2005): "Sacred Caves and Rituals from the Northern Mixteca of Oaxaca, Mexico: New Revelations." In: J. E. Brady and K. M. Prufer (ed.), In the Maw of the Earth Monster: Mesoamerican Ritual Cave Use, Austin: University of Texas Press, pp. 117–152.

Rincón Mautner, C. (2007): "Donde ataron a nuestra madre: la diosa de la tierra y el Coatepec de la Mixteca." In: B. Barba Ahuatzin/A. Blanco Padilla (eds.), Iconografía mexicana VII: Atributos de las deidades femeninas. Homenaje a la Maestra Noemí Castillo Tejero, Colección Científica Serie Antropología volúmen 511, México City: INAH, pp. 155–172.

Spores, R./Balkansky, A. K. (2013): The Mixtecs of Oaxaca: Ancient times to the present. The Civilization of the American Indian Series, volume 267, Norman: University of Oklahoma Press.

Terraciano, K. (2001): The Mixtecs of colonial Oaxaca: Ñudzahui history, sixteenth through eighteenth centuries, Stanford: Stanford University Press.

van Doesburg, S. (2004): "La antigua sociedad indígena a través de sus propios documentos: Reconstrucción del patrón de asentamiento y de la tenencia de la tierra en el pueblo de San Miguel Tulancingo alrededor de 1600." In: N. M. Robles García (ed.), Estructuras políticas en el Oaxaca antiguo: Memoria de la Tercera Mesa Redonda de Monte Albán 2002, México City: INAH, pp. 261–283.

van Doesburg, B. (2017): "The Borders on Lienzo Seler II (Coixtlahuaca II)." In: V. König (ed.), On the mount of intertwined serpents: The pictorial history of power, rule, and land on Lienzo Seler II, Petersberg: Michael Imhof, pp. 87–100.

Monumentality by numbers

Sebastian Hageneuer & Sophie C. Schmidt

Introduction

Monumentality can be defined in different ways: it involves a combination of great technical ingenuity, high levels of skill, the devotion of vast amounts of time to building, the type and range of the resources, and the sheer size of the task (Brunke et al. 2016: 250). As one can see in this volume, the range of objects and tasks associated with monumental endeavors is broad and manifold (Cousin or Pacheco in this volume). In this article, we do not want to (re)start a discussion about what monumentality is or is not (see Introduction to this volume), but to put forward a method of quantification. Our thesis is that if monumental buildings were common at some point in time, not all of them were truly special; or in other words, some buildings seem to be more monumental than others. It also seems that by way of calculation and statistics, we can put forward our own opinion on the title of this volume, as it appears that at least in our case, size did not matter.

If one traveled through ancient Mesopotamia in the 21st century BCE, one would feel immediately at home in all major cities, because all of them had a standardized ziggurat as their central element.[1] A recent article by Hagen Brunke has shown that building a ziggurat in the 21st century BCE, an endeavor that was executed by the king, probably did not even really impact on the economy of the state (Brunke et al. 2016: 284; Brunke 2018). The real purpose of these monumental programs could have been to keep the people – who were workers and farmers – occupied during non-harvest times, as an ancient form of a job creation scheme. The question is, if it was not a problem to create these monuments, why do we think of them as special? If we could find a way to quantify monumentality, maybe we would be able to differentiate between various kinds of monuments, and see which of them stand out and why.

---

1 Personal comment of Ricardo Eichmann during the workshop 'Size matters' (9–11 October 2017, Berlin).

In this article we use the virtual reconstructions[2] of nine tripartite houses and a quantification of the effort needed to create these buildings to find a 'normal' baseline for the correlation of size and effort to see whether, and if so how, certain monuments deviate from this norm. We intentionally include one outlier from the beginning, the so-called Stone-Cone Building. As is explained below, the structure is built with special and expensive materials and therefore deviates from the set norm. Our aim here is not to point to the obvious (expensive buildings are out of the norm), but rather to show the extent to which the deviation occurs and, as a result, argue about the meaning of the terms 'monument' and 'monumentality'.

Architectural Energetics of Uruk

The basis of this research is provided by the results of the reconstructions of monumental architecture of Uruk (modern Warka in Iraq), which were undertaken partly through the 'Uruk Visualization Project' of the German Archaeological Institute and partly through work in the research group B-2-3 'Big Buildings – Big Architecture?'[3] of the Excellence Cluster TOPOI.[4] This work took place in 2008–2013 (Uruk Visualization Project) and 2013–2017 (TOPOI) and comprised 15 different buildings from the Late Uruk Period (4th millennium BCE). All these buildings – except one from Habuba Kabira in Syria, which we included for comparison – are considered out-of-the-norm compared to others and therefore labeled as monumental or special. The aim of the TOPOI research group was not the simple reconstruction of monumental architecture, but to research the cultural significance of so-called monumental buildings (Brunke et al. 2016).

One part of the project was to reconstruct these buildings scientifically (Bator et al. 2013; Hageneuer 2014; 2016), but also to quantify the necessary building materials in order to establish the basis for a *chaîne opératoire*.[5] The results of this work were tables full of values of the materials for each building reconstructed, based on the proposed version of reconstruction (for a simplified version, cf. Table 1). As

---

2 The terms *(Virtual) Reconstruction* or *(Digital) Visualization* are used throughout this article. We define these terms for the purpose of this article as the digital recreation of an ancient building based on its primary and secondary sources to the best of our knowledge. For further information about the method used, please refer to Bator et al. 2013; Hageneuer 2014; 2016; Hageneuer/ Levenson 2018.

3 Topoi.org. (2019). [online] Available at: https://www.topoi.org/project/b-2-3/ Last accessed 8 January 2019.

4 We are very thankful for the support and collaboration through the Excellence Cluster and with the research group B-2-3 of TOPOI itself, which was always open to new ideas and helpful in countless meetings and discussions.

5 Publication with all the calculated results is in preparation.

these values are based upon virtual reconstructions and are therefore themselves virtual numbers, the question of the usefulness of the calculations arises, especially if we consider that the period these architectures are coming from, the Late Uruk Period (4th millennium BCE), has only scarce remains, sometimes only preserved up to a couple of centimeters. We know little about these buildings and their purpose. All reconstructions, although scientifically researched as much as currently possible, are highly hypothetical.

Table 1: List of the calculated materials for each examined reconstruction in cubic meters

	Mud bricks	Clay	Tempered Clay	Cast wall	Timber	Reed	Asphalt	Clay Cones	Stone Cones	Bottle Cones	Lime-stone
Building B	751.80	205.94	0.00	0.00	25.53	14.47	0.00	0.00	0.00	0.00	0.00
Building C	4420.61	840.68	420.76	0.00	64.54	33.00	0.00	0.84	0.00	0.00	0.00
Pillared Hall	334.40	0.00	167.55	0.00	11.74	6.26	0.00	12.27	0.00	0.00	0.00
Building F	859.71	246.06	0.00	0.00	16.75	9.54	0.00	0.00	0.00	0.00	0.00
Building G	1907.05	596.37	0.00	0.00	27.00	15.03	0.00	0.00	0.00	0.00	0.00
Building H	807.74	255.50	0.00	0.00	17.00	9.14	0.00	0.00	0.00	0.00	0.00
House H (Habuba Kabira)	149.25	89.46	0.00	0.00	7.65	3.78	0.00	0.00	0.00	0.00	0.00
White Temple	1284.82	301.40	174.85	0.00	31.44	10.32	0.00	0.00	0.00	15.49	0.00
Stone-Cone Building	58.77	2550.44	0.00	1396.88	102.82	50.10	49.31	0.00	40.48	0.00	1272.46

Nevertheless, we think that the calculation of the building materials has importance. As we focused on a special building type (tripartite houses) we could apply a certain reconstruction methodology, assuring all reconstructions underwent the same reconstruction procedure. We are therefore confident in saying that even if the reconstructions are hypothetical and thus the calculated values are as virtual as the visualizations themselves, the resulting numbers are comparable to each other and can give us some insights into the relative architectural energetics of tripartite houses in the Late Uruk Period of ancient Mesopotamia.

For the purpose of this article, we first want to take a closer look at nine of the reconstructed and processed buildings: Building B, C, F, G, H, the Pillared Hall, the White Temple, and the Stone-Cone Building of Uruk, and as a comparison House H of Habuba Kabira, all of which date to the Late Uruk Period and are of the tripartite house type. This type is defined by a central middle-hall and at least one row of rooms on either of its long sides. On one short side, the head of the building, another room served as a second hall perpendicular to the main hall. Sometimes, this room was even a secondary tripartite house, with its own side rooms (for example cf. Figure 1; Heinrich 1982: 7–13). These buildings were common in Mesopotamia from the 5th millennium BCE for private as well as for official purposes. Unfortunately, we cannot provide a detailed description of each building itself or the respective reconstruction process,[6] as space here is limited. We will provide citations to the corresponding publications and offer a condensed description of the buildings with only the information we need for the purpose of this analysis.

Buildings B, F, and H (Eichmann 2007: 250–254, 137–143, 152–159) are the simplest ones and very similar to one another as they consist of a central middle-hall with three adjoining rooms on each side and a perpendicular positioned room as the head of the building into which one could step directly from the middle hall or the adjoining side rooms. Their areas differ between 382.50 m² and 434.46 m². Building G (Eichmann 2007: 147–152) is a little bit more complex as it features two *alae* at the end of the central hall in connection to the head room, which enlarges the central space of this tripartite building. So, in addition to the three adjoining rooms on each side of the central hall, Building G had two open spaces from which you could step into the head room and occupied an area of 701.68 m². Building C (Eichmann 2007: 236–245) featured these *alae* too and also offered four adjoining rooms on each side (Figure 1). In addition, it had not only one perpendicular room as the head of the building, but rather a whole tripartite house itself with three adjoining rooms on each side. So, to enter the head room you had to pass through the side rooms of the head of the building first. With its size of 1222.88 m², it was one of the biggest buildings in Uruk and is the largest in this analysis.

All these monuments had a very simple building structure in common: mud-brick walls with clay plaster. Only Building C featured some minor decorations and possibly some painting. Also, the plastering of this building was executed with whitewashed clay (Eichmann 2007: 242–243) instead of naturally colored clay.

The Pillared Hall (Eichmann 2007: 159–172) is strictly speaking not a building of the tripartite type, as it consists only of a hall. Its size is also the smallest of the so-called monumental buildings with an area of only 210.34 m². It is considered some kind of gate building to a proposed secluded space in the center of Uruk, as well as a meeting space (Eichmann 2007: 168). We included this building regardless, because we can still utilize the same reconstruction techniques as we did with the tripartite houses before, as the Pillared Hall is simple in its architectural design. Interestingly, this building is heavily decorated with colored clay cones

---

6 Publication with the reconstruction process of the buildings described here is in preparation.

Figure 1: Plan of Building C in Uruk, 4ʰ millennium BCE (© Deutsches Archäologisches Institut)

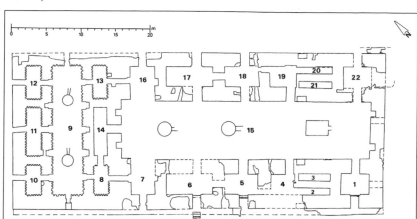

which offer a unique design on every panel on the pillars (Eichmann 2007: 166–167). Also, the plastering of the walls where no decoration was applied was carried out with an egg-yolk-yellow washed clay (Eichmann 2007: 167).

The White Temple (Eichmann 2007: 491–503; Hageneuer 2016) is part of a much larger complex as it is situated upon a multi-phased ziggurat. As our calculations focused on the tripartite building on top of this ziggurat, we can omit a description of the terrace itself. The White Temple is a building of the tripartite type with four adjoining rooms on each side, but without a head room. The walls were plastered with whitewashed clay and the building had some minor decorations in the form of bottle-shaped clay cones that were positioned in two bands on the upper outer part. Interestingly, the reconstruction of this building is based upon a model representation found within the foundations of the building itself. The dimensions of the White Temple were 387.63 m².

The Stone-Cone Building (Eichmann 2007: 364–378; Hageneuer/Levenson 2018) is the only building described here that was not constructed with mud bricks, but with some form of ancient concrete that was probably poured into a preconstructed boarding frame. Besides the unusual material for the walls, the building was heavily decorated with stone cones of different colors (Figure 2). In addition to these materials we can also add a massive foundation of mud bricks and limestone slabs to the equation as the weight of the building materials used here demanded a well-constructed base, something that was not necessary for the other buildings in this study. In contrast, Buildings B, C, and the White Temple had smaller mud-brick foundations above the ground that served to level the building layer. The visible part of the building covered an area of approx. 560 m². It consists of a middle-hall with three adjoining rooms at each side. At the head of the building, there is a recess in the center and a gateway room on one side entering into the head room. This room is special, as it is shaped like an 'L' and featured a water-proof basin of unknown function. The Stone-Cone Building is therefore expected to be an outlier and the quantification and statistics below prove this hypothesis. Nevertheless, our aim is to show how much of an outlier this building is and to suggest an interpretation of its importance.

Figure 2: Proposed reconstruction of the Stone-Cone Building in Uruk, 2012 (© artefacts-berlin.de; material: Deutsches Archäologisches Institut)

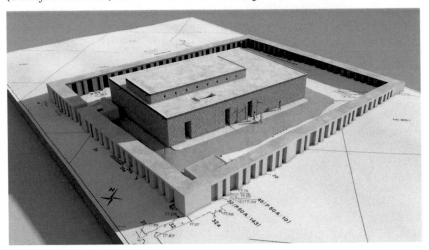

Figure 3: Proposed reconstruction of House H in Habuba Kabira, 2014 (© artefacts-berlin.de; material: Kay Kohlmeyer)

House H of Habuba Kabira (Heinrich et al. 1973; Strommenger 1980) is of interest because of the comparison of monumental architecture in Uruk with ordinary
private architecture. We choose Habuba Kabira because in the Late Uruk Period
no traces of urban architecture were found in Uruk itself. One example is found
at a distance of 1300 km in Habuba Kabira. It was constructed with mud bricks
and had no decorations. House H was a bigger complex, but its eastern part consisted of a complete tripartite building with three side rooms to the west and two
to the east (Figure 3). The head of the building was divided into a smaller and a
bigger room to the north. The area of that part was approx. 130 m² and therefore
the smallest tripartite building in this study.

All these buildings (except House H of Habuba Kabira) are termed monumental due to their size, decoration, or proposed public function. Certainly, these
buildings are bigger or more decorated than private houses and in the case of the
Stone-Cone Building, the decoration was of great importance.

Effort estimation

In the previous section, we presented the reconstructions in question and the
respective calculated volumes of different building materials (Table 1). In this section, we analyze the relative effort for each building in order to see in what capacity different building materials and volumes are connected to a possible effort or
energy used in constructing the buildings. This involves moving beyond the volumes of building materials to find a comparable value for the effort of creating
this monumental architecture. Normally, we would achieve this through a complete *chaîne opératoire*, in which we track every expenditure related to the building
process – from getting the resources to finalizing the building (see Buccellati in
this volume). For the purpose of this article, we decided to simplify the process of
calculation as we do not seek exact figures for expenditures,[7] but rather comparable values between the buildings examined. We want to propose this simplified
method in order to offer a quick and accessible way to compare expenditure calculations. As mentioned above, these calculations do not claim to be exact or even
true, but to offer a method of comparison. We created a list of factors of effort
for each step in the building process to multiply with the calculated volumes of
different building materials. Again, this is not to be understood as an exact result
for the expenditure of human labor but more as an estimate to put the different
building steps in relation to each other (Table 2).

---

7 This work is currently part of an ongoing PhD by Felix Levenson.

Table 2: List of factors, representing the relative effort of each building step

Process	Factor
Clay for plastering and flooring	1
Reed for roofing or flooring	1
Tempered Clay for plastering (white and egg-yolk yellow)	2
Creation of sun dried mud-bricks (Riemchen, see Eichmann 2007: 16 ff.)	4
Clay & bottle cones	4
Timber for roofing and some staircases	7
Stone-cones of different colour	8
Other materials like limestone or asphalt	12
Cast walls of the Stone-Cone Building	16

Clay and reed are resources that are available in abundance in the Mesopotamian plains (Coockson 2009: 12; Levey 1959: 149). This is the reason why nearly all the architecture was built from these two materials from the 8th millennium BCE (Coockson 2009: 11). The knowledge of processing clay was common and therefore the simplest task in our list (factor 1). Clay was used for plastering the mud-brick walls and roofs in order to keep the occasional rain from damaging the building. Reeds, on the other hand, were used to cover the roofs before a thick package of clay was applied to seal the surface (van Beek 2008: 293–294). Occasionally, reed was also used as a basis for mud-brick walls, as we can see with the Stone-Cone Building (Eichmann 2007: 371).

For some buildings (Pillared Hall, Building C, and the White Temple) tempered clay was used to plaster the building in order to give it a different color. For the Pillared Hall, an egg-yolk-yellowish color was detected (Eichmann 2007: 167–168). It is not yet clear what temper caused the coloring of the clay in this manner, only that it did not preserve very well. The White Temple and Building C, however, were covered with a whitened clay plaster that was made of chalk, which turns white during the calcination of limestone. As the tempering of the clay would have taken more effort than the simple processing of natural clay, we decided to assign a factor of 2 to this step.

The creation of sun-dried mud bricks was a bit more complex, because the collected clay had to be tempered (Coockson 2009: 31), put in forms to give them the desired size, and left to dry on wide empty fields (Hageneuer/Levenson 2018: 113) that were probably not located on site. The transport of the sun-dried mud bricks is therefore also part of this factor. Hagan Brunke completed such calculations for the mud-brick construction of a ziggurat in the 21st century BCE. Not only did he include the creation of the mud bricks, but also their transportation onto the site, the payment of the workers involved, and the masonry work (2018: 30–34). Taking these numbers into consideration, we feel quite confident in assigning a factor of 4 to the production of mud bricks and the creation of the walls of our buildings.

Clay and Bottle Cones as they appear in Building C, the Pillared Hall, and on the White Temple are made from normal clay but need additional firing, for which one would have needed fuel in the form of dung and wood. The process of creating these items was not complicated, but the additional steps of firing and processing these decorations led us to assign the factor 4.

Various sources tell us that the roofing in ancient Mesopotamia was carried out as a combination of timber, reed, and clay packages (Cookson 2009: 64–68; Heinrich 1935: 21; Heinrich/Seidl 1968: 7; Miglus 1999: 237; Pfälzner 2001: 126). It is known that timber was a rare resource and would have been utilized sparingly. To construct a roof, one needs at least two kinds of timber: thick beams that span over the width of the bigger rooms to support the roof and smaller beams to lay on top or to cover smaller rooms. The relation between both types is approximately two to three times more smaller beams than bigger ones. The bigger beams could reach a length of 7 m and probably more (Eichmann 2007: 244) and are therefore costlier in terms of energy than smaller beams, which could be found and transported much more easily. The transportation costs of these bigger beams were very high, as they had to be imported from far away, probably Lebanon, Turkey, or Iran (Kuniholm 1997: 347). The smaller ones are of local origin and compensate for the high energetic value of the transportation of the bigger beams. As an estimate, we decided on an averaged factor of 7 that includes mainly the transportation of the timber from distant sources, but also the smaller beams as well as the timber-work necessary for construction.

One of the last items on the list are the stone cones, which were only used for the Stone-Cone Building. These were made from limestone of different colors. They had to be cut, processed, and transported to the site, where the cones most probably were smoothed before they were put into the still-wet cast wall of the Stone-Cone Building. The shaping of the cones was done very roughly and would not been particularly time-consuming. We do not know the exact origin of these stones, but as we do not know of any limestone sources in the vicinity of Uruk itself, we can only suggest that the transport was of long range. Therefore, we decided to apply the factor 8 to this production step. As the cones were small and easily transported, we assigned a lower value than for the limestone blocks, which essentially had the same source but were much harder to transport.

Some other materials were more difficult to process. Asphalt or bitumen was available at the surface in some areas of the Ancient Near East (Connan 1999: 34, Figure 1). For the Late Uruk period, the sole source of bitumen, based on analysis of bitumen remains in nearby Tell el-Oueili, seems to have been Hit-Abu Jir, an area located to the west of Baghdad, over 400 km away (Connan 1999: 41) but reachable via the river Euphrates. Although a trade route for the common use of bitumen was established, this resource had to be transported over a great distance. We therefore assigned a factor of 12 to the energy effort of obtaining the bitumen and processing it. We also included the limestone that was used in the foundation of the Stone-Cone Building in this 'others' category, as the source and transport would have been the same as for the cast stone material (see below) and therefore relied heavily on transportation.

The main building material of the Stone-Cone Building was made from carbonate rock which had to be transported from the closest source, which was at least 50 km away and only reachable by land (Boehmer 1984: 147). The production stages for creating the cast wall material were complex and involved a lot of different steps (Hageneuer/Levenson 2018: 113–115). As a result of studying the production process, we agree with an estimated triple to quadruple effort in creating this building material in comparison to traditional mud bricks (Hageneuer/Levenson 2018: 115). Hence, we decided to assign the highest factor of 16 to this material.

After exploring several possibilities for using the assigned factors in our calculations, we realized that the results differed very little if the individual factors were increased or decreased, but rather more if the order was changed. As we are looking at factors describing effort in creating different building materials, this makes sense, as these factors are proportionally defined by their relation to each other. It is twice as costly to create clay cones as colored clay, whether these factors are 4 and 2 or 19 and 10 does not matter in terms of our analysis, which aims to compare different buildings made from the same materials.

Therefore, we conclude that for this analysis the exact factors are not of as much importance as the assignation of a well-established rank system. For this reason, we are confident that these factors represent a good evaluation of effort in regard to the respective building steps and can serve as a tool of analysis until the complete *chaîne opératoire* is established.

Quantitative Analysis

In the following analysis,[8] we look at several points to identify out-of-the-norm monuments within a group of out-of-the-norm buildings. Two steps are necessary here:

---

8 All calculations discussed in this chapter were realized with R 3.3.4 (R Core Team 2017). Code and data are available under the DOI 10.17605/OSF.IO/3AJ7V.

1. A quantitative analysis of the building materials in order to see which production steps demand the greatest effort;
2. A regression analysis to see if there is a relationship between volume and effort and, if so, how predictable it may be.

The first step is comparing the different amounts of materials used for the different buildings. They are listed in Table 1 and visualized in the stacked bar plot (Figure 4).

It is no surprise to see that mud bricks are the most important building material in almost all tripartite buildings. Clay used as plaster was needed just as often, but of course the volume required was smaller. Also, all buildings included reed and wood in their construction, as described above.

Figure 4: Stacked bar plot showing mass of different materials used in the building process of the different buildings

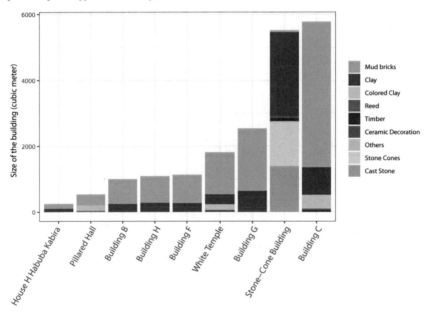

Interesting here are two monuments that do not conform to the others. When building the Pillared Hall, people did not use normal clay at all but rather a tempered clay, mud bricks, and clay cones ornamentation. This shows a creative way of aiming at singularity without changing much in the construction process in comparison to the buildings B, H, F, G, and House H of Habuba Kabira, which are very similar in their material.

The Stone-Cone Building, in contrast, shows distinct features in its material composition. Almost no mud bricks were used but much more clay and rare materials (cast stone, asphalt, and limestone), as well as the stone cones it was named for. Here we can observe a vastly different building process from that of the other monuments.

Concerning size, an impressive range can be observed. The virtual reconstructions of the two smallest tripartite buildings (Habuba Kabira House H and the Pillared Hall) are only 225 and 485 m³, whereas the reconstructions of the two largest tripartite buildings (the Stone-Cone Building and Building C) are 10–20 times as big (5521.26 m³ and 5780.43 m³ respectively).

As has been argued above, the effort involved in constructing the buildings depended on the materials used. We therefore created a graph comparing the effort involved in using the different materials scaled to 100 % for each building (Figure 5). This enables the viewer to easily compare the composition of efforts in relation to the different materials used in the building processes, independent of the absolute effort that went into erecting the monument.

Figure 5: Stacked bar plot (scaled to 100 per cent) showing effort needed for different materials by building

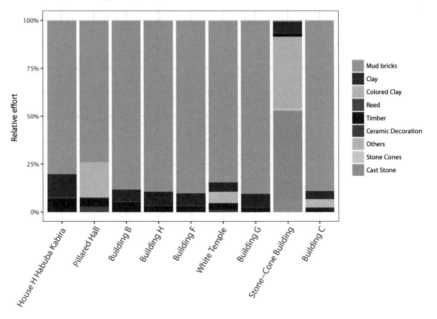

The largest part of constructing the tripartite buildings was always the processing of mud bricks – except for the Stone-Cone Building. We see that the large amount of bricks used insured their great impact on the effort involved in constructing the building. Clay and tempered clay also have a recognizable impact, but as they were much easier to produce it is relatively small. It is noticeable that the effort involved in building with timber was quite low, and with reed the effort was almost negligible.

The Stone-Cone Building, the White Temple, and the Pillared Hall are buildings on which decoration was recorded. Though this ornamentation has an impact on the effort involved in construction, it is easy to see that this impact is small. This may not be surprising for the ceramic decorations because they are easy to produce (clay and bottles cones: effort factor 4), but the stone cones built into the Stone-Cone Building also show very little impact, less than might have been expected considering that the effort factor assigned to them was double that of the ceramic decoration (stone cones: effort factor 8). This shows that although decoration may be a highly visible aspect of a monumental building, due to the small amounts needed in comparison to the masonry work, decorations had no significant impact on the overall effort calculation of the building process. In light of these findings, it is interesting to note that so few buildings were decorated. It seems effort might have been more important than appearance.

As in the analysis before, the Stone-Cone Building is a special case as there are two categories of material built into it which were not recorded in the other buildings. The categories 'other materials' (consisting of asphalt and limestone) and 'cast stone' have a huge impact on the effort of the construction. As there were also large amounts of material used in the building (see Figure 6 and Table 1) this is not surprising *per se*, but the high amount – 38 per cent for 'other materials' and 53 per cent for cast stone – (together more than 90 per cent of all the effort in building this monument) is quite impressive. It raises the question as to why these materials were chosen and why this amount of effort was put into the construction of the Stone-Cone Building (Hageneuer/Levenson 2018). This building also exemplifies how low the effort for clay production was, which was the largest class of material used in the building process for the Stone-Cone Building (46 per cent) but nonetheless has so little impact on the effort (only 6 per cent).

We may conclude that the effort involved in constructing a monument lies in erecting the walls and less in roofing, plaster, decoration, or similar constructions.

Lastly, the relation between effort and the size of the tripartite buildings is investigated. First, we plotted the relative effort index against the size of the buildings in cubic meters (cf. Figure 6). There is a correlation between the size of a building and the effort involved in its creation, except for the Stone-Cone building, which is the second largest (after Building C) but has by far the highest cost in effort. To analyze this further, a linear regression was calculated between the two variables. The linear regression creates a "best-fit straight line" (Drennan 2009: 205), which describes the general trend between these two variables. The R^2-value then evaluates how good this fit is. R^2 describes the proportion of the variance in the dependent variable that is predictable from the independent variable. It is calculated using the residuals, which are the difference between a value that is predicted by the regression line and the actual measured value. R^2 is the sum of the squares of the residuals divided by the variance of the predicted values. It can take values between 0 and 1, where 1 is the best fit possible and the trend has little or no variance (Drennan 2009: 209–210; Baxter 2015: 63–79). Next to this evaluation of the strength of the correlation between the two variables, a p-value was calculated to describe the statistical significance of the findings. We chose a linear regression as a starting point, because it fits to the hypothesis that the effort involved in creating a monument should directly and linearly correlate to its size.

Figure 6: Comparison of two linear regression models fitted to the variables effort and size

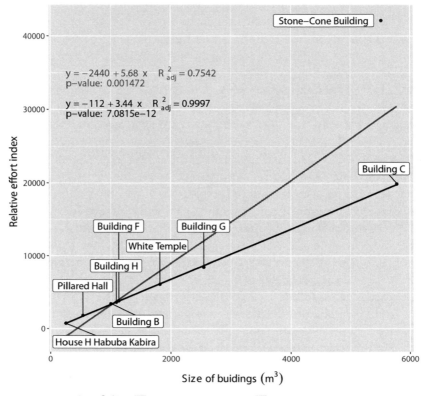

The results of our analysis are visualized in Figure 6. There are two main observations we want to point out in this figure. Firstly, if all tripartite buildings are evaluated together and a linear regression is calculated, only buildings B, F, and H are near the best-fit line and the Stone-Cone Building is an obvious outlier in effort. An R^2-value of 0.75 might be considered a fair fit of the trend line to the data, but just by looking at the plot it becomes obvious that a better fit might be found, either with a non-linear regression or if the Stone-Cone Building is removed from the calculation. To try a non-linear regression, we used the 'loess' (Local Polynomial Regression Fitting) method, which is a smoothing algorithm that downweighs outliers (Baxter 2015: 80–82) and a generalized additive model (GAM). Using these non-parametric regression methods did not improve the R^2-value (R^2 of 0.72) and the resulting best-fit line could not be reasonably explained. Therefore, we returned to the linear regression and removed the Stone-Cone Building. As explained above, the structure had been built with special building materials and therefore was an expected outlier. We had included it in our earlier analysis to test this expectation. To take it out of the calculation proved to be the best way to achieve a near perfect best-fit line: the second linear regression that was calculated without the Stone-Cone Building created an extraordinarily good fit ($R^2 = 0.9997$).

Residual analysis of the first linear regression confirmed that the Stone-Cone Building is responsible for almost all the variance if included in the regression. P-values for both linear regression lines are highly significant. Therefore, we conclude that the Stone-Cone Building is a special case, where the effort required to build it does not correspond linearly to its size.

On the other hand, we can see that the building costs of all the other tripartite buildings do correspond almost perfectly with their size (see the linear model without the Stone-Cone Building in Figure 6). Costs increase with size by a factor of 3.44. This is, of course, dependent on the way effort is calculated.[9]

Not perfectly aligned are the Pillared Hall, Building B, and Building C, which are slightly costlier than the linear model suggests, and the Building G, which is slightly cheaper in effort. Looking back at the materials used for building, it is easy to see that the slight increase in effort for the Pillared Hall is a result of the decoration and colored clay used on the building. In Building B a little bit more timber was utilized even though it is small in size, and in Building C colored clay replaced the natural clay. Building G is the third largest building but composed of mud bricks and a relatively large amount of clay, which is very cheap, therefore the effort in construction was a little less than might have been expected.

To conclude this analysis, we state the following: a linear relationship between size and effort of construction can be found for most tripartite buildings except for the Stone-Cone Building. The effort, the material type, and the amount of building materials used for this construction are unusual, which we could illustrate using a quantitative approach and linear regression modeling.

---

9 If one takes a closer look at the formula which describes the linear relationship for the buildings without the Stone-Cone Building one notices the Y intercept (value of Y where the regression line crosses the X-axis) of -112, meaning that to 'build a building of size 0 cubic meters' a value of -112 is estimated on the effort-scale. Considering we are dealing with values for effort of more than 40,000 this is quite near the realistic value of 0.

Monumentality vs. Monuments

Our analysis shows that in a comparison of size versus effort, most of the build-ings seem to follow an estimated line. It seems only natural to assume that similar buildings show a linear relationship if their sizes are compared to their building efforts, as the more these buildings grow, the more resources, transportation, and workers are needed. However, the interesting cases of this statistical analysis are not the items that comply with this estimation, but the ones that do not, like the case of the Pillared Hall, which is of very small size but is extensively decorated.

In this concluding section, we want to draw attention to two buildings. The first one is the private house H in Habuba Kabira, which we find in the lowest sec-tion of our graph (Figure 6). Although the tripartite house of this building is only part of a bigger structure, the relationship between size and effort holds true. We can see here that a normal private house does not differ much from a monumen-tal tripartite building like Building C of Uruk regarding material used and effort compared to size. Of course, the resources and human labor needed for Building C were much higher and therefore we speak of a monument, but we can also assume that the authority responsible for Building C had greater resources available than the private person in Habuba Kabira. Interpreting the regression model of our graph as normal or expected, we can therefore suggest that bigger buildings do not necessarily mean greater noteworthiness in relation to the respective owner. It can be expected that a king would construct a bigger building than a private person. Now, if we define monumentality not by size or cost, but by singularity and exceptionality, 'something that stood out' to people, we must look at buildings that do not follow the estimated line. This brings us to the Stone-Cone Building.

As we have already seen, the Stone-Cone Building is special in many respects, but our quantitative analysis confirms that it stands out from the other exam-ples of our study due to the special building materials used instead of mud bricks. We may define monumental architecture by certain categories or factors (see the Introduction to this volume), but they might not have been of importance in antiq-uity. In this analysis we propose that the factor of size might not have played a role. In our opinion, we clearly need to distinguish between usual monuments and out-of-the-norm monuments and therefore true monumentality as we term it today with all its connotations.

The Stone-Cone Building's construction effort deviates from the best-fit line of the other monuments by a factor of more than two. It was therefore more than twice as expensive as expected regarding its size. This shows clearly that the con-struction of the Stone-Cone Building was an act of exceptional effort and impor-tance, which is a sign of true monumentality.

To summarize we want to recall that we are still talking about monuments with an extraordinary function and symbolic value. Nonetheless, we believe that there is a difference in monuments and monumentality such that within the realm of extraordinary buildings, we still find monuments of exceptional value. These could represent a form of monumentality that might be of higher importance than others, though perhaps not as visible on first sight. To use George Orwell's well-known adage: all monuments are monumental, but some are more monumental than others.[10]

Bibliography

Bator, S./van Ess, M./Hageneuer, S. (2013): "Visualisierung der Architektur von Uruk." In: N. Crüsemann/M. van Ess/M. Hilgert/B. Salje (eds.), Uruk. 5000 Jahre Megacity, Petersberg: Michael Imhof, pp. 365–371.

Baxter, M. (2015): "Notes on Quantitative Archaeology and R." https://www.aca demia.edu/12545743/Notes_on_Quantitative_Archaeology_and_R (last accessed March 31, 2018).

van Beek, G. W. (2008): Glorious mud! Ancient and Contemporary Earthen Design and Construction in North Africa, Western Europe, the Near East, and South-west Asia, Washington D. C.: Smithsonian Institution Scholarly Press.

Boehmer, R. M. (1984): "Kalkstein für das urukzeitliche Uruk." In: Baghdader Mit-teilungen 15, pp. 141–147.

Brunke, H./Bukowiecki, E./Cancik-Kirschbaum, E./Eichmann, R./van Ess, M./ Gass, A./Gussone, M./Hageneuer, S./Hansen, S./Kogge, W./May, J./Parzinger, H./Pedersén, O./Sack, D./Schopper, F./Wulf-Rheidt, U./Ziemssen, H. (2016): "Thinking Big. Research in Monumental Constructions in Antiquity." In: G. Graßhoff/M. Meyer (eds.), Space and Knowledge. Topoi Research Group Arti-cles, eTopoi. Journal for Ancient Studies, Special Volume 6, Berlin: Edition Topoi, pp. 250–305.

Brunke, H. (2018): "Großbaustellen in Sumer – Aufwand und Kosten." In: K. Rheidt/ W. Lorenz (eds.), Groß Bauen – Großbaustellen als kulturgeschichtliches Phä-nomen, Kulturelle und technische Werte historischer Bauten, Basel: Birkhäu-ser, pp. 27–36.

Connan, J. (1999): "Use and trade of bitumen in antiquity and prehistory: molecular archaeology reveals secrets of past civilizations." In: Philosophical Transac-tions of the Royal Society of London B: Biological Sciences 354, 1379, pp. 33–50.

Coockson, B. C. (2009): Living in Mud, Istanbul: Ege Yayinlari.

Drennan, R. D. (2009): Statistics for Archaeologists. A Common Sense Approach. Second edition, Heidelberg et al.: Springer. DOI 10.1007/978-1-4419-0413-3

Eichmann, R. (2007): Uruk – Architektur I. Von den Anfängen bis zur frühdynas-tischen Zeit, AUWE 14, Rahden/Westf.: Marie Leidorf.

---

10 Orwell 1945: "All animals are equal, but some are more equal than others."

Hageneuer, S. (2014): "The visualisation of Uruk – First impressions of the first metropolis in the world." In: W. Börner/S. Uhlirz (eds.), Proceedings of the 18th International Conference on Cultural Heritage and New Technologies 2013, CHNT 18, 2013, Wien: Museen der Stadt Wien – Stadtarchäologie, pp. 1–12.

Hageneuer, S. (2016): "Le Temple blanc d'Uruk sur sa haute terrasse." In: P. Quenet (ed.), Ana ziqquratim. Sur la piste de Babel, Strasbourg: Presses Universitaires de Strasbourg, pp. 112–113.

Hageneuer, S./Levenson, F. (2018): "Das Steinstiftgebäude in Uruk – ein gescheitertes Experiment?" In: K. Rheidt/W. Lorenz (eds.), Groß Bauen – Großbaustellen als kulturgeschichtliches Phänomen, Kulturelle und technische Werte historischer Bauten, Basel: Birkhäuser, pp. 109–21.

Heinrich, E. (1935): Sechster vorläufiger Bericht über die von der Deutschen Forschungsgemeinschaft in Uruk-Warka unternommenen Ausgrabungen (= UVB VI), Berlin.

Heinrich, E. (1982): Die Tempel und Heiligtümer im alten Mesopotamien, Textteil, Berlin: de Gruyter.

Heinrich, E./Seidl, U. (1968): "Maß und Übermaß in der Dimensionierung von Bauwerken im alten Zweistromland." In: Mitteilungen der Deutschen Orient-Gesellschaft 99, pp. 5–54.

Heinrich, E. et al. (1973): Vierter vorläufiger Bericht über die von der Deutschen Orient-Gesellschaft mit Mitteln der Stiftung Volkswagenwerk in Ḥabuba Kabira (Ḥububa Kabira, Herbstkampagnen 1971 und 1972 sowie Testgrabung Frühjahr 1973) und in Mumbaqat (Tall Munbaqa, Herbstkampagne 1971) unternommenen archäologischen Untersuchungen, erstattet von Mitgliedern der Mission, Mitteilungen der Deutschen Orient-Gesellschaft 105, pp. 5–68.

Kuniholm, P. I. (1997): "Wood." In: E. M. Meyers (ed.), The Oxford Encyclopedia of Archaeology in the Near East, Volume 5, Oxford: Oxford University Press, pp. 347–349.

Levey, M. (1959): "Clay and its technology in Ancient Mesopotamia." In: Centaurus 6/2, pp. 149–156.

Miglus, P. A. (1999): "Städtische Wohnarchitektur in Babylonien und Assyrien." In: Baghdader Forschungen 22, Mainz.

Orwell, G. (1945): Animal Farm, http://www.gutenberg.net.au/ebooks01/0100011h.html (last accessed June 6, 2018).

Pfälzner, P. (2001): Haus und Haushalt. Wohnformen des dritten Jahrtausends vor Christus in Nordmesopotamien, Damaszener Forschungen 9, Mainz.

R Core Team (2017): "R: A language and environment for statistical computing. R Foundation for Statistical Computing." https://www.R-project.org/ (last accessed June 11, 2018).

Strommenger, E. (1980): Habuba Kabira. Eine Stadt vor 5000 Jahren, Mainz: Philipp von Zabern.

Texts in the City: Monumental Inscriptions in Jerusalem's Urban Landscape

Jeremy Smoak & Alice Mandell

> And the sign said,
> the words of the prophets
> are written on the subway walls
> And tenement halls
> And whispered in the sounds of silence.
> *Lyrics by Paul Simon*, The Sound of Silence
> *lyrics © Universal Music Publishing Group*

1. Introduction

In October 2017, we were invited to join a TOPOI seminar entitled 'Size Matters – Extra-Large Projects in the Ancient World' hosted at Freie Universität in Berlin. The discussions addressed recent theoretical work on the topic of monumentality. We were chosen to address the specific topic of monumental writings in the ancient southern Levant. A key take away from the week's discussion was that while 'size matters', monuments are much more than large buildings. Monuments and monumental writings function as portals that connect times and spaces and sites where memories are constructed and commemorated. Perhaps no southern Levantine monumental structure illustrates this quality as well as the temple in Jerusalem. This structure was destroyed in 587 BCE, and yet, its religious and cultural importance led to its rebuilding in 515 BCE. Although this second structure was then destroyed in 70 CE, many communities still revere its legacy. The Western Wall, which is one of the remaining retaining walls of the Second Temple has become, in its own right, a focal point of pilgrimage and prayer. The power of this structure in the imagination of many communities also led to the construction of Christian and Muslim religious structures in Jerusalem that pay homage to elements of this ancient Israelite temple (Ousterhout 1990; Amitzur 1996). Most notably the al-Aqsa Mosque and the Dome of the Rock both commemorate and claim this space in tribute to the ancient temple of Solomon (Grabar 1959).

When we considered how best to adapt these fruitful discussions of monumentality to our own area of specialty, we decided to focus upon key monumental writings from the time of the First Temple. We noted incongruity between the highly technical terminology used to described monuments and their inscriptions, and the more theoretical focus of our discussions at the 'Size Matters' seminar. Typically, scholars of Northwest Semitic languages employ several characteristics to define a text as monumental: 1) monumental inscriptions are professionally written in stone and are connected to people of power, and 2) they memorialize individual achievements as well as royal-sponsored projects.[1] Recent studies, however, have brought increased theorizing over what the terms *monumental* and *monumentality* imply about the nature and function of monumental objects and their relationships to materials, places, and memory (Osborne 2014; Scarre 2011; Parker 2003; Harmanşah 2011; Wu 1995). They move the study of monuments and monumental texts beyond the observation that *monuments* are somehow bigger than other spaces, objects, and structures. This more theoretical approach investigates what physical, material, historical, and social factors cause this difference. As such, scholars emphasize that the adjective *monumental* does not necessarily refer to a materially large object, but rather to an object or place that stands out because of its execution, meaning, and impact on viewers (Pauketat 2014; Rigney 2004; 2010). It is true that structures that we consider to be monumental typically are built in a more spectacular manner, and are often feats of technical skill. Yet, there may be nothing materially different between them and the other structures or objects around them. For example, the destroyed space of the Temple Mount no longer held the two ancient Jewish temples in 638 CE. And yet, the associations of this space with key figures in Islamic history and the legacy of the two temples led early Umayyad caliphs to build monumental structures on this very site. As this example shows, the monumentality of structures and objects may instead derive from their complex histories and the value that past and present communities ascribe to them.

In the following essay, we outline how recent theory on spatiality, materiality, visual design, and memory might be applied meaningfully to the study of the corpus of monumental inscriptions from the Iron Age Levant. After synthesizing

---

1 See most notably the use of the category 'monumental' in the various editions of Northwest Semitic inscriptions in Hallo, W./Younger, K./Hoffner, H. (eds.) (2000), Context of Scripture: Monumental Inscriptions from the Biblical World, Leiden: Brill. Hallo defines monumental texts quite expansively as texts created "for all time, whether royal or private, building or votive or mortuary, weights or seals, rediscovered on their original tone and metal surfaces or preserved in copies on clay and papyrus" ("Introduction: The Bible and the Monuments," Context of Scripture, volume 2, xxiv). However, in the field of Northwest Semitics, inscriptions in stone that are not seen as royal tend to be classified as non-monumental. For example, the Iron Age inscriptions found in the family tomb complexes at Khirbet el-Qom and Khirbet Beit Lei, which are also from Iron Age Judah are not classified as monumental texts in the majority of studies. Perhaps because they are written in a way deemed less professional and planned they have been studied as graffiti and exemplars of 'popular' or vernacular writing.

key scholarship in the study of monumentality, we introduce five points on monumentality and apply them to two well-known inscriptions from Iron Age Jerusalem: The Royal Steward Inscription and the Siloam Tunnel Inscription (switch the order to reflect the order of our discussion in the article) both of which are dated to the late 8th-early 7th centuries BCE. The first inscription that we examine – the Royal Steward Inscription – was placed over the doorway of an elite tomb in the Silwan necropolis outside of Jerusalem. This text mentions the tomb owner and his female consort, both non-royal figures (*Silw* 1) (Avigad 1953: 137–152; Ussishkin 1993: 247–254; McCarter 2000; Dobbs-Allsopp et al. 2004: 403–405; Renz 1995: 264–265; Suriano 2018: 201–205). The second inscription – the Siloam Tunnel inscription – does not name any one person, but celebrates a feat of engineering: the completion of an underground water channel in Jerusalem (Aḥituv 2005: 15–20; 2008: 19–25; Dobbs-Allsopp et al. 2005: 499–506; Younger 1994). While we might assume that this commemorative text was placed in a large public space, it was inscribed onto the interior rock surface of an underground water tunnel in the City of David – a place not easily accessible for the majority of audiences.

Both inscriptions were cut from local limestone, were professionally executed, and commemorated non-royal figures. And yet, they had vastly different functions and were set in very different settings. The more cursive script style and the location of the Siloam Tunnel inscription inside of a tunnel led some to categorize it as a monumental graffito (Schniedewind 2004: 72–73). As William Schniedewind (2004: 73) adds about the Siloam Tunnel Inscription, "[...] this inscription is not a simple graffito. Although not a royal inscription, the wall on which it appears was carefully prepared and its letters are elegantly carved into the hard limestone." The Royal Steward Inscription, by contrast, is less cursive in script style, and was placed in a more accessible location on the lintel of a tomb entrance. Yet, we begin our study by emphasizing that both inscriptions were not installed in publicly prominent locations typical of royal monumental inscriptions.

A focus upon the spatiality, materiality, and visual design of these two inscriptions also offers a different perspective into the 'palace-temple' paradigm. The 'palace-temple' paradigm tends to limit monumentality to those texts produced by elites (or the institutions that they represent) which are set into stone in spaces designed for large viewing audiences. Our approach differs by examining how the Royal Steward and Siloam Tunnel inscriptions functioned as part of the urban landscape of Jerusalem and how their design indexed professional expertise. Monuments curate memories and experiences, which means that such texts also monumentalized non-royal stories and memories in ancient Judah. In different ways, these two texts monumentalized their respective spaces by creating a type of linguistic urban space within the capital city of Judah.

The point that we hope to establish is that *scale – not size – matters*. For this reason, we argue for a broader perspective on monumentality that includes *scale, space, spectatorship, graphic design, and materiality.* This essay, then, ultimately makes a methodological argument, namely, that an object's monumentality proceeds from its site of display in a larger setting, its interactions with people, and the way in which it affects time in the sense that it stimulates memories that people carry away with them.

2. Are there monumental writings in Ancient Israel and Judah?

It might be helpful to begin by asking why these two inscriptions should be considered monumental texts. As discussed, the terminology of monumental appears frequently as a general way to characterize lapidary texts from the Iron Age Levant written in local alphabetic scripts and that are from a royal provenance. Importantly, several studies do use the terminology of monumentality as a way to characterize the production of the objects (Naveh 1982a: 198; 1968: 68–69). For instance, Joseph Naveh (1987: 3) differentiates "memorial" texts from the shorter texts that might also serve a commemorative function (i. e., "graffiti," "votive," or "burial inscriptions of epitaphs"):

> Memorial stelae were erected by kings and rulers to glorify their deeds which are sometimes described as the fulfillment of divine will. Despite their subjective nature, these inscriptions contain important historical data. Here, too, we find curses against whosoever would damage the monument or deface the inscriptions (Naveh 1987: 3).

Christopher Rollston offers a more robust definition, describing monumental texts as those which are professionally written and are commissioned by elites:

> The term "monumental inscription" is often used to refer to inscriptions commissioned by kings and high officials and which were intended to be permanent, enduring and (to some degree) public. Often these inscriptions were carved into stone. Within monumental inscriptions, the scribe or stonemason who was doing the chiseling would attempt to ensure that the lines of the inscription were fairly straight, of approximately the same length, and with fairly consistent spacing between the letters. The letters of a monumental inscription are normally carefully formed, in terms of the morphology and the stance of the letters. (Rollston 2016: 114)

Other studies use this terminology to describe the audience of these inscriptions. In his efforts to classify the different types of inscriptions from the Levant, Alan Millard (1972: 99) characterized monumental inscriptions in the following way: "These are texts intended for public display as enduring records. As it happens, the Siloam Tunnel Inscription alone can be counted a worthy representative of its class in Hebrew." Seth Sanders (2009: 139), however, notes the unusual location of this inscription and describes it instead as a "hidden memorial to anonymous collective experience." He observes,

> Rather than identifying themselves with the ruler and addressing an anonymous audience in the king's voice, they identify themselves as texts: *spr* or *dbr*. They tell the stories of independent professionals who mediate images and languages: craftsmen and prophets [...] skilled communicators quickly adapted the monumental styles and scripts to represent different types of agents: the collective craft, religious and kin groups to which they themselves belonged (Sanders 2009: 161).

He views the Siloam Tunnel Inscription as a new type of monument that appears in the 8th century that focuses on the achievements of non-royal protagonists and is written in a narrative style (Sanders 2009: 161).

As these examples show, the secondary literature in our field indicates that the designation monumental is defined in different ways. In some cases, it is applied to lapidary inscriptions without much discussion of what this terminology implies about the ontology and function of these texts and what makes them monumental. This is especially apparent in those studies that categorize the Siloam Tunnel Inscription as a monumental text and compare it to those royal monumental inscriptions from regions neighboring Israel and Judah (see Rollston 2016: 139). Alternatively, other studies connect its importance to the auspices of royal public projects. Commenting on the importance of the Siloam Tunnel Inscription, Lawrence Stager and Philip King (2001: 220) state, "At the south end of the tunnel, not far from the Pool of Siloam, a *monumental* Hebrew inscription was incised on a specially prepared wall panel of the tunnel" (italics ours). Several sentences later, they continue, "Surprisingly, the *monumental* inscription does not bear the name of King Hezekiah in whose reign the tunnel was certainly constructed" (italics ours).

We also note that when we turn to the script of these two texts it is not always clear what is meant by the designations 'lapidary' or 'monumental'.[2] For this reason, Vanderhooft's definition of monumental is especially refreshing because he includes those inscriptions typically designated as 'graffiti'. He observes that such graffiti "use a type of monumental script, or a rough version of it" (i. e., the Judean tomb texts from the sites of Khirbet el-Qom and Khirbet Beit-Lei) (Vanderhooft 2014: 110). Vanderhooft's approach has the added benefit of including inscriptions

---

2 Indeed, Naveh questioned the development of a distinct Hebrew lapidary script, arguing that the script overall moves to a more cursive style regardless of the medium of the inscription (e. g., hence, the cursive letter forms on stone inscriptions from the Moabite Stone [1982b: 66–69]).

on a range of durable materials (i. e., metal, ivory, and clay) that were crafted to make such statements about the power or status of their owner (Vanderhooft 2014: 109). His observations form a helpful starting point because they reevaluate the heuristic value of the terminology monumental vs. lapidary.

We would expect the designation lapidary script to refer to the style of script used in stone inscriptions, or to a style of script that developed from the practice of writing in stone. The inscriptions under consideration here, however, demonstrate that in certain cases monumental inscriptions attest to the use of a more cursive style. This raises the question of whether or not the choice of a more or less cursive script is a reflection of aesthetic, the function of the text, the level of training of the mason, or some other social, political, or cultural dynamic. While some classify the Siloam Tunnel inscription within the category of royal inscriptions, several studies observe that its cursive script style more closely resembles the script style of non-lapidary texts of tomb graffiti.[3] Yet, it is executed in a way that suggests that it was a meticulous and planned inscription and it is a commemorative text (Schniedewind 2004: 72–73).

Other much less complete texts that contain very little content, on the other hand, are identified as monumental or of a royal provenance, mainly due to their medium (stone) and their less cursive style (i. e., the Ophel Inscription; the 'City of David' inscription; the Samaria Stele) (Naveh 1982a: 195–198; 2000: 1–2; Cross 2001: 44–47; Sukenik 1936: 156). The assumption is that such texts come from a royal provenance and are therefore monumental. However, when we turn to the corpus of funerary inscriptions carved in stone in tombs and caves from the same period (8th-7th centuries) we see a tendency to classify these inscriptions as graffiti rather than monumental texts (Khirbet Beit Lei and Khirbet el-Qom) (Naveh 1979; Mandell/Smoak 2016). All of this raises the more fundamental question: what makes one stone inscription a graffito and another stone inscription a monumental text? In the following section, we give further definition to what the terminology of monumentality conveys about the social function of these texts by focusing upon scale, space, spectatorship, graphic design, and materiality. By

---

3 See the comments by K.A.D. Smelik about the script of the inscription, "It is important to note that the text was not written in monumental but in a cursive script. This points to a person who was accustomed to write on papyrus or on shards (ostraca). It is unlikely that the stonemasons had this experience." (Smelik 2011: 105). John Healy makes similar observations about the script of the Siloam Tunnel Inscription: "There are certain tendencies to a more cursive style, but almost all our sources are inscribed on stone and pots and we have very little information about writing on soft materials. A good example of a stone inscription is the Siloam tunnel inscription (eighth century BC), which is probably meant to be a formal monumental inscription but actually contains many cursive features, with down-strokes curving to the left. The cursive form seems to have been normal and there may have been no Hebrew tradition of royal inscriptions requiring a monumental script." (Healy 1990: 226).

bringing these aspects of monumentality into the discussion, we show how the adjective monumental refers to the ability of objects to transcend space and time and consequently live in the memories, emotions, retellings, reenactments, and biographies of their audiences. They continue to be relevant because they compel their audiences to write biographies about them or to graft them into personal, familial, or cultural narratives.

a. Scale

The corpus of inscriptions from the southern Levant is much smaller in number and is less impressive in overall size and execution than the wealthier regions of the ancient Near East. Indeed, one might ask the question of whether or not those inscriptions that scholars deem monumental are truly so in comparison to the much larger and voluminous corpora in Egypt, Anatolia, Syria, and Mesopotamia.[4] To this we point to our study of monumentality more broadly, which underscores that *scale, not size*, matters. *Monumentality is not a matter of size, but scale in significance to surrounding objects, spaces, and texts and their cultural importance.* The monumentality of the buildings, objects, and inscriptions from the Iron Age southern Levant reflects the political development of the region into small territorial states.

This also means that the monumentality of an object or inscription is partially determined by its audience or, perhaps better, the interactions between an object and its audience. Indeed, while the majority of monumental inscriptions are found on large stones, we should be careful not to exclude those inscriptions of smaller scale written on permanent and enduring media that allow their words to transcend space and time. An object's monumentality is not located in or determined by its size. Rather, as James Osborne (2014: 4) stresses, "we can only consider an object's monumentality in the context of its relationship to the community of which it forms a part". This means that in certain cases the tiniest of objects may be considered monumental precisely because the ascription of monumentality is always a negotiation between the object's agency and the agencies of groups of people over time (Osborne 2014: 13). We might point to the two silver amulets discovered at the site of Ketef Hinnom in Jerusalem to illustrate this point. Although they contain microscopic inscriptions on their surfaces contemporary audiences have monumentalized their meaning by incorporating their significance within wider narratives about the history of writing in ancient Judah (Barkay 1992; Barkay/Vaughn/Lundberg/Zuckerman 2004). Despite their tiny sizes, they have become monumentally significant to contemporary discussions of the composi-

---

4 See the discussion of the comparison of monuments and monumental inscriptions in Israel and the wider Near East in Hallo (2000).

tion of the biblical texts, the study of Hebrew epigraphy, and reconstructions of Israelite religion (Smoak 2016).

This also means that when we look at inscriptions or those texts embedded into monumental structures, we should consider their scale and social capital. We might pay greater attention to the scale of a text in relation to the physical structure into which it was set. And, when possible, we might ask how such inscriptions dominated the physical surface or structure of their built settings. We can ask how their placement and display on specific buildings sought to monumentalize the spaces in which such buildings sat. We can contrast such busy text-displays with those texts placed on key architectural junctures, or that are marked as monumental in the way that they are set apart, either in isolation from other texts or by key iconography. We can look to the way in which the Behistun trilingual inscription of Darius stands apart visually and materially from its environs. Its height and location suggest that it was designed for a viewing rather than a reading audience. Travelers would have perceived this inscription as it emerged from the natural rock formations, thus reminding them of the power of Darius to carve the landscape.

b. Space

Monuments employ their surrounding landscapes to project their meanings (Glatz 2014). There is often an inextricable relationship between monuments and their natural settings. As Goldhahn writes, monuments

> help to shape the perception of the landscape. At the same time as the monument is materialized in the landscape, the landscape is materialized in the monument. This dialectic process is essential; the materials used in monument construction – wood, earth, turf, sand, fire cracked stones, ash charcoal, seaweed, beach sand, snails, etc. – are gathered from specific places in the landscape and are incorporated into a new composite construction in the form of the monument" (Goldhahn 2008: 59).

They shape the perception of the natural topography of a region by making landscape and place communicate to audiences. As we will demonstrate, both the Royal Steward and Siloam Tunnel inscriptions were set into stages that purposefully integrated both natural and constructed landscapes.

When we examine the choices underlying the placement of inscriptions into monumental structures, it is clear that the scale and layout tend to be determined by a concern for both present and future audiences. In his study of pre-historic monuments, Chris Scarre (2011: 16) writes,

> Locations were chosen to draw attention both to the monument itself and to the place where it was built [...] these may already have been places of mythological or sacred significance, or locations of assembly and ceremonial performance. The construction of monuments gave those associations novel and enduring form.

His approach takes seriously the spatial relationship between monuments and their audiences and leads us to consider how *monuments and monumental inscriptions generate viewing spaces and choose their audiences*. Those monumental inscriptions placed in public spaces – roads, plazas, parks, etc. – were designed with a broader and more dynamic viewing audience in mind. As Greg Woolf (1996: 25) emphasizes, "[...] monuments do imply a sense of posterity, of viewers and readers to come, whose progress through the public spaces or along the public roads where monuments were often set up, might be arrested, and who might then pause to read, and to remember". This approach has the advantage of anticipating the transformation and changes in the natural, built, or social environment that might strip away or strengthen the social weight of a monumental text. We can look to the change in meaning of the Siloam Tunnel Inscription which, once 'discovered' and brought to the surface in 1880, has for many scholars become iconic of Hezekiah's preparations for siege as well as literacy, scribalism, and the royal chancellery in Jerusalem. That is, it is now valued by the academic community for different reasons than its original inception.

c. Spectatorship

This brings us to our next point, that the bodies that interact with monuments and monumental inscriptions play active roles in shaping their meanings. Ultimately, it is the audiences of monumental texts that give them enduring meaning – with a change in a generation, monuments can derive new and sometimes unintended meanings. The people who engage with monumental inscriptions bring with them memories and the knowledge of landscapes, terrain, and travel, which become connected to their experiences of such texts. Monumental inscriptions differ from other text types because they are designed to represent a place where multiple hands, minds, and memories converge. Once they are formed and embedded into a physical space, they become a point of reference that connects the present to past generations, landscapes, and power structures. In this way, a monumental inscription freezes time in the sense that it displays in one time and place the process of controlling, harnessing, and building the natural landscape into an object. The transformation of a natural landscape into a built environment also indexes the ability of a community to compress time into a single display.

d. Graphic design

We have alluded to the ways in which monuments and monumental inscriptions create a dialectic between their graphic design aesthetics and their physical settings. This dialectic works to transition the experience of viewers from the realm of landscape and built environment to the realm of memory. Now we will address in more specific detail how this process occurs. That is, how an audience's experience with the combination of the space of the monument and its graphic design forges a memory that transcends time and space. By graphic design we mean the compositional elements of a text (e. g., shape, color, texture pattern, and script) that communicated its function, value, and provenance to audiences (see Kress/van Leeuwen 1996; Thomas 2014: 60; Mandell/Smoak 2018).

There is a tendency, however, to study the graphic design of monumental inscriptions for what they might be interpreted to reveal about script development, regional variation, and political ideologies. These are important questions, but they tend to neglect that design refers to many facets of the visual aspects of a text. A good design is one that holds in tension the knowledge and expertise of the designer with the expectations of any given audience. The design represents the meeting point between three interests: the person who commissioned the text, the designer, and the audience (Smith/Schmidt 1996). Moreover, the design of an inscription brings together economic forces, artistic choice, and technological expertise.

The study of graphic design and the visual display of texts in the modern period offers us a vocabulary and methodology to better understand the multimodality of ancient monumental writings. Jeff Bezemer and Gunther Kress (2008: 174) describe design as "the practice where modes, media, frames, and sites of display on the one hand [...] and the characteristics of the audience on the other are brought into coherence with each other". This definition is important because it stresses that the non-linguistic, or 'paragraphemic' aspects of a text (i. e., the choices in layout, materiality, and overall graphic design) are not ancillary to the linguistic content of a text, but rather are an inseparable part of its message. The study of the design of the scripts on these inscriptions should also pay close attention to how the design of the text intends to interact with the text's other modes, including display, color, shape, and size. As Jennifer Dickson (2015: 508) explains,

> Visual cues such as text formatting, font choice, and choice or manipulation of orthography and writing systems produce complex indexical meanings that are part of the "content" of a piece of writing, just as intonation, volume and prosody become part of the contextually embedded meaning of a spoken utterance.

The Siloam and Royal Steward inscriptions are, in their present form, unaccompanied by any image. As will be discussed, the variation in cursive script style in these inscriptions and other monumental writings of this period should be included as an aspect of their design, rather than a mere indication of their date or provenance (e. g., from a professional vs. non-professional milieu). We would argue that their script style was an equally important factor in their design as the words of these texts. We look to recent work on writing that considers the script ideologies at play in a text, which consider graphic variation to be "a socially relevant communicative practice" (Spitzmüller 2012: 256). In other words, the choice of script style was determined by the text and its audience. For this reason, we include the iconicity of script style as a communicative property of these inscriptions (Sebba 2015: 208–227). The script employed was identifiable as one used in official and royal projects and in administrative bureaucratic communication. When used in these more local displays of power, this script style signaled high status and social prominence.

e. Materiality

A focus upon the materiality of inscriptions offers a corrective to the tendency to study such texts only for what they reveal about the development of script traditions and the history of literacy in ancient Judah. Materiality refers to "an approach that prioritizes the physicality (material) of objects or sites and examines the relationships between people, objects/monuments and actions, allowing the exploration of social networks and meanings" (Williams/Kirton/Gondek 2015: 13). Materiality encompasses both a focus upon how writing or inscribing a material was a material act as well as the way in which written things became material artifacts after they were inscribed (Berti/Bolle/Opdenhoff/Stroth 2017: 3–4). This approach calls for a more holistic examination of a monumental text as an 'object'. It also means thinking more broadly about how such monumental writings functioned as "social agents" (Gell 1998: 17–19).

A focus upon materiality also paves the way for greater emphasis upon the planning and production of monumental objects and inscriptions. Monuments and monumental inscriptions encode messages about the relationship between professional skill and the power of those who erect them by commandeering labor and raw materials. Stone monuments and monumental inscriptions give enduring voice to the ability to draw together knowledge, resources, and skill into one place and time. As Kyle Keimer (2015: 193) observes,

> Those who control the knowledge of working with such a stone (i.e., the kings who commission the masons) make specific statements about their legitimacy, power, and permanency precisely because they are able to have such a hard stone

sculpted and incised. The results are not only pieces of art, but they also further the rhetoric of the monarch, both through the shape and display of the object itself and in the inscription that is incised into it.

As we discuss below, a focus upon the materiality of monumental inscriptions has the added benefit of reframing the study of these texts from the standpoint of their professional manufacture. While there is a tendency to connect such texts to royal auspices, more effort needs to be directed toward understanding them as stages where technological advances, professional skill, organized labor, *and individual and collective agency* was expressed.

3. The monumentality of the Royal Steward inscription

The Royal Steward inscription is a monumental funerary epitaph for a Jerusalem official discovered over the lintel of a tomb east of the ancient Iron Age city. In 1870 Clermont-Ganneau's explorations outside of Jerusalem led him to this inscription (1899: 305–313; see also Diringer 1934: 106). The tomb is part of a larger complex of burials on the eastern slopes of the Kidron Valley across from the Ophel Hill and the City of David. This necropolis was used by Judean elites during the period of the late monarchy. The inscription was carved into the outer-façade of a tomb complex preserved in the modern-day village of Silwan (Ussishkin 1993: 247–254). The relationship between the city of the dead and spaces of the living elite of Jerusalem was a by-product of the way in which these burial complexes mirrored elite compounds on the other side of the Kidron Valley.

When we turn to our key points on monumentality, our first observation considers this text as an integral part of the tomb complex. Viewing this inscription would have entailed a consideration for the larger space of the tomb complex, and its location in the necropolis. We will also address the broader message about the power that its location on the eastern hill would have projected to its audience. First, however, we will address its materiality and scale. The block of limestone that makes up the outer-façade of the tomb measures 8 m in width by 4 m in height. This three-line inscription was set into a panel that was about 1.32 m in length and was engraved above the main entrance of the tomb (Avigad 1953: 137). The placement of the text is significant, as it became the central sign complex that a person would encounter when approaching the inner chamber. The inscription reads

This [is the tomb of PN-]iah, the royal steward. There is neither silver nor gold [he]re, [but] only [his bones] and his concubine's bon[es] w[ith] him. Cursed be the one who opens this (tomb).

Figure 1: Drawing of the Silwan necropolis and Kidron Valley (Avigad 1953, 138; courtesy Israel Exploration Journal)

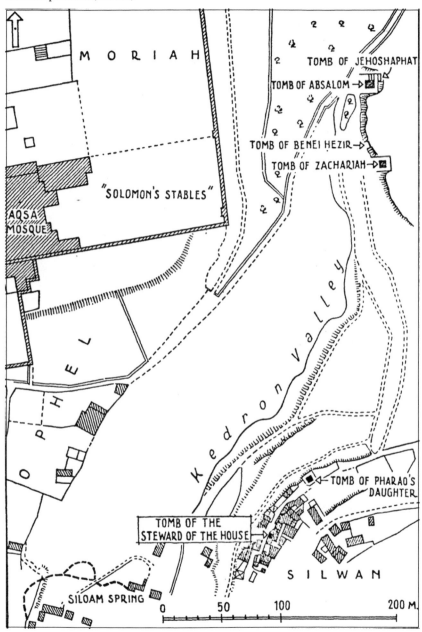

This inscription memorializes the status of the tomb owner who served "over the house" and offers a warning to those approaching the tomb. Much of the discussion of the inscription surrounds its possible relationship to Isaiah's rebuke of Shebna, one of Hezekiah's officials (Avigad 1953: 151; Willis 1993: 60–67; Dobbs-Allsopp et al. 2004: 404; Hays 2010: 558–573; 2015: 233–234). Scholars looked to the prophetic rebuke in Isaiah 22: 15–19 to reconstruct the personal name in this inscription. The relevant parts of the rebuke read,

> [15] Thus the Lord, Yahweh Almighty says:
> Go, say to this steward,
> To Shebna the palace administrator:
> [16] What are you doing here and who gave you permission
> To cut out a grave for yourself here,
> Hewing your grave on the height
> And chiseling your resting place in the rock?
> [17] Beware, Yahweh is about to take firm hold of you
> And hurl you away, you mighty man.
> [18] He will roll you up tightly like a ball
> And throw you into a large country.
> There you will die
> And there the chariots you were so proud of
> Will become a disgrace to your master's house.
> [19] I will depose you from your office,
> And you will be ousted from your position.

If indeed there is a connection between this biblical text and the tomb of the Royal Steward then it is possible to read the prophet's rebuke as directed toward the very monumentality of the tomb. Our more cautious view is that the prophet's rebuke, at the very least, admonishes about the practices associated with elite funerary monuments. Matthew Suriano (2018: 100–108) has recently provided fresh analysis of the linguistic aspects of this inscription that addresses the textual landscape created by such writings in this necropolis. As Suriano (2018: 108–110) argues, the references to "here" and "the height" in v.16 point toward the construction of monumental tombs in the Silwan necropolis. That is, the prophet's rebuke captures the way that such a tomb's monumentality was expressed by its spatial setting and its visibility to the inhabitants of Jerusalem. He writes,

> unlike other cemeteries, such as those in the Hinnom Valley and the northern necropolis, which were probably obscured in Jerusalem's urban topography because they were largely underground and unobtrusive, the standing monuments of Silwan would have visibly marked ancient Jerusalem's eastern horizon (Suriano 2018: 110).

Christopher Hays stresses that the prophet's rebuke may have also been directed toward the individual nature of such elite tombs, noting, "They are large and characterized by fine stonework and by features reflecting their builders' intention that they be used only for themselves and not for their descendants" (Hays 2010: 561). Such observations are important because they draw attention to the statement that this monumental tomb made within Jerusalem's natural and built environments, that is, how spectatorship played a role in its monumentality. The Silwan necropolis spoke to the power of Jerusalem's nobility to harness and transform the natural landscape into a built space. The monumentality of the tomb was not merely expressed by its *size*, the reference to elites, or the employment of a professional scribe and/or mason to create this text. Its monumentality was also expressed in the space that it occupied as the focal point of the tomb and that tomb's prominent position up on the eastern ridge of the Kidron Valley. The monumentality of the Royal Steward Inscription was also expressed by the integration of natural and constructed landscapes into its edifice.

When we look more closely at Isaiah's rebuke, it is clear that it addresses the way in which such monuments tapped into the associations of both the natural and built space of the necropolis. The language of v.16 relates the constructed "tomb" (*qbr*) to the "height" (*mrwm*) of the ridge and the "dwelling" (*mškn*) to the "rock" (*slʿ*) of the Kidron cliff. The repetition of the word "here" (*ph*) draws further attention to the action that is rebuked – namely, the transformation of the "height" and the "rock" into a "tomb" and a "dwelling". The prophet is critical of the way in which the tomb's monumentality has turned the height of the natural rocks into a spectacle. The prophet is also dismissive of the way in which the tomb's design contributed to its monumentality. Verse 16 invokes technical terminology that refers to the execution of the tomb into the rock of the cliff. The verse repeats the verb "hew" (*ḥṣb*) twice and employs the verb "carve" or "engrave" (*ḥqq*). This terminology conveys a sense of the design of the tomb as well as its relationship to the natural limestone of the ridge. Although the biblical text does not appear to refer to the inscription on this or other tombs specifically, the use of the verb "engrave" (*ḥqq*) can refer to the act of writing. Seen in this context, the prophet's rebuke is framed as a performance of *counter-monumentality*. After describing the erection of the tomb on the "height" and the "rock," the prophet condemns the official Shebna by using language that is associated with the dismantling of monumental architecture. Isaiah states that Yahweh will "hurl down," "thrust down," and "tear down" Shebna, his station, and his office.

When we return to this specific inscription, its artistically exquisite design upon the lintel of the tomb forms an excellent case study in monumental writing. Graphically, the repetition of carefully executed letter-forms projects a message of order, direction, and stability. Graphic designers would refer to this artistic technique as an effect of "repetitive-expectancy," which creates a 'rhythm effect' and an appearance of 'organized movement'" (Bradley 2013: 39). These visual aesthetics convey notions of a high-level of planning, ordered progression, and organized movement and control. Moreover, the engraved letters on this lintel are among the largest examples of writing in the corpus of inscriptions from the Iron Age southern Levant. Thus, the artistic design and scale of the letters compel audiences to wonder how much time and effort went into its production.

Again, rather than focus solely upon the material or script or individual that commissioned the text, our analysis also considers how its design and spatial associations contributed to its monumentality. We view the very placement of the inscription in a prominent display setting over the entrance of the tomb to have conveyed a significant part of its monumentality. The inscription begins by identifying the name of the deceased and his title, the Royal Steward or "the one over the house". Our first observation is that the placement of this text above the lintel, or over the house of the deceased, may be a visual play on the title of the interred: "over the house" i. e., a steward. The placement of a text into a prepared space above the entrance of a tomb door lintel is a common feature in extant funerary inscriptions from this region (e. g., the outer door of the Tomb of the Pharaoh's Daughter door lintel and within the family tomb at Khirbet el-Qom, over an interior chamber [Tomb 1]) (Suriano 2018: 101–102; Dever 1970–1971). We would note, however, that the words "who is over the house" in the Royal Steward text are stretched out and fill the exact center of the prepared lintel space. The spacing is unusual in that it separates the definite article from the word "house".

The relationship between the spatial arrangement of this and other tombs of this period and dwellings is well established. As Suriano (2018: 105) writes, the Royal Steward is claiming the space of the tomb, the house of the dead. We think, moreover, that the placement of the tomb owner's title, even if incidental, in the central space of the lintel ("over the house") would have created a stronger connection between this text and the status of the person that this tomb represented. Their responsibilities in life filled the focal point of this inscribed space, immediately over the doorway of their tomb. In this way, the display location of the inscription gave non-linguistic expression to the very language found in the text.

We now turn to the internal graphic design elements, including the arrangement of the letters, and how they impact the scale of the words set into the lintel inscription. The mason who produced the inscription bannered the text into (nearly) two straight lines of well-arranged alphabetic letters. Thinking about this from the perspective of visual culture demands that we think about the opposition of empty and full spaces and the execution of letter forms and scribal marks as displays. The letters are grouped into word units through the opposition of empty and full spaces. We also observed that there appears to be an interest in spacing the words of the text so that they stretch across the carved space of the lintel. This arraignment produces an image that is dense with writing while the downwards vertical stokes of certain letter forms pull the eye down to lower lines of text, thus creating an image of continuous script. The shape, spacing, and slanting of the letters blurs the line between art and writing as the eye is drawn to the aesthetics of certain letters. For instance, the elongation of the tails on the letters *alef*, *resh*, *waw*, and *resh* that make up the word "cursed" (*'rwr*) produces an image of a word that stands taller than the other words in the inscription. We also note that these letter forms appear to be straighter. While we can of course attribute this to a phase in script, thinking about writing as a part of the monumental design of the tomb requires us to think about non-literate audiences, who may have only recognized this word, which is attested in other tomb contexts (e. g., Beit Lei). The graphic design of these specific letters has the effect of bolding the word in a way that is analogous to the use of all caps in the word 'STOP!'

People who interacted with the inscription had to lift their heads and eyes to see the words. The inscription was out of their reach above the doorway to the tomb. The prominent position of the inscription *over* the doorway combined with the width of the inscription conveyed messages about social hierarchies and boundaries. The vertical height of the letters on the inscription converged with the height of the inscription on the lintel to convey the power of the individual buried within the tomb. The ontology of the inscription as one well-designed large slab of limestone gave enduring testimony to the deceased's ability to stand in a position above those whom he commissioned to construct the tomb. The inscription's location over the doorway placed the words of the deceased in a hierarchical relationship to those who read them.

In death, as in life, "the one over the house" spoke authoritatively to the inhabitants of Jerusalem. If there is indeed a connection between this tomb and Isaiah's rebuke of Shebna, the prophet's condemnation to "hurl down," "thrust down," and "tear down" the royal steward take on added meaning against the background of the display setting of the inscription. We are not suggesting that the prophetic attack refers to the inscription specifically. But the reference to Yahweh "tearing down" Shebna from his office would have taken on concrete meaning against the backdrop of the inscription displayed over the tomb. Indeed, it becomes easy to imagine that the inscription might have been the concrete target of the threats to "hurl down," "thrust down," and "tear down" when we consider the way that it identified the tomb with "the one over the house". Generally speaking, the prophet's rebuke counter-monumentalizes the inscription by decrying "the one who is above".

Figure 2: Drawing of the Royal Steward Inscription (Avigad 1953: pl. 9; courtesy of the Israel Exploration Society)

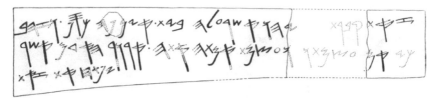

When we move to the script of this inscription, it is typically described as written in a 'monumental' or 'lapidary' style, which implies an opposition to ink-based and more ephemeral writings. However, the extant inscriptions from Judah during the 8th century are marked by their increasingly curved execution.[5] In addition, certain letters exhibit a 'tick' on their right-hand side that originated in the stroke of a stylus using ink, which carried over to certain stone inscriptions. For example, the *'alef* on the Siloam Tunnel Inscription has no tick, but it is written with two horizontal and nearly parallel strokes; the bottom stroke on the right stops at the vertical stroke. The *zayin* is written with a tick and the *mem, nun,* and *kaf* curve upwards. These features of the script style of the Siloam Tunnel Inscription contrast noticeably with certain features on the Royal Steward Inscription. For these reasons, we see a breakdown in the terminology used for stone and monumental inscriptions, which display varying degrees of a cursive script style (see Cross 1962a: 18). For example, while the Royal Steward text is written in a more cursive script than the Ophel Stone Inscription (see Figure 2), it is not as cursive in style as the Siloam Tunnel Inscription. For this reason, we must return to Naveh's observation that the letters used in these inscriptions exhibit a range of cursive/non-cursive forms, or what he called "formal styles" (Naveh 1987: 8; see also the comments on cursive vs. lapidary script in Keimer 2015: 204–206). This variation was conditioned by the skill of the scribe/mason, the type of text, and, equally important, *the desired aesthetic or graphic design of the inscription.* As Kyle Keimer (2015: 197) emphasizes,

> [...] each inscription has captured in stone the subjective decisions of the mason responsible for its production [...] When the technology and practicality behind the production of an inscription are considered, it becomes possible to comment on

---

5   This is the hallmark feature that most identify as signaling the appearance of an 'Old Hebrew' script and the age of script differentiation along national and linguistic lines. Because this script is first found on the Moabite stela the degree to which this was a marker of national identity at this early stage can be debated. Most notably, we point to the fact that the curve of the *kaf, mem,* and *nun* in the Moabite Stone are diagnostic features that differentiate this script from those written using the Phoenician script.

why a script appears a certain way and not just how an inscription looks and what the inscription itself says.

To this, we would add that scripts are not neutral vehicles of communication, but work with the linguistic modes of a text to convey meaning (Spitzmüller 2012: 256–260).

In some cases, the letter forms that are cursive and akin to what we would expect of a script conditioned by the social context and technologies used to produce a text. In the field of linguistics, it is accepted that a dialect can operate in various registers (i. e., the situational variation that can occur within a language variety) (Biber and Finegan 1994: 6). Perhaps we might also consider how the 'registers' of script selected for such purposes were determined by the social setting of the text and its material, rather than limiting the 'cursive' or 'non-cursive' or 'lapidary' vs. 'cursive' debates to the date of the text or the technologies used to create it.

The above discussion also points to the need for further consideration of how scripts encode and convey more than chronological and political messages. Script styles possess not only diachronic information, but they are informed by individual decisions about their aesthetics and desired function and other considerations (see Zuckerman/Swartz Dodd 2003; Kaufman 1986). The moment of the execution of writing is, after all, reflective of the choices that individuals made to create a text. This means that regardless of the intention of the person funding or sponsoring these texts, their design was largely the product of those crafting such objects.[6] Those people producing such inscriptions worked backwards, so to speak. They visualized the desired effect that the words, script, medium, and viewing space would have upon an audience.

4. A monumental feat: The Siloam Tunnel inscription

The Siloam Tunnel Inscription was placed in a subterranean tunnel on the interior wall of a public works project under the City of David. The text commemorates the technological feat of a group of workers who tunneled a water system from the Gihon Spring to a large public pool on the southern end of the Iron Age city (Younger 1994: 551). The inscription does not mention any one person by name, but instead it commemorates the creation of the tunnel (Dobbs-Allsopp et al. 2005: 397). It celebrates the moment when the two teams of workers, working from opposite ends of the tunnel, met each other underground (Sasson 1982: 113; Faust 2000: 5). The inscription reads,

---

6 For further discussion of the motivations behind certain script choices, see Lehmann (2008) and Keimer (2015: 209).

[...] the breaking through. And this was the manner of the breaking through: While [the hewers were wielding] the pick, each one toward his fellow, and while there were still three cubits to be tunnel[ed through, there was hea]rd the sound of each one calling to his fellow, for there was a fissure in the rock on the right and [on the left]. At the time of the breakthrough, the hewers struck, each to meet his fellow, pick against [p]ick. And then the waters flowed from the spring to the pool for twelve hundred cubits. And a hu[nd]red cubit was the height in the rock above the heads of the hewer[s].[7] (Dobbs-Allsopp et al. 2005: 499)

The location of the inscription in a subterranean setting has caused substantial discussion about its function (see Garbini 1969; Parker 1994; Shea 1988; Sanders 2009: 139).

If we speak of the inscription as a display, it was certainly a display for the workers and those with knowledge of the tunnel, but not a display for the public at large (Parker 1997: 39). Why, then, do we classify this inscription as monumental? This was a hidden text and in this way it stands apart from the majority of texts that many scholars deem monumental. Given the monumental nature of creating this water tunnel, we might have expected the inscription to have been located outside of the tunnel, at its entrance perhaps, or next to the pool to which it leads. The inscription is located about 6–7 m inside the southern end of the tunnel. This location challenges assumptions about the spectatorship of monumental writing involving audiences that encountered them in large, urban spaces.

Indeed, the few scholars who do not classify the inscription as a monumental inscription do so precisely because it makes no mention of a king or an official who might have commissioned its production or organized the labor for the tunnel. While there is some evidence that a second inscription might have been planned for that purpose, the content of the inscription indicates that it functioned for a more narrow audience (see comments in Rendsburg/Schniedewind 2010: 191). It marks a specific moment in time when the masons cutting through the eastern ridge of the capital city managed to meet (Dobbs-Allsopp et al. 2005: 397). We emphasize at the outset that the setting of the inscription within the tunnel captured an important element in its monumentality. It is set within the technological feat itself and as a result a large part of its monumentality derives from its physical embeddedness within the technological feat that it describes.

The fact that the inscription does not mention a royal figure, an elite, or deities does not negate its monumentality. Here we have a text that narrates a *monumental feat*. That is, the inscription commemorates one of the most significant technological advances in tunneling technology in the ancient world (for a description of

---

7   For key treatments, see Schniedewind (2004: 72–73); Aḥituv (2005: 15–20; 2008: 19–25); Dobbs-Allsopp et al. (2005: 499–506); Younger (1994).

the engineering, see Gill 1991; Lancaster/Long 1999; Frumkin/Shimron 2006; Sneh/ Weinberger/Shalev 2010). The tunnel that the workers cut into the rock of the City of David was the longest tunnel produced in the Near East to that point in history. It measures a total of 533 m in length (about 1700 ft.), making it significantly longer than any of the tunnels from the Levant dating to the same time period (for a description of the tunnel, see Ussishkin 1976; 1995). The water tunnel at the site of Gibeon by comparison only measures about 50 m in length and is the second longest water tunnel in Israel during the Iron Age (Frumkin/Shimron 2006: 228). Similar tunnel projects carried out in Assyria used a method of connecting intermediate shafts in order to form long tunnels (Aḥituv 2008: 22).

The Siloam tunnel was an extraordinary accomplishment because it did not use shafting to connect the different parts of the tunnel but instead only relied upon acoustic sounding between a surface team and the subterranean teams for the entire route of the tunnel. The project required expertise in acoustic technology, hydrogeology, and architecture. The labor not only involved two teams cutting toward one another from two different sides of the City of David, but also a surface team who used acoustic tools to direct the subterranean teams toward the desired outlet. In addition, the tunnel evidences expertise in the use of plaster on the floor and sidings of the tunnel in order to mitigate the potential loss of water in the karstic rock. All of this highlights the great technological advance that this tunnel represented (see Parker 1994). The inscription was not a commemoration of the construction of a tunnel only, but also of a significant technological advancement that involved the pooling of tremendous expertise and labor for a project that would bring significant benefits to the citizens of the city.

An emphasis upon the great technological feat of the tunnel shapes the way that we look at the function of the inscription. While it is tempting to describe the inscription as a retelling or narrative of the tunneling project, we note the importance that references to expertize knowledge play in the text. The inscription repeats references to the technologies, tools, and professionals involved in the project: "breakthrough", "picks", "excavators", "struck", etc. In this way, the inscription is not so much a description of the story of the tunneling as it is a description of the completion of the project and testament to the expertise and technologies involved (for similar suggestions, see Parker 1997: 39; Younger 1994: 552–553).[8] The inscription celebrates the sophisticated technology and professional labor that was brought together for the project, highlighting the final moment when water flowed from the Gihon to the Siloam Tunnel. Particularly noteworthy in this

---

8 So, Parker (1997: 39), "The inscription is told from the point of view of someone caught up in the success of the project (the actual meeting of the two parties) and impressed by its scale (the measurements). The structure and content of the inscription betray both an emotional engagement in the outcome and a sense of pride in the success of an exceptional technical achievement."

regard are the references to the use of acoustic technology in the inscription. The inscription recalls the "sound" of the workers that the excavators heard in the tunnel as they tunneled. Here we have – if Frumkin and Shimron and others are correct – a commemoration of the sophisticated use of acoustic technology to guide the excavators (Frumkin/Shimron 2006: 232; see also Puech 1974: 201–202).

As we noted above, the inscription is not so much a story or narrative of the project as it is an overture to the tools, technology, and professionals involved in the project. It does not tell us who commissioned the project, when, or why, but rather speaks to the people who made it. Important also is the way that the inscription draws specific attention to measurements. Line three refers to the acoustics that the workers heard while they were still *three cubits* apart. Line four alludes to knowledge of directionality: *north and south*. Line four describes the length of the flow of water *(one thousand two hundred cubits)*. Finally, line four describes the height of the rock above the heads of the excavators as *one hundred cubits*. In this way, the last line of the text commemorates the accomplishment of the surface team to communicate with the excavators some hundred cubits below. As this description of the text reveals, the monumentality of the inscription lies in large part in the way that it celebrates and commemorates pioneering expertise in engineering, hydraulics, and acoustic technology. The tunnel was a monumental feat that involved the pooling of the highest level of professional skill for the creation of the longest tunnel in the region. The location of the inscription *within* the tunnel in which the breakthrough took place formed an important part of the way that this aspect of its monumentality was expressed (see Aḥituv 2008: 23). The inscription's monumentality was expressed by its location at the meeting point of the different professional teams and the outcome of their labors.

The script style of the inscription has long taken center stage in discussions of the history and development of a national Hebrew script (see Hendel 1996: 233–237; van der Kooij 1987: 103–107).[9] Many studies note that use of a cursive script in the inscription is unusual, as it deviates from the lapidary style expected on such a stone monument. Vaughn noted that several of the letter forms evident in the inscription most resemble the script of 7th-century BCE Hebrew seals and administrative texts (i. e., the Samaria Ostraca) (1999; cited in Schniedewind 2015: 407). It is also noteworthy that the script style of the Siloam Tunnel Inscription differs from the style of other monumental inscriptions from Jerusalem during the same period (i. e., Ophel Inscription and the fragment of a monumental inscription from the City of David). What we have on the Siloam Tunnel Inscription is a script style that more closely resembles the cursive style used in administrative texts, which reflect the use of ink writing implements. The scribe and/or mason who produced

---

9 For further discussion of the paleography of the inscription, see Naveh (1982b: 90–95); Cross (1979: 75).

the inscription adapted the letter forms typical of an administrative style to a stone inscription. The result is a unique *graphic design* that locates an extended text with a lot of technical and professional terminology in a densely compacted rectangular space. The professional expertise demonstrated by the scribe's ability to space out the letters evenly, include word-dividers at the appropriate places, and arrange the text into four lines of equal length paralleled the professional expertise of the engineers who carried out the project. The script style with its wide use of cursive forms gives voice to and celebrates the trade and achievements of a professional elite within the capital city.[10] It gives iconic and concrete voice to the accomplishments of non-royal professionals beyond their own lifetimes.

Perhaps the strongest reflex of the monumentality of the inscription is found in its various discussions and retellings in contemporary scholarship (Parker 1997: 40–42; Stager/King 2001: 220; Schniedewind 2004: 72–73; Hadley 2012). As we noted at the outset of this study, monumental inscriptions define themselves in large part by how effectively they lend themselves to local memories, cultural narratives, and political histories. Such inscriptions possess an ability to transcend time and act as portals that connect past, present, and future audiences. One of the most noticeable features of the Siloam Tunnel Inscription is the way that contemporary scholars connect its importance to the history of the reign of Hezekiah and his conflict with the Assyrian empire in the late 8th century BCE. Even though the inscription itself does not mention the king or its relation to the historical events of this period, its location in the tunnel and its description of the technological feat of bringing water to the city are readily connected to Hezekiah's preparations for an Assyrian siege. Certain studies, however, situate the time frame of this project either earlier than Hezekiah's reign (Reich/Shukron 2011: 147–157; for a summary, see also Russell 2017: 103–105) or later to the reign of Manasseh (Sneh/Weinberger/Shalev 2010: 61–63; see also Knauf 2001: 281–287).

Some of the scholarly discussion tends to overlook the significance of the technological language in the inscription in favor of locating its significance within the broader political and biblical history of the Neo-Assyrian Period. This tendency obfuscates an important part of the inscription's monumentality which is, intimately related to its local and professional import. In this inscription, we have civil engineers commemorating their craft by carving their most monumental professional achievement into the wall of the tunnel. The inscription memorialized the feat by focusing the memory of those who worked on the tunnel upon the final stage of the product and the benefits that it brought to the city. The inscription

---

10 See the comments by Rendsburg and Schniedewind (2010: 119), "The writing employed here differs from the standard genres of royal palace and priestly temple writing; rather, the inscription is a work of engineers, craftsmen and labourers whose aim was to commemorate their accomplishment".

did not commemorate a public spectacle, but instead a technological feat that was accomplished by a select group of elite professionals who possessed a specific type of knowledge. This was a closed display text of sorts in that its audience was those professional architects, engineers, laborers, and geologists who collaborated on the project. This display recorded their engineering plans, tools, and labors that were employed in the tunnel. The location of the inscription inside the tunnel formed the appropriate way to celebrate their technical skill. And, while it is commemorative, the inscription also anticipates 'forward-looking relationships', such as the relationship between the tunnel project and the larger needs of the city. In this way, the text connected this specific group of engineers and stone masons to future generations in the city who benefitted from their labor.

5. Conclusion

The present study has sought to add new dimensions to the way that our field defines and describes the monumentality of inscriptions. The terminology of monumental is often applied to stone inscriptions and monuments, however, there is little effort to interact with new theoretical insights about what such terminology conveys regarding their function and evolving meaning. We have also stressed that while most studies agree that the Royal Steward and Siloam Tunnel Inscriptions are monumental texts, there is no real consensus about why that is. Monumentality is defined using the following terminology: public, display, commemorative, expensive, lapidary script, formal script, monumental script, durable, scribal, professional, large, stone, royal, etc. However, there is less consideration for why inscriptions that possess such traits are considered monumental, or how to classify those texts that do not meet these criteria but fulfilled similar social roles. Some studies attempt to connect such inscriptions to royal scribes, or focus on their execution in stone, or highlight aspects of their script. As recent scholarship on monumentality shows, however, monumental texts can be non-royal, non-lapidary, inscribed in a more cursive script, and set within hidden or less-accessible display locations. In order to offer a more integrated approach to monumental inscriptions we have therefore considered the roles that *scale, space, spectatorship, graphic design, and materiality* play in the Royal Steward and Siloam Tunnel Inscriptions to create meaning. These two texts employ writing to shape perceptions of the spaces in which they were installed and to *monumentalize* the technologies and expertise that went into their production.

The Royal Steward and Siloam Tunnel Inscriptions offer different perspectives on the variety of forms that monumental inscriptions might take within an urban landscape. The Royal Steward Inscription gave enduring visual and linguistic expression to the relationship between the Silwan necropolis and the City of David, the place of Jerusalem's administrative elite. Monumental inscriptions function as microcosms of the convergences of power, skill, technology, and labor. As Sarah Jackson and Joshua Wright (2014: 136) summarize, "monuments carry out human intentions and meanings even when their creators are not present, or are long gone [...] They extend the work of people by directing interaction, thought and experiences of the landscapes they inhabit." The ability to engrave monumental structures with Hebrew writing on both ridges of the city made a statement about the boundaries of the city and the ability of the city's elite to harness technology and expertise to shape the landscape. Inscribing the exterior of his tomb formed a most effective way for the Royal Steward to live beyond the *space* and *time* of the capital city. In this way, monumental writing enabled Jerusalem's elite to leave an enduring record of their power over the realms of life and death.

The Siloam Tunnel Inscription showcases a different expression of monumentality. It memorializes the expertise and labor of professionals who cut a massive tunnel under the monumental structures of Jerusalem. It records in stone the highly professional knowledge and skill required to accomplish such a monumental feat. The work of the tunneling had obvious and enduring benefits for the city that were set out in public at the pool. We can think of the effect of the tunnel, the water coursing into the urban space of the city, as the public display of the tunneling feat. The inscription, by contrast, was hidden within the darkness of the tunnel and communicated to a much more narrow audience. Rather than view this location as incidental, we believe that the underground tunnel formed the perfect location for expressing a form of elite professional knowledge – 'knowledge of the guild' – needed to cut such a tunnel. We also view the more cursive script used in this text as another mode by which it communicated to Jerusalem's engineering elite. Once set into stone, this intricate and fluid script gave enduring expression to the professionals able to work in stone in such an advanced manner.

References

Aḥituv, S. (2005): Ha-ketav we-ha mikhtav, Jerusalem. (Hebrew)

Aḥituv, S. (2008): Echoes from the Past: Hebrew and Cognate Inscriptions from the Biblical Period, Jerusalem: Carta.

Altman, R. (2007): "Some Notes on Inscriptional Genres and the Siloam Tunnel Inscription." In: Antiguo Oriente 5, 35–88.

Amitzur, H. (1996): "Justinian's Solomon's Temple in Jerusalem." In: M. Poorthuis/ C. Safrai (eds.), The Centrality of Jerusalem: Historical Perspectives, Kampen: Kok Pharos, pp. 160–175.

Avigad, N. (1953): "The Epitaph of a Royal Steward From Siloam Village." In: Israel Exploration Journal 3, pp. 137–152.

Barkay, G. (1992): "The Priestly Benediction on Silver Plaques from Ketef Hinnom Jerusalem." In: Tel Aviv 19, pp. 139–192.

Barkay, G./Lundberg, M./Vaughn, A./Zuckerman, B. (2004): "The Amulets from Ketef Hinnom: A New Edition and Evaluation." In: Bulletin of the American Schools of Oriental Research 334, pp. 41–71.

Berti, I./Bolle, K./Opdenhoff, F./Stroth, F. (2017): "Introduction." In: I. Berti/K. Bolle/F. Opdenhoff/F. Stroth (eds.), Writing Matters: Presenting and Perceiving Monumental Inscriptions in Antiquity and the Middle Ages, Berlin: Walter de Gruyter, pp. 1–11.

Bezemer, J./Kress, G. (2008): "Writing in Multimodal Texts: A Social Semiotic Account of Designs for Learning." In: Written Communication 25, pp. 166–195.

Bradley, S. (2013): Design Fundamentals: Elements, Attributes, and Principles, Boulder: Vanseo Design.

Brown, R. (2006): "Inscribing Colonial Monumentality: A Case Study of the 1763 Patna Massacre Memorial." In: The Journal of Asian Studies 65/1, pp. 91–113.

Canepa, M. (2014): "Topographies of Power: Visualizing the Visual, Spatial and Ritual Contexts of Rock Reliefs in Ancient Iran." In: Ö. Harmanşah (ed.), Of Rocks and Water: Towards an Archaeology of Place. Joukowsky Institute Publications 5, Oxford, pp. 53–92.

Cross, F. (1962a): "Epigraphical Notes on Hebrew Documents of the Eighth-Sixth Centuries B. C.: III. The Inscribed Jar Handles from Gibeon." In: Bulletin of the American Schools of Oriental Research 168, pp. 18–23.

Cross, F. (1962b): "Epigraphical Notes on Hebrew Documents of the Eighth-Sixth Centuries B. C.: II. The Murabbaʿât Papyrus and the Letter Found Near Yabneh-Yam." In: Bulletin of the American Schools of Oriental Research 165, pp. 34–46.

Cross, F. (1979): "Two Offering Dishes with Phoenician Inscriptions from the Sanctuary of ʿArad." In: Bulletin of the American Schools of Oriental Research 235, pp. 75–78.

Cross, F. (2001): "A Fragment of a Monumental Inscription from the City of David." In: Israel Exploration Journal 51, pp. 44–47.

Demsky, A. (2007): "Reading Northwest Semitic Inscriptions." In: Near Eastern Archaeology 70, pp. 68–74.

Demsky, A./Bar-Ilan, M. (1988): "Writing in Ancient Israel and Early Judaism." In: M. Mulder (ed.), Mikra: Text, Translation, Reading and Interpretation of the Hebrew Bible in Ancient Judaism and Early Christianity. Compendia Rerum Iudaicarum ad Novum Testamentum. Section 2: The Literature of the Jewish People in the Period of the Second Temple and the Talmud, Volume 1, Assen-Maastricht; Philadelphia: Van Gorcum; Fortress, pp. 1–38.

Dever, W. G. (1970–1971): "Iron Age Epigraphic Material from Khirbet el-Qôm." In: Hebrew Union College Annual 40–41, pp. 139–204.

Dobbs-Allsopp, F./Roberts, J./Seow, C.-L./Whitaker, R. (2004): Hebrew Inscriptions: Texts from the Biblical Period of the Monarchy with Concordance, New Haven: Yale University Press.

Faust, A. (2000): "A Note on Hezekiah's Tunnel and the Siloam Inscription." In: Journal for the Study of the Old Testament 90, pp. 3–11.

Frumkin, A./Shimron, A. (2006): "Tunnel Engineering in the Iron Age: Geoarchaeology of the Siloam Tunnel, Jerusalem." In: Journal of Archaeological Science 33, pp. 227–237.

Frumkin, A./Shimron, A. (2011) "The Why, How and When of the Siloam Tunnel Reevaluated: A Reply to Sneh, Weinberger, and Shalev." In: Bulletin of the American Schools of Oriental Research 364, pp. 53–60.

Garbini, G. (1969): "L'iscrizione di Siloe e gli 'Annali dei re di Guida'." In: Annali dell'Università degli Studi di Napoli "L'Orientale" 19, pp. 261–263.

Gilibert, A. (2011): Syro-Hittite Monumental Art and the Archaeology of Performance. The Stone Reliefs at Carchemish and Zincirli in the Earlier First Millennium BCE, Topoi – Berlin Studies in the Ancient World 2, Berlin; Boston: Walter de Gruyter.

Gill, D. (1991): "Subterranean Waterworks of Biblical Jerusalem: Adaptation of a Karst System." In: Science 254, pp. 1467–1471.

Gitin, S./Dothan, T./Naveh, J. (1997): "A Royal Dedicatory Inscription from Ekron." In: Israel Exploration Journal 47/1-2, pp. 1–16.

Glatz, C. (2014a): "Places in the Political Landscape of Late Bronze Age Anatolia." In: Ö. Harmanşah (ed.), Of Rocks and Water: Towards an Archaeology of Place. Oxford: Oxbow, pp. 140–168.

Glatz, C. (2014b): "Monuments and Landscape: Exploring Issues of Place, Distance, and Scale in Early Political Contest." In: J. F. Osborne (ed.) Approaching Monumentality in Archaeology, IEMA Proceedings, Albany: State University of New York Press, pp. 109–134.

Glatz, C./Lourde, A. (2011): "Landscape monuments and political competition in Late Bronze Age Anatolia: An investigation of costly signaling theory." In: Bulletin of the American Schools of Oriental Research 361, pp. 33–66.

Grabar, O. (1959): "The Umayyad Dome of the Rock." In: Ars Orientalis 3, pp. 33–62.

Goldhahn, J. (2008): "From Monuments in Landscape to Landscapes in Monuments: Monuments, Death and Landscape in Early Bronze Age Scandinavia." In: A. Jones (ed.), Prehistoric Europe – Theory and Praxis, New York: Blackwell, pp. 56–85.

Hackett, J./McCarter, P./Yardeni, A./Lemaire, A./Eshel, E./Hurvitz, A. (1997): "Defusing Pseudo-Scholarship: The Siloam Tunnel Ain't Hasmonean." In: Biblical Archaeology Review 23/2, pp. 41–50.

Hadley, J. (2012): "2 Chronicles 32:30 and the Water Systems of Preexilic Jerusalem." In: I. Provan/M. Boda (eds.), Let Us Go Up to Zion: Essays in Honour of

H. G. M. Williamson on the Occasion of His Sixty-Fifth Birthday, Leiden: Brill, pp. 273–284.

Hallo, W. (2000): "Introduction: The Bible and the Monuments." In: W. Hallo/K. Younger (eds.), The Context of Scripture: Volume II: Monumental Inscriptions from the Biblical World, Leiden: Brill, pp. xxi–xxvi.

Halpern, B. (2001): David's Secret Demons: Messiah, Murderer, Traitor, King. Grand Rapids: Eerdmans.

Harmanşah, Ö. (2011): "Monuments and Memory: Architecture and Visual Culture in Ancient Antolian History." In: S. Steadman/G. McMahon (eds.), The Oxford Handbook of Ancient Anatolia, 10,000–323 B. C. E., New York: Oxford University Press.

Harmanşah, Ö. (2014): "Stone Worlds: Technologies of Rock-Carving and Place-Making in Anatolian Landscapes." In: A. Knapp/P. van Dommelen (eds.), The Cambridge Prehistory of the Bronze and Iron Age Mediterranean, Cambridge: Cambridge University Press, pp. 379–393.

Harmanşah, Ö. (2015): Place, Memory, and Healing: An Archaeology of Anatolian Rock Monuments, New York: Routledge.

Harmanşah, Ö. (2018): "Graffiti or Monument? Inscription of Place at Anatolian Rock Reliefs." In: C. Ragazzoli/Ö. Harmanşah/C. Salvador/E. Frood (eds.), Scribbling through History: Graffiti, Places and People from Antiquity to Modernity, London: Bloomsbury Academic, pp. 49–64.

Harmanşah, Ö. (2019): "Rock Reliefs and Landscape Monuments." In: A. Gunter (ed.), A Companion to Ancient Near Eastern Art, London: John Wiley & Sons, pp. 483–505.

Hays, C. (2010): "Re-excavating Shebna's Tomb: A New Reading of Isa 22, 15–19 in Its Ancient Near Eastern Context." In: Zeitschrift für Alttestamentliche Wissenschaft 122, pp. 558–575.

Hays, C. (2015): A Covenant with Death: Death in the Iron Age II and Its Rhetorical Uses in Proto-Isaiah, Grand Rapids: Eerdmans.

Healy, J. (1990): "The Early Alphabet." In: J. Hooker (ed.), Reading the Past: Ancient Writing from Cuneiform to the Alphabet. London: British Museum Publications, pp. 197–257.

Hendel, R. (1996): "The Date of the Siloam Inscription: A Rejoinder to Rogerson and Davies." In: Biblical Archaeologist 59, pp. 233–237.

Hess, R. (2006): Writing about Writing: Abecedaries and Evidence for Literacy in Ancient Israel." In: Vetus Testamentum 56/3, pp. 342–346.

Hojer, L. (2008): "Concrete Thought and the Narrative Wall: Graffiti – Monument and Ruin." In: F. Tygstrup/U. Ekman (eds.), Witness: Memory, Representation and the Media in Question. Copenhagen: Museum Tusculanum Press, pp. 243–299.

Hollander, A./Schmid, U./Smelik, W. (eds.), (2003): Paratext and Megatext as Channels of Jewish and Christian Traditions: The Textual Markers of Contextualization, Boston: Brill.

Hoskins, J. (1986): "Agency, Biography and Objects." In: C. Tilley/W. Keane/S. Keuchler/M. Rowlands/P. Spyer (eds.), Handbook of Material Culture. London: Sage, pp. 74–84.

Jackson, S./Wright, J. (2014): "The Work of Monuments: Reflections on Spatial, Temporal and Social Orientations in Mongolia and the Maya Lowlands." In: Cambridge Archaeological Journal 24/1, pp. 117–140.

Kaufman, S. (1986): "The Pitfalls of Typology: On the Early History of the Alphabet." In: Hebrew Union College Annual 57, pp. 1–14.

Keimer, K. (2015): "The Impact of Ductus on Script Form and Development in Northwest Semitic Inscriptions." In: Ugarit-Forschungen 46, pp. 189–212.

Kooij, G. van der (1987): "The Identity of Trans-Jordanian Alphabetic Writings in the Iron Age." In: A. Hadidi (ed.), Studies in the History and Archaeology of Jordan. Volume 3, Amman: Department of Antiquities, pp. 107–121.

Koller, A. (2012): The Semantic Field of Cutting Tools in Biblical Hebrew: The Interface of Philological, Semantic, and Archaeological Evidence, Washington, D. C.: The Catholic Biblical Association of America.

Kreppner, F. (2002): "Public Space in Nature: The Case of Neo-Assyrian Rock Reliefs." In: Altorientalische Forschungen 29, pp. 367–383.

Kress, G./Van Leeuwen, T. (1996): Reading Images: The Grammar of Visual Design, London: Routledge.

Lancaster, S./Long, G. (1999): "Where They Met: Separations in the Rock Mass near the Siloam Tunnel's Meeting Point." In: Bulletin of the American Schools of Oriental Research 315, pp. 15–26.

Lehmann, R. (2005): "Space-syntax and Metre in the Inscriptions of Yahamilk, King of Byblos." In: O. Al-Ghul & A. Ziyadeh (eds.), Proceedings of Yarmouk Second Annual Colloquium on Epigraphy and Ancient Writings, 7th–9th October, 2003, Irbid: Yarmouk University, pp. 69–98.

Lehmann, R. (2008): "Calligraphy and Craftsmanship in the Ahirom Inscription: Considerations on Skilled Linear Flat Writing in early 1st Millennium Byblos." In: Maarav 15/2, pp. 119–164.

Lemaire, A. (1987): "Notes d'épigraphie nord-ouest sémitique." In: Syria 64, pp. 205–216.

Lemaire, A. (1992): "Writing and Writing Materials." In: D. Freedman (ed.), The Anchor Bible Dictionary, Volume 6, New York: Doubleday, pp. 999–1008.

Lemaire, A. (2001): "Schools and Literacy in Ancient Israel and Early Judaism." In: L. Perdue (ed.), The Blackwell Companion to the Hebrew Bible, Oxford: Blackwell, pp. 207–217.

Lemaire, A. (2014): "A History of Northwest Semitic Epigraphy." In: J. Hackett/W. Aufrecht (eds.), 'An Eye for Form': Epigraphic Essays in Honor of Frank Moore Cross. Winona Lake,: Eisenbrauns, pp. 5–29.

Levi della Vida, G. (1968): "The Shiloaḥ Inscription Reconsidered." In: M. Black/G. Fohrer (eds.), In Memoriam Paul Kahle, Berlin: Walter de Gruyter, pp. 162–166.

Machinist, P. (2018): "Royal Inscriptions in the Hebrew Bible and Mesopotamia: Reflections on Presence, Function, and Self-Critique." In: S. Jones/C. Yoder (eds.), 'When the Morning Stars Sang': Essays in Honor of Choon Leong Seow on the Occasion of his Sixty-Fifth Birthday, Berlin: Walter de Gruyter, pp. 331–364.

Mandell, A./Smoak, J. (2016): "Reconsidering the Function of Tomb Inscriptions in Iron Age Judah: Khirbet Beit Lei as a Test Case." In: Journal of Ancient Near Eastern Religions 16, pp. 192–245.

Mandell, A./Smoak, J. (2018): "Reading beyond Literacy, Writing beyond Epigraphy: Multimodality and the Monumental Inscriptions at Ekron and Tel Dan." In: Maarav 22/1-2, pp. 79–112.

McCarter, P. (2000): "The Royal Steward Inscription." In: W.W. Hallo/K.L. Younger (eds.), The Context of Inscription, Volume 2, Leiden: Brill, p. 180.

McCarter, P. (2008): "Paleographic Notes on the Tel Zayit Abecedary." In: R. Tappy/P. McCarter (eds.), Literary Culture and Tenth-Century Canaan: The Tel Zayit Abecedary in Context, Winona Lake: Eisenbrauns, pp. 45–59.

Millard, A. (1972): "The Practice of Writing in Ancient Israel." In: Biblical Archaeologist 35/4, pp. 98–111.

Millard, A. (1985): "An Assessment of the Evidence for Writing in Ancient Israel." In: J. Amitai (ed.), Biblical Archaeology Today: Proceedings of the International Congress on Biblical Archaeology, Jerusalem, April 1984, Jerusalem: Israel Exploration Society, pp. 301–312.

Millard, A. (1995): "The Knowledge of Writing in Iron Age Palestine." In: Tyndale Bulletin 46, pp. 207–217.

Modiano, R./Searle, L./Shilingsburg, P. (eds.), (2004): Voice, Text, Hypertext: Emerging Practices in Textual Studies, Seattle: University of Washington Press.

Montgomery, J. (1934): "Archival Data in the Book of Kings." In: Journal of Biblical Literature 53, pp. 46–52.

Montgomery, J. (1951): A Critical and Exegetical Commentary on the Book of Kings. International Critical Commentary, Edinburgh: T. & T. Clark.

Na'aman, N. (1998): "Royal Inscriptions and the Histories of Joash and Ahaz, Kings of Judah." In: Vetus Testamentum, pp. 333–349.

Naveh, J. (1979): "Graffiti and Dedications." In: Bulletin of the American Schools of Oriental Research 235, pp. 27–30.

Naveh, J. (1982a): "A Fragment of an Ancient Hebrew Inscriptions from the Ophel." In: Israel Exploration Journal 32, pp. 195–198.

Naveh, J. (1982b): Early History of the Alphabet: An Introduction to West Semitic Epigraphy and Palaeography, Jerusalem: Leiden: Magnes: Brill.

Naveh, J. (2000): "Hebrew and Aramaic Inscriptions." In: D. Ariel (ed.), Excavations at the City of David 1978–1985, Directed by Yigal Shiloh, Volume 6: Inscriptions, Qedem 41, Jerusalem: Hebrew University.

Naveh, J. (2001): "Hebrew Graffiti from the First Temple Period." In: Israel Exploration Journal 51, pp. 194–207.

Nelson, R./Olin, M. (2003): "Introduction." In: R. Nelson/M. Olin (eds.), Monuments and Memory; Made and Unmade, Chicago; London: The University of Chicago Press, pp. 1–10.

Norin, S. (1998): "The Age of the Siloam Inscription and Hezekiah's Tunnel." In: Vetus Testamentum 48, pp. 37–48.

Osborne, R. (1987): "The Viewing and Obscuring Power of the Parthenon Frieze." In: Journal of Hellenic Studies 107, pp. 98–105.

Osborne, J. F. (ed.) (2014): Approaching Monumentality in Archaeology, IEMA Proceedings, Albany: State University of New York Press.

Ousterhout, R. (1990): "The Temple, the Sepulchre, and the Martyrion of the Savior." In: Gesta 29/1, pp. 44–53.

Parker, H./Rollston, C. (2016): "The Epigraphic Digital Lab: Teaching Epigraphy in the Twenty-First Century C. E." In: Near Eastern Archaeology 79, pp. 44–59.

Parker, G. (2003): "Narrating Monumentality: The Piazza Navona Obelisk." In: Journal of Mediterranean Archaeology 16/2, pp. 193–215.

Parker, S. (1994): "Siloam Inscription Memorializes Engineering Achievement." In: Biblical Archaeology Review 20, pp. 36–38.

Parker, S. (1997): Stories in Scripture and Inscriptions: Comparative Studies on Narratives in Northwest Semitic Inscriptions and the Hebrew Bible, New York: Oxford University Press.

Pauketat, T. (2014): "From Memorials to Imaginaries in Monumentality of Ancient North America." In: J. F. Osborne (ed.), Approaching Monumentality in Archaeology, IEMA Proceedings, Albany: State University of New York Press, pp. 431–446.

Puech, E. (1974): "L'inscription du tunnel de Siloé." In: Revue Biblique 81, pp. 196–214.

Reich, R./Shukron, E. (2011): "The Date of the Siloam Tunnel Reconsidered." In: Tel Aviv 38, pp. 147–157.

Rendsburg, G. (2007): "No Stelae, No Queens: Two Issues Concerning the Kings of Israel and Judah." In: D. R. Edwards/C. T. McCullough (eds.), The Archaeology of Difference: Gender, Ethnicity, Class, and the "Other" in Antiquity: Studies in Honor of Eric M. Meyers, Boston, pp. 95–107.

Rendsburg, G./Schniedewind, W. (2010): "The Siloam Tunnel Inscription: Historical and Linguistic Perspectives." In: Israel Exploration Journal 60, pp. 188–203.

Renz, J. (1995): Die althebräischen Inschriften, Teil 1, Text und Kommentar, Handbuch der althebräischen Epigraphik 1, Darmstadt: Wissenschaftliche Buchgesellschaft.

Richards, C. (1996): "Henges and Water: Towards an Elemental Understanding of Monumentality and Landscape in Late Neolithic Britain." In: Journal of Material Culture 1/3, pp. 313–336.

Rigney, A. (2004): "Portable Monuments: Literature, Cultural Memory, and the Case of Jeanie Deans." In: Poetics Today 25/2, pp. 361–396.

Rigney, A. (2010): "The Dynamics of Remembrance: Texts between Monumentality and Morphing." In: A. Erll/A. Nünning (eds.), Companion to Cultural Memory Studies: An International and Interdisciplinary Handbook, Berlin: Walter de Gruyter, pp. 343–353.

Rollinger, R. (2015): "Royal Strategies of Representation and the Language(s) of Power: Some Considerations on the Audience and the Dissemination of the Achaemenid Royal Inscriptions." In: S. Procházka/L. Reinfandt/S. Tost (eds.), Official Epistolography and the Language(s) of Power: Proceedings of the First International Conference of the Research Network Imperium & Officium, Wien: Austrian Academy of Sciences Press, p. 117–130.

Rollston, C. (2010): Writing and Literacy in the World of Ancient Israel: Epigraphic Evidence from the Iron Age, Archaeology and Biblical Studies 11, Atlanta: Society of Biblical Literature.

Rollston, C. (2012): "An Old Hebrew Stone Inscription from the City of David: A Trained Hand and a Remedial Hand on the Same Inscription." In: J. Lundberg/S. Fine/W. Pitard (eds.), Puzzling Out the Past: Studies in Northwest Semitic Languages and Literatures in Honor of Bruce Zuckerman, Leiden: Brill, pp. 189–196.

Rollston, C. (2014): "Northwest Semitic Cursive Scripts of Iron II." In: J. Hackett/W. Aufrecht (eds.), An Eye for Form: Epigraphic Essays in Honor of Frank Moore Cross, Winona Lake: Eisenbrauns, pp. 202–234.

Rollston, C. (2015): "Scribal Curriculum during the First Temple Period: Epigraphic Hebrew and Biblical Evidence." In: B. Schmidt (ed.). Contextualizing Israel's Sacred Writings: Ancient Literacy, Orality, and Literary Production, Atlanta: Society of Biblical Literature Press, pp. 71–102.

Rollston, C. (2016): "Epigraphy: Writing Culture in the Iron Age Levant." In: S. Niditch (ed.), The Wiley Blackwell Companion to Ancient Israel, Boston: Wiley Blackwell, p. 131–150.

Rosenberg, S. (1999): "The Siloam Tunnel: A Feat of Survey." In: A. Faust et al. (eds.), New Studies on Jerusalem: Papers of the Fifth Conference, 23 December 1999, Jerusalem: Yad Y. Ben Zvi, pp. 3–20.

Russell, S. (2017): The King and the Land: A Geography of Royal Power in the Biblical World, Oxford: Oxford University Press.

Sanders, S. (2008): "Writing and Early Iron Age Israel: Before National Scriptures, Beyond Nations and States." In: R. Tappy/P. McCarter (eds.), Literate Culture and Tenth-Century Canaan: The Tel Zayit Abecedary in Context. Winona Lake: Eisenbrauns, pp. 97–112.

Sanders, S. (2009): The Invention of Hebrew. Traditions, Urbana: University of Illinois Press.

Sass, B. (2005): The Alphabet at the Turn of the Millennium: The West Semitic Alphabet ca. 1150–850 BCE. The Antiquity of the Arabian, Greek and Phrygian Alphabets. Journal of the Institute of Archaeology of Tel Aviv Occasional Publication 4. Tel Aviv: Emery and Claire Yass Publications in Archaeology.

Sasson, V. (1982): "The Siloam Tunnel Inscription." In: Palestine Exploration Quarterly 114, pp. 111–117.

Scarre, C. (2011): "Monumentality." In: T. Insoll (ed.), The Oxford Handbook of the Archaeology of Ritual, Oxford: Oxford University Press, pp. 9–23.

Schniedewind, W. (2004): How the Bible Became a Book: The Textualization of Ancient Israel, Cambridge: Cambridge University Press.

Schniedewind, W. (2013): A Social History of Hebrew: Its Origins through the Rabbinic Period, New Haven: Yale University.

Schniedewind, W. (2015): "Problems in the Paleographic Dating of Inscriptions." In: T. Levy/T. Higham (eds.), The Bible and Radiocarbon Dating: Archaeology, Text and Science, London: Equinox, pp. 405–412.

Sergueenkova, V./Rojas, F. (2016): "Asianics in Relief: Making sense of Bronze and Iron Age Monuments in Anatolia." In: The Classical Journal 112/2, pp. 140–178.

Shafer, A. (2015): "The Present in Our Past: The Assyrian Rock Reliefs at Nahr el-Kalb and the Lessons of Tradition." In: A. Archi/M. Biga/L. Verderame (eds.), Proceedings of the 57th Rencontre Assyriologique Internationale, Rome 4–8, July 2011, Winona Lake: Eisenbrauns, pp. 491–499.

Shaheen, N. (1977): "The Siloam End of Hezekiah's Tunnel." In: Palestine Exploration Quarterly 109, pp. 107–112.

Shea, W. (1988): "Commemorating the Final Breakthrough of the Siloam Tunnel." In: Y. L. Arbeitman (ed.), On Focus. A Semitic/African Gathering in Remembrance of Albert Ehrman, Amsterdam; Philadelphia: John Benjamins, pp. 431–442.

Smelik, K. (2011): "A Literary Analysis of the Shiloah (Siloam) Tunnel Inscription." In: G. I. Davis, J. K. Aitken, K. J. Dell, and B. A. Mastin (eds.), On Stone and Scroll: Essays in Honour of Graham Ivor Davies, Berlin: Walter de Gruyter, pp. 101–110.

Smith, J./Schmidt, D. (1996): "Variability in Written Japanese: Towards a Sociolinguistics of Script Choice." In: Visible Language 30, pp. 46–71.

Smoak, J. (2016): The Priestly Blessing in Inscription and Scripture: The Early History of Numbers 6: 24–26, Oxford: Oxford University Press.

Smoak, J. (2017): "Inscribing Temple Space: The Ekron Dedication as Monumental Text." In: Journal of Near Eastern Studies 76/2, pp. 319–336.

Sneh, A./Weinberger, R./Shalev, E. (2010): "The Why, How, and When of the Siloam Tunnel Reevaluated." In: Bulletin of the American Schools of Oriental Research 359, pp. 57–65.

Stager, L./King, P. (2001): Life in Biblical Israel. Library of Ancient Israel, Louisville: Westminster/John Knox.

Stavrakopoulou, F. (2013): Materialist Reading: Materialism, Materiality, and Biblical Cults of Writing." In: J. Barton/K. Dell/P. Joyce (eds.), Biblical Interpretation and Method: Essays in Honour of John Barton, Oxford: Oxford University Press, pp. 223–242.

Sukenik, E. (1936): "Note on a Fragment of an Israelite Stele Found at Samaria." In: Palestine Exploration Fund Quarterly Statement 68/3, p. 156.

Suriano, M. (2018): A History of Death in the Hebrew Bible, Oxford: Oxford University Press.

Thomas, E. (2014): "The Monumentality of Text." In: J. F. Osborne (ed.), Approaching Monumentality in Archaeology, IEMA Proceedings, Albany: State University of New York Press, pp. 57–82.

Ussishkin, D. (1975): "The Original Length of the Siloam Tunnel in Jerusalem." In: Levant 8, pp. 82–95.

Ussishkin, D. (1993): The Village of Silwan: The Necropolis from the Period of the Judean Kingdom, Jerusalem: Israel Exploration Society and Yad Izhak Ben-Zvi.

Ussishkin, D. (1995): "The Water Systems of Jerusalem during Hezekiah's Reign." In: M. Weippert/S. Timm (eds.), Meilenstein: Festgabe für Herbert Donner zum 16. Februar 1995, Harrassowitz Verlag: Wiesbaden, pp. 289–307.

Vanderhooft, D. (2014): "Iron Age Moabite, Hebrew, and Edomite Monumental Scripts." In: J. Hackett/W. Aufrecht (eds.), 'An Eye for Form': Epigraphic Essays in Honor of Frank Moore Cross. Winona Lake: Eisenbrauns, pp. 107–126.

Vaughn, A. (1999): "Palaeographic Dating of Judaean Seals and Its Significance for Biblical Research." In: Bulletin of the American Schools of Oriental Research 313, pp. 43–64.

Williams, H./Kirton, J./Gondek, M. (2015): "Introduction: Stones in Substance, Space and Time." In: H. Williams/J. Kirton/M. Gondek (eds.), Early Medieval Stone Monuments: Materiality, Biography, Landscape, Woodbridge: The Boydell Press, pp. 1–34.

Willis, J. (1993): "Historical Issues in Isaiah 22, 15–25." In: Biblica 74, pp. 60–67.

Woolf, G. (1996): "Monumental Writing and the Expansion of Roman Society in the Early Empire." In: Journal of Roman Studies 86, pp. 22–39.

Wu, H. (1995): Monumentality in Early Chinese Art and Architecture, Stanford: Stanford University Press.

Younger, K. (1994): "The Siloam Tunnel Inscription: An Integrated Reading." In: Ugarit-Forschungen 26, pp. 543–556.

Zuckerman, B./Swartz Dodd, L. (2003): Pots and Alphabets: Refractions of Reflections on Typological Method." In: Maarav 10, pp. 89–133.

Contributors

Autenrieth, Sabrina N.
Universiteit Leiden, Department of Archaeology
Sabrina Autenrieth is a PhD researcher within the VICI Project: 'Economies of Destruction. The emergence of metalwork deposition during the Bronze Age in Northwest Europe, c. 2300–1500 BC' at the Faculty of Archaeology in Leiden. Her research focuses on Late Neolithic to Middle Bronze Age metalwork depositions in the river landscape of the Rhine, encompassing the synergy between object, body, landscape and material within the practice of relational depositions.

Bernbeck, Reinhard
Freie Universität Berlin, Institut für Vorderasiatische Archäologie
Reinhard Bernbeck teaches at the Freie Universität Berlin Western Asian archaeology. He is co-editor of Ideologies in Archaeology (with Randall H. McGuire) and Subjects and Narratives in Archaeology (with Ruth van Dyke).
Past excavations include prehistoric sites in Iran, Turkmenistan, Turkey, and Jordan. He has also carried out fieldwork at Nazi camps and World War I sites in Berlin and surroundings. He co-edits the online journal Forum Kritische Archäologie. His interests include past political economies and the political-ideological dimensions of archaeology today. Apart from academic positions he has also worked with the International Committee of the Red Cross in humanitarian missions in the context of the Afghanistan conflict.

van Boekel, Dieuwertje
Universiteit Leiden, Department of Archaeology
Dieuwertje has concluded her Research Masters degree at Leiden University in the field of Ancient Native American cultures. After graduation she started working as an archaeologist for 'ADC Archeoprojecten' in the Netherlands, where she now leads and collaborates with a number of Dutch research projects, ranging from Mesolithic campsites to historic city centres.

Buccellati, Federico

Freie Universität Berlin, Institut für Vorderasiatische Archäologie

Federico Buccellati, Near Eastern Archaeologist, is a researcher at the Freie Universität Berlin as well as at the Alexandria Archive Institute. He has served as Field Director of the Mozan/Urkesh Archaeological Project since 2008, and is Deputy Director of the International Institute for Mesopotamian Area Studies (IIMAS). His research interests lie in 3rd and 2nd millennium Syro-Mesopotamia, particularly architecture and the archaeological record, as well as theoretical and digital aspects of archaeology.

Bußmann, Richard

Universität zu Köln, Institut für Afrikanistik und Ägyptologie

Richard Bussmann studied Egyptology, Ancient Near Eastern Studies and Theology at the universities of Heidelberg, Berlin and Göttingen. He received his PhD in Egyptology from Free University Berlin in 2007. In 2010, he held a post-doctoral research fellowship at Cambridge University. From 2010 to 2016, he was a lecturer in Egyptology and Egyptian Archaeology at University College London. Since 2016 he is a professor in Egyptology at the University of Cologne. His research interest is in social archaeology during the Bronze Age in Egypt, urbanism in North-Eastern Africa and comparative approaches to early complex societies. Richard Bussmann co-directs the fieldwork project Zawyet Sultan: archaeology and heritage in Middle Egypt. He is the author of Die Provinztempel Ägyptens von der 0. bis zur 11. Dynastie: Archäologie und Geschichte einer gesellschaftlichen Institution zwischen Reisdenz und Provinz and Complete Middle Egpytian: A New Method for Learning Hieroglyphs. Reading Texts in Context.

Butterlin, Pascal

Université Paris 1 Sorbonne Pantheon, Intitute d'archéologie du Proche-Orient

Pascal Butterlin is teaching ancient Near East archaeology at Université Paris 1 Panthéon-Sorbonne. He has excavated in Syria for 25 years and directs the Mari Project since 2004. His main focus of research is urban history from the first cities to the imperial capitals of Mesopotamia.

Cousin, Laura

UMR 7041 Archéologies et Sciences de l'Antiquité, Nanterre (ArScAn – HAROC)

Laura Cousin received her Ph. D. in Ancient History from the Paris-I University (2016). She wrote a dissertation entitled Babylon, City of the King in the First Millennium BC, which was awarded by the Dissertation Prize 2017 of the French Society of Urban History (SFHU). Specialist in the history of Babylonia in the first millennium BC, she is currently associate researcher of the UMR 7041 "Archéologies et Sciences de l'Antiquité", équipe "Histoire et Archéologie de l'Orient Cunéiforme" (ArScAn – HAROC, Nanterre, France).

Delitz, Heike

Universität Bamberg, Fakultät Sozial- und Wirtschaftswissenschaften, Soziologie
Heike Delitz is Privatdozentin (PD) at the University of Bamberg, Germany, where she teaches courses on sociological theory. Here recent book Kollektive Identitäten was published with transript in 2018. From 2019 until 2022, she will work on a book about different "architectural modes of collective existence", thanks to a research project funded by the German Research Foundation (DFG).

Gleiter, Jörg H.

Technische Universität Berlin, Institut für Architektur
Jörg H. Gleiter (Prof. Dr.-Ing. habil., BDA) is the head of the chair of architectural theory and the managing director of the Institute for Architecture of Technische Universität Berlin. He has studied in Tübingen, Berlin, Venice, and New York. 1989–1995 professional experience in New York and Berlin. I was twice a fellow in residence at Kolleg Friedrich Nietzsche in Weimar with visiting professorships in Venice, Tokyo, Weimar, Bozen-Bolzano, and Providence (RI). Gleiter is the founder and editor of the book series ArchitekturDenken. Among his publications are Traditionelle Theorie. Architekturtheorie 1863–1938 (Berlin 2018); Architektur und Philosophie (ed. together with Ludger Schwarte, Bielefeld 2015); Ornament Today. Digital. Material. Structural (ed. by Jörg H. Gleiter, Bolzano 2012); Urgeschichte der Moderne (Bielefeld 2010); Der philosophische Flaneur. Nietzsche und die Architektur (Würzburg 2009). His research focusses on architecture theory and philosophy, critical epistemology of architecture, architecture semiotics, critical theory of ornament, Friedrich Nietzsche.

Hageneuer, Sebastian

Universität zu Köln, Archäologisches Institut
Sebastian Hageneuer, Near Eastern Archaeologist, works as a research assistant at the Archaeological Institute at the Universität zu Köln. In 2010, he received his degree in Near Eastern Archaeology. Since 2013, he is part of a research group that focuses on the significance of size in the architecture of the Ancient Near East.

van der Heyden, Sylva

Technische Universität Berlin, Institut für Kunstwissenschaft und Historische Urbanistik
Sylva van der Heyden is an art historian with special interests in 18th and 19th century and its reception history, graphic prints and objects made with uncommon materials. She was part of a research group within the Excellence Cluster TOPOI (Berlin) focusing on the topos of the reception of the greatness of the ancient and modern Rome (2013–2019).

Hof, Catharine

Technische Universität Berlin, Historische Bauforschung und Baudenkmalpflege

Catharine Hof is a postdoctoral researcher at the German Archaeological Institute (DAI). She is also a lecturer in 3D-Visualization of historic monuments at the Technical University of Berlin (TU Berlin) where she is also working as a researcher. She received her D.Eng. in architecture with a work on historic wooden constructions from the Karlsruhe Institute of Technology (KIT). Recently she has habilitated herself at the TU Berlin with a thesis on the City Wall of Resafa (in press). Working areas cover: China, Ethiopia, Germany, Italy, Israel, Poland, Turkey, Sudan, Syria and Yemen. All postdoctoral research has been generously supported by a variety of third-party funders leading to several conference contributions and articles. A research fellowship of the Free University of Berlin – TOPOI allowed her to work on the Large Cistern of Resafa addressed here. Her main focus of historical and archaeological research is on architecture in Late Antiquity in the East and on Nubian Meroitic settlement development in northeast Africa. She is particularly interested in the development of construction techniques and the transfer of building knowledge.

Lane, Rachael

University of Sydney

Rachael Lane is a PhD candidate at the University of Sydney. Her work focuses on the philosophy, history and theory of archaeology with a special interest in landscapes and monumentality of Angkorian Cambodia.

Levenson, Felix

Freie Universität Berlin, Institut für Vorderasiatische Archäologie

Felix Levenson is a PhD researcher at the Freie Universität Berlin at the Institut für Vorderasiatische Archäologie and an associated member of the former Cluster of Excellence 264 TOPOI. His research focuses on the social meaning of architecture and memory work in the Ancient Near East. He is currently focused on "networks of knowledge" between Mesopotamia and Ancient Iran in the 4th millennium BCE and on memory work and the creation of historical narratives in the Ancient Near East.

Mandell, Alice

Johns Hopkins University, Department of Near Eastern Studies

Alice Mandell is the Albright Chair of Biblical and Ancient Near Eastern Studies at Johns Hopkins University. She is a specialist in biblical literature, northwest Semitics, the history of the ancient Levant, and sociolinguistic approaches to the study of writing.

Mogetta, Marcello
University of Missouri, Institute of Ancient Mediterranean Studies
Marcello Mogetta (PhD, University of Michigan) is Assistant Professor of Roman Art and Archaeology in the Department of Ancient Mediterranean Studies at the University of Missouri, Columbia. His teaching and research focus on 1st millennium BCE Italy, investigating the cultural implications of Rome's early expansion through the lens of urbanism, architecture and building technology. His work on the origins of Roman concrete pays particular attention to the complex and ambiguous relationship between the formation of a distinctive Roman material and visual culture, foreign influence from the broader Mediterranean context, and the agency of non-Roman patrons and builders in the process. He co-directs field projects at the Latin site of Gabii (Gabii Project) and in Pompeii (Venus Pompeiana Project), and has been collaborating with the Capitoline Museums and the MU Museum of Art and Archaeology (Hidden Treasure of Rome project) to study a Roman Republican-era pottery collection using advanced digital imaging.

Pacheco Silva, Mónica
Freie Universität Berlin, Berlin Graduate School of Ancient Studies, Landscape Archaeology and Architecture
Monica Pacheco was a TOPOI doctoral fellow and participates in the PhD program "Landscape Archaeology and Architecture" (LAA) at Berlin Graduate School of Ancient Studies (BerGSAS) and finished her PhD in 2019. With prior studies in Archaeology in Mexico, she graduated from the University of Hamburg with a major in Mesoamerican studies and minors in Ethnology and History of Art. Her research project entitled "The representation of space and place in Mesoamerica: The Lienzo Coixtlahuaca/Seler II in the Berlin Ethnology Museum" correlates the topographic and archaeological data with the geographical reality and the ethno-historical sources.

Schmidt, Sophie C.
Universität zu Köln, Archäologisches Institut
Schmidt, Sophie C. is a Prehistoric Archaeologist and Research Associate in Digital and Computational Archaeology at the University of Cologne, Germany. She received her degree in Prehistoric Archaeology in 2016 submitting a geostatistical master's thesis and has been teaching quantitative methods for archaeologists at the University of Cologne since. Her research interests lie with quantitative methods and the European Neolithic.

Smoak, Jeremy
University of California, Los Angeles, Near Eastern Languages & Cultures
Jeremy D. Smoak is Senior Lecturer in Near Eastern Languages and Cultures at the University of California, Los Angeles, where he teaches courses on biblical literature, Israelite religion, and classical Hebrew. His recent book The Priestly Blessing in Inscription and Scripture: The Early History of Numbers 6: 24–26 was published with Oxford University Press in 2016. His current book project examines the literary history of Solomon's temple in the book of Kings.

White, Kirrily
University of Sydney
Kirrily White is a PhD candidate at the University of Sydney. Her research focuses on low occupation density mega-settlements in prehistoric periods. A significant part of her research is the role of monumentality in sustaining group coherence and resilience.